DON'T DO IT!

A DICTIONARY OF THE FORBIDDEN

PHILIP THODY

ST. MARTIN'S PRESS
NEW YORK

St. Martin's Press, Scholarly and Reference Division, 175 Fifth Avenue, New York, N.Y. 10010

First published in the United States of America in 1997

Printed in Great Britain

ISBN 0–312–17373–3

Library of Congress Cataloging-in-Publication Data

Thody, Philip Malcolm Waller, 1928–
Don't do it: a short dictionary of the fordbidden/by Philip Thody.
p. cm.
Includes bibliographical references and index.
ISBN 0–312–17373–3
1. Social norms—Dictionaries. 2. Taboo—Dictionaries.
I. Title.
GN494T48 1997
303.3′7—dc21 96–40302
CIP

Contents

Warning

The original title of this book was *Taboos: A Dictionary Guide to the Forbidden.* However, for reasons set out in the Introduction, the present title was adopted. It is a book for the lay reader, not for the professional anthropologist.

Acknowledgements

Brian Southam suggested the idea to me and provided much information and advice. Barry Brown, Brian Ferris, Maia Green, Suzette Heald, Brian Innes, Brian Morris, Bill Johnson, Bill Mims, Michael Russell and Hugh Stappleton read through the typescript and made invaluable suggestions. All mistakes are my own.

Preface, or *How to Use this Book*

The Introduction explains how *Don't Do It!: A Dictionary of the Forbidden* came to be written. It gives a brief history of the word 'taboo', and describes the way in which it is most frequently used in modern English.

The Introduction also highlights some of the general questions raised in the five sections into which the book is divided:

I Actions
II Nourishment
III Words and Themes
IV Ideas, Books and Pictures
V Signs

These general questions include topics such as the difference between taboos and laws, the function of law in a democratic society, the role played by taboos in some earlier societies, and the place they still occupy in our own.

When a word is printed in **bold** in the text of an entry, this indicates that it can also be found as a **headword**. The interest offered by certain topics has made it inevitable that some **headwords** recur in more than one section.

When the themes discussed under one **headword** do recur in other entries, the relevant **headwords** are printed in **bold** at the end of that entry. Readers are invited to use this system of cross-referencing in order to browse. While the book can be read straight through, it is better used, as its title implies, as a kind of dictionary.

The Conclusion suggests a number of reasons for feeling pleased that modern Western society is gradually reducing the number of taboos and interdicts governing speech and conduct.

Appendix A lists some of the general topics raised in the book. It also indicates either the section or sections in which they figure, or the page or pages on which a discussion of them can be found in the **Introduction** or the Conclusion.

Appendix B provides an alphabetical list of all the headwords.

Appendix C lists the names of authors and historical figures mentioned in the text.

A list of the principal works consulted is on pp. 333–339.

INTRODUCTION

FROM DISTANT ORIGINS TO MODERN USAGE

The word 'taboo' first came into English in 1784, when Captain Cook published his account of the visit which he had made to Tahiti during his third voyage round the world. In it, he described how

> The *taboo* also prevails in Atooi, in its full extent, and seemingly with much more vigour than even at Tongataboo. For the people here always asked, with great eagerness and signs of fear to offend, whether any particular thing, which they desired to see, or we were unwilling to shew, was *taboo*, or as they pronounced the word, *tafoo*?[1]

Cook also noted how the term was used in Tahiti to designate a tree with qualities so sacred that people who touched it exposed themselves to severe, supernatural penalties.

In the technical sense which the term later acquired in the descriptions by Western anthropologists of non-European societies, it remained associated with the idea of the sacred, and especially with that of punishment. Anyone who had broken a taboo could be cleansed of the offence only by a propitiatory ceremony conducted by a priest. As Herman Melville soon realized when he visited the Polynesian island of Typee in the summer of 1842, taboos could also be infringed by people who had no idea of the offence they were committing. 'Time and again', he writes, 'I was called to order, if I may use the phrase, when I could not for the life of me conjecture what particular offence I had committed.'[2] In so far as ignorance of the law is no excuse, it is one of the few similarities between taboos and laws. One of the most celebrated incidents in literature and mythology takes place when Oedipus marries his mother Jocasta without either of them being aware they are infringing the **incest** taboo.

In our own society, that of the industrialized West, the word 'taboo' has lost almost all its magical and religious associations. In particular, it no longer has the idea essential to Margaret Mead's definition as 'a prohibition whose infringement results in an automatic penalty without human or divine mediation'.[3] Except perhaps for offences against **political correctness**, there is little likelihood nowadays of anybody who breaks what are referred to as 'taboos' incurring any kind of punishment. The word has also lost the sense which Freud thought very important, that of the sacred. In everyday language, it merely evokes something which is forbidden, generally for reasons which are hard to defend on rational grounds. The ironic tone in which the word tends to be used also has the effect of suggesting that protected status of the idea or institution is undeserved.

An immediate example of this was provided when Sir Paul Condon, the London Metropolitan Police Commissioner, commented in public in July 1995 on the statistics which showed that most muggers in the London area were black. 'Top Policeman Shatters Taboo: Condon Acts on Black Crime' ran the headline on 5 July in the *Daily Express*, and 'Met Chief Breaks Taboo to Reveal that Most Muggers are Black' on the same day in the *Daily Telegraph*. The *Guardian* commented on the misleading nature of the statistics by pointing out that they applied only to London. Figures taken nationwide showed that criminals were just as likely to be white as black. But for less progressively minded newspapers, the insistence was on the idea that race had become a forbidden topic. In their view, there was the same kind of taboo in our own society on mentioning race in public as had existed in the society of Victorian England on any open reference to sex. The implication of the headlines was that far from being criticized for breaking the taboo, Sir Paul deserved to be praised for speaking honestly about a subject which was normally hidden.

Although the irony came about only in the twentieth century, it was not long after its entry into the English language that the word 'taboo' took on the extended sense which it now has, and with which I am primarily concerned in this book. One of the first examples of this extended use took place in 1791, less than eight years after Captain Cook had first introduced the word, when the House of Commons considered adopting 'a plain declaration that the topick of France is *tabooed* or forbidden ground to Mr Burke'.[4] As early as November 1790, Burke's *Reflections on the Revolution in France* had predicted the descent of that then unhappy country first into chaos and then into tyranny. However, he had also acquired the nickname of 'the dinner bell', a term which denoted a speaker so boring that his colleagues left the chamber of the House of Commons for the dining-room the moment he rose to speak. He was, in particular, becoming so obsessive on the subject of France that a total ban was necessary to protect his colleagues against what they saw as his misplaced eloquence. The early use of the word 'taboo' in a context which evokes primarily a breach of good manners, in the sense that a gentleman does everything possible to avoid laying himself open to the charge of being a bore, suggests how far the term had already moved away from its original associations with magic and superstition and into those of the social and political life of Western Europe and North America.

This tendency continued during the nineteenth century, with the jurist and statesman James Bryce pointing out in his *American Commonwealth* (1888) that 'you cannot taboo a man who has got the vote'. It is even more marked today, when the word evokes either attitudes that are outdated and irrational, or topics that were deemed unmentionable in the past but are now being openly discussed. In August 1995, the London-based magazine *She* carried the headline 'One in Five Women Do It [earn more than their husbands]. So Why the Big Taboo?' On 29 February 1996 the *Daily Telegraph* described a television programme on the problem of male infertility as tackling 'another taboo subject'. Neither is this usage peculiar to the United Kingdom. When, in June 1970, the American journalist and novelist Tom Wolfe wrote about 'the flood of taboo thoughts' which ran through his head at 'those Radical Chic evenings', he was using the word with an irony which warned his readers that he was going to denounce a heresy. The adulation which the glitterati of New York society were bestowing on the Black Panthers was, in his view, an intellectual aberration, whatever the quasi-sacred status of this organization in certain advanced circles might be.[5]

The variety of contexts in which the term 'taboo' has come to be used by American and English writers and journalists is in this respect an almost classic example of the role played in language by loan words. One of the main functions of such words is to enable distinctions to be made that had not previously been possible, and ideas to be expressed in a new and more concise manner. In so doing, however, the loan word often loses much of its primary meaning, and takes on associations which would have caused its original users some surprise. Indeed, as is shown by the entries on **adultery** and **paedophilia**, as well as by part of the entry on **children**, the word is also sometimes used in a sense which blurs the distinction between taboos, which are for the most part irrational and hard to defend on practical or humanitarian ground, and laws, whose function in providing equal and justifiable protection for all members of society is one of the acknowledged hallmarks of civilized society.

On both sides of the Atlantic, the term 'taboo' has also become what linguistic philosophers call a 'boo word', one which the speaker endows with as automatic a weight of disapproval as the adjectives 'irrational', 'authoritarian' and 'paternalistic', or the nouns 'bureaucracy', 'consumerism' and 'fascism'.[6] When, on 4 March 1991, John Leo published in *U.S. News and World Report* an article entitled 'The Political Taboos of the '90s', he aimed not to endorse the cult of **political correctness** but to denounce it. It may have been the boo-word status of the term 'taboo' that led to the reaction of a number of anthropologists and linguists to whom my publisher Brian Southam wrote in the late 1980s asking if they would like to write a book dealing primarily with taboo words, but which also discussed taboos in general.

For the anthropologists replied, with surprising unanimity, that they did not regard the word as either meaningful or useful. One of them, in particular, wrote that

> the term itself has been dismantled over recent years (Douglas, Leach, Lévy-Strauss, et al.) and shown to be nothing more than a dustbin into which Europeans threw the most disparate materials which they did not understand,

thus anticipating the views of a reader to whom the typescript of this book was sent, and who said that

> the word is used as a dustbin for everything about other cultures that Westerners do not understand and functions as 'proof' of illogical Them and rational Us.

Both anthropologists thus created what it is tempting for me as a layman to describe as a taboo on taboos, and there is an important sense in which their reluctance to use the term is fully understandable. The word 'taboo', retaining as it does something of the disparaging self-confidence with which nineteenth-century Europeans described cultures different from their own, is a classic example of the tendency described by Talal Asad in *Anthropology and the Colonial Encounter* (1973) when he wrote that 'ever since the Renaissance, the West has sought both to subordinate and devalue other societies, and at the same time to find in them clues to its own humanity'.[7]

I should therefore make it clear that this book is not intended primarily for anthropologists. They may indeed find it, as another reader did, a text which itself provides 'raw material' for a study of 'a particular simplistic view of the world that one might characterize as "mid-twentieth-century, Western, middle-class, optimistic"'. In that respect, readers might like to use it as a text inviting them to look at the ideas that they have come to take for granted, and thus to wonder whether what I present as an increasingly taboo-free society is merely an undesirable historical accident which the passage of time will inevitably lead to disappear.

In ordinary language, the current use of the term 'taboo' does indeed designate, as is shown by the examples given of its usage in this book, so wide a range of attitudes and experiences that it is not possible to analyse it in a manner suited to an intellectually rigorous discipline such as anthropology, based as it now is on field work and observation. The care which professional anthropologists take to replace what lay observers describe as taboos in the context of the society in which they operate also precludes any attempt on their part to deal with ritual prohibitions in one book. If they eschew the use of the word 'taboo', it is to avoid giving the impression that it can meaningfully refer to practices whose nature and origins differ so much according to context that the term is virtually meaningless in any scientific sense.

Some of the examples of modern interdicts quoted in Sections IV and V of the book nevertheless suggest that we may be wrong to see our own society as entirely free from taboos, and it was partly for this reason that I could not resist the temptation to discuss a word that can be used in so many ways, has taken on so many associations, and raises so many questions about the ethics of sexuality, the role of the law, the limits to the authority of the state, or the widespread and apparently irresistible ambition of human beings to tell their fellows what not to do, to eat, to say or to think. In many contexts, and especially when they place an interdict upon sexual activities of which a particular group happens to disapprove, taboos frequently illustrate the truth of the modern rewriting of Lord Acton's comment on Robespierre: 'All power is delicious. And absolute power is absolutely delicious.'

TOWARDS A SOCIETY WITH NO TABOOS

The boo-word status of the term 'taboo' suggests that we are becoming the first society to try to base our ethical standards on wholly utilitarian criteria. We are trying, in other words, to create a situation where we forbid as few activities as possible, and to do so only when these activities can be clearly shown to cause physical or financial harm to specific individuals or to publicly identifiable groups. As the entry **paedophilia** suggests, the laws against the sexual exploitation of children are based on clearly defined and totally defensible moral principles. But we tend to regard the sexual behaviour of adults as a matter of legitimate personal choice. We restrict freedom of speech only when libel or slander can be shown to harm specific individuals, or when verbal attacks against particular groups threaten to lead to racial or religious persecution. In the increasingly secular society of the West, other forms of censorship have virtually disappeared. In the United States, the burning of the Stars and Stripes has become a constitutionally protected way of expressing dissent from government policy, and there has even been a case where the burning of a cross in front of a house which a black family had bought in a predominantly white neighbourhood was seen as the legitimate expression of political views.[8]

We continue to punish violence, and impose the same penalties on the deliberate evasion of income tax, excise duties or social security payments as on theft from specific individuals or private and public institutions. Although it is not possible to identify any individual harmed by such evasion, the damage to the community at large takes the form of the need for other people to pay more to make up for the shortfall. We continue to ban the use of certain drugs, and do so on the grounds of the definable harm which they do to the people who consume them. But we make little serious attempt to forbid the consumption by adults of **alcohol** or tobacco, and allow our young people, in the United Kingdom as well as in the United States, an unprecedented freedom of sexual and social behaviour.

We have also more or less given up trying to impose limits on the use of certain words, as well as on what topics can be discussed in the newspapers, on radio and on television. There are, it is true, conventions in the United Kingdom governing what can be shown on television before nine o'clock in the evening, and on the kind of words that can be used on the radio. But even on the BBC, these conventions are disappearing, and it would be very difficult to find an 8-year-old child in the United States or in the United Kingdom who had not been exposed to discussions in the media about **adultery**, AIDS, **contraception**, **homosexuality**, **Lesbianism**, **menstruation**, **oral sex**, the sexual abuse of children and **venereal disease**. Such children may not have a very clear idea about what is involved, and may even not be very interested in what, for the most part, are essentially adult concerns. But the idea, current as late as the 1930s, that events as natural, innocent and desirable as pregnancy or childbirth could be mentioned only by euphemisms has totally disappeared. The verbal taboos which played such an important part in people's lives in the Victorian period and in the first half of the twentieth century are also in the process of disappearing.

The idea of a society with no taboos at all, in the sense of one where the only activities which are forbidden, or indeed even frowned on, are those whose anti-social nature can be proved in a court of law, strikes some observers as a very strange one. Thinkers of a conservative persuasion argue that our own society might be healthier, and we ourselves better off as individuals, if we had not rejected so many of the apparently irrational commandments of the past. In his Maccabean lecture to the British Academy on jurisprudence, *The Enforcement of Morals* (1959), Lord Devlin argued that the law should not limit itself to punishing acts which do definable harm to particular individuals or identifiable institutions. It should also, in his view, serve as one of the principal means whereby a society articulates and makes public its general value system. 'An established morality', he declared, 'is as necessary as good government to the welfare of society', and he continued:

> The law does not discharge its function by protecting the individual from injury. Society cannot ignore the morality of the individual any more than it can his loyalty. It flourishes on both, and without either it dies. Societies disintegrate from within more frequently than they are broken up by external pressures. There is disintegration when no common morality is observed and history shows that the loosening of social bonds is often the first stage of disintegration, so that society is justified in taking the same steps to preserve its moral code as it does to preserve its government and other essential institutions.[9]

Lord Devlin's lecture expressed the key notion justifying the maintenance of taboos in a secular society that otherwise gives pride of place to the freedom of the individual to do what he likes, to act as she pleases, so long as what they do does not harm anyone but themselves. It was given in the context of the debate that led in the United Kingdom to the decriminalization in 1967 of homosexual acts between consenting adults in private. It is by no means unusual for a defence of the taboos of the past to concern itself primarily with sexual matters. In 1993, for example, the British conservative writer Peregrine Worsthorne criticized the liberal thinkers of his day for not having 'battled to uphold the minimum of sexual taboos and repressions necessary for the survival of monogamous marriage'.[10] The debate about censorship is characterized in the United States of America, as well as in the United Kingdom, by a tendency to concentrate on descriptions of sexual activity. When, as occasionally happens, commentators object to the depiction of violence in the cinema or on television, their protests are far more vigorous when the violence in question has sexual overtones.

The case for the retention of certain taboos is discussed in Section I of this book, which is concerned with attempts to ban a number of activities that disciples of John Stuart Mill would define as self-regarding, and is taken up again in the Conclusion. Although Mill does not use the word 'taboo', he puts the basic case against them in the passage of his essay *On Liberty* (1859), in which he argues that 'over himself, over his own body and mind, the individual is sovereign'. The society developed in the industrialized West is a secular democracy based on a rationally formulated legal system. Unlike taboos, laws are not arbitrary and unalterable. They are defensible on the grounds of social utility, and are subject to change. They are the conscious creation of a society whose members know which values they wish to defend and why. They can thus be altered to keep pace with the emergence of different values. Taboos, in contrast, are based neither on reason nor on experience, and are not amenable to reform. They either survive unchanged or they disappear completely.

Taboos also differ from laws in the wide variety of activities which they seek to forbid. Some of these activities, as is indicated by the length of the entries on **incest** or **homosexuality**, involve important moral and psychological questions. Others, especially those which concern dress or the use of certain words, are relatively trivial. The taboos affecting matters of clothes, table manners and fashions in language are consequently included in this book more for their entertainment value than because of the importance of the moral or philosophical issues which they might raise. They also illustrate the truth of Burke's description of human beings, in his *Thoughts and Details on Scarcity* (1795), as 'building their culture, nervously loquacious, on the edge of the abyss'. Rather than say nothing and let well alone, we cannot resist the opportunity to spin theories and issue interdicts. What the history of taboos most clearly illustrates is Pascal's notion of how terrifying we find silence.

The question of what can and cannot be seen as self-regarding activities recurs in a number of entries in Section I and is equally important in Section III. By concentrating on what people should or should not be allowed to say or print, Section III evokes the contentious issue of censorship. Section IV raises this question in a slightly different form in the entries that discuss whether certain groups, as well as certain individuals, have the right to require the law to respect their feelings by banning the expression of views which they find offensive. This question arises most frequently when the issue involved is one of religious belief, or of the respect owed to public decency.

The difficulty of laying down absolute rules also occurs in the entries in Section III. It arises in the entries on **blasphemy** or **Lady Chatterley's Lover** or James Joyce's **Ulysses** in Section IV. These entries deal with the reasons lying behind the taboos of the past, as well as with the arguments used to justify some of the interdicts of the present day. They thus call into question Lord Devlin's view that the law should be used not simply to discourage anti-social behaviour and punish crimes, but also to enforce and make explicit the traditional morality and taboos of the past. This issue is further discussed in the Conclusion.

TABOOS AS SIGNS

Although eclectic, in the sense that I try to give an account of the explanations for taboos suggested by anthropologists such as Mary Douglas, Edmund Leach, Marvin Harris and Hutton Webster, or nineteenth-century scholars like Sir James Frazer and Sir Edward Taylor, my approach is essentially a semiological one. I acknowledge the role that taboos play in religion, am struck by their obsession with sex, and share the difficulty which many other people experience in distinguishing them from superstitions. My recognition that taboos are about power is particularly clear in my comments on the current movement for **political correctness**, as well as in the entries on **contraception**, **oral sex** and **lesbianism**. I nevertheless see taboos principally as signs. Not all of them fall into this category, and a number retain a good deal of the mystery that still presides over their origin. But the idea that taboos come into their own when they signal the differences which separate one group of people from its neighbours or rivals is a useful starting-point. By forbidding certain actions in which other people too readily indulge, we show that we are not as others are. By refusing to eat foods which they too willingly consume, we demonstrate how superior we are to them through the fastidious nature of our tastes. By not using certain words, we show that we are a class above some of our fellows, as well as in a class apart.

The five headings under which I discuss taboos represent a scaling down rather than a fundamental alteration of the six categories which I had originally envisaged, and which were used in the original publicity for this book:

sex, birth and death
food, drink and excretion
dress, gestures and hairstyles
gender, race and religion
art, literature and the cinema
language, religion and science.

The change was prompted partly by the desire to leave space for other people to write about what I have found to be a fascinating topic. More particularly, however, it reflected the feeling that I was becoming increasingly like the Mr Casaubon of George Eliot's *Middlemarch*, and *Don't Do It! A Dictionary of the Forbidden* more and more like his great but uncompleted 'Key to all Mythologies'. Mr Casaubon was held up by the fact that he 'did not know the Germans'. I found an equal obstacle to a complete discussion of the phenomenon in the number, variety and overlap of the taboos available for discussion. Melville, the first American to give an account of taboos, had experienced the same problem, writing in *Typee* (1846):

> The capricious nature of the taboo is not its least remarkable feature: to enumerate them all would be impossible. Black hogs – infants to a certain age – women in an interesting situation – young men while the operation of tattooing their face is going on – and certain parts of the valley during the continuance of a shower – are alike fenced in by the operation of the taboo.[11]

Readers should therefore see this book as an appetizer. It is an attempt to refute Chamfort's remark that a man faced with a bowl of cherries always begins by eating the better ones only to end up by consuming the lot.

Leeds, 8 December 1996

NOTES

1 Quoted from p. 22 of Franz Steiner, *Taboo*, Cohen and West, London, 1956; Penguin, Harmondsworth, 1967.
2 H. Melville, *Typee: A Peep at Polynesian Life* (1846), Northwestern University Press, Evanston and Chicago, 1968, p. 91.

3 See her article in the 1937 edition of the *Encyclopaedia of Social Sciences.*

4 Quoted by Steiner in *Taboo*, Penguin, 1967, p. 27.

5 See 'Those Radical Chic Evenings', reprinted from 'Radical Chic: That Party at X's', *New York Magazine*, 8 June 1970, in Tom Wolfe, *The Purple Decades*, Farrar, Straus and Giroux, New York, 1982; Jonathan Cape, London, 1983, Picador, London, 1993; pp. 181–97.

6 There is no link between the term 'taboo' and the expression 'boo word'. The habit of talking about 'boo words' and 'hurrah words' stems from A. J. Ayer's *Language, Truth and Logic* (1936). In what became known as the emotive theory of ethics, Ayer maintained that statements such as 'Jones is a good man' or 'stealing is very wicked' did not refer to an ascertainable state of affairs in the outside world. They merely expressed an emotional attitude on the speaker's part, one which he or she expected the listener to share. They were the equivalent of saying 'Jones!' in tones of approval, in such a way as to provoke the reaction 'Hurrah!', or 'stealing' in tones of disapproval, with the intention of making one's listener say 'boo!'

7 Talal Asad, *Anthropology and the Colonial Encounter*, Humanities Press, Atlantic Highlands, NJ, 1973, p. 104. The anthropologists may also have refused because they did not want to be seen as popularizers, and were anxious to avoid being on the receiving end of the *odium theologicum* which sometimes makes itself felt in discussions on anthropological topics. In 1967, Edmund Leach declared in the Henry Myers lecture that 'only an idiot' would now take seriously Malinowski's claim that the Trobriand Islanders saw no connection between sexual intercourse and pregnancy (*Man*, January 1968, pp. 242–61; see **incest** (ii) in I). For a further indication of the temperature at which discussion can sometimes takes place among anthropologists, see the entry **cannibalism** in I, and endnote 14 to the entry **hair** in V.

8 See Nadine Strossen, *Defending Pornography*, Simon and Schuster, New York, 1995; Abacus, London, 1996, p. 41.

9 *The Enforcement of Morals* was republished in a book of the same name by the Oxford University Press in 1965. It is quoted here from Sanford H. Kadish and others, *The Criminal Law and Its Processes*, 4th edn, Little, Brown, Boston, 1983, where it is included as part of a general discussion on the justification of punishment. See also **sado-masochism** in I.

10 See *Tricks of Memory*, Weidenfeld and Nicolson, London, 1993, p. 270.

11 Melville, *Typee*, p. 244.

Section I
ACTIONS
'Don't do it, be it, or indulge in it!'

An open society is one that interferes with the actions of its citizens only when it can be clearly shown that these do definable harm to other people. This is why birth control is no longer illegal and why, in the United Kingdom and in a number of states in the United States of America, the laws against homosexual behaviour between consenting adults have been abolished. In both cases, the interdict can be seen as an example of a taboo that used to find its expression in a law but now no longer does so.

Adultery
Bestiality
Bondage
Cannibalism
Contraception
Divorce
Doors
Gestures
Hedonism
Homosexuality
Incest
Inform
Intermarriage
Lesbianism
Masturbation
Menstruation
Miscenegation
Nose
Oral sex
Paedophilia
Publish
Sado-masochism
Sex
Smoking
Speak
Stamp
Stare
Talk
Tell
Touch
Trespass
Usury
Whistle
Work

Adultery (i) The distance which the word 'taboo' has travelled since it was first introduced by Captain Cook in 1784 can gauged from an article in *The Independent* for 6 June 1995 entitled 'Discreet

Liaisons of the Bourgeoisie'. In it, the claim was made that 'Adultery used to be absolutely taboo. You could sleep with whomever you fancied, so long as neither of you were married.' A tendency to promiscuity, according to a recent declaration by the Bishop of Edinburgh, was an integral part of our genetic make-up. Married people could, the article suggested, therefore be as free and easy in their sexual behaviour as their unmarried counterparts.

The contrast between the bishop's remark and the attitude adopted by more traditional religious leaders is even more marked when one turns from the Koran* to the Old Testament.† *Sura* XXIV.2 reads:

> The fornicatress and the fornicator –
> scourge each one of them with a hundred stripes,
> and in the matter of God's religion
> let no tenderness for them seize you
> if you believe in God and the Last Day.

Leviticus, 20:10 commands that both the adulterer and the adulteress shall be put to death, and the Mosaic law prescribed stoning. However, the Koran contains nothing that has implications comparable with those of the story of the woman taken in adultery in *John*, 8:3–11.

(ii) The bishop's use of the term 'taboo' illustrated the dangers of too loose an application of Wittgenstein's dictum that the meaning of a word is its use in the language. Originally, the word 'taboo' evoked an irrational commandment of supernatural origin, whose defiance was inevitably followed by the punishment of the person who had broken it, whether she or he realized what they were doing or not. The breaking of such taboos rarely had a direct effect on other people. Adultery, in contrast, involves the conscious breaking of a promise freely entered into with another person, often in a completely secular context. It also has consequences that almost always involve pain and suffering to other people, especially children.

*A. J. Arberry's translation of the Koran is used throughout (Allen & Unwin, London, 1955; Oxford University Press, Oxford, 1964).

†The Authorized Version of the Bible (the 'King James') is used throughout.

Arthur Hugh Clough's rewording of the Seventh Commandment in *The Latest Decalogue* (1859) –

> Do not adultery commit;
> Advantage rarely comes of it

– is not the restatement of a taboo. It is a sensible piece of advice.
See also below, **paedophilia** and **children** (ii) in III.

Bestiality (i) After its condemnation of homosexuality 18:22, *Leviticus*, 18:23 commands: 'Neither shall thou lie with any beast to defile thyself therewith: neither shall any woman stand before a beast to lie down thereto: it is confusion.' The penalty laid down in *Leviticus*, 20:15 was death. In *Sexual Behaviour in the Human Male* (1948), Alfred Kinsey says of the older Hittite code, which predated the rules set out in the Old Testament, that 'the taboos on animal intercourse were not clearly the moral issues that they subsequently came to be'. He illustrates this idea by drawing attention to one of the contrasts in the Hittite code. While the penalty for a sexual act performed by a man with a pig or a dog was death, the only sanction imposed on anyone indulging in sexual contacts with a horse or mule was merely a ban on approaching the king or becoming a priest. This difference leads Kinsey to remark that 'such distinctions are strikingly paralleled by the taboos which make certain foods clean and other foods unclean'. It was not a question of right or wrong. It was one of observing a certain number of distinctions – an idea underlined by the use of the word 'confusion' in *Leviticus*, 18:23, quoted above.

No formal taboos against bestiality are listed in the works of anthropologists such as Mary Douglas, Edmund Leach, Claude Lévi-Strauss, or Hutton Webster which I have used in the preparation of this book. As with the comparable absence of taboos against **cannibalism**, this supports the view that taboos also function as signs distinguishing one tribe from another. Either all tribes in a particular area indulged in bestiality or cannibalism, in which case there were no interdicts; or the activities were so unthinkable that no taboos were necessary. The persistence into the Old Testament of the ancient Hittite prohibitions also confirms the view, set out in more detail in **pork** in Section II, that taboos had a taxonomic as well as a semiological function. Kinsey remarks that it is 'a fundamental of taxonomy that nature rarely deals in discrete categories'. It is, in contrast, precisely by introducing systematic distinctions that culture separates itself from nature. There are some foods you can eat, and some you cannot, some animals with which sexual relationships are permissible, others with which they are forbidden. Morality does not enter into it, a confirmation of the view that taboos represent a pre-ethical stage in human development.

Moral questions do not seem to have worried the 6 per cent of the total male population of the United States whom Alfred Kinsey and his team of researchers found in the 1940s to be involved in animal contacts during early adolescence. They tended to be farm boys in the western and south-western states, who were with animals all day and were often introduced to sex by seeing them coupling. They also had few opportunities for anything else, and the frequency declined to 1 per cent after the age of 20; except for 'one case of a male past 80 years of age who had had such contacts regularly throughout the whole of his life'. Bestiality was also, Kinsey points out, the least frequent form of sexual activity.[1]

(ii) Throughout medieval Europe, the penalty for bestiality was death. As late as 1750, in Vanves, to the south of Paris, Jacques Ferron was hung for cohabiting with a she-ass. The animal was acquitted. Sir Edward Coke refers in the *Institutes of the Laws of England* (completed in 1644) to 'a great lady who had committed buggery [US sodomy] with a baboon and conceived by it', but makes no reference to the birth of a child. In English law, bestiality remained a felony, assimilated with witchcraft and sodomy, until the nineteenth century. The last execution took place in 1835, and the death penalty was not abolished until 1861. In 1806, as Carolyn Conley reported in *The Unwritten Law: Criminal Justice in Victorian Kent* (1991), more men were hung for sodomy than for murder.

Although the courts were, as she comments, 'pragmatic if misogynistic about sexual assaults on women', sexual acts between men or between men and animals were, quite literally, unspeakable. The Criminal Registry and the *Central Criminal Court Sessions Papers* 'indicated charges of bestiality, buggery and sodomy with ellipses: b . . . st . . . y, b . . . y, and s . . . y'. The taboo was also powerful enough to affect the sentencing policy of the courts.

While assaults on women and children were, as Carolyn Conley put it, 'easily ignored or dismissed as mere trifles, indecent assault on adult males, once made public, could not be excused'.[2] It is a specific case of taboos being, at best, indifferent to the welfare of women, if not actually hostile to them, and concerned with upholding distinctions seen as important to men. In *The Criminal Prosecution and Capital Punishment of Animals* (1906) E. P. Evans comments on how odd it was that the Christian lawgivers who adopted the Jewish code against intercourse with animals should have enlarged it to include the Jews themselves. 'Men and women convicted of copulating with a human being who was not a Christian', he writes, 'were put to death, together with their partners.'[3]

Under the Sexual Offences Act 1967, it remains an offence in the United Kingdom 'to commit buggery with another person or with an animal'.[4] The word 'bestiality' does not figure in the index in either of the two main guides to criminal law in the United States: Sanford H. Kadish, Stephen J. Schulhofer and Monrad G. Paulsen, *Criminal Law and its Processes* (1983) or James Vorenberg, *Criminal Law and Procedure* (1981). The New York statute against sodomy in the case of *People* v. *Onore*, in Kadish *et al.*, *Criminal Law and its Processes*, refers only to 'deviant conduct with another person'. As in the United Kingdom, the law thus makes no distinction in this respect between human beings and animals. It is the act of anal penetration itself which is illegal.

See below, **homosexuality**.

Bondage 'For some lovers', wrote a journalist in *Cosmopolitan* in June 1992, 'a touch of the taboo is required to lift the experience into the superlative. These include bondage, spanking, and sex in public places.' There was, however, a note of caution: 'If you find these a turn off, stop them.'

Cannibalism (i) Oscar Wilde pointed out that although the commandment in *Exodus*, 20:12 instructs children to honour their parents, there is no equivalent requirement on parents to love and honour their children. When an action is instinctive and natural, there is no need for laws or commandments to enforce it, and there is a parallel to Wilde's observation in the difficulty of finding accounts or records of taboos against cannibalism. Taboos exist only when there is an activity in which a significant number of people are tempted to indulge. If there are virtually no records of taboos forbidding cannibalism, then it is tempting to argue that the instinctive revulsion we have against eating members of our own species is so powerful that there is no need to supplement it by formal interdicts. The word 'cannibalism' figures in the most comprehensive study of taboo, Hutton Webster's *Taboo: A Sociological Study* (1942), in only two contexts: that of its supposedly magical ability to enable the strength of the vanquished enemy to pass into the veins of his conqueror; and as a practice forbidden to women.

Leviticus, 11:3–24 forbids a wide range of foods to the Israelites, from the bat to the vulture and the swine to the swan (see **pork** in II). But the only mention of human beings as a possible source of food is in *Leviticus*, 26:29, where the Lord uses it as a threat: 'And ye shall eat the flesh of your sons, and the flesh of your daughters shall ye eat.' The possibility of Israelites indulging in cannibalism of their own accord is also significantly absent from the crimes enumerated in *Deuteronomy*, 27:15–27, which include, in addition to moving one's neighbour's landmark, smiting one's neighbour secretly, and perverting the judgements of the stranger, the fatherless and widow, together with five types of **incest**. The Koran condemns eating the dead bodies of human beings, placing it on the same plane as conspiring – *Sura* XLIX.10:

> And do not
> spy, neither backbite one another;
> would any of you like to eat the
> flesh of his brother dead?

– already condemned in *Sura* LVIII.10. But there is, once again, no particular insistence on the idea that eating people is wrong, with the rules on what Muslims may not eat being summarized in *Sura* V.2–5:

> Forbidden to you are
> carrion, blood, the flesh of swine,
> what has been hallowed to other than God,
> the beast strangled, the beast beaten down,

the beast fallen to death, the beast gored,
and that devoured by beasts of prey –
except you have sacrificed duly –
as also things sacrificed to idols,
and partition by the divining-arrows
that is ungodliness.

In spite of its title, Brian Marriner's *Cannibalism: The Last Taboo* (1992)[5] does not talk about formal taboos against cannibalism, either in past history or in modern times. Instead, the book analyses the phenomenon in terms either of necessity or of criminal insanity, describing how, in 1972, sixteen members of an amateur rugby team kept themselves alive by eating the bodies of the other passengers who had been killed on impact when the aeroplane carrying them from Argentina to Chile crashed in the Andes. Brian Marriner also gives gory details of how three German cannibals, Georg Karl Grossman, Fritz Haarmaan and Kark Denke, butchered and consumed their victims. But except for survival cannibalism, when the choice lies between eating the dead bodies of other humans or dying of starvation, he provides few modern examples of cases where cannibalism is not preceded by murder. At no point does he provide a detailed list of taboos against cannibalism that suggest it is something which normal human beings might do quite spontaneously unless instructed otherwise, in the way that they might wear clothes made of a mixture of wool and linen, drink wine, make graven images, go to bed with their cousin, or make love to a member of the same sex (see **mix** and **alcohol** in II, **images** in IV, **incest** and **homosexuality** below; see also the quotation about the dog in the night-time from Conan Doyle's *Silver Blaze* in **apples** in II).

(ii) The word 'taboo' is equally absent from the index of the controversial book which called into question the very idea that formal or ritualized cannibalism had ever existed, William Arens's *The Man-Eating Myth: Anthropology and Anthropophagy* (1979). Like other observers, Arens admits the possibility of 'survival cannibalism': human beings eating their fellows in order to stay alive. However, he points to the lack of hard evidence for institutionalized or ritualized cannibalism and comments: 'like the poor, cannibals are always with us but happily just beyond the possibility of actual observation'.[6] More particularly, he criticizes modern anthropologists for perpetuating what he presents as the myth originally propagated by Christian missionaries anxious to prove the barbaric nature of the people they had already decided either to convert or destroy.

In the fifth of her Reith lectures, published as *Managing Monsters* (1994), Marina Warner took up the argument of *The Man-Eating Myth* in an even more aggressively political form. In her view, cannibalism was a myth invented by European colonizers at the beginning of the age of exploration. Writing that 'empirical support for cannibalism as a routine form of sustenance has never been found', she argued in 'Cannibal Tales: The Hunger for Conquest' that

> Cannibalism is used to define the alien but actually mirrors the speaker. By tarring the savage with the horror of cannibalism, settlers, explorers, colonisers could vindicate their own violence – it's a psychological manoeuvre of great effectiveness.

For her, it is the European invaders and exploiters who are the genuine devourers of other people. It is we who destroy their culture at the same time as we kill them off physically in order to satisfy our own greed. The myth of cannibalism justifies the brutal reality of colonialism.[7]

Perhaps unwisely, William Arens did not limit himself to drawing the attention of his readers to the apparent absence of hard evidence for the existence of cannibalism as a systematic way either of obtaining nourishment or of performing rituals. He also made a sustained attack on what he presented as the way anthropologists themselves went about their work. This led to a number of criticisms of his book, of which one of the most sustained was a review article by Ivan Brady which appeared in the September 1982 number of the *American Anthropologist*. Ivan Brady, the reviews editor for the section 'Social and Cultural Anthropology', argued that

> it should be remembered that Arens's book is less an attempt to set the record straight on cannibalism (where it does or does not occur and why) than it is an indictment of anthropology for swallowing such tales whole and parading them around in

> the literature as facts when most of the evidence turns out on inspection to be unsubstantiated impressions, rumours, innuendo, ethnocentrism, plagiarism and so forth.

In particular, Dr Brady picked out for unfavourable mention Arens's comment on the progress of anthropology itself, and especially his contention that 'much of the excitement and optimism of an earlier era has been replaced by a contemporary sense of futility and outright cynicism on the part of many anthropologists', and that 'despite assurances to the contrary, scholars in all fields occasionally have functioned as little more than purveyors of attractive pedestrian myths'.[8]

It is a shade disappointing, especially when *The Man-Eating Myth* had also been described by P. G. Rivière in 1980 in *Man*, the journal of the Royal Anthropological Institute, as 'a bad book', characterized by being prepared with 'little work and less scholarship',[9] to discover that Dr Arens's critics did not come up with a plethora of hard evidence to prove that either ritualized cannibalism, or the eating of human beings as a regular means of obtaining protein, had been witnessed by a series of reliable observers, and could therefore be seen as an attested fact of human behaviour. So concerned were anthropologists about the tone and implications of Arens's book that a special symposium of the American Anthropological Association entitled 'The Ethnography of Cannibalism' was held in December 1980 in Washington, DC, and the papers given at it were published by the Society for Psychological Anthropology three years later.[10] However, here again, only one participant, Fitzjohn Porter Poole, claimed actually to have witnessed acts of cannibalism, and the overall effect of the controversy stirred up by Arens's book was to confirm a comment made by Jean-Pierre Castile in another article in the *American Anthropologist* when he cast doubt on Michael Harner's thesis that the Aztecs indulged in cannibalism primarily because there were few other sources of protein: 'I cannot say that it is proven that no such thing occurred, but I do insist that he [Harner] has not proven that it did.'[11]

There is an intriguing contrast here between the views of professional anthropologists and those put forward by writers such as Robert Ardrey, who had shown no hesitation in claiming in *The*

Territorial Imperative (1969) that cannibalism has been 'a prevalent pastime throughout all of human record', and pointed out that in some of the earliest human remains to have been excavated in China, from the caves of Chou Kou Tien, the skulls can be seen to have been forced open to extract the brains.[12] His book was not, however, mentioned in the publications sparked off by *The Man-Eating Myth*, any more than was Chapter 32 of *Typee: A Peep at Polynesian Life* (1846), in which Herman Melville described the 'disordered members of a human skeleton, the bones still fresh with moisture, and with particles of flesh clinging to them here and there', which he came across in one of the taboo groves on the island. He had no particular ideological axe to grind, and seems to be describing institutionalized or even ritualized cannibalism, though the same may not have been true of the Dutch missionary mentioned by Edward Schneider in his letter to the *Times Literary Supplement* quoted in the entry **camels** in Section II.

The argument about *The Man-Eating Myth* tended to concentrate instead on what methods of observation were or were not valid in anthropological enquiry. This has only a marginal interest for the study of taboos. These are interdicts about whose existence there can be no doubt, being attested as they are in a wide variety of anthropologists' reports, as well as in books such as the Bible or the Koran. There was, nevertheless, an interesting coincidence in the publication in the same issue of the *American Anthropologist* in which Dr Brady's review-article had appeared of an equally long article entitled 'Kuru or Cannibalism?'. Kuru, a disease current in the Fore region of the Eastern Highlands of New Guinea, and which has similarities to Creutzfeldt-Jakob's disease, had commonly been attributed to cannibalism, and especially the habit of eating the brains of already deceased human beings.

The evidence for this attribution, however, was now revealed as open to question, and the authors of the article, Lyle B. Steadman and Charles F. Merbs, wrote that the most likely source for the disease was not in the brains or bodies eaten 'but simply the handling of corpses of infected kin and affines'. They nevertheless concluded their article by describing cannibalism as 'one of the most abominable activities imaginable', and commented that 'perhaps because cannibalism, like incest, is indeed possible, people must be regularly reminded of its destructiveness'.[13] This may well be true, and may well explain the difficulty of finding formal taboos against it. The horror that we feel at the very idea of eating members of own species is so great that we do not need to be told not to do it. In Melanesia, the eating of the corpses is part of a funerary rite and is therefore difficult to classify as cannibalism in the normal sense of the word.[14]

See also **human beings** in II, and **homosexuality** in IV.

Contraception (i) The Judeo-Christian tradition differs from other world religions as much in its taboos against birth control as in its former success in persuading the legislator to introduce laws against **homosexuality**. Once a Hindu has begotten a son, there is no rule against preventing further births. The Koran contains no ban either on homosexuality or on contraception. Like Confucianism, Shintoism gives great importance to the family. Neither religion forbids birth control.

As with the ban on **homosexuality**, the Judeo-Christian taboo on the deliberate avoidance of impregnation goes back to the Old Testament. It is based on the account in *Genesis*, 38:8 of Onan's refusal to conform to the custom known as the levirate, whereby a man had to marry his brother's widow if she had not yet borne children. For after Er, Judah's firstborn, had been wicked in the sight of the Lord, so that 'the Lord slew him', Judah said to Onan:

> Go in unto thy brother's wife, and marry her, and raise up seed to thy brother.
>
> And Onan knew that the seed should not be his; and it came to pass, when he went unto his brother's wife, that he spilled it on the ground, lest that he should give seed to his brother.
>
> And the thing which he did displeased the Lord: wherefore he slew him also.

A prohibition on anything likely to reduce the number of future warriors matches the general ethos of the Old Testament, described by Aldous Huxley in 1937 as 'the history of the cruelties and treacheries of a Bronze Age people, fighting for a place in the sun under the protection of its anthropomorphic tribal deity'.[15] The French law of 1920 banning the sale of contraceptive devices and all advertisements for them stemmed from comparable considerations. Although it matched the teaching of the Catholic Church, it was not inspired by it. France had been a secular republic since 1905. However, it had also lost almost a million and a half men in the First World War, and had had so low a birthrate throughout the nineteenth century that it could keep enough men in the trenches only by refusing to allow them to go on leave. The birthrate between 1914 and 1918 had thus been so disastrously low that there was a perceived need to make women have as many children as possible in order to make up for 'the empty years'. The 1920 law was nevertheless not successful in increasing the birthrate. Between 1914 and 1939, only immigration prevented a net decline in the French population. When the law was rescinded in 1967, it was because the taboo had become impossible to enforce. It was not because the French government now thought that enough babies were being born.

(ii) The right of couples in the United Kingdom and the United States to choose the method by which they limited the number of children they had was not won overnight. In 1824, John Stuart Mill was arrested for distributing birth control literature to the poor in London. In 1834, a Bristol publisher was prosecuted and fined for selling Charles Knowlton's *The Fruits of Philosophy; or The Private Companion of Young Married People.* When first published in the United States in 1832, this book had evoked the comment from the *Boston Medical and Surgical Journal* that 'the less is known about it among the public at large, the better it will be for the morals of the community', and Knowlton, who added to his other offences the fact of being an outspoken free-thinker, was twice prosecuted. On the first occasion, he was fined $50; on the second, he was sentenced to three months in prison. In the United States, Arthur Comstock was successful in 1873 in having Congress pass an Act banning contraception. Theoretically, this remained in force until 1965, when the Supreme Court ruled in *Griswold* v. *Connecticut* that the laws against contraception violated the constitutional right to privacy.

In 1916, Margaret Sanger was briefly imprisoned for opening the first birth control clinic in New York. She owed her subsequent acquittal partly to the support which she gave to what was then the popular eugenics movement. Her slogan: 'More children for the fit, fewer children to the unfit. That is the chief issue in birth control'[16] echoed the views of the moral majority of her time. Until the *Griswold* v. *Connecticut* decision, a number of states in North America allowed condoms to be sold only if the purchaser had the intention of using them to protect himself against a sexually transmitted disease. If the object was to prevent contraception, the sale was illegal. In spite of the fact that the AIDS epidemic has brought the sheath back into fashion, its use as a means of preventing the spread of disease is not yet accepted by the Roman Catholic Church. The borderline between prophylaxis and contraception is too narrow. However, on 12 February 1996, the French bishops issued a statement saying that the use of the sheath was permissible as a measure intended to halt the spread of the AIDS virus. The conservatively minded newspaper *Le Figaro* described the bishops' decision as the lifting of a taboo.

In the United Kingdom, Marie Stopes survived the attempt to ban her *Married Love* in 1916, and went on to found the first birth control clinic, in Holloway, London, on 17 March 1921. She may have been helped by the fact that like Margaret Sanger and a number of other early apostles of birth control, she too was a convinced eugenicist. She also offered advice only to married couples. In 1930, she saw her ideas officially accepted when the Ministry of Health authorized the opening of further clinics, again only for married women, as well as the establishment of the National Birth Control Council. After expressing disapproval in 1908 and 1920, the Anglican Church changed its mind in 1958 and said that the practice was acceptable in the case of married couples. It was not until 1965 that the Brooke Advisory Clinic, initially based only in London, began to supply contraceptives to unmarried women.

(iii) The attitude of the Roman Catholic Church offers the unusual example of a taboo being supported by a more elaborate and intellectually consistent ideology than exists in most religions. Already, in the fourth century AD, St Augustine was arguing in *Marriage and Concupiscence* that those who used 'an evil deed' or 'an evil prayer' to prevent contraception were married in name only, and categorically condemning those who used 'poisons of sterility'.[17] The Church's present position was stated in its clearest form in the words of the 1968 encyclical *Humanae Vitae*, which placed a ban on 'every action which, either in anticipation of the conjugal act or its accomplishment, or in the development of its natural processes, proposes, whether as an end or as a means, to render procreation impossible'. This restatement of the traditional teaching of the Church marked a refusal by Pope Paul VI to accept the recommendation of the commission appointed by his predecessor in 1963, and which is said to have been about to accept that chemical or mechanical means of birth control could be morally licit. It is fully consistent with the Catholic concept of natural law, which involves a view of sexuality as given by God exclusively for the purposes of procreation.

In the 1950s, the salacious mention of contraception in Barbara Cartland's *Guide to Married Life* (1954) led it to be placed on the Irish Republic's Register of Prohibited Books. In 1957, a similar fate was visited upon an issue of *Woman and Home* when it broke the same taboo by referring to the possibility of limiting the size of one's family by artificial means. It is nevertheless unusual, even in Ireland, for Catholic families to have more children than their Protestant or agnostic neighbours. The ban on the use of artificial modes of contraception has therefore ceased to provide a badge of ideological identity.[18]

The taboo on contraception is unusual in the total coincidence between its origin and function. In both cases, the object was to ensure that there were enough people to fulfil the injunction addressed to the first human beings in *Genesis*, 1:28: 'Be fruitful, and multiply, and replenish the earth, and subdue it: and have dominion over the fish of the sea, and over the fowl of the air, and over every living thing that moveth upon the earth.' Now that this mission has been over-accomplished, the taboo persists as an almost classic illustration of Freud's contention, in *Totem and Taboo*, that one of the main objects of taboos is to prevent people enjoying themselves. Were there to be a prize for the taboo whose survival beyond the point where it was useful has caused most unhappiness, frustration and unnecessary suffering, and which nowadays represents the greatest threat to the ecology of the planet, the ban on artificial methods of contraception would win hands down.

See below, **hedonism**, **miscegenation** and **oral sex**; also **contraception** in III and IV; **menstruation** in IV; the remarks about power in the Introduction; and section (iii) of the Conclusion.

Divorce The Catholic Church is unique among Christian denominations, as, indeed, among other world religions, in placing an absolute ban on divorce. The doctrine finally defined at the Council of Trent in 1560 is based on the injunction in *Mark*, 10:9: 'What therefore God hath joined together, let not man put asunder.' It also stems from the ruling in *Matthew*, 5:32 and *Luke*, 16:18 that a man who 'puts his wife away' and takes another commits adultery. Similarly, I *Corinthians*, 7:10 enjoins husbands not to 'put away' their wives, and instructs wives to whom this has happened not to take another husband. *The Catholic Encyclopedia* writes that

> There are two fundamental theological evils in civil divorce and separation. The trial of a baptised person and the verdict for and against divorce and separation is an invasion by the state of the right of the church to hear and judge matrimonial causes, and the verdict of divorce is the exercise of a power which the state has not received from God.

During his period as general manager and director-general of the BBC (1922–38), Lord Reith showed that his Presbyterian background did not make him unsympathetic to all aspects of Catholic doctrine. He refused to allow any divorced person to introduce the Epilogue.

Although the Prophet said that 'of all things licit, the most hateful to God is divorce', Islamic law allows four ways in which a marriage can be dissolved: by mutual consent; by request of the wife; on varying grounds including 'the husband's impotence, apostasy, madness, dangerous illness, or some other defect in the marriage'; or through repudiation by the husband. Although this is a unilateral decision which he does not need to explain, it must be pronounced while the wife 'is in a state of purity [*tuhr*], that is, not menstruating'. If she is pregnant, it cannot take effect until 'an allotted time after the child is born'.[19] In *The Concise Encyclopedia of Islam* (1989), Cyril Glassé points out that a number of Islamic countries are taking steps to mitigate the inferior position in which this places women.

It is a tribute to the skill of Evelyn Waugh that he succeeds, in the closing pages of *Brideshead Revisited* (1945), in constructing a highly moving plot around a belief in the indissolubility of marriage to which some twentieth-century observers would give the status of a taboo.[20]

Doors Among senior ranks of the British Diplomatic Service, one does not knock before walking into a colleague's room. While this may be to avoid implying that she or he might be involved in improper activities, the custom does not exist in other ministries. It thus fulfils one of the central functions of taboos: that of establishing and marking a difference.

See **pork** in II and **images** in IV.

Gestures The Puritan revolution of the seventeenth century laid great emphasis on *Matthew*, 5:37: 'Let your communication be, Yea, yea; Nay, nay; for whatsoever is more than these cometh of evil.' This inspired the refusal of members of certain sects such as the Quakers to swear on the Bible, and to insist instead on affirming. It changed the English from being as voluble and gesticulative a race as the Italians into a people who looked down on jabbering foreigners and prided themselves on their sobriety of speech.

Hedonism (i) In spite of Calvin's insistence that 'man becomes happy through self-denial', not even his most austere followers placed a ban on the pleasure afforded by eating and drinking. There are too many references in the Bible to the importance of feasts as an occasion for praising God through His works. The taboo on the pursuit of sexual activity for pleasure alone survives in the view, said to be peculiar to Judeo-Christianity, that it is wrong to indulge in non-procreative sex. This is expressed in the interdiction by the Roman Catholic Church on all forms of artificial birth control. It recurs in the reasons given in *The Catholic Encyclopedia* for the ban on homosexuality:

> The homosexual act by its very essence excludes all possibility of transmission of life; and an act which cannot fulfil the procreative purpose of the sexual faculty is, therefore, an inordinate use of that faculty.

(ii) The taboo on the favourable presentation of sexual experience lingers on in the debate about censorship. The view that it is wrong to make people more interested in sex than they already are was put by a psychiatric witness, Dr Tarumniaz, when the state of Delaware bought an action in 1951 against the film *Hollywood Peep Show*. It was, in his view, wrong to depict certain sexual activities, lest

> A happily married individual, who is considered a mature adult individual, seeing such films, becomes seriously concerned with whether he is obtaining the necessary gratification of his sex desires from his normally endowed and inclined wife. It may deviate him into accepting that there is something which arouses him to become interested in an abnormal type of sexual satisfaction which he had perhaps from this picture.

The judge agreed and the film was banned.

Dessie Kellegher's wife Kay, in the film of Roddy Doyle's *The Snapper* (1993), would have seen what Dr Tarumniaz meant. However, neither Dessie nor his wife would have agreed with him that it was a bad idea to get new ideas about sex. For when the Kelleghers' teenage daughter Tina finds herself pregnant, her father Dessie feels that he ought to find out a little bit more about sex and babies, and borrows a book from the local library. Later, when he and his wife are in bed, he suddenly dives down under the sheets, and in response to his wife's question of what has got into him, tells her to wait. After what is clearly a session of cunnilingus, she tells him, with a slight but obviously satisfied smile, that she can now see.

The fact that the action of *The Snapper*, like that of the other plays in *The Barrytown Trilogy* (1992–4), takes place in a suburb of Dublin reveals a shift of attitudes in a city where it was still difficult, in the 1960s, actually to buy a copy of James Joyce's *Ulysses*. In spite of the persistence of its ban on contraception, the Catholic Church has clearly not been able to maintain its power to regulate other details in the sexual life of the citizens of the Irish Republic. Dessie, for example, borrows the book from the public library, a fact which shows a remarkable change in church–state relationships in a country where the Church was still powerful enough in 1980 to ensure that no mention was made of **contraception** in the Health (Family Planning) Act.

(iii) It is an open question whether the universal availability of books such as Alex Comfort's *The Joy of Sex* (1969) has made people happier. As long ago as 1963, Mary McCarthy argued in one of the essays reprinted in *The Humanist in the Bathtub* that what she called 'the tyranny of the orgasm' was compelling women not only to make more sexual efforts than they would have chosen if left to themselves, but also to feel guilty if they did not obtain the right result. She thus presented an implicit argument in favour of a taboo on the nature and amount of what might be called the sexual propaganda available, and Dr Eustace Chesser observed, in *The Sexual, Marital and Family Relationships of the English Woman* (1956), that whereas it was shameful, before 1914, for a woman to admit to experiencing pleasure in intercourse, the situation nowadays is that many women 'feel ashamed if they do not experience an orgasm'.[21] A related idea was expressed in stronger terms by Sally Cline in *Women, Passion and Celibacy* (1993). In her view, women's orgasms are 'a form of manipulated emotional labour which women work at in order to reflect men and to maintain male values', and Nadine Strossen summarizes the attitude of a number of American feminists, when she writes that 'sexual intercourse, and even female orgasms, are essentially forced on women through media manipulation in order to please men'.[22] A recurrent theme in Germaine Greer's *Sex and Destiny: The Politics of Human Fertility* (1984) is that Western women offer their menfolk the spectacle of repeated orgasms as a replacement for the children which our modern obsession with birth control prevents them from giving to their sexual partner.

An article in The *Sunday Telegraph* for 30 July 1995 entitled 'The Beach Book' offered a reminder of how fully taboos in this area have disappeared in the industrialized West. The article evoked the spectacle of Mr and Mrs Holiday-Maker going off together, she with her suitcase full of the recent novels by Jackie Collins, Shirley Conran, Jilly Cooper or Judith Krantz. After she has spent the morning reading, and they retire for a lie-down after lunch, Mr Holiday-Maker reflects on the 'unusually bold behaviour' of his wife, 'not to mention her unsuitable insistence on trying to involve in her activities the complimentary basket of exotic fruits provided by the hotel'.

See **contraception** (iii) above, **oral sex**, **homosexuality**, **Lesbianism** and **sado-masochism**, together with the comments of Henry Davis SJ quoted under **sex** below. A certain hostility to hedonism is visible in the arguments mentioned in IV as having been used to oppose the publication of *Lady Chatterley's Lover*.

Homosexuality (i) The Judeo-Christian taboo against sexual relations between men goes back to *Leviticus*, 18:22: 'Thou shalt not lie with mankind as with womankind: it is abomination.' *Leviticus*, 20:13 commands the death penalty. The taboo was reaffirmed in *Romans*, 1:18 and 1:26–8, where St Paul presented both Lesbianism and male homosexuality as a punishment visited by God upon 'all ungodliness and unrighteousness of men, who hold the truth in unrighteousness'. 'And likewise also the men', he writes,

> leaving the natural use of the woman, burned in their lust one toward another; men with men working that which is unseemly, and receiving in themselves that recompense of their error which was meet.

The penny catechism of the Roman Catholic Church continues to classify sodomy, together with wilful murder, the oppression of the poor, and the attempt to defraud workers of the fruits of their labour, as one of the 'four sins that cry to Heaven for vengeance'.[23] On 2 August 1995, the *Guardian* reported Robert Mugabe, President of Zimbabwe, as saying that homosexuals should have no right in society at all, and declaring:

> If we accept homosexuality as a right, as it is being argued by the association of sodomists and sexual perverts, what moral fibre shall our society ever have to deny organised drug addicts, or even those given to bestiality, the right they might claim and allege they possess under the rubrics of 'individual freedom' and 'human rights', including the freedom of the press to write, publish and publicise their literature on them?

The word 'homosexuality' was coined in 1869 by a German doctor called Hongrois Benkelt. It did not come into common usage until the 1890s, when what Michel Foucault called the 'taxonomical impulses of the nineteenth century' led to the change he describes in *The History of Sexuality* (1980). During the Middle Ages, he argued, the civil and the ecclesiastical authorities had used the 'utterly confused' category of 'sodomy' to condemn practices as different from one another as sex between men or between women, sex between men and women not sanctioned by marriage, sex bent on preventing contraception, or sex between humans, whether men or women, and animals. Now, however, he claimed, the homosexual had ceased to be 'a temporary aberration' and become 'a species, a personage, with a past, a case history, and a childhood, with a life style and a morphology, with a particular anatomy, and possibly a mysterious physiology'.[24]

This change is reflected in the vocabulary used to define those afflicted with what Proust saw as the curse of possessing a female soul in a man's body. Until the late nineteenth century, the term used was 'bugger' or 'sodomite', and the Marquis of Queensberry, the father of Lord Alfred Douglas, was as out-of-date in his vocabulary as he was inaccurate in his spelling when he left a card at Wilde's club, the Albemarle, on 18 February 1895, reading 'To Oscar Wilde, posing as a Somdomite' (sic).[25] Until the early nineteenth century, there was no difference between predominantly Catholic countries such as France or Italy and Protestant ones such as Great Britain or the United States. However, the Napoleonic Code of 1804 took a fairly lenient view, and the activity ceased to be an offence in countries influenced by it such as France, Italy, Belgium and Spain.

(ii) In 1961, the Illinois state legislature, as Rollin M. Perkins and Ronald A. Boyce put it in *Criminal Law* (1982),

> removed sodomy from the category of crime in that state except to the extent that criminal sanctions are needed to protect (1) the individual against forcible acts, (2) the young and immature from sexual advances by older persons and (3) the public from open and notorious conduct which flouts accepted standards of morality in the community.

By 1982, California, Iowa and New Jersey had done the same.[26] The success of events such as Gay Freedom Day, which on 24 June 1990 brought over 300,000 people out on to the streets of

San Francisco, means that it is sometimes difficult to enforce the laws against homosexuality on the statute book of the states which still retain them.

Nevertheless the Gay Liberation Front, formed in 1969, has enjoyed only partial success in altering the official legal position in the United States as a whole. Its formation occurred after New York City police staged a weekend raid on 27 June 1969 on the Stonewall Inn, and a serious riot ensued when drag queens, Lesbians and homosexuals fought back and attracted support from spectators. In 1992, laws against 'crimes against nature', 'the infamous crime against nature', 'the abominable and detestable crime against nature' were still on the statute book in twenty-four of the fifty states.[27] In 1986, an unsuccessful attempt was made in *Bowes* v. *Hardwick* to have the laws against homosexuality declared unconstitutional by the Supreme Court. On 30 June, by a judgment of five to four, the court declared that 'the constitutional guarantee of personal liberty and privacy does not protect private homosexual conduct between consenting adults', and upheld against constitutional challenge the Georgia anti-sodomy laws which banned oral or anal sex. In 1990, Supreme Court Justice Lewis Powell, who cast the fifth, decisive vote in favour of the constitutionality of the Georgia laws in the *Bowes* v. *Hardwick* case, was reported as having said that he was wrong, and that homosexuals should benefit from the right to privacy.[28] The matter nevertheless remains within the discretion of the legislature of each individual state. In 1996, laws against anal and/or oral sex were on the statute book in the twenty-four states of Alabama, Arizona, Arkansas, North Carolina, South Carolina, Florida, Georgia, Idaho, Kansas, Louisiana, Maryland, Massachusetts, Mississippi, Missouri, Montana, Nevada, Oklahoma, Oregon, Rhode Island, Tennessee, Texas, Virginia, Utah and the District of Columbia.[29] However, *The New York Times* for 21 January 1996 reported that eighty-seven counties or cities have civil rights ordinances extending protection to homosexuals, and that similar laws exist in California, Connecticut, Hawaii, Massachusetts, Minnesota, New Jersey, Rhode Island, Vermont and Wisconsin. The situation is clearly a complicated one, in that some states (e.g. Massachusetts) have laws banning homosexuality but protecting homosexuals.

In recent years, argument in the United States has concentrated on the right of homosexuals to serve in the armed forces and on their eligibility to receive various benefits. In 1988, the Helms amendment forbade disease control centres to fund activities which 'promote or encourage, directly or indirectly, homosexual sexual activities'. In 1989, the Fair Housing Act said that no disability allowances were to be paid in cases of 'homosexuality, bisexuality, paedophilia, transvestism, exhibition, voyeurism, compulsive gambling, kleptomania, pyromania and gender-identity disorders'.[30] In 1993, President Clinton was unsuccessful in implementing his campaign promise to have the laws excluding homosexuals from the armed services rescinded. However, a compromise was reached whereby the authorities agreed not to ask about the sexual preferences of those wishing to serve their country in uniform, and homosexuals agreed not to broadcast their tastes. The 'Don't ask/don't tell' policy was also extended as far as day-to-day practice was concerned to the slogan 'Don't tell/don't touch'.

(iii) In theory, what the 1828 law called 'the abominable crime of Buggery committed with either Mankind or with any Animal' was punishable under English law by death. Forcible buggery is punishable as rape. Although it remains an offence in the United Kingdom for a man to commit consensual buggery (US sodomy) with a woman, there have been no prosecutions since the 1828 act became law.[31] Since the 1828 law did not explicitly mention such activities as mutual masturbation, the presupposition until 1885 was that these were not criminal offences. A consequence of the Labouchère amendment of 1885, which extended the prohibition by making all sexual acts between males illegal, was the sentence of two years' hard labour passed in 1895 on Oscar Wilde. Henry du Pré Labouchère (1831–1912) was a zealous but undiscriminating legislator, who proposed amendments with little thought as to their consequences. It is thus possible that the most famous imprisonment for a sexual offence of a writer in a Western democracy was the result more of an accident than of any systematic crusade against homosexuality.

As late as 1953, the writer Peter Wildeblood was sent to prison in England for two years for taking part in homosexual acts with adults, and he later commented, in *Against the Law* (1957), that

'Britain and America are almost the only countries in which such behaviour constitutes an offence' and added:

> In America the law is reduced to absurdity by the fact that it applies officially, also, to a variety of acts between men and women, whether married or not; it has been estimated that a strict application of the law would result in the imprisonment of two-thirds of the adult population, and as a result it is seldom invoked, even against homosexuals.[32]

In 1967, homosexual acts committed in private between consenting adults aged 18 or over ceased to be illegal in the United Kingdom. The criminal law is no longer based on the assimilation between sodomy and heresy originally established by St Jerome in the fourth century AD. Buggery (US sodomy) continues to be an offence if it takes place in public, a ruling which applies especially if it is committed in a public lavatory to which other people have access. It is also an offence 'on a merchant ship by a member of the crew of that or of any other United Kingdom merchant ship'.[33] Supporters of the gay rights movement in Britain see themselves as still victimized by the taboo against homosexuality in three ways: whereas heterosexual activity is legal at the age of 16, homosexuals have to wait until they are 18; professed homosexuals are not allowed to serve in the armed forces, a ruling which might, when conscription was in force in the United Kingdom between 1916 and 1918 and again between 1939 and 1963, have led to a surprising increase in the declaration of interest in members of the same sex; and the open expression of homosexual feelings is more rigorously pursued than heterosexual acts by the laws against conduct likely to cause a breach of the peace.[34] The example offered by the state of Hawaii, which recently accepted as legal a form of marriage carried out between two members of the same sex, has not yet been widely followed. However, it is under consideration in Holland and Denmark. On 27 February 1996, Bishop Walter Righter was placed on trial by the Episcopalian Church for ordaining a professed homosexual as a deacon.

(iv) Homosexuality is tolerated in most of the Arabic countries influenced by the teaching of Islam. Muhammad was well acquainted with the story of Lot, referring in *Sura* XXI.73 to the inhabitants of Sodom as 'an evil people, truly ungodly', and approving in *Sura* XXVI.170–4 of the destruction of the city. But the Koran contains no condemnation of homosexuality that is as explicit as *Leviticus*, 20:13, and a fourteenth-century *hadith*, or saying attributed to the Prophet, (see **images** in IV) claims that 'God pays no attention to a man who has slept with a man, nor to a woman who has slept with a woman'.[35] Homosexuality is not banned in either Hindu, Buddhist or Shinto culture, and Bret Hinsch maintains in *Passions of the Cut Sleeve: The Male Homosexual Tradition in China* (1990) that it was 'widely accepted and even respected' for long periods in Chinese history, and comments that

> just as Edward Gibbon observed that all but one of the first fourteen emperors of Rome were either bisexual or exclusively homosexual, for two centuries, at the height of the Han period (206 BC–AD 220), China was ruled by ten openly bisexual emperors.[36]

Since the prime concern of the peasants was to have enough children to ensure a plentiful supply of labour to work the land, homosexuality remained an activity restricted to what Dr Hinsch calls 'the rich and privileged', and there are few mentions of **Lesbianism** in Chinese literature.

Although homosexuality was not seen as unnatural in classical Greece, and there was, as Paul Veyne observes, 'no ritual taboo against pederasty' in ancient Rome,[37] it would be misleading to see either society as offering the same total freedom in sexual matters that characterized San Francisco before the outbreak of the AIDS epidemic. K. J. Dover points out in *Greek Homosexuality* (1978) that in sexual relations between men in fifth-century Athens, 'the reciprocal desire of partners belonging to the same age category is virtually unknown'. In spite of the fact that it was 'taken absolutely for granted that close contact with a beautiful, grateful, admiring young man' was 'a virtually irresistible temptation' for members of his own sex, the relationship between an elder man and a boy was not strongly physical. What mattered was the affection which the older man succeeded in making the boy feel for him.[38]

Taboos frequently offer an insight into the tastes and values of the society which adopts them. One of the most frequent features of homosexuality in contemporary Britain and America is a liking for rough trade. In the traditional Japan described by Ruth Benedict in *The Chrysanthemum and the Sword* (1946), homosexuality was tolerated so long as it was discreet and did not prevent a man from carrying on a family. But while adult men would seek out boy partners, they considered the passive role to be beneath their dignity.[39] Similarly, in the classical world of Greece and Rome, any free citizen who allowed himself to be buggered by a slave lost all claim to social prestige. In the macho society of ancient Rome, fellatio, whether given or received, was the basest form of self-humiliation; and cunnilingus even more so. In our own society, the former is said to be one of the most common practices among male homosexuals. Brutus, 'the noblest Roman of them all', loved a boy so beautiful that reproductions of him were to be seen everywhere in the city. His attractiveness, however, like that of the Greek epheboi, disappeared the moment the hair grew on his upper lip.

See **Lesbianism** and **paedophilia** below; **poofter** and **queer** in III, **homosexuality** and the entry on *The Well of Loneliness* in IV; **hair** in V.

Incest (i) In 1970, Edmund Leach called the incest taboo 'the great event with which culture began', and wrote in 1979 that 'if ten modern anthropologists were asked to designate one universal human institution, nine would be likely to name the incest prohibition'. In 1949, in *The Elementary Structures of Kinship*, Claude Lévi-Strauss went so far as to describe it as 'the corner stone of human society',[40] and the impression given by most anthropologists is that the incest taboo is an even more important sign of our humanity than the development of language, the use of tools, or the obligation we feel to care for the old and the infirm.

Anthropologists also maintain that the origins of the incest taboo had nothing to do with procreation. On the contrary, they insist, they were purely social. If members of the tribe did not marry out, and thus strengthen it by acquiring new allies, it would soon become extinct. It is a view encapsulated in the slogan 'Marry out or die out', and one which the English nineteenth-century anthropologist Edward Tylor summarized when he wrote in 1881:

> In the course of evolution, human societies had the choice of giving their womenfolk away to create political alliances or of keeping their womenfolk to themselves and getting killed off by their numerically superior enemies.[41]

For Lévi-Strauss, exogamy is essential to the peaceful relationships between bands or clans on which social life is based. The exchange of women is a necessary step to the exchange of goods and services on which civilized life depends.

Anthropologists consequently tend to reject the popular view that the taboo on sexual activity between blood relations originates in an awareness of the genetic dangers of in-breeding. They point out that in the more robust societies which preceded our own, and in which the incest taboo originated, sickly children died too quickly to leave any offspring. In-breeding would thus not have the cumulative and visible effects which it can produce in our own more protective culture. When Bronislaw Malinowski visited New Guinea between 1914 and 1918, he rapidly received the impression, as he puts it, that the Trobriand islanders had not yet 'grasped the fertilising virtue of seminal fluid' and saw the testes as having a purely decorative function. But although the Trobriand islanders apparently refused to accept that there was any link between the sexual act and the birth of a child, they saw brother–sister incest as 'the supreme taboo' and centred the sexual education of their children round the need to respect this interdict.[42]

One of the many problems which the incest taboo sets is that of explaining why, if it dates back to so rational an ambition as the desire to extend one's social acquaintance, the physical revulsion against incest itself is so strong. It is this revulsion that makes the alternative explanation put forward by biologists initially so attractive. They present the incest taboo as genetic in origin as well as in function, with Richard Dawkins arguing in *The Selfish Gene* (1989) that members of species as different from one another as quails and lions quite instinctively avoid mating with those with whom they have grown up.[43] If human beings behave in the same way, he maintains, it is because the ambition of our genes to perpetuate themselves has always given us the same instinctive awareness as other animals that mating with anyone to whom one is closely related will produce imperfect offspring. Since it would be a disadvantage to our genes to be lodged in their next incarnation in a potentially non-viable body, they have always led us to act in such a way as to avoid the danger, and continue to do so. Genes have the same need of a large pool in order to ensure their genetic survival as a human community does of a large number of allies in order to ensure its prosperity as a viable social group.

In his 1991 Reith lectures, Steve Jones summed up the most commonly held view of the function of the incest taboo when he commented that the most important invention for improving the quality of the human stock in rural England was the bicycle. It enabled young men to go easily to the next village in search of a bride to whom they were not related. But what may well be true of the usefulness of exogamy to contemporary human beings could easily not apply to its origins. The origins of the incest taboo among humans could well have been purely social, and based on the idea that all societies can profit from what is metaphorically as well as literally known as new blood. While Richard Dawkins may be right about quails and lions, other animals seem totally indiscriminate in their copulations. If left to themselves, cats, dogs and rabbits couple with members of their own species with what seems, to the human observer, to be a complete disregard either of ties of blood or of possible genetic consequences.

The existence of an instinctive revulsion against incest was nevertheless called into question in 1985 by Patricia Whelehan in her review in the *American Anthropologist* of Joseph Shepherd's *Incest: A Biosocial View* (1983). While admitting that the origins for the taboo might well be twofold, with learned behaviour induced by social rules reinforcing an already existing innate disposition not to mate with those to whom one was closely related, she pointed out that incest was, in the United States, 'probably the most under-reported and misreported crime because of the horror associated with it, and statistics vary by reports'. It was 'estimated that 10% to 14% of our children under 18 years of age have been involved in incestuous relationships'. Sibling incest, she wrote, is 'believed to be the most common; father/daughter incest is the most reported'. This led her to argue that incest is hardly a rare phenomenon, and implicitly to support the view that the origins of the incest taboo are purely social. For how, she asked, could the frequency of such behaviour possibly fit in with the existence of 'an innate aversion, on biological grounds, to avoid sex within these dyads'?[44]

The importance of incest as a literary theme, briefy discussed in IV, bears out how complex, passionate and puzzled our attitudes towards it can be.

(ii) The incest taboo raises other problems in addition to the disagreement it inspires between anthropologists and biologists, the wide range of attitudes adopted towards it in different societies, and the impossibility of arriving at a satisfactory explanation either for its absence or its occurrence. It is so far from being universal that in certain families in some ancient societies, most notably that of the Incas and the early Egyptians, marriage between brother and sister was compulsory. The idea that some families had so inherent a greatness, and so important a social role to fulfil, that they could never permit themselves to indulge in exogamy, survived for a remarkably long time. In Elizabethan England, it led to the conviction that Lucrezia Borgia shared her bed with her brothers because there was nobody else worthy enough to be her mate.

There are also a number of societies in which marriage to a blood relative is either compulsory or highly recommended, and in which the consequent defiance of the incest taboo is not limited to the great ones of this earth. An African proverb among the Tswana people of Botswana runs 'Child of my father's younger brother: marry me that the cattle may return to the kraal.' In certain Muslim societies, a girl must marry her father's brother's son unless he takes the initiative in renouncing his claim to her.[45] This is partly to keep the property within the family, and partly to avoid diluting the emotional ties which keep the family together. If, as Jared Diamond contends in *The Rise and Fall of the Third Chimpanzee* (1991), human behaviour is most instructively interpreted in terms of the evolutionary advantages which it bestows on the individuals practising it, there is no contradiction between the explanation of the incest taboo as a social mechanism and the modern insistence on its usefulness as a biological device for avoiding the genetic dangers of in-breeding. For a sociobiologist, as the term itself implies, the two considerations cannot be separated.

They are mutually supportive, not intellectually incompatible. Our society benefits from gaining a large number of members with different acquired attitudes and skills, as well as with new inherited mental and physical characteristics. The biological group to which we belong profits from the acquisition of a wider and potentially more fertile gene pool.

(iii) The starting-point for the most recent book on the subject, Françoise Héritier's *Les deux soeurs et leur mère* (1994), is what she calls 'l'inceste du deuxième type' (second-type incest), the taboo which forbids a man from having sexual relations with two sisters, or with a mother and her daughter. Like other anthropologists, she sees the taboo on incest as fundamental to the vision which human beings have of themselves, and explains it in essentially psychological terms. The first step in our understanding of ourselves and our place in the world, she argues, lies in the distinction we make between what is ourselves and what is not ourselves. What the sexual act primarily involves is the mingling of ourselves with another person, and she illustrates what she means by quoting Hamlet's reply to Gertrude in Act IV, scene iii: 'man and wife is one flesh'. Since the woman with whom one has slept 'becomes' oneself, it would be almost the equivalent of **masturbation** in the sense of sex with oneself, then to sleep with her sister or mother.[46] Françoise Héritier also quotes an example from the Middle Ages to illustrate how the breaking of the incest taboo was seen as having disastrous consequences not so much for the couple themselves but for the whole community to which they belonged. For when Count Geoffroy Martel d'Angers married his cousin Agnès, and the whole town of Angers was 'consumed in a terrible fire', there was no doubt in anyone's mind that this was punishment sent from heaven.[47]

(iv) An alternative approach to the incest taboo is to compare it with the various taboos on food and drink. One of their functions, as I argue in **pork** in Section II, is to distinguish a tribe from its less fastidious neighbours. But taboos are also taxonomic, in that they place a ban on substances that do not clearly belong to a specific and immediately identifiable group. They thus help to divide the world into satisfactory categories. This is equally true of the taboo on incest. A mother is a mother, not a mother and a wife. A brother is a brother, not a brother and a husband. Great though the affection between cousins can sometimes be, few families are so large that they cannot benefit socially from bringing in more members from the outside, and thus enabling relationships to be more varied and interesting.

Whoever it may have been who drew up the incest taboo – and it is a defining characteristic of taboos that they have no known author (see **serviette** (i) in Section III) – the attitude which was expressed presupposed a powerful tendency among human beings not to want to leave the immediate family circle, a kind of psychological centripetal instinct which the inventors of taboos saw as their duty to resist. As any sensible parent of nervous offspring knows, apron strings and umbilical cords are made to be cut, and Jared Diamond does not agree with the view that the origins of the incest taboo lie in natural antipathy. What he suggests is that its origins more probably lie in the reaction of society as a whole against the tendency of human beings to be strongly attracted to people who most resemble them. 'Our actual behaviour', he writes in *The Rise and Fall of the Third Chimpanzee* (1992), 'is summed up by a popular song of the 1920s':

> I want a girl
> Just like the girl
> That married dear old Dad

and he continues:

> The reason we tend to resemble our mates is that many of us are looking for someone who reminds us of our parent or sibling of the opposite sex, who in turn resembles us. As children, we already begin to develop our search image of a future sex partner, and that image is heavily influenced by the people of the opposite sex whom we see most often. For most of us, that is our mother (or father) and sister (or brother), plus close childhood friends.[48]

It is, in his way of interpreting human behaviour, because human beings have always felt the need to fight against this tendency that they created the incest taboo.

A Table of Kindred and Affinity, discussed below in the entry **intermarriage**, bears witness to the awareness which human beings have also had of the need never to separate sexual relationships from the creation of appropriate social ties. It is not only because Jewishness can be transmitted only through the mother that there is such concern when a Jewish boy decides to marry out. It is because marriages with members of other faiths weaken the sense of group identity which has been a major factor in enabling the Jews to survive in face of such long and persistent persecution.

In her article in the 1968 *Encyclopedia of the Social Sciences*, Margaret Mead gives an emotional and moral overtone to the incest taboo when she talks about the danger created by divorced parents, each with children from a former marriage, living together in the same house. 'The co-existence in the same household', she writes, 'of non-biologically-related adults and siblings' means that the family may become

> the setting for cross-generational reciprocal seduction and exploitation rather than fulfilling its historic role of protecting the immature and permitting the safe development of strong, consanguineous ties in a context where sex relationships are limited to spouses.

Because of the traditionally greater sexual freedom accorded to males, this is more likely to take the form of the seduction of stepdaughters by stepfathers than of stepsons by stepmothers, and Françoise Héritier's analysis of the Woody Allen case offers an intriguing account of how violently we can feel that the incest taboo has been infringed even when no biological relationships are involved, and when there is no question of the seduction of a person who is sexually immature. For although there was a thirty-year age gap between Woody Allen and Sun Yi, both of them were adults in the eyes of the law, and neither Woody Allen nor Mia Farrow was biologically related to Sun Yi. She was Mia Farrow's adopted daughter, and Woody Allen himself did not even have a formal social relationship with her, since at no point was he married to Mia Farrow. His relationship with Sun Yi was, in Françoise Héritier's view, nevertheless widely seen as incestuous and condemned as such, proof for her of the way in which our 'collective imagination' is 'saturated by second-order incest'.[49]

There may, however, be a more straightforward explanation in the feeling that sexual relationships should not take place between people so widely separated by age. Although there is a strong possibility that any children born to Sun Yi and Woody Allen would, in spite of the age gap between them, not only have been physically attractive but witty and amusing as well, we feel that it is somehow wrong for a man to sleep with a girl young enough to be his daughter; or, for that matter, for a man to make love to a woman old enough to be his mother. However unjustified the comments of many journalists on the Woody Allen case may have been, they are a reminder of how difficult it can be to distinguish taboos on incest from the laws which protect the young from sexual exploitation by the old, whether within a family situation or outside it.

So humane an intention is unlikely to have been the original aim of any taboo, and some are very difficult to distinguish from superstitions. The Anyanja of Nyasaland believed that a man having intercourse with his sister or his mother before setting off to war thereby rendered himself bulletproof.[50] The taboo can also, however, occasionally have a more prosaic use. On 8 August 1995, *The Independent* reported how an Indonesian villager had been sentenced to produce 100 sacks of cement after being convicted of incest, and added: 'There is a serious shortage of cement in Indonesia.'

See below, **intermarriage**, **miscegenation** and **sado-masochism**; also **homosexuality** and **incest** in IV.

Inform Most school children resemble members of the Mafia in observing the 'omertá', or the rule of silence. In *The World of the Public Schools* (1971), George Macdonald Fraser describes as 'unbelievable' the written code of honour at West Point which lays down that a cadet is '*obliged to inform*' on any of his fellows who lies, cheats or steals. The rule of silence is a taboo whose origins are as clear as its functions. Nothing destroys a group's identity more quickly than the betrayal of its secrets.

Intermarriage (i) The problem of explaining the taboo on incest purely in genetic terms recurs when one turns to the laws in both Christian and Islamic countries governing whom one may and may not legally marry.

Thus the order for the Solemnization of Matrimony in the

Book of Common Prayer of the Church of England gives the first reason for marriage as 'the procreation of children, to be brought up in the fear and nurture of the Lord, and to the praise of his holy Name'. This consideration nevertheless seems marginal in earlier versions of a* Table of Kindred and Affinity, the list of people whom one may not legally marry according to the rites of the Church of England. This gives the impression of having been devised almost as much with the social implications of marriage in mind as with the need to procreate healthy children by the avoidance of in-breeding. The original version, drawn up in 1563 by Archbishop Parker, did not limit the ban on marriages to those which might take place between people who were biologically related to each other, such as mothers and sons, fathers and daughters, brothers and sisters, first cousins, uncles and nieces, and nephews and aunts. Article 6 also stated that a man could not marry his father's brother's widow, and article 21 forbade him to marry his deceased son's wife.

The importance for the seventeenth-century English Christian of article 18, forbidding a man to marry his deceased brother's wife, can be judged by Shakespeare's clear assumption that his audience will share the revulsion that Hamlet feels at the fact that the man whom his mother has married is not only his father's murderer but also his father's brother. Although there are no ties of consanguinety between Gertrude and Claudius, it is as much the incestuous nature of their union as the crime that made it possible that inspires the fury Hamlet feels when his father's ghost tells him what has happened. (See also note 57 below.)

The starting-point for a Table of Kindred and Affinity is in *Leviticus*, 18:6–18. This contains, side by side with rules against marrying blood relations such as mother, father, sisters, brothers, aunts, uncles and cousins, interdicts on sexual relationships with relatives by marriage such as sisters-in-law and daughters-in-law. An important clue as to the reason why there is no genetic basis for a number of the interdicts lies in the now obsolete meaning of the word 'affinity' as 'closeness', illustrated by the frequency

* 'A' and not 'the'; presumably with the implication that there may be other versions.

with which one still speaks of 'spiritual affinity', the concept evoked in the ban placed by the Roman Catholic church on a man's marrying his godmother or a woman's marrying her godfather. Since marriage has always been regarded as a social contract as well as a formalization of a sexual relationship, it was always seen as important to do two things: prevent people contracting alliances with those to whom they were already close, and who did not therefore need to be brought into the fold; avoid adding another and perhaps incompatible layer to an already existing relationship. It is confusing to have a wife who is also one's son's widow, or a husband who is also the widower of one's father's sister.[51]

The Koran contains a list of people whom one may not marry which is similar to a Table of Kindred and Affinity, and characterized by the same mixture of associated concerns that seems to have inspired the original taboos against **incest** and a Table of Kindred and Affinity. In addition to forbidding marriage to blood relations such as mothers, daughters, sisters, aunts and nieces, the Koran also bans marriage to foster-mothers and foster-sisters, as well as to what *Sura* IV.25 calls

> your mothers who have given suck to you
> your suckling sisters, your wives' mothers,
> your step-daughters who are in your care
> being born of the wives you have been in to –
> but if you have not been in to them
> it is no fault in you – and the spouses
> of your sons who are of your loins

There is also a rule against marrying women who have already married, except those taken prisoner in a *jihad* – a 'war under the orders of the righteous Imam against those who persecute the Faith'. The further prohibition on marriage to 'a woman whom your father married' could mean a widowed stepmother, again not a blood relative with whom it might be genetically dangerous to have children, but someone with whom you nevertheless already have a contractual relationship with strong emotional overtones.

Although incestuous relationships are rarely conducted with the aim of producing children, some societies carry the argument that certain marriages are inadvisable on genetic grounds to the point where they give the incest taboo the force of law. In Scotland, with a strength of language that recalls Montaigne's view that incestuous unions are likely to be more passionate than normal ones, the old Scots of the 1567 Act called incest an 'abhominabill, vile and fylthie lust'. This 1567 Act was transformed in 1986 into a new law based upon the view expressed in 1980 by the Scottish Law Memorandum when it said that 'intercourse between certain persons should be prohibited because the offspring are more likely to exhibit certain physical and mental abnormalities'.[52] While this may be true, there is some inconsistency in the fact that such a law would punish a 35-year-old uncle who has had a vasectomy for having consensual sex with his 33-year-old cousin or with his 23-year-old niece. This latter idea may, like the relationship between the 50-year-old Woody Allen and the 20-year-old adopted daughter of his mistress, not be an emotionally attractive one. There is an understandable feeling that there should not be too wide an age gap between sexual partners. But there can be no objections to such relationships on biological grounds.

(ii) The psychologist Anthony Storr comments that 'it is harder to fall in love with those one is used to, or incest would be commoner than it is'.[53] His view echoes the quip that a Table of Kindred and Affinity is based on natural antipathy. The fact that biologically unrelated children adopted into the same family are not allowed to marry each other is a ruling which strikes most of them as an example of superfluous zeal on the legislator's part. But although, as Anthony Storr points out, there are relatively few marriages between children who have grown up together in the kibbutzim, this aversion may just as easily stem from overfamiliarity as from any awareness, however obscure, of the genetic disadvantages of consanguineous marriages.

In France, as in Scotland, the state is stricter than in England, since the Church of England seems to have followed the example offered by its absence from the list of prohibitions in *Leviticus*, 18 in not banning marriages between first cousins.[54] In the United States of America, the law plays a comparable role in requiring people to marry someone to whom they are not biologically related. Only eighteen states allow marriage between first cousins, and some of these require proof that at least one of the partners in the marriage is infertile. 'In our society', write Ivan

Nye and Felix M. Bernardo in *The Family: Its Structure and Interaction* (1973),

> members of the nuclear family are prohibited from marrying one another. In addition, the incest taboo against intermarriage between a person and his mother, father or sibling is also extended to grandparents, uncles, aunts, nieces and nephews. Moreover, in two thirds of our states, laws exist that preclude intermarriage between first cousins.[55]

The parallel between what is officially the secular republic of the United States of America and the canon law of the Roman Catholic Church, which forbids marriage between first cousins unless a special dispensation has been obtained from the bishop, is coincidental. It nevertheless emphasizes how the taboos on incest and the laws on intermarriage can stem, as Patrician Whelehan suggests (see above, **incest** (i)), from a mixture of social and biological considerations. The canon law of the Roman Catholic Church originated in a period when there was no scientific knowledge of genetics. The laws in the United States were almost certainly based at least in part on a modern awareness of the possible dangers of in-breeding.

(iii) The notion that there are possible genetic disadvantages in marriage to a blood relative seems to have been unknown in classical times. No ancient historian attributes Cleopatra's extraordinary behaviour at the battle of Actium to the idea that she was suffering from the kind of mental weakness which a modern observer would attribute to the fact that she was the product of at least four generations of consanguineous marriage. The idea that there are inherited dangers in marriage between close relatives nevertheless occurs quite early in the Christian era. In the sixth century AD, Pope Gregory the Great answered a query from St Augustine about consanguineous marriages with the observation that such unions tended to be barren, and the Church consequently discouraged marriages between first cousins long before the rationalists of the eighteenth century began to interest themselves in the question.[56] It was only much later, after the implications of the experiments carried out by Gregor Mendel (1822–24) had begun to be absorbed into scientific discourse that the geneticists of the late nineteenth and early twentieth centuries were able to explain events such as the failure of Toulouse-Lautrec's legs to mend properly after his fall when aged 14 by the fact that his mother and father were first cousins.

(iv) Article 18 of the original Table of Kindred and Affinity, which forbade a man to marry his deceased brother's wife, offers the rare example of a taboo being invented for a specific social purpose, and one with clear political intentions. Elizabeth I had come to the throne in 1558, and her right to rule depended on her being recognized as the legitimate child of Henry VIII and Anne Boleyn. This, in turn, required that the annulment of Henry's first marriage to Catherine of Aragon, who was the widow of his deceased brother Arthur, be fully in keeping with the teachings of the Church. It was a ruling hard to justify by reference to the Old Testament, where in *Genesis*, 38:8–10 it is precisely Onan's refusal to follow the custom of the levirate, whereby a man is required to marry the infertile widow of his dead brother, which attracts such wrath from God that He slays him.[57] The prohibition nevertheless remained in force until 1928, and the campaign for its abolition was one of the great liberal causes in late nineteenth- and early twentieth-century England.[58]

See **incest**, above; and as a literary theme in IV.

Lesbianism Sexual activity between women is condemned in *Romans*, 1:26 for the same reason as homosexuality. In order to punish those who grew 'vain in their imaginations', God 'gave them up unto vile affections: for even their women did change the natural use into that which is against nature'. Theoretically, the laws still existing in certain American states against **oral sex** make Lesbians liable to criminal prosecution. I have not been able to find examples of such charges being brought. The absence of laws in England against sexual relationships between women is said to have originated in an access of timidity. Although the possibility of extending the Labouchère amendment (see above, **homosexuality**) to women was discussed, nobody could be found brave enough to explain to Queen Victoria what such relations might involve. The matter was raised again in 1921, when the Scottish Conservative lawyer Frederick Macquiston moved a Private Member's motion to the Criminal Law Amendment Act to the effect that

> Any act of gross indecency between female persons shall be a misdemeanour and punishable in the same manner as any such act committed by male persons under section eleven of the Criminal Law Amendment Act 1885.

In spite of the objection by another MP to the effect that 'to adopt such a clause would harm by introducing into the minds of perfectly innocent people the most revolting thoughts', the clause was passed in the Commons on 4 August 1921 by 148 to 53, only to be defeated in the Lords.[59]

One advantage of the absence of laws against Lesbianism was that two women could share a house, and give physical signs of affection for each other, without arousing comment.* This nevertheless had the disadvantage of making it difficult for Lesbian women to acknowledge their sexuality. Monica Still, who had met and fallen in love with her partner Maya while working as a nurse during the Second World War, gave an interview in *The Independent* for 26 April 1995 in which she said: 'It came as a relief finally to take the decision that men were out. In those days, it was quite a brave decision to make. Lesbianism was virtually unheard of. There were no books about Lesbianism to read; no helpline to call.'

See **Lesbianism** in III, the comments by Dr Tarumniaz in **hedonism** above, and the entry on *The Well of Loneliness* in IV.

Masturbation St Thomas Aquinas saw it as a greater sin than fornication, a view implicitly endorsed by the devices adopted by nineteenth-century parents to prevent their sons from masturbating. These included an iron cage lined with spikes, and an electric circuit which rang a bell in the parents' bedroom if their son had an erection.[60] As late as 1940, the United States Naval Academy at Annapolis 'considered evidence of masturbation sufficient grounds for refusing admission to a candidate'[61]; and when, in December 1994, the US Surgeon-General, Dr

* So, of course, in the late nineteenth century, could men. Victorian and Edwardian men would have greeted the suggestion that there was anything sexual in Holmes and Watson sharing digs together with the same shocked incredulity as Watson does when the idea is put to him in the Billy Wilder film *The Private Life of Sherlock Holmes* (1970).

Jocelyn Elders, said that masturbation at least had the advantage of limiting the spread of AIDS and avoiding teenage pregnancies, there was such an outcry that President Clinton had to demand her resignation. She immediately resumed her duties as Professor of Paediatrics at the University of Arkansas, President Clinton's home state.

This attitude reflected Baden-Powell's view, expressed in *Rovering to Success* (1910), that masturbation 'cheats semen of getting its full chance of making up the strong, manly man you would otherwise be'. Jocelyn Elders's critics would also have seen eye to eye with John Harvey Kellogg, who considered masturbation 'the vilest, the basest, the most degrading act a human being can commit', likely to cause tuberculosis, heart disease, epilepsy, dimness of vision, insanity, idiocy and death. Indeed, so great was Kellogg's horror that in 1906 he 'introduced a number of foods designed to promote health and decrease interest in sex, one of which was called Corn Flakes'.[62] In *Pornography and Obscenity* (1930), D. H. Lawrence described masturbation as 'certainly the most dangerous sexual vice that society can be affected with, in the long run'. He thus differed from the traditional Japanese view, which Ruth Benedict described in *The Chrysanthemum and the Sword* (1946). For them, what she called 'auto-eroticism' was 'a pleasure about which they feel no guilt'. They considered it, as she put it, to be 'sufficiently controlled by assigning it to a minor place in the decorous life'.[63]

Although warnings about masturbation seem to have been principally aimed at men, and more especially at boys, there are cases when girls have been discouraged by very violent means, of which the compulsory wearing of chastity belts is one of the mildest.[64] The frequency with which *olisboi*, or artificial phalluses, feature in the decoration of ancient Greek vases – one of which depicts a woman carrying a container full of them – suggests that female masturbation was an established practice in fifth-century Athens. If this was indeed the case, attitudes were clearly different from those which prevailed in Victorian times, when

> a number of medical experts complained that the craze for the newly invented bicycle was a thinly diguised desire for the illicit pleasures of masturbation.[65]

In the twentieth century, the women of the Chukchee tribe in Siberia are said to masturbate with the long calf muscle of the reindeer.[66]

Two comments by women quoted in *The Hite Report: A Nationwide Study of Female Sexuality* (1976) highlight the persistence and the importance of Christian taboos in this area: 'Given the historic horror of our culture for masturbation, I suppose being able to masturbate and not be upset by it in others is no small degree of freedom'; 'Being Catholic, I was brought up to think that I should not obtain power or pleasure from my body, nor should anyone else.' The *Hite Report on Male Sexuality in America* (1978) follows the example of the earlier report on female sexuality by depicting masturbation as quite widespread; and both insist that it should be seen as natural and enjoyable. Both acknowledge that it produces feelings of guilt and inadequacy. Neither mentions the disadvantage which 'the solitary vice' shares with **incest**: it does not increase one's social acquaintance.

See **sexual activity** in IV.

Menstruation (i) Although marital infidelity, sexual impotence and homosexuality were not taboo subjects for the comic playwrights of fifth-century Athens, they did draw the line at jokes about menstruation; thus putting it, though for different reasons, on the same level as the plague which broke out in the second year of the Peloponnesian war (431–404 BC). Women living in one of the pre-literate, taboo-ridden societies where the fact of menstruating placed them virtually in the same category as somebody who had committed a crime must have had something of the same awareness of the inherent injustice of the universe as Oedipus, who commits a crime which he and his parents have made every effort to avoid. Women are seen as criminals for something which the female body does and which is completely natural.

It is by no means unusual for taboos to be directed against women. On the Polynesian island of Typee, Herman Melville came across a set of groves which were

> defended from profanation by the strictest edicts of the all-pervading 'taboo', which condemned to instant death the sacrilegious female who should enter or touch its sacred precincts,

> or even so much as press with her feet the ground made holy by the shadows that it cast.

Melville found this quite contrary to common sense, and commented of another episode: 'I could not for the life of me understand why a woman should not have as much right to enter a canoe as a man.'[67]

Tom Wolfe's comment in his satirical 'Vignette' entitled *Primitive Cultures* about 'the importance of Diedrich's discovery of the Luloras, the tribe that made women climb trees and remain there during their menstrual periods', does not exaggerate the nature of the taboos said to have been discovered by anthropologists. Among the Guarani Indians of South America, a menstruating girl is sewn up in a hammock as if she were a corpse, but with a tiny aperture allowing her to breathe. She is then suspended over a smoking fire for several days until she is considered to have been purified.[68] Pliny the Elder (AD 23–79) wrote in his *Historia Naturalis* (AD 77) that menstrual blood turned new wine sour, caused grafts and cuttings to wither away, and claimed that dogs which lap up menstrual blood go mad, with their bite acting as a poison for which there is no cure.

It is easy for us to laugh at such ideas, to find an element of exaggeration in the suggestion reported by Henry Beard and Christopher Cerf in *The Official Politically Correct Dictionary and Handbook* (1992) that the word 'menstruate' should be replaced by 'femstruate', and to feel that Penelope Shuttle's and Peter Redgrove's *The Wise Wound: Menstruation and Everywoman* (1978) contains more than an element of exaggeration. We live in a culture where advertisements for sanitary towels, advertised in suitably discreet terms as early as July 1888 on the back page of *The Antiquary*, have become as common as those for washing powder. The situation of a woman unfortunate enough to be born on a South Sea island, or in parts of tribal Africa or in certain Islamic societies, would have been very different.

(ii) *The Wise Wound* (1978) is one of the fullest accounts available of attitudes towards menstruation, and is written from a resolutely feminist viewpoint. It argues that traditional, male-dominated society has consistently refused to accord women their true place, and has done so because of the privileged access to wisdom which the natural rhythm of their bodies makes available to them. This has helped to produce a society which is 'aggressively anxious', and whose 'systematic menstrual ignorance' has led it to become 'one of the most bellicose in modern history'. Neither do its joint authors, Peter Redgrove and Penelope Shuttle, make any secret of their debt to Carl Jung (1875–1961) or of their hostility to traditional Christianity, and they write that 'the Christian devil was a representation of the animus of the menstruating woman, in so far as the Christian ethic has satanised woman and her natural powers'.[69] In their view, the widespread taboos with which men have surrounded menstruation express fear and jealousy, and will disappear only when the balance of power between the sexes finally changes.

In a similar vein, the American painter Judy Chicago describes in her autobiography, *Through the Flower: My Struggle as a Woman Artist* (1992), how she protested against the taboos on menstruation by designing what she called a 'Menstrual Bathroom', in which 'under a shelf full of all the paraphernalia with which a culture "cleans up" menstruation, was a garbage can filled with the unmistakeable marks of our animality'. One could not, however, walk into the bathroom. Rather, one 'peered through a veil of gauze', a fact which recalls the role so often played by taboos as devices to separate the worlds of nature and of culture. On another occasion, Judy Chicago decided to do a 'menstruation lithograph', but found the pre-existing images in society too strong. It was, she wrote, 'an image of a woman's hand pulling a bloody Tampax out of her vagina', and she added: 'I tried to make the image as overt as I could, but even then other people interpreted the Tampax as a bloody penis, a testament done to our perceptive powers by the absence of an image of female reality.'[70]

(iii) In 1981, in an article in *The American Anthropologist*, Dr Barbara B. Harrell, a first-year resident physician in the department of obstetrics and gynaecology at the University of Washington hospital, put forward a very different view, and one which seemed at times to be framed as a deliberate criticism of the attitude adopted by Judy Chicago, Penelope Shuttle and Peter Redgrove. She suggested that because it was the physiological norm for American women to have a more or less regular

28-day cycle, Western anthropologists had tended to exaggerate the role played in pre-industrial societies both by menstruation itself and by attitudes towards it. Pointing out that 'in pre-industrial societies as a whole, lactation is prolonged and intensive, while menstruation is correspondingly uncommon', she argued that menstrual months 'occupy less than one fourth of a pre-industrial woman's reproductive span'. Because, in modern Western society, the 'cyclic surging of powerful female hormones' leads women to function in 'a heightened sexual state', we are led to give far more importance both to menstruation itself and to the taboos surrounding it. 'Our femaleness', she writes in conclusion, 'need not be inextricably bound up with recurent menstrual flow. We need not rationalise our distaste for this monthly nuisance, and we can reject menstruation if we wish, without rejecting our sexuality. Perhaps this understanding can help western scholars move away from the concept of "the normal monthly period", and closer to the origins of physiologic and symbolic womanhood.'[71]

See also **illness** in III and **menstruation** in IV.

Miscegenation (i) Some of the more ideologically minded defenders of apartheid based their doctrines on biblical precedent. So, too, did a number of the supporters of the segregationalist laws establishing 'separate but equal' facilities for whites and blacks in the USA. In South Africa, as in the Deep South, both groups saw the commandment 'Thou shalt not let thy cattle gender with a diverse kind', like the ruling that he 'that giveth any of his seed unto Moloch' shall 'surely be put to death' (*Leviticus*, 19:19; 20:2), as offering support for their policies. This was especially the case when the quotations were seen in the context of the insistence throughout the Old Testament on the need for the chosen people to keep themselves apart.

Many sects, and some religions, offer an ideological parallel to the laws on racial segregation by insisting that their followers marry within the faith. Social and family life can be very difficult for Jews who marry out and wish to remain in touch with their parents and family friends. Since full membership of the Jewish community can be acquired only through the mother, the situation is sometimes particularly difficult when a Jewish boy marries out. Even if his wife converts to Judaism their children cannot be fully Jewish. Tensions can also arise from the fact that Judaism has never sought to make converts, so that Gentiles wishing to adopt the religion of their Jewish partner are not always made to feel that they are full members of the Jewish community. If there is a mixed marriage between a Catholic and a Protestant, the Catholic Church continues to insist that the children be brought up in the faith. *Sura* II.220 tells Muslims to marry only converts to Islam:

> Do not marry idolatresses, until
> they believe; a believing slavegirl
> is better than an idolatress, though
> you may admire her. And do not marry
> idolaters, until they believe.

Sura LX.10 also instructs Muslims not to allow their wives to marry out:

> And if any of your wives slips away from you
> to the unbelievers, and then you retaliate,
> give those whose wives have gone away the like
> of what they have expended. And fear God, in
> whom you believe.*

(ii) There still remain, especially in as class-ridden a society as that of the United Kingdom, strong prejudices against marriage between members of different social classes. Although the action of John Braine's *Room at the Top* (1957) takes place in the England of the early 1950s, the advice which his Aunt Emilie gives him – 'Get one of your own class, lad, go to your own people' – can still be heard in the 1990s. Comparable views surface in a more extreme form in Japan, where the *baraku* class of manual and service workers still have such low prestige that, as Edward Pilkington reported in *The Guardian* for 2 August 1995, 'half of the proposed marriages between *baraku* and non-*baraku* are stopped by the non-*baraku* family'. One of the taboos which D. H. Lawrence broke in *Lady Chatterley's Lover* – see the entry in Section IV – concerned sexual relationships between different classes, which

* Polygamy is authorized in *Sura* IV.1–2. The other instructions concern dowries.

for a long time were considered socially acceptable only if an upper-class man took a mistress from outside his own class in order to acquire sexual experience before marrying 'one of his own kind'.

The ban on marriage, or indeed on any form of sexual relationships between members of different ethnic or ideological groups, seems at first sight a mirror image of the taboo on **incest**. Whereas this encourages exogamy, in that it forbade sexual relationships within the group, laws against miscegenation gives pride of place to the opposite practice of endogamy. There is, however, an important difference. The insistence that members of a tribe or family must marry out presupposes that they will, by so doing, form alliances with groups of comparable or perhaps even greater prestige. The ban on miscegenation, in contrast, is based on the notion that the dominant group must keep itself pure by refraining from sexual relations with members of other groups which were judged to be inferior. The dictionary definition of miscegenation as 'interbreeding, intermarriage or sexual intercourse between different races' has a neutrality to it which hides the racial and social implications which it has in practice. The same is implicitly true of taboos against members of a religious or even a political group marrying out. It would require a very unusual combination of circumstances for a Protestant family, whether in Northern Ireland or elsewhere, to consider that a son or daughter had improved their social position by marrying a Catholic; and vice versa.

In the past, miscegenation was always seen as a worse offence when a woman involved herself with a member of the subordinate group than when a man did. Male European colonizers frequently came out without their wives. It was therefore seen as natural for a colonizer to take a woman from the colonized group, and even to marry her according to the customs of her country. This is what happens in Puccini's *Madame Butterfly*, when Pinkerton marries Cio-Cio-San in a Japanese ceremony, only to discard her when he is married according to the laws of the United States to Kate. The presupposition that males from the subordinate group always longed for a woman from the dominant group led in the Deep South to the kind of lynch-mob mentality described by authors such as Richard Wright (1908–60) or William Faulkner (1897–1962). In the popular fiction of the nineteenth and early twentieth centuries, the term 'half-breed' was almost invariably prefaced by the adjective 'treacherous'. In 1967, as Noel Perrin points out in *Dr Bowdler's Legacy* (1992), the Nancy Drew mystery *The Secret of the Leaning Chimney* (1949) was expurgated, and the terms 'half-breeds' and 'half-castes' omitted.

In *Sex and Destiny: The Politics of Human Fertility* (1984), Germaine Greer points out that Marie Stopes went so far as to say, in an interview published on 19 April 1934 in *The Australian Women's Weekly*, that 'all half-castes should be sterilised at birth. Thus painlessly and in no way interfering with the individual's life, the unhappy fate of he who is neither black nor white is prevented from being passed on to unborn babies.'[72]

See above, **incest**; **mix** in II; **political correctness** in III; and ***Lady Chatterley's Lover*** in IV.

Nose In 1995, in one of his 'Letters from America', Alistair Cooke drew the attention of his English audience to what he described as the custom whereby North Americans did not blow their noses in public. Instead, he commented, they wiped them, reserving the noisy act which is performed in public by most Europeans for the privacy of the bathroom.

It is not, however, a taboo widely known in New York State, and may have been characteristic of an older generation of upper-class Americans. This distinction would be supported by the fact that in her novel *Love and Friendship* (1983), Alison Lurie makes her wealthy and upper-class heroine, Emily Stockwell Taylor, express surprise when her husband, who comes from a much less privileged background, does blow his nose when in a room with other people.

European visitors to the United States can thus breathe a sigh of retrospective relief. They have not, in blowing their noses, been as rude as anyone would be nowadays in any society if they put into practice Erasmus's view in his *De civilitate morum puerilium libellus* (1534; 'On the Behaviour of Boys') that it is perfectly acceptable to fart in public.

Oral sex (i) The laws against **homosexuality** in Alabama, Arizona, Arkansas, North Carolina, South Carolina, Florida, Georgia, Idaho, Kansas, Louisiana, Maryland, Massachusetts,

Mississippi, Missouri, Montana, Nevada, Oklahoma, Oregon, Rhode Island, Tennessee, Texas, Virginia, Utah and the District of Columbia impose the same penalties on oral sex between men and women as they do on sexual relationships between men. In the early 1990s, the English jurist Clive Stafford met a man in a prison in Georgia who was serving five years for consensual oral sex with his wife. In 1995, Auberon Waugh reported in the *Daily Telegraph* on the case of an English schoolteacher who had received a ten-year jail sentence in Melbourne, Florida, for allegedly fellating four of her black students.[73] The taboo represented by these laws may not be based on a universal reaction. Of the women interviewed for the *Hite Report: A Nation-wide Study on Female Sexuality* (1976), 42 per cent described themselves as having regularly experienced orgasm during oral stimulation. In *The Hite Report on Male Sexuality* (1978), 90 per cent of the men who were asked if they enjoyed oral sex with a woman replied 'Yes', a reply which confirms the frequency with which fellatio is said to be one of the services most frequently required from prostitutes.

Bonaparte was quite keen on oral sex, and wrote to Josephine in 1798, after the battle of Rivoli: 'You know I never forget the little visits, you know, the little black forest . . . I kiss it a thousand times and wait impatiently for the moment I will be in it.'[74] For Napoleon, the legal ban on cunnilingus in twentieth-century America would have justified Freud's remark in *Totem and Taboo* (1919) that taboos 'mostly concern matters which are capable of enjoyment, such as freedom of movement and unrestrained intercourse'.[75] His enthusiasm for the practice is paralleled by the account of fellatio in John Updike's *Memories of the Ford Adminstration* (1992). Early on in the story, the narrator Alfred Clayton describes how his 'perfect love partner' Genevieve Brent

> tucked back her black hair so that a gleam of face showed in the faint light from the streets and found my prick with her mouth and despite my squeamish, chivalrous, insincere efforts to push her off ruthlessly sucked and hand-pumped me into coming, into helplessly shooting off (like fireworks in a chaste fifties movie as a metaphor for sex) into a warm wet dark that was her tiny little head.[76]

It is clear that the equation of fellatio with cannibalism by the theologian Tertullian (*c.*160–*c.*230)[77] played little part in Genevieve Brent's world-view. She also differed from Charlie Chaplin's first wife, Lita, who strongly objected to oral sex, and cited Chaplin's insistence as one of the grounds for the divorce she obtained in 1926. In 1927, this led the review *La Révolution Surréaliste* to publish a translation of an article purportedly written by Chaplin and which had originally appeared in the New York based magazine *Transition*. In it, Chaplin claimed that all married people went in for oral sex, and that he couldn't see what all the fuss was about.[78]

The passage from Updike's *Memories of the Ford Administration* illustrates how taboos on the description of sexual behaviour have disappeared from the American novel, just as they have done from the theatre in Britain and the United States. The first part of Tony Kushner's *Angels in America*, 'Millennia Approaches' (1992), has been going for only twenty minutes, and the word 'fuck' been used some thirteen times, when Prior Walter says to Louis Ironson: 'You don't notice anything. If I hadn't spent the last four years fellating you, I'd swear you were straight.'

Although unmentionable in public in England until the 1980s, and even the 1990s, oral sex can now be referred to in a very matter-of-fact way. Vanessa Feltz, criticizing what she called 'the great contraceptive con' in the August 1995 issue of *She*, enumerated all the disadvantages of the pill, the coil and the sheath. Commenting that 'caps and cunnilingus are mutually exclusive', she continued: 'Any twit attempting to combine them will be struck dumb for up to a month while the spermicide commences its fatal bombardment of his tongue cells.' She made no comment on the mystery surrounding the availability from vending machines in airport and motorway lavatories of fruit- or chocolate-flavoured condoms. Does this availability represent an attempt on the part of the men to encourage their sexual partners to indulge in an activity by which they would not otherwise be tempted? Or does the fact that the same flavours are available from the machines in the women's lavatories point to the universal popularity of an activity which can be rendered even more enjoyable by a hint of peach, raspberry or vanilla? Or is it that it would be too expensive to have two kinds of vending machines, one for the women's **loo** and one for the men's?

(ii) There are a number of possible reasons for the absence of any mention of oral sex from the interdicts in *Leviticus* and *Deuteronomy*. It may have been through prudery. It may have been because the practice was seen as occurring mainly among homosexuals, whose activities were taboo anyway. Alternatively, though less probably, it may have been because oral sex could be legitimized as a prelude to penetrative and therefore potentially fertile activity, and not as an exclusive substitute for it. Or, again, it may have been because the ancient Israelites, like Philip Swallow's wife Hilary before she meets Morris Zapp in David Lodge's *Changing Places* (1975), had not reached that level of sophistication in their sexual lives.[79] There is no mention of oral sex in the standard works on taboos by Ray B. Browne, Mary Douglas, Radcliffe-Brown, Franz Steiner and Hutton Webster available in most libraries.

Laurence Stone pointed out in a review in the *London Review of Books* on 3 August 1995 that Shere Hite had recruited the people who replied to her questionnaire from 'readers of sexually-oriented magazines like *Playboy* and *Penthouse*', and argued that the figures in her reports should therefore be treated with some scepticism. The more recent studies to which he referred reveal a society with less adultery and fewer homosexuals – 2.3 per cent of the population of the USA as against the alleged 9 per cent – than both Hite surveys suggest. However, it remains one in which revulsion against oral sex seems to be a minority reaction. Although men can be heard making the comment that cunnilingus leaves a nasty taste in the mouth, it is unusual for them to wish to translate an aesthetic preference into a moral interdict.

The taboo status of oral sex reinforces the general point about taboos made in the entries in Section II on **pork** and **mix:** that they are devices for maintaining distinctions. In both men and women, the external genitalia – the penis and the vulva – also serve for natural elimination by the passage of urine and ought therefore to be kept separate from the mouth, the organ for absorbing nourishment. The most frequent complaint against cunnilingus is not a moral or even an aesthetic one. It is an essentially hedonistic objection, in that the practice is accused of exciting without satisfying.[80] The distaste expressed for oral sex may also go back to the period when it was practised as a second best because of the absence of reliable contraception. The taboo against it does not seem to have been based on the dangers summed up in the line 'It's the world's biggest dick/it don't matter, just don't bite it', and which led the 1990 single '100 Miles and Running' by Niggaz With Attitudes to be banned by the UK distributors W. H. Smith and HMV.

See above, **homosexuality**; and **contraception** in Section III.

Paedophilia (i) The *Guardian* for 21 February 1996 published a long article by Jonathan Freedland on Gerald Hannon, a professor at Toronto's Ryerson University, who had attained considerable notoriety by maintaining that there was nothing wrong with sexual relationships between adults and children. Freedland described Hannon as 'speaking out on society's most sensitive taboo', and reported him as saying that there was basically no difference between a child-sex ring and a junior ice hockey team. Hannon's contention in this respect was that

> Both involve children and adults. Both involve strenuous physical exercise (adult coaches taking the role of the adult lover). Both involve danger. Both involve pleasure. Yet we approve of children's hockey and deplore child-sex rings.

It is not an outstandingly convincing parallel, and the use of the word 'taboo' in the introduction to the article blurs the issues. As in the case of the quotation from *The Independent* quoted above in the entry on **adultery**, the word 'taboo' implies that objections to the practice of child sexuality are irrational and prejudiced. The term 'taboo' has taken on so strong an ironic tinge that no writer using it in modern Britain or America can do so without giving the impression of thinking that the ban should disappear. There are, however, so many rational and humane objections to paedophilia that the description of opposition to the practice as a 'taboo' is decidedly misleading.

The body of Jonathan Freedland's article does not support Hannon's views. It draws attention to the objections formulated by Hannon's opponents, especially the writer Judy Steed, and makes no attempt to dismiss the very obvious arguments against adults having sex with children: that it involves requiring children to do something which they do not understand, and to make choices quite beyond the range of their mental and psychological development; that the initiative for such relationships invariably comes from the adult, and seeks to increase what is almost always his pleasure; that such relationships are thus almost invariably exploitative; and, perhaps most important, that they have no long-term future. Once the child grows up, the paedophile inevitably moves on to other, younger partners. The child is then left with the understandable feeling of having been exploited and cheated.

It would be tedious to rehearse all the other objections that justify the existence in most countries of laws against sexual activities between adults and children under 16. These laws are based on the eminently rational grounds that they defend the weak from the strong, a role very rarely performed by any taboo. At first sight, the fact that Hannon appears concerned solely with relationships between men and young boys seems to make his arguments even less attractive. There is a strong temptation to say that a sexually maturing boy of 15 who finds an older woman able and willing to initiate him sexually is to be envied and perhaps even congratulated. The law in the United Kingdom, however, sees matters differently, establishing as it does the same maximum sentence of ten years against either a man or a woman having sexual intercourse with either a girl or a boy under 16. What is lacking in each case is informed consent, just as what is present is sexual exploitation.

The only way in which these purely rational objections can be described as 'taboos' is in the context of the taxonomic function traditionally fulfilled by taboos in other contexts. This function is illustrated by the taboos on **incest** and **oral sex** analysed above, and recurs in the entries **mix** and **pork** in Section II. Incest taboos seek to avoid confusion in relationships between members of the same family, those on oral sex maintain a defensible separation between different parts of the body, while the taboos on what foods certain groups may or may not eat make distinctions between different kinds of nourishment. The same taxonomic function is performed by the laws forbidding sexual relationships between adults and children. The only acceptable relationships between adults and children are those of the care and protection which the older and stronger owe to the younger and weaker. They are not relationships between equals, and cannot, by definition, be so. Sexual relationships, in contrast, can be emotionally valid only between equals.

(ii) The existence of laws against paedophilia casts doubt on Gerald Hannon's claim that his attempt to justify it ought to be protected by the traditions guaranteeing academic freedom, and that he is justified to use his position as a university teacher to advance his thesis. Since paedophilia is against the law in Canada, as indeed in most countries, it is from one point of view as though he were defending shop-lifting or burglary. But although academic freedom has not normally been seen as extending to the defence of illegal activities, supporters of the Hannon thesis can point out that he is not the only university teacher to have put forward ideas which were against the law in the society in which he happens to be living. Academics who attacked apartheid in South Africa, or defended Jews in Hitler's Germany, were highly praised outside the society which they were criticizing. Why then should Hannon, who is not himself a practising paedophile, not be seen as a progressive reformer on the lines of those who argued against the laws against **contraception** or **homosexuality**? There are, as he points out, other societies in which sexual activities between adults and children were regarded as the norm. Why should we refuse to entertain the idea that our own society might profit from a move in their direction? Perhaps, Hannon could argue, the fact that the word 'taboo' is used to describe objections to child sexuality is an indication that this is already happening. Might we not reach a situation where the current 'taboo' against child sexuality strikes us as being as quaint a survival of archaic attitudes as our former ban on **homosexuality**?

We know relatively little about Indonesian society, one of those which Hannon maintains have abolished the 'taboo' against paedophilia, and even less about the attitude of the children supposedly required by custom to have sex with adults. We know enough about Greek sexual customs (see above, **homosexuality**, (iv)) to know that the limits placed on it were far more rigorous than the total absence of rules envisaged by Hannon. We also have enough evidence about how unhappy children are made by being abused sexually to be fairly sure that Hannon is wrong to argue that they keep happy memories of what happened. There is, however, one attested exception.

In 1916, André Gide took Marc Allégret, the son of a French Protestant pastor, on a trip to London. The discovery of the affair had a disastrous effect on Gide's marriage, and broke his wife Madeleine's heart. Marc, who was 16 at the time, nevertheless remembered the relationship with gratitude, and wrote about Gide with considerable affection in the memoirs which he published in 1973. Neither did it impede his sexual development. In 1955, he helped to discover Brigitte Bardot; and in 1957, directed the film *L'Amant de Lady Chatterley*.

See **homosexuality**, above; **mix** and **pork** in II; and **homosexuality** in IV.

Publish The normal rule governing advancement in academic life, especially in the United States, has always been 'Publish or Perish'. The American religious sociologist Andrew M. Greeley nevertheless speaks of violating what he calls 'the ecclesiastical taboo against priests, particularly young priests, setting pen to paper' by publishing his first book, *The Church in the Suburbs* (1958), when he was still at the 'infantile age of twenty-nine'.[81] Priests, in the discipline to which he was expected to submit, were required to communicate solely with their own flock, and not with a wider public, and even then to do so only by word of mouth. The taboo on their publishing books and articles was intended to emphasize how they differed from the laity. It also preserved the monopoly enjoyed on the dissemination of the printed word by the Vatican. A bishop's pastoral letter to parishes is read out to the congregation, not circulated in pamphlet form.

Father Greeley again blurred the boundaries between ecclesiastical and secular learning when he broke what he calls 'the long taboo against diocesan priests from Chicago attending the University of Chicago'. His decision to obtain 'professional training in the social sciences' was a comparable violation of what he calls 'the rules of amateurism and mediocrity – the notion that any priest can do anything – at the core of clerical culture' and his attitude both to publishing and to professionalism strikes an audible chord in observers of what used to happen in England. In some Oxford and Cambridge colleges, it was at one time a truth universally acknowledged that no gentleman ever allowed his name to appear in print.

Sado-masochism (i) The only occasion when sado-masochism attracted the attention of the law was in England in 1990. In what was known as 'Operation Slammer', a number of sado-masochistically inclined homosexuals were successfully prosecuted for committing assaults on one another. Although the possibility of participation had been discreetly advertised, everything happened in private. No minors or women were present, and everyone had fully agreed in advance to what they knew was going to take place. Their appeal, in which some of the defendants pleaded guilty to aiding and abetting assaults on themselves, was rejected in 1992, with the House of Lords implicitly taking the view trenchantly expressed by Lord Devlin in his Maccabean lecture *The Enforcement of Morals* (1959), when he argued that the law cannot neglect the private behaviour of individuals even when this does no harm to other people. Lord Devlin illustrated the logic of his argument when he pointed out that 'consent of the victim is no defence to a charge of murder', and argued that

> The reason why a man may not consent to the commission of an offence against himself beforehand or forgive it afterwards is that it is an offence against society.[82]

What the decision by the House of Lords did not take into account is the argument that the men submitting to the ill-treatment did not regard it as such. It was, for them, a means of obtaining pleasure; though not of the same kind as offered by rugby football or boxing. It was sexual in nature, and there are analogies between the implications of Operation Slammer and Macaulay's remark that the seventeenth-century Puritans banned bear-baiting not because it caused pain to the bear but because it gave pleasure to the spectators. The tendency of taboos to set out to stop people enjoying themselves sexually in a way which they prefer but of which society disapproves is equally noticeable in the entries on **contraception**, **hedonism**, **homosexuality** and **oral sex**.

There is no similarity between the arguments used in the prosecutions to which Operation Slammer gave rise and those invoked when the suggestion is made that professional boxing should be banned. There, it is not a question of preventing boxers from enjoying themselves. It is one of stopping them from inflicting permanent damage upon one another. The argument is not that the activity itself is wrong. There has been no sustained campaign to ban either amateur boxing or rugby football, both of which can cause quite serious injuries. The argument is that society has the right and duty to prevent people from earning money by deliberately hurting one another. There was, in contrast, no question of money in Operation Slammer, and no suggestion that the harm inflicted would be as permanent and irreversible as the brain damage from which boxers tend to suffer. Neither, since the activities for which the men arrested under Operation Slammer were prosecuted took place in private, was there any question of their causing an affray or behaving in such a way as to cause a breach of the peace. Eleven of the men involved were nevertheless sentenced to periods of imprisonment of up to four and a half years. Twenty-six others were cautioned. The violence they inflicted on one another had, in the eyes of the law, the disadvantage of being not only sexual but homosexual. There are no records of similar charges being made against female prostitutes who offer flagellation as one of their basic services.

In December 1995, the Law Commission for England and Wales recommended that acts of sado-masochism should no longer be regarded as criminal offences. A decision by the English Appeal Court reported in the *Daily Telegraph* for 1 March 1996 took a step towards implementing this recommendation when it cleared a man who had branded his initials on his wife's bottom of the charge of causing actual bodily harm. Lord Justice Russell accepted the wife's view that these initials were 'a desirable personal adornment', and said that her desire to be marked in this way was 'no less understandable than piercing nostrils and even tongues for the purposes of inserting jewellery' (see **pins** in V). In March 1996, a London jury reached a comparable decision when it acquitted Martin Church of the charge brought against him under the 1751 Act Against Keeping a Disorderly House. The defendant admitted that whippings, spankings and minor beatings took place, and that the adults attending dressed up in fetish clothing. However, he denied that the activities were orgies conducted for gain, and stressed their purely voluntary nature.[83]

A central factor distinguishing both these cases from Operation Slammer was that they concerned heterosexual relationships. The relaxation of the laws against homosexuals in both the United Kingdom and the United States has not removed the various prejudices against them. The case dismissed by Lord Justice Russell not only took place with the full consent of husband and wife, and in the privacy of their own home, but also without anyone else knowing; the matter came to light only when the wife's doctor reported it to the police. In Operation Slammer, an advertisement had been placed in a magazine inviting interested and consenting adults to ring a particular number. There was thus, for the prosecution, an analogy with the charge of committing an offence against public decency mentioned above under **homosexuality** (iii). Like the 1990 recommendation of the Law Commission, the decision of the Appeal Court marks a further step towards a legal system based on John Stuart Mill's dictum in *On Liberty* (1859) that 'over himself, over his own body and mind, the individual is sovereign'. If the practices involved in sado-masochism cease to be punishable by law, it will be for reasons analogous to those inseparable from the concept of freedom of speech as defined in 1929 by Oliver Wendell Holmes when delivering a dissenting judgment in *United States* v. *Schwimmer*:

> If there is any principle of the Constitution that more imperatively calls for attachment than any other it is the principle of free thought – not free thought for those who agree with us but freedom for thought we hate.

This was not, however, the view taken in February 1997 by the European Court of Human Rights at Strasbourg. In rejecting the appeal which three of the accused had made against the prison sentence imposed on them the Court ruled that the laws under which they were convicted were 'necessary in a democratic society' for the protection of the health as well as the morals of its members.

(ii) The scarcity of formal taboos against sado-masochism sets something of a problem for the sociobiologists. They maintain that the incest taboo is what Gregory Leavitt, writing in *The American Anthropologist* [84], calls a 'cultural reflection of natural selection processes', arguing as Richard Dawkins does that we have a natural aversion for incest which stems from our innate awareness that it is likely to produce sickly offspring. But if Freud is right, and sado-masochism is indeed the most widespread of all the perversions, it is hard to explain why the evolutionary instincts supposedly lying at the root of the incest taboo have not created a comparably powerful set of taboos against it; or, for that matter, against other forms of sexual activity such as fetishism and homosexuality which, by their very nature can produce no offspring at all.

At the S-M pub in Berlin, you get put in the stocks and lashed before being allowed to order your pint. In the *Guardian* for 5 February 1996, Linda Grant argued that in contemporary Britain, sado-masochism is 'not just voguish but sanctioned by the mainstream'. Her statement that 'in the nineties, the dominatrix has become the icon of the sexual woman; the message she is giving out is one of power – over herself and over men' is nevertheless hard to reconcile with her recognition, later in the same article, that 'in the real world of prostitution, it is the paying customer who calls the shots, the man with the cash'. The difficulty which Sacher-Masoch experienced in finding a woman prepared to play the dominating role in which he sought to cast her is reflected in the plethora of cards in the telephone booths of central London advertising the services of Miss Whiplash. There would scarcely be so many of these cards on display if the men wishing to use the services they offer could have their needs satisfied by a wife or girlfriend whose inclinations exactly matched their desires.

In *Misogynies* (1985), Joan Smith pointed to a marked absence in the contemporary cinema of taboos likely to protect women against the tendency of 'slasher' films such as *Jagged Edge* (1985), *Blow Out* (1981), *Body Double* (1984), or *Dressed to Kill* (1980) to make money by exploiting the depiction of violence against women. In this respect, she argued, a whole sector of the modern entertainment industry was profiting from the disappearance of earlier prohibitions; she wrote

> The Stallone films, and war films like Clint Eastwood's *Heartbreak Ridge* (1986), do not break any taboos. There is no universal prohibition on men beating up other men in our society. The man who gets involved in the odd punch-up at closing time

is a bit of a lad. Thousands of people turn up at the Albert Hall to watch two men pound each other to pulp in the name of sport.

See also **sado-masochism** in IV.

Sex In spite of the turning away of Moses from his wife after he has become the prophet of the Lord, suspicion of sex is not part of the modern Jewish tradition. Ideally, the rabbi should be married, in order that he may better advise married couples as to the conduct of their own lives.

A marked preference for chastity is visible in St Paul's reluctant endorsement of marriage in I *Corinthians*, 7:9: 'But if they cannot contain, let them marry: for it is better to marry than to burn'. The traditional view of the Church that sex was intended only for procreation inspires the taboo on **contraception**. It was expressed in its clearest form by Henry Davis SJ in his *Moral and Pastoral Theology* (1938) when he declared that 'it is grievously sinful in the unmarried deliberately to procure or accept even the smallest degree of venereal pleasure'.[85] This view is echoed by Robin Lane Fox's summary of Christian teaching on sex in the Middle Ages. It was, he writes in *The Red Lamp of Incest* (1983), 'a mortal sin to embrace one's wife too passionately', and he quotes Montaigne as saying that one of the dangers of incestuous love is that it is likely to be highly passionate.[86] In *The Body and Society: Men, Women and Sexual Renunciation in Early Christianity* (1988), Peter Brown quotes the advice of Tertullian to his fellow Christians: 'By continence, you will buy yourself up a great stock of sanctity, by making savings on the flesh, you will be able to invest in the Spirit.' Celibacy also had the advantage, for the clergy, of setting them apart from the rest of society, and justifying their power as well as their privileges. Because they had mastered the body, they had the right to own property and the right to be obeyed. The ban against Catholic priests having sex may also have performed a semiotic function by distinguishing them from rabbis, and continues to mark a difference between them and members of the Protestant clergy.

The influence of St Paul's suspicion of sexual pleasure is detectable in the views expressed in the *Lady Chatterley* trial and in the taboos on **oral sex**. It remained alive long enough to exercise a strong if contrary influence on the views of the pop singer Madonna, who in January 1996 told Bob Guccione Jr, in an interview published in his magazine *Spin*, that 'when you are raised to believe that anything having to do with sex is forbidden and taboo, then of course that's all you want to know about'. 'Catholicism', she added, 'is a very masochistic religion', and she continued: 'I somehow equate God and religion and sacrifice with taboo and sexuality.'[87]

Although Christianity is the most puritanical of religions, it does not have a monopoly of a preoccupation with sex. Like the taboos which it is one of its functions to study, anthropology is much concerned with the subject as well, a point made in a recent book by two anthropologists, Don Kulick and Margaret Wilson, entitled *Sex, Identity and Erotic Subjectivity in Anthropological Fieldwork* (1995). As Don Kulick remarked, speaking of the year or so spent studying a remote tribe in a non-industrial society, the indispensable *rite de passage* whereby one becomes a proper anthropologist: 'The biggest taboo is the sexuality of the fieldworker. What one is supposed to do about sex for a whole year, far away from one's normal life and sexual partner(s), is never touched on in courses on anthropological fieldwork.' Both he and Margaret Wilson were, he added, risking their own careers in daring to broach the subject, and he made a further comment which is relevant to the entry **primitive** in III and **Eurocentrism** in IV. 'Anthropology', he wrote, 'traffics in sex; it absolutely revels in it – but only as long as the sex being scrutinised is *their* sex, the sex of the Other, the sex of the people we study.'[88]

A comment on the view that chastity was especially desirable in women occurs in Christopher Fry's verse play *The Lady's Not for Burning* (1949), of which the action is set in 'the thirteenth century more or less'. When Alizon Eliot describes how her father

> thought he would never be able to find enough husbands
>   for six of us, and so he made up his mind
> to simplify matters and let me marry God.
> He gave me to a convent

her recollection attracts a question from Richard, an orphaned clerk:

What showing did he think he would make as God's father-in-law?

See above, **masturbation** and **sado-masochism**.

Smoking It is easy to sympathize with Frederick J. Simoons's comment in his study of food avoidances in the old world, *Eat Not This Flesh* (1961), that if consumer habits were governed by reason, Americans would give up tobacco. In April 1996, a step was indeed taken towards the fulfilment of his ambition to 'generate strong group emotions and the support of powerful institutions which forbid its use'. The American Cancer Society protested violently against two photographs in *Playboy* magazine depicting the supermodels Kate Moss and Stephanie Seymour smoking cigarettes.[89]

It is nevertheless a mark of taboos that it is very difficult to invent them, and the prohibitions on smoking in public have taken the form of laws created by the state and regulations imposed by organizations. The ban on smoking in aircraft is also justifiable on the grounds of safety as well as of hygiene, considerations frequently absent from traditional taboos. If taboos do happen to fulfil a useful purpose, this is generally by accident. Up to now, the only prohibitions on smoking which even remotely recall taboos concern its postponement in the United Kingdom until after the loyal toast, and the view that ladies do not smoke in the street. The latter is a means of reinforcing class distinctions not based on money. It is a definition of a lady that if she does have to smoke, she is sufficiently capable of deferred gratification to wait until she is alone. The former exists primarily to show respect to the Crown, and is an example of a taboo playing a semiological role by its sudden removal.

Thus the statement 'You may now smoke' marks the end of the formal part of the meal. A different part of the evening has now begun. Guests may go to the loo. They may also move their chairs, and go and talk to people next to whom they would have liked to be sitting. Alternatively, they may now go and greet the friends whom they were relieved to have noticed, at the beginning of the evening, had been placed at some distance from them, hoping as they do so that their enthusiasm will appear unfeigned. All the diners must also steel themselves to listen to the after-dinner speech.

Speak In certain American military academies, first-year cadets may never address a cadet in the second, third or fourth years without having been spoken to first. In the Citadel military academy in South Carolina, where in 1995 Shannon Faulkner, a woman, won the right to enter but was made to find the course too tough and left after she had had to spend four days in the infirmary, first-year cadets are allowed to say only three things to their seniors: 'Sir, yes sir'; 'Sir, no sir'; 'Sir, excuse me sir'.

Taboos of this kind serve to emphasize differences, and are not limited to military academies and English public schools. If someone is in the presence of a member of the British royal family, there is the same taboo on being the first speak as on any form of physical contact. When, in 1887, Guy Wethered was president of Oxford University Boat Club, no new Blue was allowed to speak to an old Blue unless first addressed.[90] Recruits to the British Navy during the Second World War were still taught not to address an officer unless he spoke to them first, a rule justified at the time by the argument that the officer might be involved in giving a complicated order which he might get wrong if interrupted.

See below, **talk**.

Stamp *Sura* XXIV.30 of the Koran instructs women not to

> stamp
> their feet, so that their hidden ornament
> may be known.

It is hard, for readers afflicted with **Eurocentrism**, to avoid thinking of the Victorian advice to young ladies to keep their skirts long, on the grounds that 'ankles may arouse the most overwhelming passions'.

See also **veil** in V.

Stare In chapter VII of Kingsley Amis's second novel, *That Uncertain Feeling* (1955), the narrator realizes when idly watching a young man combing his hair that he has 'violated the unspoken code which prohibits the eye from resting on a stranger for more than two seconds'. He avoids having to fight the young man who 'sheathes his comb in a little case which also contained a nail-file' (equivalent in the South Wales of the 1950s to the 'nerd pack' mentioned in **pens** in V) by claiming to be a boxer disqualified for hitting low in the recent final of the University of Wales boxing tournament.

The rule against looking too closely at somebody, and even more against pointing at them, is an example of a taboo merging into good manners. Everyone has the right to privacy, which includes the private space by which he or she likes to be surrounded. Ideas of how much private space people need nevertheless vary from culture to culture. In *The Silent Language* (1959), E. T. Hall comments that 'in Latin America, the distance is smaller than in the United States. In fact, people cannot speak comfortably unless they are very close, a closeness which evokes aggressive or erotic intent in the USA. The result is that when they approach, we move away, and they think we are cold, reserved and unfriendly.'[91]

In most countries, it is a sensible precaution to follow the advice given by the police and 'avoid eye contact' when walking along a street which may contain criminal or hostile strangers.

Talk (i) When General Schwarzkopf ate his first meal as a cadet, or Plebe, at West Point in the early 1950s, he was not allowed to talk. You had, he recalls in *It Doesn't Take a Hero* (1992), 'to eat sitting to attention on the front six inches of your chair. No conversing, no looking around. You had to cut your food, put down your knife, take a bite, and put down your fork while you chewed.' You also had a 'first classman' bellowing in your ear, telling you: 'Keep your eyes to yourself, dumbjohn!' or 'That was too big a bite!' The scene is reminiscent of the initiation ceremonies performed in the tribal societies of Africa or Polynesia, or at English public schools.

The aim of such ceremonies is to carry out the policy which anthropologists call 'extrusion', the process by which the young person is removed from the world of childhood and the family and prepared for initiation into the official, adult life of the tribe. This involves the temporary surrender of all free will, and the readiness to follow orders, as the Jesuits put it, *perinde ac cadaver*, as though you were a corpse. The taboos by which the tribe affirms its identity then become second nature to the new member.

(ii) Although some topics are universally avoided in modern European or American society, few taboos vary more between different cultures than those governing conversation. **Death** and **money** are widely taboo (see the entries in Section III), and the hostess who said that she did not allow her guests to discuss their children, their pets, their health or their holidays was immediately recognized as a model for her sex. She permitted politics and religion, so long as she was allowed to blow the whistle if the exchanges became too lively. These were topics on which women could express a view as well. But she imposed an absolute ban on any attempt to tell jokes. As Tom Wolfe remarks in his 'Vignette' *The Invisible Wife*, a woman in American society is 'not expected to launch into disquisitions or actually *tell long stories herself*'.[92] This explains the taboo in certain circles in England on the telling of jokes, whether risqué or not, in mixed company. If jokes are allowed, especially risqué ones, women have even less chance of playing a part in the conversation than they do now.

(iii) It is in the way conversations organize themselves that the taboos separating English-speaking from Latin cultures show themselves most clearly. In a party of six, or even eight, the person speaking at a dinner table in England or America can count on a reasonably attentive audience for up to three minutes. In France, Italy or Spain, the other members of the group think that they have lost face if they do not start up an alternative conversation with their neighbour within fifteen seconds of the first person beginning to talk.

Ray B. Browne comments in his *Forbidden Fruits: Taboos and Tabooism in Culture* (1984) that 'silence is not a universal common courtesy; it is a relative thing, a culturally determined and culturally variable taboo'.[93] In the United Kingdom, the lecturer in a university finds a resigned passivity, punctuated by the occasional yawn. In the United States, the male lecturer enjoys sustained attention, followed by the ultimate compliment of questions, and this courtesy is even more noticeable when the lecturer is a woman. In France, it is normal behaviour for students to talk audibly to one another throughout the lecture, generally without even bothering to notice whether the person addressing them is male or female.

Touch The acronym M.T.F. (Must Touch Flesh) is more than a warning to young girls in the theatrical profession against lecherous producers who appear to suffer from an uncontrollable urge to fondle them. It reflects the Western view that body contact must be avoided, even among relatives and especially among close male friends. It is a taboo which strikes visitors from Islamic countries as decidedly odd.

British visitors to North America also notice a difference in the way shop assistants make change. Whereas it is not unusual, in the United Kingdom, for the person making change to press the coins into the purchaser's palm, this hardly ever happens in Canada or the United States.

See above, **stare**.

Trespass The occurrence in *Deuteronomy*, 19:14 of the commandment

> Thou shalt not remove thy neighbour's landmark, which they of old time have set in thine inheritance, which thou shalt inherit in the land that the Lord thy God giveth thee to possess it

supports Sir James Frazer's suggestion that taboos may have had the advantage of giving rise to the concept of private property. The placing of the commandment in so early a book as *Deuteronomy*, close to its instruction in 14:21 not to 'seethe the kid in his mother's milk', suggests a taboo rather than a law. So, too, does its obvious concern, which it again shares with taboos, to establish clear distinctions.

The concept of private property is a basic constituent of the civil law of virtually all societies. That of trespass, in contrast, is less clearly defined, both in the sense of going on somebody's land and in that of encroaching upon the exclusive right to offer certain services. In his article 'Taboos and Taboo-Breakers in Architecture', in Ray B. Browne's *Forbidden Fruits: Taboos and Tabooism in Culture* (1984), Dennis Alan Mann comments that 'since professions are fundamentally conservative, perpetuating their own self-interests, then the function of taboos in protecting and enhancing those interests will remain, albeit in another form'. His remark is especially applicable to the tendency of male-dominated professions such as engineering, dentistry and medicine – like architecture itself – to enforce a taboo against the entry of women.

Franz Steiner commented of Captain Cook's surprise at finding so many taboos in Polynesia that they 'would not have seemed so remarkable to a Spaniard as to a northern Protestant'.[94] The view that taboos fit better into Latin than into Anglo-Saxon culture comes out in the much later date at which women obtained the right to vote in France, Spain and Italy. One of the major functions of taboos has always been to impose an inferior status on women, to exclude them from certain activities, and to ban their participation in certain professions. In *Womansword* (1989), Kittredge Cherry noted that the world's longest underground tunnel, the Seikan, was completed without a single woman setting foot in it, not even one of the women members of the Japanese parliament who had authorized its construction.[95] Among the Chukchee of Siberia, women skin and prepare the slaughtered reindeer, but are not allowed to eat it. They are told, instead, 'Being a woman, eat crumbs'.[96] In the field of the spiritual life, it has taken Christian culture a long time to recover from St Paul's injunction in I *Corinthians*, 14:34–5:

> Let your women keep silence in the churches: for it is not permitted unto them to speak; but they are commanded to be under obedience, as also saith the law.
>
> And if they will learn anything, let them ask their husbands at home: for it is a shame for women to speak in the church.

When, in 1934, General Evangeline Booth was appointed head of the Salvation Army, she became the first woman to lead an international religious organization.

Usury (i) *Psalm*, 15:5 bestows as much praise on a man for not putting out his money to usury as for not taking reward against the innocent. *Deuteronomy*, 23:19 is more openly condemnatory, certainly as far as relationships between Jews are concerned, clearly stating: 'Thou shalt not lend money upon usury to thy brother: usury of money, usury of victuals, usury of anything that is lent upon usury.' Verse 20, however, allows usury on loans to non-Jews, presumably mitigating in advance the statement in *Ezekiel*, 18:13: He that 'hath given forth upon usury, and hath taken increase: shall he then live? he shall not live: he hath done all these abominations: he shall surely die: his blood shall be upon him.' Verses 275–280 of *Sura* II of the Koran forbid what the translation calls 'Riba', or the charging of interest. It also sentences to hellfire anyone who, having once charged interest but abandoned the practice, then goes back to it. Anyone following the commandment not to charge interest may nevertheless keep the capital sum which is then returned to him.

The question is naturally that of defining usury, considered by Jewish commentators on the Bible as excessive interest rather than a reasonable payment to the lender for doing without his money or property for a certain period. During the Babylonian captivity, the Jews came into contact with a culture at which 20 per cent per annum was the norm, and regarded this as excessive. The prohibition became more extensive with the advent of Christianity, and the disappearance of the distinction between usury, in the sense of an exorbitant charge for goods or money loaned, and a fair rate of interest to reward the lender for the temporary surrender of his property. *Luke*, 6:35 – 'But love ye your enemies, and do good, and lend, hoping for nothing again; and your reward shall be great' – was given precedence over the implications which could be read into the Parable of the Talents in *Matthew*, 25:14–29. There, the master who went on a journey to a far country reproves the servant who buried the one talent entrusted to him in the ground by telling him, 'Thou oughtest therefore to have put my money to the exchangers, and then at my coming I should have received mine own with usury', the implication clearly being that making money work for you is a perfectly legitimate activity.[97]

The emphasis on *Luke*, 6:35 led to the decision by the Council of Nicea in 325 to forbid priests to charge interest on loans. At Carthage, in 345, this was extended to laymen. In 1179 Pope Alexander III excommunicated all manifest usurers, and at Vienne, in 1331, it was declared that anyone who considered that the practice of usury was not sinful should be punished as a heretic. In contrast, the twelfth-century Jewish philosopher Maimonides interpreted *Deuteronomy*, 23:20 as saying that for Jews to charge interest to Gentiles was part of the written law. It thus became natural for the Jews to act as moneylenders in Christian society, especially in the light of the taboo preventing Christians from receiving any interest on the loans which they might make. It was, in any case, hard for Jews to do much else, since the Diaspora had deprived them of the lands which the Talmud had commanded them to cultivate, and the Christians would not allow them to buy any more.

(ii) It was not only the teaching of St Luke which led to the interdict on Christians receiving interest on loans. It was also an inheritance from Greece and Rome. Plato held that the wealth accumulated by usury divided the state by setting the rich against the poor. Aristotle argued that since money did not breed, it was unnatural to enable it to accumulate by the charging of interest on loans. St Thomas Aquinas followed Cicero in seeing money as a 'fungible' good, one whose nature it was to be consumed by the process of being used. It was therefore against nature for it to grow through being used as a loan. It was only with the Italian Renaissance that the idea developed that it was reasonable to charge interest on the loan of money which was being put to use for productive purpose, as distinct from one intended to finance immediate consumption. The Protestant Reformation, with its insistence on the virtues of thrift and hard work implied in the Parable of the Talents, completed the process whereby the rule against charging interest disappeared and the taboo vanished.

See also **money** in III.

Whistle The ban on whistling when on board ship or back-stage in the theatre is an example of how close taboos can sometimes be to superstitions. There is nevertheless a difference, in that while there is no evidence that you can make the wind blow by whistling, you can easily cause an accident in the theatre by whistling back-stage. Stage hands traditionally communicate with one another by whistling, so that an ill-timed whistle from a member of the cast might cause a piece of scenery to fall on somebody's head.

Whistling, Cyril Glassé observes, is

> forbidden in Islam, doubtless because of its association with sorcery and the casting of spells in pre-Islamic times, for which

reason it is still popularly considered to be 'communication with the Djin'. It also has connotations of mindlessness or vulgarity.[98]

It is also alleged to be impossible for homosexuals to whistle. When, in Cyril Connolly's parody *Bond Strikes Camp* (1963), M. comes across this idea in a paper analysing Bond's potential weaknesses, he purses his lips and whistles softly under his breath to reassure himself. According to Michael Baker's *Our Three Selves: a Life of Radclyffe Hall* (1985), Radclyffe Hall could not whistle either. She was also of less aristocratic lineage than her heroine and alter ego, the Stephen Gordon of *The Well of Loneliness* (1919). It will be recalled by admirers of Richmal Crompton that William Brown is frequently reproved by his father for whistling. A more sexually streetwise parent might have been sufficiently reassured to utter a note of congratulation. **Political correctness** now assimilates what used to be known as 'wolf-whistling' to sexual harassment.

Work In England, the taboo on saying that you enjoy your job is as absolute as the ban on admitting that you have learned to do something difficult by constant practice. The aristocratic ethos which still permeates English society insists that you should present skill at any activity, but especially sport, as in-born. In 1963, Flanders and Swann acknowledged the Englishness of this taboo on visible effort by singing of foreigners that

> They argue with umpires, they cheer when they've won,
> And they practise beforehand, which ruins the fun.

This taboo does not exist north of the Tweed or the Bristol Channel, or on the other side of the Atlantic. However, a report in the *Telegraph* of 23 March 1996 described a report coming out of Japan which suggested that it might one day develop there. The belief that the best possible entry into this world was to be born Japanese and male had ceased to be universal. The men in Japan were beginning to feel restive at the obligation to spend a great deal of time drinking (see **alcohol** in II). They found the requirement to take an obsessive interest in sport increasingly irksome, and longed to rebel against the taboo on shedding **tears** in public. They were also no longer prepared to work twelve hours a day, six days a week. These were all requirements from which Japanese women were in the enviable position of being free.

NOTES

1 Alfred Kinsey, and others, *The Sexual Behaviour of the Human Male*, W. B. Saunders and Company, Philadelphia and London, 1948, pp. 392, 262 and 673.
2 Carolyn Conley, *The Unwritten Law: Criminal Justice in Victorian Kent*, Oxford University Press, Oxford, 1991, pp. 187–8.
3 Quoted from Clellan Ford and Frank A. Beach, *Patterns of Sexual Behaviour*, Eyre and Spottiswoode, London, 1952, p. 154.
4 J. C. Smith and Brian Hogan, *Criminal Law*, Butterworth, London, 1987, p. 481.
5 B. Marriner, *Canibalism: The Last Taboo!*, Arrow Books, London, 1992.
6 W. Arens, *The Man-Eating Myth: Anthropology and Anthropophagy*, Oxford University Press, Oxford, 1979, p. 166. The long and generally favourable review in the *Times Literary Supplement* by Rodney Needham on 25 January 1980, gave rise to a lively correspondence in which the question was debated as to whether human flesh, when cooked, was like pork or like buffalo. See also **beef** in II.
7 M. Warner, *Managing Monsters: Six Myths of Our Time*, Vintage, London, 1994, pp. 73–4. A rather different view was expressed by Michael Harner in the *American Ethnologist*, vol. 4, March 1977, pp. 117–35, in which he maintained in his article on Aztec human sacrifices that the desire of Western observers to combat ethnocentrism and portray native peoples in the best possible light has led them to minimize the importance of such practices.
8 *American Anthropologist*, vol. 84, no. 3, September 1982, pp. 595–611 (601).
9 pp. 203–5.
10 Edited by Donald Tuzi and Paula Brown. For a review, see the *American Anthropologist*, vol. 6, no. 87, 1985, pp. 427–8, in which James G. Flanaghan draws attention to the fact that only one of the participants claimed actually to have witnessed acts of cannibalism. Indeed, several contributors offered support to Arens's basic thesis, with Donald Tuzin writing (pp. 70–1) that 'for the Arapesh, "cannibalism" is an image of unthinkability par excellence', Carol P. MacCormack observing (p. 51) that 'accusations of cannibalism are clearly a political weapon', and Shirley Lindenbaum pointing out

that 'accusations of cannibalism emerge as a recurrent idiom of Sherbro political theatre'.

In one of the earlist discussions of the subject, Montaigne pointed out in his essay 'Des Cannibales' (1580) that it was much less barbarous to eat human flesh than to torture people and burn them alive, a practice which he noted was frequently inspired in the Western Europe of the sixteenth century by religious zeal.

11 *American Anthropologist*, vol. 82, no. 2, June 1980, pp. 389–91.

12 R. Ardrey's *The Territorial Imperative*, Fontana, London, 1969, p. 285.

13 *American Anthropologist*, vol. 84, no. 3, September 1982, pp. 611–27. The article was a review of the recently published *Kuru: Early Letters and Field Notes from the collection of D. Carleton Gajdusek*, edited by Judith Farquhur and D. Carleton Gajdusek, Raven Press, New York. An account of the symptoms of Kuru is given by Rupert Furneaux in the chapter of *Primitive Peoples* (David and Charles, Newton Abbot and London, 1975), where he reports what he calls the 'stone age men of New Guinea' as attributing the disease which they refer to as 'laughing death' either to sorcery or to the shock of the new ideas imported by Europeans.

14 I am grateful to Dr Maia Green, of the Univerity of Manchester, for drawing this distinction to my attention.

15 A. Huxley, *Ends and Means*, Chatto and Windus, London, 1937; collected edition, 1946, p. 298.

16 Quoted in Jonathon Greene, *The Encyclopedia of Censorship*, (New York, 1988), Facts on File, Oxford, 1990, p. 194.

17 Quoted by C. Wood and B. Suitters, *The Fight for Acceptance*, MTP, London, 1970, pp. 63–5.

18 Thus the American sociologist Andrew Greeley comments in *The Crooked Lines of God: Authors of Their Own Lives*, University of California Press, Berkeley, 1990, p. 125, on how his fellow Catholics

> reject the official teaching of the Church on birth control, premarital sex, abortion, and other related matters, although they oppose homosexuality, extra-marital sex, and abortion on demand, in about the same proportion as do white American Protestants.

As far as the reliance on the rhythm method for limiting the number of births, there may be sound medical reasons for them to be suspicious of it and to defy the taboo on the use of chemical or mechanical techniques. In the novel *How Far Can You Go?* Secker and Warburg, London, 1980, published in the United States under the title *Snakes and Ladders*, David Lodge describes how one of his characters, the doctor Edward, comes across the hypothesis in the medical journals that genetic defects 'are more likely to occur with couples deliberately restricting their intercourse to the post-ovulatory period'.

19 Cyril Glassé, *The Concise Encyclopedia of Islam*, Stacey Publications, London, 1989.

20 For a full treatment of the problems and practice of divorce, see Roderick Phillips, *Putting Asunder: A History of Divorce in Western Society*, Cambridge University Press, Cambridge, 1988.

21 Quoted by Germaine Greer in *Sex and Destiny*, Secker and Warburg, London, 1984, p. 212.

22 See N. Strossen, *Defending Pornography: Free Speech, Sex and the Fight for Women's Rights*, Simon and Schuster, New York, 1995, pp. 110 and 112.

23 Paragraph 1867 of the full, revised Catechism of the Catholic Church (1992) now gives this star marking to five sins, quoting chapter and verse for each: wilful murder is the killing of Abel by Cain in *Genesis*, 4:10; the sin of Sodom is punished by the fire and brimstone rained down on the Cities of the Plain in *Genesis*, 19:24; the cry of the Israelites oppressed in Egypt occurs in *Exodus*, 3:7–10; the need to give charity to the widow and orphan is emphasized in *Exodus*, 22:22; and depriving the labourer of the fruits of his work is condemned in *Deuteronomy*, 24:14–15. For more details about Sodom and Gomorrah, see the entry **homosexuality** in Section IV.

24 M. Foucault, *The History of Sexuality*, translated by Robert Hurley, Pantheon, New York, 1980, Introduction, pp. 43, 110. For a further discussion of nineteenth-century attempts to define homosexuality, see Chapter 9, 'The Medicalization of Homosexuality' in David F. Greenberg, *The Construction of Homosexuality*, University of Chicago Press, Chicago and London, 1988.

25 See Richard Ellmann, *Oscar Wilde*, Hamish Hamilton, London, 1987, p. 243. For a discussion of the origin of the word 'sodomite' see the entry **homosexuality** in IV.

26 Rollin M. Perkins and Ronald N. Boyce, *Criminal Law*, Foundation Press, Mineola, NY, 1982, p. 468.

27 See Margaret Cruickshank, *The Gay and Lesbian Liberation Movement*, Routledge, London, 1992, p. 191. This represents a change from the situation set out in a footnote to p. 235 of the fourth edition of Sanford H. Kadish and others, *The Criminal Law and Its Processes: Cases and Materials*, Little, Brown, Boston, MA, 1983, which states that consensual sodomy between adults in private had been

decriminalized in twenty-two states. The description of homosexual acts is taken from Appendix B, pp. 281–92 of *The Homosexual in America: A Subjective Approach*, by Donald Webster Cory, Greenberg, New York, 1951.

28 For details of the *Bowes* v. *Hardwick* case, see *The Congressional Quarterly Almanach*, 1986, 4A, p. 11, and Jonathan Goldberg's Introduction to his anthology of essays, *Reclaiming Sodom*, Routledge, New York and London, 1994, in which he points out on p. 9 that 'the act involved in *Bowes* v. *Hardwick* was not anal sex; it was a blow job interrupted by the arrival of a policeman in Michael Hardwick's bedroom'. For Justice Lewis Powell's view, see Cruickshank, *The Gay and Lesbian Liberation Movement*, p. 191. Kadish, *Criminal Law and Its Processes* gives a long extract from the judgment in the 1980 case of *People* v. *Onofre*, in which the defendants were convicted of 'consensual sodomy' under the New York statute and each appealed to the Appellate Division, which reversed their convictions on finding that the law against sodomy was unconstitutional.

29 Information supplied by the Gay/Lesbian Hot Line in New York.

30 *Congressional Quarterly Almanach*, 1988, p. 710; 1989, p. 244.

31 Smith and Hogan, *Criminal Law*, 1992 edn, p. 477. Fenton Bressler, *Sex and the Law*, Waterton, London, 1985, p. 25.

32 P. Wildeblood, *Against the Law* (1956), Penguin Books, Harmondsworth, 1957, p. 9.

33 See Smith and Hogan, *Criminal Law*, 1992 edn, p. 478.

34 These and other issues are fully discussed in Michael Rose, *Homosexuality: A Philosophical Inquiry*, Blackwell, Oxford, 1988.

35 See p. 61 of Marc Daniel's essay, 'Arab Civilization and Male Love', in Goldberg, *Reclaiming Sodom*. While there is an element of special pleading in all the essays collected in this volume, Marc Daniel does acknowledge the existence of an alternative tradition of intense hostility towards homosexuality in Islamic culture. He attributes this at least partly to attitudes towards women current in Arab society, writing that 'Muhammed shared the contempt of his countrymen towards homosexuals, thought of as "women" and consequently inferior'.

36 Bret Hinsch, *Passions of the Cut Sleeve*, University of California Press, Berkeley and Oxford, 1990, p. 35. As Dr Hinsch explains on p. 53, the term stems from an episode in the life of the Emperor Ai. Just as William of Orange, as Churchill puts it in *A History of the English-Speaking Peoples* (1956), showed a certain 'indifference to women', so the Emperor Ai 'did not care for them', preferring the charms of his favourite, Dong Xian. One day, as the two men were asleep in the

same bed during the daytime, Dong Xian lay stretched out on the emperor's sleeve. Rather than disturb him, Ai released himself by cutting off the sleeve of his own garment.

37 Paul Veyne, 'Homosexuality in Ancient Rome', in *Western Sexuality: Practice and Precept in Past and Present Times*, edited by Philippe Ariès and André Béjin, translated by Anthony Foster, Blackwell, Oxford, 1985, p. 21.

38 See K. J. Dover, *Greek Homosexuality*, Duckworth, London, 1978, pp. 16 and 164.

39 R. Benedict, *The Chrysanthemum and the Sword*, Charles E. Tuttle, Vermont and Tokyo, 1946, p. 188.

40 See Edmund Leach, *Lévi-Strauss*, Fontana Modern Masters, Collins, London, 1970, p. 103 and his statement in William, Lessa and Evon Vogt, *A Reader in Comparative Religion: An Anthropological Approach*, Harper and Row, New York, 1979, p. 55.

41 Quoted in Leach, *Lévi-Strauss*, p. 103.

42 B. Malinowski, *The Sexual Life of Savages*, Routledge, London, 1929, pp. 155 and 143. There has been considerable discussion as to whether Malinovski was right on this point. In *The Journal of the Polynesian Society*, vol. 85, no. 2, 1976, pp. 243–255, Torben Monberg said that the Trobriand islanders now laughed at the idea that anyone should have thought they were so ignorant, and explained Malinowski's mistake by arguing that he had not asked the question in a form that they understood. In the late 1960s, the question had already inspired a lively correspondence in *Man*, the journal of the Royal Anthropological Society. In the Henry Myers Memorial Lecture for 1967, Edmund Leach had maintained that the belief in parthenogenesis among the Trobriand islanders was a dogma, comparable with the belief in the Virgin Birth of Jesus Christ among Roman Catholics, and argued that the Trobriand islanders had freely admitted to other anthropologists that the cause of pregnancy in animals other than men is copulation. In the June 1968 issue of *Man*, pp. 242–61, Melford E. Spiro disagreed, reporting how he had recently asked fifty people in the Trobriand Islands, and received the same answer as Malinowski. He also reported how a comparable belief that pregnancy is caused by spirits can be found among the Tully River aborigines in Australia.

43 R. Dawkins, *The Selfish Gene* (1976), Oxford University Press, Oxford, 1989, p. 294.

44 Joseph Shepherd, *Incest: A Biosocial View* was published by the Academic Press, New York, 1983. Patricia Whelehan's review appeared in the *American Anthropologist*, no. 87, 1985, pp. 677–8.

45 I. M. Lewis, *Social Anthropology in Perspective*, Penguin, Harmondsworth, 1976, p. 238.

46 Françoise Héritier's book *Les deux soeurs et leur mère: Anthropologie de l'inceste* published by the Editions Odile Jacob, Paris, 1994, has not yet been translated into English, and I am conscious of summarizing a long and complex argument. For her quotation from *Hamlet*, see p. 364. For the idea of sexual intercourse joining together the bodily humours of the two participants, and thus making them one body through the mingling of their blood, see pp. 90, 123, 134 and 220. See p. 237 for the link with the idea that the woman ejaculates during orgasm, thus mingling her 'sperm' with that of her partner. For the analogy with masturbation and other essentially sterile practices, see p. 365.

47 *Les deux soeurs et leur mère*, p. 114. For a comparable but more complicated example from the Muslim world, see p. 321 of the same book.

Françoise Héritier is not one of the professional anthropologists who commented unfavourably on the typescript of this book. When I wrote to say how interesting I found *Les deux soeurs et leur mère*, and to ask when it was going to be translated into English, she did not reply to my letter. Neither did the French historian Marc Ferro, when I wrote to regret that I could not attend the public lecture entitled 'Taboos in History' which he gave at the Institut Français de Londres on 5 November 1996. I was particularly interested to know whether he was talking about the role played by taboos in human history or about the existence, in historical studies, of a number of taboo subjects. However, since he did not acknowledge the receipt of my letter, I was not able to find out. As I discovered in 1987, when writing to the French scholar Michel Contat to ask a question about Sartre, senior French academics observe a taboo against replying to letters from unknown Englishmen. It is a taboo that affords an insight into the French national character comparable in its revelatory quality with the one vouchsafed by the behaviour of French students in lecture theatres mentioned at the end of the entry **talk** later in this section.

48 J. Diamond, *The Rise and Fall of the Third Chimpanzee* (1991), Vintage edition, London, 1992, p. 89.

49 Héritier, *Les deux soeurs et leur mère*, p. 356.

50 Hutton Webster, *Taboo: A Sociological Survey*, Stanford University Press, Stanford, CA, 1942, p. 163.

The literature on the incest taboo is naturally enormous. In addition to the other books and articles mentioned, Paul Bohannon and

John Middleton's *Marriage, Family and Residence*, Doubleday, Garden City, NY, 1968 contains some valuable articles, especially by Jack Goody.

51 A Table of Kindred and Affinity has been revised on a number of occasions, to the point where almost all the bans can be interpreted as justified in the light of modern genetics. See note 54, below.

52 See Vikki Bell, *Interrogating Incest: Feminism, Foucault and the Law*, Pluto Press, London, 1993, p. 130.

53 See his essay 'The Individual and the Group' in *The World of the Public School*, introduced by George Macdonald Fraser, Weidenfeld and Nicolson, London, 1977, p. 102.

54 Articles 24 and 25: 'A man may not marry his brother's daughter or his sister's daughter' (i.e. his niece). Articles 22 and 23 also forbid him from marrying his father's sister or his mother's sister (i.e. his aunt). Until the reform of 1949, article 29 forbade a man from marrying his wife's brother's daughter, and article 30 his wife's sister's daughter. These were not his first cousins; a first cousin is the son or daughter of the father's or mother's brother or sister.

Although a Table of Kindred and Affinity has been revised several times there are still thirteen prohibitions that are not based upon what modern genetics tells us about the dangers of in-breeding. Until 1949 there were thirty different kinds of relation between whom marriage was forbidden; this figure was then reduced to twenty-five, the interdict being lifted from marriage between a man and the wife of his father's deceased brother, the sister of his former wife's mother, or the wife of his brother's deceased son; and between a woman and the equivalent male relations. The 1949 revision, like that carried out in 1960, nevertheless maintained the ban on marriage between a man and his mother-in-law, his mother-in-law's mother, his great-niece, or his granddaughter; and between a woman and the equivalent male relations. Fairly characteristically, the Alternative Service Book of 1980 does not include the present version of a Table of Kindred and Affinity, and my remarks are based on the edition of the Book of Common Prayer published by Eyre and Spottiswoode in 1968. See also note 58 below.

55 I. Nye and F. M. Bernardo, *The Family: Its Structure and Interaction*, Macmillan, New York, 1973, p. 43. The penalties for incest are less clearly laid down. Until 1908, it was dealt with in England and Wales by the ecclesiastical courts. Under the Sexual Offences Act 1956, it is an offence for a man to have sexual intercourse with a woman he knows to be his granddaughter, daughter, sister or mother. However, a custodial sentence is imposed only when the woman in question is

under 16, or is mentally defective. Sweden is the only country so far to have decriminalized incest.

56 See H. F. Muller, 'A Chronological Note on the Psychological Explanation of the Avoidance of Incest', from the *Journal of Religious Psychology*, vol. 6, 1913, pp. 294–5. For a full account of the present state of play in the argument between anthropologists and sociobiologists, see Gregory C. Leavitt, 'Sociobiological Explanations for the Incest Taboo', *The American Anthropologist*, vol. 92, no. 4, December 1990, pp. 971–993. For a refutation of the supposed universality of the incest taboo, see Russell Middleton, 'A Deviant Case: Brother–Sister Incest and Father–Daughter Marriage in Ancient Egypt', *American Sociological Review*, 27, 1962, pp. 603–11. For a discussion of attitudes towards animal husbandry, see Nicholas Russell, *Like Engend'ring Like: Heredity and Animal Breeding in Early Modern England*, Cambridge University Press, Cambridge, 1986.

57 *Leviticus*, 20:10–21, laying down the penalties for various forms of sexual misdemeanours, punishes adultery, bestiality and homosexuality with death, and also imposes the death penalty for various forms of incest, including sex between a man and his father's wife and a man with his daughter-in-law. However, the punishment for a man who has sex with his brother's wife – it is not stipulated whether the brother is alive or dead – is simply that they will be infertile. In *Les deux soeurs et leur mère*, Françoise Héritier also speculates as to whether the interdict on a man marrying his wife's sister might not be linked to the desire to avoid a man and the sister-in-law with whom he is having an adulterous relationship laying a plot to murder his wife. Conversely, although there is no indication in the text that Gertrude and Claudius had been lovers before the murder of old Hamlet, the speed of their 'o'er hasty marriage' becomes easier to understand if there had been an earlier liaison between them.

The uncertainty on this point is one of several differences between the plot of *Hamlet* and the intriguing echoes which it so often evokes of the Orestes legend. Like Hamlet, Orestes has the duty to avenge his father's murder, and to kill the man who usurped his throne. However, there is no doubt about the fact that Aegisthus has already become Clytemnestra's lover while Agamemnon is away at the Trojan war, and their plot to kill him is based on a desire for vengeance which is different in each case and has no parallels in the plot of *Hamlet*. While Clytemnestra wishes to punish her husband for sacrificing her daughter Iphigenia in order to obtain favourable winds for the expedition to Troy, Aegisthus is motivated by the desire to carry on the family feud which began when Agamemnon's father,

Atreus, killed the two elder sons of his brother, Thyestes, and served them to him in a pie. Aegisthus is Thyestes' younger, surviving son, and therefore Agamemnon's cousin. The incest theme which is so dominant in Hamlet's reproaches to his mother is much less marked in the plot of Aeschylus's *The Orestian Trilogy* than it is in Shakepeare, and is not mentioned by Orestes as one of the motives for his action. An even more striking difference lies in the Ghost's insistence to Hamlet that he must not harm his mother, but 'leave her to heaven'. The horror of the Orestes legend lies precisely in the fact that Orestes kills his own mother, Clytemnestra; Gertrude's crime, in Hamlet's eyes, lies as much in what he sees as the incestuous nature of her relationship to Claudius as in her possible connivance in his crime.

58 It was given some publicity by an episode in the Huxley family. John Collier's first wife Marion, who was Thomas Henry Huxley's third child and second daughter, went mad and died in November 1887; he married her younger sister, Ethel, in 1889. This enabled Collier to say, of the founder of the Huxley clan and grandfather of Julian and Aldous, 'Yes, I married two of his daughters.' Ethel used article 18 in the 1559 version of a Table of Kindred and Affinity in a dispute with the Inland Revenue. She considered it wrong that her income should be assessed in common with that of her husband, and told a somewhat startled official at Somerset House: 'Young man, I would have you know that I am not married to the Honourable John Collier.' See Ronald Clarke, *The Huxleys*, Heinemann, London, 1968, p. 110.

59 *Hansard*, 1921, vol. 145, p. 1805. Quoted in Elaine Showalter, *Sexual Anarchy*, Bloombury, London, 1990, p. 119. See also H. Montgomery Hyde, *The Other Love*, Heinemann, London, 1970, p. 1.

60 See G. Rattray Taylor, *Sex in History*, Thames and Hudson, London, 1953; Panther paperback, London, 1965, p. 60 and p. 220.

61 Kinsey, *The Sexual Behaviour of the Human Male*, p. 264.

62 See Bernie Zilbergerld, *The New Male Sexuality*, Bantam Books, New York and London, 1992, p. 115.

63 Benedict, *The Chrysanthemum and the Sword*, p. 188.

64 In paragraph 479 of *The Book of World Sexual Records*, Star edition, London, 1975, G. L. Simons quotes appalling details from books by Alex Comfort, Richard von Krafft-Ebing and others.

65 See Allen Guttmann, *The Erotic in Sports*, Columbia University Press, New York, 1996, p. 1.

66 Ford and Beach, *Patterns of Sexual Behaviour*, p. 167; and Dover, *Greek Homosexuality*, plate R. 414.

67 See Melville, *Typee* (1846), Northwestern University Press and the Newberry Library, Evanston and Chicago, 1968, pp. 91–2 and 132.
68 Quoted by Simons in *The Book of World Sexual Records*, from F. Henriques, *Love in Action*, Panther Books, London, 1975. For Tom Wolfe, see *The Purple Decades*, Picador, London, 1993, p. 333. For a full account of taboos on menstruation, see Hutton Webster, *Taboo: A Sociological Survey*, Stanford University Press, Stanford, CA, 1942, pp. 65–7, and Penelope Shuttle and Peter Redgrove, *The Wise Wound: Menstruation and Everywoman*, Gollancz, London, 1978; Penguin Books, Harmondsworth, 1980.
69 Shuttle and Redgrove, *The Wise Wound*, Penguin edn, p. 126.
70 See Judy Chicago, *Through the Flower: My Struggle as a Woman Artist*, Women's Press, London and New York, 1982, pp. 88 and 138. The radical Austrian artist Otto Muehl (born 1926) used to do an act in which he cracked an egg over the pudenda of a menstruating woman and then ate it (the egg, that is).
71 *The American Anthropologist*, vol. 83, no. 4, December 1981, pp. 796–823.
72 Greer, *Sex and Destiny*, p. 310.
73 See Adam Sampson, *Acts of Abuse: Sex Offenders and the Criminal Justice System*, Routledge, London, 1994, p. 8, and *Daily Telegraph*, 14 and 16 October 1995.
74 Quoted on p. 187 of Evangeline Bruce, *Napoleon and Josephine: An Improbable Marriage*, Weidenfeld and Nicolson, London, 1995.
75 Sigmund Freud, *Totem and Taboo* (1919), Penguin Books, Harmondsworth, 1938, p. 41.
76 J. Updike, *Memories of the Ford Administration*, Knopf, New York, 1992, p. 176.
77 See Paul Veyne's article in Philippe Ariès and Georges Duby, *A History of the Private Life from Pagan Rome to Byzantium*, translated by Arthur Goldhammer, Belknap Press, Harvard University Press, Cambridge, MA, 1990, p. 12.
78 See *Documents Surréalistes*, edited by Maurice Nadeau, Éditions du Seuil, Paris, 1948, pp. 85–94. The frequency of its practice in Hollywood is suggested by the remark allegedly made by Marilyn Monroe when she finally became a star: 'Thank God. I shall now never have to suck another cock.'
79 See p. 230 of the Penguin edition (1978) of David Lodge's novel *Changing Places* (1975):

> 'Sorry I hit you about the head when you started, you know, that kissing stuff. Not very sophisticated, you see.'
> 'I like that. Now Désirée –'

> Hilary lost a little of her radiance. 'Could we not talk about your wife, please?'

The reference also evokes an early conversation between Morris and his wife, on p. 40, after she has told him that she can 'never be a fulfilled person as long as she was married to him'.

> 'What have I done?' he demanded rhetorically, throwing his arms about.
> 'You eat me.'
> 'I thought you liked it.'
> 'I don't mean that, trust your dirty mind. I mean psychologically.'

Page 143 of Shere Hite's *The Hite Report: A Nation-wide Study of Female Sexuality*, Macmillan, New York, 1976; Collier/Macmillan, London, 1976, claims that 'it is generally accepted by Bible scholars that the earliest Jewish tribes mentioned in the Old Testament accepted cunnilingus and homosexuality as a valid part of life and physical relations, as did the societies around them – which were not, for the most part, totally patriarchal'. This is not a view frequently mentioned in traditional biblical scholarship, and the book to which the authors of the Hite Report refer – Judd Teller, *Jews: Biography of a People* – is not in the British Museum's catalogue of printed books.

80 See pp. 232–4 of the Hite Report (see above, n. 79).

81 Greeley's, *The Crooked Lines of God*, p. 138. The taboo may, however, be less absolute than Father Greeley suggests and may merely lie in the need for anyone in holy orders to obtain permission before publishing. In the 1940s, Thomas Merton, a Trappist monk in Kentucky, was required to secure permission to write from his superiors; perhaps they wished to profit from the fact that he had been an editor before being ordained as a priest. In 1971, the Jesuit William Johnston wrote a book called *Christian Zen*.

82 Lord Devlin's lecture was reprinted by the Oxford University Press in 1965. Other passages are quoted in the Introduction, where it is presented as putting forward the central case for the maintenance of taboos in a secular society otherwise based on the idea that an individual whose behaviour does no harm to other people is free to dispose of his or her mind and body as he or she thinks fit.

Supporters of Lord Devlin's view underline the contradictions in Western society's attitude towards drugs. They point out that while we allow alcohol and tobacco, both of which can damage people's health and which impose a high economic burden on society by the illnesses to which they give rise, we continue to ban substances such as marihuana or cocaine; and argue that this inconsistency is a defect to be expected in a society which cannot make its mind up on what the role of the law should be. The word 'taboo', however, is very rarely used either by those who think that all drugs should be decriminalized or by defenders of the status quo. Its absence is an indication of the extent to which discussion on the role, scope and limits of the law is based in modern society on practical considerations. The majority of people who consume alcohol do not do so to excess, and do not damage their health. This is certainly not true of drugs such as cocaine, and may well not be true of cannabis, marijuana or other drugs still officially classified as dangerous. Part of the case for defining taboos as rules forbidding self-regarding activities rests on the fact that while laws can make rational distinctions of this type, taboos cannot.

A review of Lord Devlin's lecture in *The Times Literary Supplement* for 7 August 1965 quoted the ironic comment by his best-known opponent, H. L. A. Hart, about 'the innocuous conservative principle that there is a presumption that common and long-established institutions are likely to have merits not apparent to the rationalist philosopher'. Lord Devlin's view that 'most men take their morality as a whole . . . to destroy the belief in one part of it will probably result in weakening the belief in the whole' has analogies with the views expressed in **handbag** in III.

For details of the 1992 case involving sado-masochism, see Sampson, *Acts of Abuse*, 1994, p. 2. The case was fully reported in *The Independent* for 20 December 1990 and the *Guardian* for 6 March 1992.

83 The *Guardian* 30 March 1996.
84 December 1990, p. 983.
85 Quoted in Keith Connell, *Irish Peasant Society: Four Historical Essays: Catholicism and Marriage in the Century after the Famine*, Clarendon Press, Oxford, 1988, p. 137.
86 Robin Lane Fox, *The Red Lamp of Incest*, Notre Dame Press, Notre Dame, IN, 1983, p. 115 and p. 122.
87 Quoted from the *Guardian*, 22 January 1996.
88 *The Times Higher Education Supplement*, 3 November 1995. Don Kulick and Margaret Wilson, *Sex, Identity and Erotic Subjectivity* is published by Routledge, London, 1995. An entertaining account of other problems encountered by an anthropologist doing field work can be found in Nigel Barley's *The Innocent Anthropologist*, British Museum Publications, London, 1986; Penguin, Harmondsworth, 1988.
89 See p. 116 of Frederick J. Simoons, *Eat Not This Flesh: Food Avoidances*

in the Old World, University of Wisconsin Press, Madison, Wisc., 1961; the *Guardian*, 4 April 1996.

90 *The World of the Public School*, Edited by George Macdonald Fraser, p. 154.

91 Quoted in Elizabeth Rouse, *Understanding Fashion*, Blackwell Scientific Publications, Oxford, 1989, p. 21.

92 Wolfe, *The Purple Decades*, p. 336.

93 See Ray B. Browne, editor, *Forbidden Fruits: Taboos and Tabooism in Culture*, Bowling Green University, Bowling Green, Ohio, 1984, p. 8.

94 F. Steiner, *Taboo*, Cohen and West, London, 1956; Penguin, Harmondsworth, 1967, p. 23.

95 K. Cherry, *Womansword: What Japanese Words Say About Women*, Kodansha International, Tokyo and London, 1989, p. 28. This taboo may, of course, also have been inspired by the view frequently held by men exercising dangerous professions such as mining or deep-sea fishing that the presence of women is unlucky. If that were the case, it would be another example of the difficulty of distinguishing between taboos and superstitions.

96 See Simoons, *Eat Not This Flesh*, p. 110.

97 If Christ was talking about the currency used in the Greek world, the sums involved in the Parable of the Talents are quite large. As Professor Finley points out in Appendix 2 of the 1972 edition of Rex Warner's translation of Thucydides's *The Peloponnesian War*, the Parthenon cost 470 talents and it was 'an unusually expensive building, all in marble'. There were 60 minas to the talent, and 100 drachmas to the mina. A skilled workman in fifth-century Athens earned a drachma a day, and it is improbable that the value of money had increased between the age of Pericles and that of Christ.

98 Glassé, *The Concise Encyclopedia of Islam*, p. 213.

Section II

NOURISHMENT

'Don't eat or drink it!'

Just as they refuse certain sexual partners on the grounds that a relationship with them is incestuous, human beings place a ban on certain foods. They do not always do so for purely hygienic reasons. They also seek to impose an order on the natural world and to clarify their relationships with other groups. Better, however hungry you may be feeling, to eat something which you know is in keeping with the customs of your tribe, than yield to blind appetite and forfeit your right to membership. Better, as well, if you are unsure about the category to which the food belongs, to make sure that it is a pure and unmixed specimen of an unambiguous type.

Alcohol
Apples
Bananas
Beef
Birds
Blood
Butter
Camels
Cats
Cheese
Chicken
Chips
Coconut oil
Cow
Dog
Duck
Eels
Eggs
Fat
Fats
Fox
Fried
Ginko
Goat
Horse
Human beings
Lamb
Meat
Mix
Pork
Raw
Rodents
Salt
Seafood
Snails
Sugar
Swans
Watermelon

Alcohol (i) *Sura* V. 90 of the Koran says:

> O believers, wine and arrow-shuffling,
> idols and divining-arrows are an abomination,
> some of Satan's work; so avoid it; haply
> so you will prosper.[1]

The apparent contradiction in the statement in *Sura* XLVII.15 that

> This is the similitude of Paradise
> which the godfearing have been promised:
> therein are rivers of water unstaling,
> rivers of milk unchanging in flavour,
> and rivers of wine – a delight to the drinkers

is resolved if the passage is interpreted symbolically.

It is not unknown for certain Muslims to disapprove of the consumption of alcohol to the point where they refuse to share a meal with agnostics, Christians or Jews if wine is being served to their fellow guests. Because the room in which the Cercle français at the University of Coventry, UK, holds its meetings is used on other occasions by the Islamic society, the French society is not allowed to serve wine to its members. A legend in Russian history insists that one of the founders of the nation, Vladimir (*c.* 956–1015), adopted Christianity because the taste which the Russians had already acquired for alcohol made the faith of Islam unacceptable to them.

The word itself is Arabic in origin, transcribed as 'kohl' or 'koh'l' and meaning fine powder or essence. In his essay 'Wine When It Is Red' (1908), G. K. Chesterton showed what would now be seen as the height of political incorrectness when he wrote:

> it is interesting to realize that our general word for the essence of wine and beer and such things comes from people who have made particular war upon them. I suppose that some aged Moslem chieftain sat one day at the opening of his tent and, brooding with black brows and cursing in his black beard over wine as the symbol of Christianity, racked his brains for some word ugly enough to express his racial and religious antipathy, and suddenly spat out the horrible word 'alcohol'.

Islam was a late arrival among the religions of the Middle East, with the Koran, 'literally the Word of Allah',[2] being dictated to the Prophet Muhammad during his stay in Mecca between AD 610 and 622, and subsequently at Medina between 622 and 632. The religion which he founded had to distinguish itself from Christianity, its major proselytizing rival, with which it shared a number of the legends, myths and taboos of the Old Testament. It did so partly by banning pork, whose acceptability already distinguished the Christians from the Jews, but more particularly by placing a taboo on wine, which from the miracle of Cana in Galilee onwards (*John*, 2:1–10) plays a central role in the Christian sacraments. Although wine also has a high sacramental importance for Jews, Judaism is not a religion that seeks to make converts. The Islamic taboo against alcohol was thus almost certainly aimed primarily at Christianity.

In the United States, the Black Muslims avoid alcohol, do not eat any of the foods banned in the Old Testament or the Koran, and reject more than a dozen vegetables which were part of the staple diet on slave plantations. Total abstainers in the Christian Churches include the Baptists, the Christian Scientists, the Seventh Day Adventists, the Jehovah's Witnesses and the Mormons, who also eschew both tea and coffee. These sects also share the ambition to separate themselves very clearly from other denominations. They justify their ban on alcohol by maintaining that when Christ performed his first miracle and changed water into wine at the wedding feast in Cana of Galilee, the drink in question was unfermented grape juice. Objections to alcohol also led two nineteenth-century American publishers to remove any mention of beer from Thomas Hughes's *Tom Brown's Schooldays* (1857).[3]

(ii) Taboos on drink can serve as social markers as much by their absence as by their existence. Paul Fussell notes how American society of the 1980s contained a number of attractively relaxed groups of people whom he dubs in his *Caste Marks: Style and Status in the USA* (1984) 'category X'. Their drinking habits were characterized by a equal absence of taboos and discrimination, in that in parties given in these circles, 'all the wine brought by guests, no matter the quantity, is inevitably consumed'.[4] The leading guide to social customs in twentieth-century America, Miss Manners, comments that the habit of drinking all the wine is also true of 'spaghetti dinner parties of impoverished graduate students'. She nevertheless points out that in other circles, 'it is presumed that the host will provide all the goodies and that the guest's reward is emptying the host's larder and cellar'.[5] This is consistent with the idea that the bringing of wine or other consumable gifts to a dinner party is part of an exchange ceremony, serving the same function of creating or cementing social ties that Lévi-Strauss gives as the explanation for the exchange of women between different tribes in pre-literate society.

The role which taboos play in making social distinctions more explicit is further discussed in Sections III and V. In Arthur Pinero's play *The Second Mrs Tanqueray*, first performed in 1893 and considered in the England of the time as a masterpiece of social realism, the *déclassé* status of the company which Aubrey Tanqueray finds himself keeping after he has married Paula is indicated by the fact that one of their dinner guests is constantly wondering when he can have a whisky and potash. If a gentleman drank anything apart from port after dinner, it was brandy.

In the 1960s, English visitors to the United States could be taken aback when strong cocktails were followed by a choice between black coffee or iced water when the food was served. It was a custom which went further than the traditional view that only low alcohol drinks such as wine or beer should accompany a meal eaten at table, and may well be unusual in the coincidence between its original intention and subsequent function. It arose in Prohibition days, when dinner guests could be tempted to take advantage of the illicit cocktails and wine offered in private houses and consume too much of both. The taboo on alcohol at table sought to discourage the excessive bonhomie that this might create. Anyone drinking either iced water or black coffee after a highball knows how rapidly any cheerfulness evaporates.

For Chesterton, see **political correctness** in III and **Eurocentrism** in IV.

Apples (i) There is no mention in the Bible of an apple being the forbidden fruit eaten by Eve. It is merely referred to

(*Genesis*, 3:3) as 'the fruit of the tree which is in the midst of the garden'. The apple nevertheless plays so central and nefarious a role in Judeo-Christian mythology that its non-taboo status recalls the conversation in Sir Arthur Conan Doyle's short story *Silver Blaze*:

> 'Is there any point to which you would wish to draw my attention?'
> 'To the curious incident of the dog in the night-time.'
> 'The dog did nothing in the night-time.'
> 'That was the curious incident.'

As Holmes is quick to realize, the failure of an event to take place when there seems to be every reason to expect it can be just as significant as its actual occurrence.

English authors of the eleventh century refer to the apple as the fruit by which the serpent tempted Eve, and medieval and Renaissance painters frequently include an apple in the depiction of the incident leading to the Fall. Milton makes Satan (*Paradise Lost*, 1667, Book X, lines 485–7) say:

> Him by fraud I have seduced
> From his Creator, and, the more to increase
> Your wonder, with an apple!

Why, then, did the apple never become the subject of a generalized taboo supplementing the ban originally placed on it by God? Theologically, the fruit had the worst possible associations, second only to those of the serpent who made such cunning use of it. Why did these associations never lead anyone to place on the fruit itself the same kind of taboo that Jews and Muslims place on **pork**, or Hindus on **beef**, and which Western culture in general places upon snakes?

Although there used to be a virtual taboo on garlic in traditional English cooking, fruits and vegetables are very rarely at the receiving end of taboos, and there is an immediate, commonsense explanation of why apples have always been, as it were, absolutely kosher: they are so obviously healthy that nobody in his right mind would ever want to forbid people from eating them. Pythagoras, it is true, forbade his followers to eat beans, and in *The Greek Myths* (1955) Robert Graves quotes Herodotus as saying that there is a taboo on men planting beans because of a possible link with ghosts. Graves also notes that the Greeks based their belief that red-coloured berries brought bad luck on the story of Demeter and Persephone (see **chrysanthemums** in V). But there are few other examples of any foods other than meat and fish attracting a taboo. It is consequently very tempting to use the universal acceptability of apples, in spite of their negative theological connotations, to support the popular view that the only foods which ever become the subject of a taboo are those which offer a serious danger of making you ill.

The only alternative explanation for the non-taboo status of apples is one which has the effect of parodying the idea of taboos functioning as signs. It runs as follows: in Christian mythology, though for reasons we do not understand, the apple came to play a central role in the story of the Fall, the incident whose importance is reflected by Cardinal Newman's graphic description of it, in his *Apologia pro vita sua* (1864), as the 'vast, aboriginal catastrophe lying at the root of human adventure'. But apples did not grow in the Middle East during the period when Christianity was developing its theology, and the religions of the Middle East were devising ways of distinguishing themselves from one another. The fruit did not therefore offer a convenient sign whereby Christianity could, at one and the same time, express one of its central doctrines and enable its believers to show themselves how they differed from the followers of other religions. One of the main functions of taboos, as shown by the entry **pork** below, has always been to mark off a particular group as different from its neighbours. But for all the negative associations later given to it in Christian mythology, the apple was not around at the right moment in history to play the same role as fermented grape juice does for Muslims: a form of nourishment to be ostentatiously rejected.[6]

(ii) The Judeo-Christian tradition presents the human adventure as beginning with the breaking of a taboo, an act of cowardice whereby the man puts the blame on the woman (*Genesis*, 3:12): 'And the man said, The woman whom thou gavest to be with me, she gave me of the tree, and I did eat.' In 1992 the British classical scholar Robin Lane Fox commented on the coincidence in time between the emergence of the myth of Pandora's box and the story of Eve's behaviour in the garden of Eden. In Hesiod's poetry too, he writes, 'a story of origins is combined with a myth of the first woman, Pandora, as the origin of mankind's miseries. In the history of women, the eighth century BC is a dark and all too inventive era.'[7] However, although the Koran places no comparable responsibility on Eve, the position of women in Islam has not been notably better than the place assigned to them by traditional Christianity.

In 1893, for the World's Columbian Exhibition held in Chicago, the American artist Mary Cassatt designed a mural in which the central panel 'depicted women plucking the fruits of knowledge from trees in an orchard and handing them down to their daughters'. Unfortunately, the mural was lost, an event which the twentieth-century painter Judy Chicago describes as 'a fitting symbol for our own lost heritage'.[8]

See below, **butter**, **chicken**, **lamb**, **pork** and, for shellfish, **seafood**; see **watermelon** for an unusual taboo; see also below, **chips**, **fats** and **fried,** for the claim that the food taboos of late twentieth-century Europe and North America are based on health and hygiene.

Bananas In *Travels in a Strange State: Cycling across the U.S.A.* (1994), Josie Drew notes how the plethora of bananas in Hawaii – the island contains more than seventy species – has given rise to a large number of myths about them. It is considered bad luck to dream about them, to carry them, or to take them on a fishing trip. 'An old taboo', she notes, 'not only prohibited women from eating with men but also forbade them (under penalty of death) to eat bananas along with coconuts.'[9]

See below, **coconut oil**.

Beef Ideally, Buddhists are vegetarians, so they no more eat beef than they do pork or chicken. The Institutes of Manu, set down between AD 100 and 300, forbid the slaughtering of cattle, and give beef the same taboo status that **pork** has for Jews and Muslims. The Indian mutiny of 1857 is said to have been sparked off by the rumour that the new cartridges distributed to the non-European troops, and which had to be bitten open before the powder was inserted into the breech block, had been greased both with pork and with beef fat, thus causing equal offence to Muslim and to Hindu regiments.

Archaeological evidence suggests that beef was eaten on the Indian sub-continent until 100 BC or thereabouts, and the passage in the Institutes of Manu which forbids men to eat of the flesh of the cow may have initially been inspired by ecological considerations. It is a waste to eat cows and bullocks, which are not only valuable as a source of manure, but can also can pull ploughs and carts. Since the highest caste in India, the Brahmins, accept the doctrine of Ahimsa, or respect for life, and tend to be vegetarians, the taboo may have been strengthened for reasons of snobbery. Upwardly socially mobile members of other castes frequently imitate those with whom they can never merge, but whose general prestige makes their life-style highly desirable. Frederick J. Simoons notes how, in the 1950s, 'in Keraket Tahsil, in Uttar Pradesh, a Hindu caste of untouchables, the Bhars, renounced pig keeping in an attempt to raise their status'.[10]

A comparable tendency is visible nowadays in Europe and North America, where **fried** food has become socially taboo, and a fashionable diet is low in calories, consisting of vegetables, fruit, rice and pasta. Neither is it unusual for subgroups within a particular culture to use taboos about who may eat what food with whom as social markers. Brahmins do not accept food cooked by members of lower castes, which they see as polluting. In 1955, the wife of an assistant lecturer at Glasgow University, anxious to repay some of the hospitality which she and her husband had received at the professor's table, invited him to dinner. She was informed that he never dined out with junior colleagues. His sister, however, softened the blow by adding that she would be pleased to take tea with the assistant lecturer's wife if they could find a mutually convenient time.

There is no ban in Indian culture on the products of the cow such as milk, butter or cheese, and Hindus make a ritual distinction between food which is *pakka* – the origin of 'pukka', as in 'pukka sahib', a real gentleman, and the RAF 'pukka gen', reliable information – and food which is *kacca*. The former is prepared with clarified butter, and Brahmans will eat nothing else. The latter is boiled in water, and is acceptable only by inferior castes.

Vegetarians can draw comfort from the fact that even in Chinese culture, where there seem to be no taboos at all on what people may eat, butchers are held in low esteem.

Birds The birds presented as unclean in *Leviticus*, 11:13–19 include vultures, kites and ravens, the owl, the night hawk and the cuckow, the little owl, the cormorant and great owl, the swan, the pelican, the gier eagle, the stork, the heron, the lapwing and the bat.

All scavenger animals are unclean, and there seems to be a general disinclination to eat carnivores. This offers a contrast to the rarity, noted above, of fruits or vegetables being at the receiving end of taboos, and the taboo status of pigs may stem from the fact that they are omnivorous. The widespread concern in the United Kingdom and elsewhere in 1996 about 'mad cow' disease can be attributed in part to the idea that it is seen as wrong for a naturally graniverous animal such as the cow to be fed products derived from the flesh of other animals. Gentiles quite frequently refuse prawns or shrimps on the grounds that they live off the dead of other species.

A number of food taboos are explicable by reference to the remark by Robin Lane Fox quoted under the entry **mix**, below: that in order to be acceptable, an animal had to belong clearly to a specific and definable category. Thus the bat is unclean because it is notoriously difficult to classify it as either a bird or a mammal. Owls are peculiar because they fly only at night. Like **swans**, pelicans lack the quality which makes the **chicken** acceptable, namely that of being able to jump up when walking on land (see *Leviticus*, 11:21). It is this which clearly marks the chicken as a land animal, not one which occupies an intermediary status between land and water. It is because it is not clear whether swans and pelicans belong to the water or to the land that they are seen as unclean.

See, however, **duck** below; and **eels** and **seafood**.

Blood The development of Shintoism from the eighth century AD onwards in feudal Japan brought with it the view that anyone and anything connected with blood was unclean. According to the 1974 edition of the *Encyclopedia Britannica*, this gave rise to the custom of eating raw fish. In AD 741 a law was passed forbidding the killing of cattle or horses for food. This was almost certainly for ecological reasons. The Japanese realized earlier than Western Europeans that the same area of ground could provide much more food if it was used to grow vegetables than when taken up with livestock.

Leviticus, 17:14 explains the commandment in *Deuteronomy*, 12:16 and elsewhere not to consume blood by pointing out that it is 'the life of all flesh', and therefore sacred. Since, however, the command is immediately followed by the instructions to the Children of the Lord in *Deuteronomy*, 14:1 not to 'cut themselves' or 'make any baldness between your eyes for the dead', it may also have been inspired by semiological considerations as much as by ecological ones. In *Tar Baby* (1981), the American novelist Toni Morrison makes Sydney Childs say to the feckless William Green: 'I am a Phi-l-a-delphia Negro mentioned in a book of the same name. My people owned drug stores and taught school when yours were still cutting their faces open so as to tell one from the other.'[11] Like the refusal to cut themselves, the observance of the commandment not to drink blood was one of the means whereby the Israelites made themselves what *Deuteronomy*, 14:2, calls 'a peculiar people unto himself', different from the other, heathen tribes with which they came into contact, and superior to them.

See below, **chicken** and **lamb**.

Butter If, when entertained to tea, the socialist pioneer Sidney Webb (1859–1947) allowed his hand to stray towards the butter dish, his wife Beatrice would sternly remind him: 'We do not eat butter.' Her taboo was inspired more by the view that Sidney ought not to live for pleasure alone than by considerations of health. The Webbs lived in a pre-cholesterol age.

See below, **fats**.

Camels It may have been because of the commandment not to eat them in *Leviticus*, 11:4 that a saying attributed to the Prophet in Morocco runs: 'He who does not eat of my camels does not belong to my people.'[12]

A readiness to eat certain foods can be just as certain a sign of membership of a group as the determination to abstain from them. Edward Shneider, Professor of English at California State University, described in a letter to the *Times Literary Supplement* on 2 February 1980 how a nineteenth-century Dutch missionary visiting New Guinea in 1853 was offered human flesh in ritual hospitality by the Toba Bataks. When he declined, he was reproved by his hosts, who pointed out to him that although he might be able to speak Batak, he could not really be seen as one of them if he persisted in his refusal.

Muslims do not seem to have been held back from eating the beast which provided their main means of transportation by considerations of the kind which led Hindus to confer a sacred status on **cows**. See **cannibalism** in I and **beef** above.

Cats Since cats are the most fastidiously clean of all animals, there can be no hygienic reasons for not eating them. However, in Kipling's *Just So Stories* (1902), the Cat that Walked by Himself is humanized by his ability to catch mice and entertain the baby. This makes him one of the family, and creates the same feeling that it is wrong to eat cats which lies at the root of the American and Western European taboo on eating **dogs** or **horses**. It is almost as if you are eating your own children.

Cheese According to Hastings *Encyclopedia of Religion and Ethics*, cheese was banned as a possible ingredient for the Eucharist for fear of making it a real, as distinct from a symbolic, meal.

Chicken Chickens are rarely the subject of a taboo in cultures influenced by the religions of the Middle East. However, the Angami Naga in Indonesia forbid their priests to eat chicken, and both chicken and **eggs** are avoided in south-east Asia, Tibet and Mongolia, perhaps because of their association with witchcraft. The cock is frequently used in magical ceremonies, especially those associated with voodoo cults. **Eggs** are seen as too closely connected with the various problems of human fertility and infertility. It is possible that chicken were originally domesticated in order to be used either for divination or for cock-fighting.

In the Jewish culinary tradition, chicken is the most kosher

(Hebrew *kasher* = right) of all meats.* This is based upon *Leviticus*, 11:21 'Yet these may ye eat of every flying creeping thing that goeth upon all four, which have legs above their feet, to leap withal upon the earth.' However, as in the Islamic tradition, the chicken has to be killed in accordance with certain rules. In particular, all its blood must be drained from it before it is cooked, as in the taboo on consuming blood in *Deuteronomy*, 12:16: 'Only ye shall not eat the blood: ye shall pour it upon the earth as water.'

In 1991, an outbreak in the United Kingdom of salmonella poisoning gave credence to the view that this particular ruling, like a number of other Islamic or Judaic taboos affecting food, has sound hygienic justification. Imperfectly cooked chickens, in which there were still traces of blood, were shown to contain the salmonella virus, while those that were thoroughly cooked did not. The instruction in *Deuteronomy*, 12:16 to drain the carcase of blood may not have had its origins in an awareness that this was a good way of avoiding food poisoning. It is much more likely to have been inspired by a desire to differentiate oneself from the heathen. But as in the case of **pork**, a taboo which may well have had its origins in the desire to give out a sign showing oneself as different came to perform a very useful hygienic function. The same is true of the rules of slaughtering animals in strict accordance with the halal principles of Islamic law. They, too, have a strong prophylactic function, whatever may have been their semiotic or religious origin.

The usefulness of Islamic or Jewish food taboos as a means of reducing the risk of food poisoning supports the implicit defence of taboos put forward by Lord Devlin in the passage from his Maccabean Lecture *The Enforcement of Morals* (1959) quoted in the Introduction. Indeed, one might even argue that many taboos represent an accumulated 'wisdom of the ages', which it would be

* The awareness among Gentiles of the meaning of the word 'kosher', 'acceptable to the point of being excellent', is reflected in phrases in British English such as 'he has a right kosher French accent' – i.e. one which makes him sound like a Frenchman. In the United States, the word tends to imply 'totally honest', 'above board', 'undoubtedly legitimate'.

Because American and European culture has had a more intimate association with Judaism than with Islam, the word 'halal' has not yet come to be used in this way. In contrast, in British society at any rate, the experience of the Raj has given the word 'pukka' (see **beef**) the same connotations in British English as 'kosher'.

unwise to jettison on the grounds that some of the more general interdicts enshrined in traditional taboos are hard to justify on intellectual grounds and constitute an excessive interference with the liberty of the individual. The matter is further discussed in the Conclusion, and the question of the relative absence of food taboos recurs below in the entry **lamb**.

Chips (i.e. french fries) It is partly for social reasons that french-fried potatoes have acquired the status of a taboo food in the British middle class, especially among those of its members who wish to emphasize how different they are from the petty bourgeoisie or the proletariat. The title of Arnold Wesker's play *Chips with Everything* (1962) is intended to evoke the monotony and lack of imagination of the food offered to the British working class, in which chips are automatically served with everything from bacon and eggs to spaghetti bolognese. Chips themselves thus serve as a symbol of the poverty of the cultural diet which bourgeois society forces upon the deprived proletariat, and are refused by the more enlightened members of the bourgeoisie for that very reason. The taboo is also defended by the health argument and the incompatibility between eating chips and staying thin.

See below, **fats**, **fried**, **meat**, **salt** and **sugar**; also **fat** in V.

Coconut oil In *Taboo* (1956), Franz Steiner quotes Sir James Frazer as reporting that in the Marquesas Islands, 'a woman engaged in the preparation of cocoa-nut oil was taboo for five days or more, during which she might have no intercourse with a man'.[13] It is a good example of a taboo which, in Western terms at any rate, defies all rational explanation. See also above, **bananas**.

Cow See above, **beef**. The Hindu taboo on eating it gives the expression 'sacred cow'. See **shibboleth** in III.

Dog Although dogs are not mentioned as taboo either in *Leviticus* or *Deuteronomy*, references to them in the Old Testament are invariably unfavourable. They would also be covered by the general interdiction in *Leviticus*, 11:26–7 against eating 'the carcasses of every beast which divideth the hoof, and is not cloven-footed, nor cheweth the cud . . . whatsoever goeth upon his paws among all manner of beasts that go on all four.' In Islam, dogs are considered to be ritually unclean. According to the Maliki school of law, anybody touching one must therefore then be cleansed by the lesser ablution of *wudu*. An exception is made for hunting dogs, Cyril Glassé says, and it is 'lawful to eat game caught by a trained hunting dog if the dog is released with the pronunciation of the *basmalah*'.[14]

The Marjuma of Nigeria affirm their ancient way of life against the intrusion of Christianity and Islam by continuing to eat dog flesh. Since Jews, Christians and Muslims all refuse to eat dog, the taboo is not a sign whereby the different religions originating in the Middle East distinguish themselves one from another. The Western refusal to eat dogs is best explained by what is known in the United Kingdom as the Rover complex, a term derived from the name frequently given to a favourite dog. It is impossible, on walking past supermarket shelves in Europe and North America stacked high with dog food, not to admire the Chinese. Because it is a waste of food feeding them, the Chinese kill any dogs that do not do a useful job of work. They then eat them because it is a pity not to use the meat. The inhabitants of Thailand regard dog as the greatest luxury, seeing **eels** as the best water meat, and dog as the best land meat. In Macao, the most popular breed in casseroled dog is the black-tongued chow.

A minor example of Saussure's insistence on the arbitrary nature of signs is provided by the term 'hot dog', adopted by the Mexicans in the linguistic calque of '*pero caliente*'. We never think of dogs when eating a hot sausage sandwich, any more than we recollect that until 1917, when the United States declared war on Germany, they were known far more widely than they are today as 'frankfurters'. Nobody knows why hamburgers kept their name in spite of the same anti-German feeling.

See below, **horse**.

Duck While the principles detectable in the interdicts set out in *Leviticus*, 11:13–19 are perfectly consistent, they do not have a predictive value. If they did, then ducks would not be acceptable; although they fly, they also waddle on land and swim on the water. Thus the difficulty in attributing them to a clear and unambiguous category, which make **eels** and **seafood** unclean, is the same.

However, in *The Complete International Jewish Cook Book* (1976), Evelyn Rose gives a recipe for roast duck.

See above, **birds** and below, **mix**.

Eels Clearly banned in *Leviticus*, 11:10 – 'All that have not fins and scales' – and subject to the same general reprobation as snakes, banned in 11:42: 'Whatsoever goeth upon the belly, and whatsoever goeth upon all four, or whatsoever hath more feet among all creeping things that creep upon the earth, them ye shall not eat.' In the East End of London and the seaside resorts of the UK's South Coast, most Gentiles manage to overcome the repulsion allegedly associated with creeping or slimy creatures when faced with jellied eels.

Eggs In the first of his stories, 'Jeeves Takes Charge' (1921), Bertie Wooster describes how Lord Worplesdon, the father of Lady Florence Craye, the first fiancée whom his manservant saves him from marrying,

> came down to breakfast one morning, lifted the first cover he saw, said 'Eggs! Eggs! Eggs! Damn all eggs!' in an overwrought sort of voice, and instantly legged it for France, never to return to the bosom of his family. This being, mark you, a bit of luck for the bosom of the f., for old Worplesdon had the worst temper in the county.

Lord Worplesdon's proclamation of a personal taboo has found few followers, and in other cultures the egg has erotic associations which complement our custom of using it as a fertility symbol at Easter. Among the Tembu, the Fingu and the Ngumi of the Congo basin, it is a standard sexual advance for a woman to tell a man 'I shall cook eggs for you.'[15] It is improbable that the custom whereby the landladies offering bed and breakfast in Scotland and Ireland serve two eggs to the man but only one each to his wife and children has the same connotations.

Taboos are not, however, entirely consistent. In *The Wise Wound* (1978), Penelope Shuttle and Peter Redgrove refer to an African taboo which forbids women who wish to be fertile to eat eggs, and add: 'Witches are said to sail on broken egg-shells; a menstrual image.'[16]

Frederick J. Simoons notes in *Eat not This Flesh: Food Avoidances in the Old World* (1961) that Arabs see eggs as paupers' food, and that they are 'widely avoided' in south-east Asia, Tibet and Mongolia.

See above, **chicken**.

Fat *Leviticus*, 7:23–4 commands the Israelites not to eat the fat of either ox, sheep or goat, but to burn it as an offering to God. *Leviticus*, 17:6 explains why when it commands the priest to 'sprinkle the blood upon the altar of the Lord at the door of the tabernacle of the congregation, and burn the fat for a sweet savour unto the Lord'. *Sura* VI.148 introduces a slight modification when it forbids Muslims to eat the fat of oxen and sheep 'save what their backs carry'.

Sacrifices to the gods in Homer also involved burning the fat, and the tradition of lighting a candle as an offering to God or to the Virgin Mary may go back to the idea in *Leviticus* that the burning of fat was an appropriate sacrifice.

Fats Once Western Europe began its economic recovery in the early 1950s, all fats and fatty foods became increasingly taboo. This marked a distinct change from the situation immediately after the end of the Second World War, when the highest praise bestowed on a Camembert in the Paris of 1949 was still '45% *de matières grasses*' (fat content 45 per cent). In England, **butter** had only just ceased to be rationed, and children were urged to eat cream on the grounds that they needed 'building up'. Medical orthodoxy now imposes a powerful taboo on any foods likely to increase cholesterol levels, and treats with contumely any suggestion that such levels might be genetically determined.

See **butter** and **chips** above, and **fried** below.

Fox Oscar Wilde's description of fox-hunting as 'the unspeakable in full pursuit of the uneatable' is a reminder of how human beings can spend an immense amount of time, energy and money in the pursuit of an animal which is then not eaten. Huntsmen explain the refusal to eat the fox by the argument that it is vermin. If this is the case, it is hard to explain the taboo against simply shooting or trapping it. In the days when cavalry existed in order to add a touch of elegance to what would otherwise have been merely a vulgar brawl, fox-hunting was praised for the valuable training it provided in riding fast over difficult terrain.

The taboo probably stems from an aristocratic rejection of utility, and is akin to the cult of what anthropologists call the potlatch. This is the ostentatious destruction, especially by the chief of a host tribe among the Native Americans of the north-west, of a vast pile of food in order to demonstrate his wealth by displaying how much he can afford to waste. By not eating the fox, the huntsmen and their ladies remind themselves and other people of how rich they are, and of how little they therefore need the flesh of the animal that they have taken so much trouble to kill.

In the United Kingdom, the same argument applies to stag-hunting. The venison on sale in shops or available in restaurants comes either from deer farms or from animals which have been shot as part of the culling process. The runnable stag is fed to the hounds, not to the men who have pursued it. In the United States, in contrast, the word 'hunting' normally implies killing animals with rifles. As the film *The Deer-Hunter* (1978) makes clear, it tends to be a lower-class activity. When shot, the deer are quite frequently eaten, and even turned into sausages.

The otter is another animal which, in England at any rate, is not eaten when caught at the end of the hunt. What matters is being able to afford to take part in the chase, and hunting on horseback is widely used as a means of social differentiation and exclusion in the Loire Valley, Virginia and New England as well as in the United Kingdom.

These social considerations nevertheless do not offer an entirely satisfactory explanation of the refusal to eat the fox. John Peel, the hero of the well-known English hunting song, lived in Cumbria, and hunted on foot. He was an ordinary farmer, and neither a genuine nor a would-be member of the aristocracy. But neither he nor the friends who hunted with him ever ate the foxes they caught, and it is hard to see, if their main preoccupation was to protect their chickens and get rid of vermin, why they did not simply shoot the animal. The potlatch argument also fails to explain the other high-prestige activities which involve the slaughter of animals, and where the kill is eaten. These include **duck-**, pheasant-, snipe- and partridge-shooting, and there is a similarity between these activities and hunting on horseback in that it is essential to wear the right clothes.

See **newness** in V.

Fried Grills and roasts are socially OK. So, too, is any meat cooked slowly, whether as a stew on the top of the stove or in a closed dish, or casserole, in the oven itself. Terms such as *boeuf bourguignon*, *goulash*, Irish stew, or hotpot thus all carry a positive social connotation, the latter two because they have the additional advantage of suggesting a lack of social ostentation, stemming from the fact that the ingredients aren't flashily expensive and the cook has taken a lot of trouble over preparing the meal. Grills also are socially OK, because the meat, when grilled, is kept intact, retains its natural juices and authentic taste, and is not contaminated by contact with fat from another animal or with an alien substance such as vegetable oil. In stews and casseroles – another fashionable if not always accurate term is *boeuf Stroganoff* – the juices of the meat are absorbed into the vegetables, producing a mutual and pollution-free enrichment. Frying for immediate consumption, which is not really found in the best houses, is naturally different from the light frying of meat over a high heat before it is put into a casserole or stew.

Frying itself is taboo for the same reason as **chips**: it is the way poor people cook their food, having inefficient grills and lacking the time to prepare complicated dishes. Like hamburgers, fried foods offer instant oral gratification. They are thus socially taboo on grounds immediately recognizable to anyone brought up in the Protestant tradition of self-denial: anything providing pleasure without effort must be wrong.

See **fats** above, **mix** below and **serviette** in III.

Gingko It is unusual for non-Asian Americans to eat the fruit of the gingko tree, because they do not like the smell. Its taste is nevertheless quite mild, not unlike a kiwi fruit. When the fruits of the female gingko trees along Riverdale Avenue in New York are ripe, Korean families collect them with sticks and nets, and eat them as a delicacy.

Goat Nigel Barley reports in *The Innocent Anthropologist* (1986) that while homosexuality is unknown among the inhabitants of Dowayoland, in East Africa, blacksmiths are seen as odd because they will eat goats and monkeys. He then adds, apparently distancing himself from his profession, 'an anthropologist will explain that this is because both are too close to humans. Eating them, therefore, is the culinary equivalent of incest or homosexuality.'[17]

This is unlikely to be the reason why goats are not normally eaten in England or North America, and they form part of the staple diet in country areas of southern Italy, Turkey and Greece as well as in North Africa. The most frequently offered explanation is that the meat is too tough. However, since few people will confess to having tried it, this explanation is not convincing, and is not in fact true. Since there are not many goats in England or North America, it is more probably because of its unfamiliarity, and the relative cheapness and availability of other meat. There may also be a reminiscence of the biblical separation between the sheep and goats, with the goat being a symbol for the unchosen, and even for the pariah. Goat's cheese, in contrast, is highly prized and on sale in all the better supermarkets. This is because it goes well with cheap red wine, whose taste it hides. It also has a peasant authenticity about it which reminds northern Europeans of their holidays in Mediterranean countries. Like goat's milk, it can be consumed by people who are lactose intolerant.

Horse Together with **dog** (see above), horse is probably the most taboo meat among western Europeans and North Americans. The fact that it is regarded with especial repugnance by Spaniards may stem from the influence of Islamic culture, where the association of the horse with mounted warriors has endowed it with quasi-magical qualities.

Like dogs, horses also fail to meet the requirement in *Leviticus*, 11:3–7 about dividing the hoof and chewing the cud. They are thus not acceptable to Jews. Anglophone Gentiles sometimes justify the taboo on grounds of hygiene: dogs are dirty, horsemeat is alleged to give you cancer. Dogs are indeed dirtier than cats, but we don't eat cats either. Both are domestic animals, kept as pets, and therefore endowed with near human qualities. To eat them would therefore be akin to **cannibalism**. There is no evidence to support the cancer argument, and the Swiss, a highly health-conscious nation, have a dish called *fondue bourguignonne*, which differs from the traditional *fondue* in that instead of small pieces of cheese, it is horsemeat which is cut into cubes and cooked in hot oil at the table.

A literary explanation for the unacceptability of both horse and dog in Western society is offered in Kipling's *Just So* story 'The Cat that Walked by Himself' (1902), mentioned above under the entry **cats**. After the dog has becomes First Friend to man, the horse become First Servant. Other works of imaginative literature provide further evidence for the humanization of horses, with Anna Sewell's *Black Beauty: The Autobiography of a Horse* (1877) carrying on from the tradition established in the fourth book of *Gulliver's Travels* (1717), where the Houyhnhnms far exceed men – the Yahoos – in wisdom and virtue. Like cats and dogs, horses are so much part of the family that to eat them would be akin to cannibalism. Horses also differ from other farm animals in being trained to perform a wide variety of tasks. Like bullocks, cows, pigs and sheep, they are not bred solely to be eaten.

The Western taboo on eating horses may date from the anxiety of Islam, Judaism and Christianity to distinguish their followers from the pagans who ate horses as part of their sacred rites. It can also be traced back to the days when horses were the main source of manure and the principal means of locomotion and traction. They would therefore no more be eaten by Europeans than the equally useful **cow** is in modern India. However, Frederick C. Simoons casts doubt on this explanation by pointing out that Asian people such as the Mongols, who are very dependent on horses, eat them as a central part of their diet.

In the modern, industrialized West, horses are linked with high-prestige leisure pursuits: riding, fox-hunting, eventing, flat-racing, point-to-point and steeple-chasing. To eat them would thus be to confuse two areas of activity: entertaining yourself with your social equals in the open air; and sitting down to a family meal indoors. It is socially OK to eat other high-prestige animals such as grouse, partridge or pheasant. They are bred solely to be shot. Horses are not. In countries where they do form an acceptable part of people's diet, their meat is not normally sold in the ordinary butcher's shop, but at a special shop with the symbol of a horse's head above the door.

Although there are horsemeat shops more or less everywhere in France, they are more frequent in the poorer areas. They are harder to find in the more socially prestigious parts of France such as Provence or the Dordogne where the British like to spend their holidays. There, the diet is based on olive oil, fruit, vegetables and wine, all of which derive their non-taboo status from the belief that they keep cholesterol levels down, and thus help to avoid heart attacks. In France itself, horsemeat is seen as greatly inferior to beefsteak, and is much cheaper. This led the first Napoleon officially to categorize it as 'food for the poor'. On 13 February 1996, horsemeat steak was advertised on the loudspeaker system of the *Monoprix* in the rue Gambetta in Lille for 56 francs a kilo. Beefsteak was 107. Middle-class French people are conscious of how eating horsemeat would link them with the Belgians, a generally low-prestige nation, given to eating **chips** (= french fries) with mayonnaise.

See **chips**, **fats** and **fried** above, and **mix** and the closing remarks on **pork** below.

Human beings The opening of Kipling's *Just So* story 'How the Whale Got his Throat' (1908) offers a rare example of humour in the literary treatment of the eating of human beings which is free of black overtones:

> And the small 'Stute fish said in a small 'stute voice, 'Noble and generous Cetacean, have you tasted Man?'
> 'No,' said the Whale. 'What is it like?'
> 'Nice,' said the small 'Stute fish. 'Nice but nubbly.'

In Thackeray's poem 'Little Billee' (1843), the cabin boy saves himself from being eaten by gorging Jack and guzzling Jimmy by spying land just as he is about to be killed. He was more fortunate than the non-fictional Richard Parker, who on 25 July 1884 was murdered and eaten on the high seas 1,600 miles off the Cape of Good Hope by Thomas Dudley and Edwin Stephens. They were found guilty of murder at Exeter Crown Court on 6 November of the same year, and the death sentence confirmed on appeal. It was commuted to one of six months' imprisonment, presumably on the grounds that Richard Parker was on the point of death when he was killed and would almost certainly not have survived for the four days which elapsed between his death and the moment when Dudley and Stephens were picked up by a passing vessel.[18] In W. S. Gilbert's 'The Rhyme of the Nancy Bell' (1869), the narrator explains his statement

> Oh, I am a cook and a captain bold,
> And the mate of the *Nancy* brig,
> And a bo'sun tight, and a midshipmite,
> And the crew of the captain's gig

by the fact that he had eaten them all.

Swift exploited the full emotional potential of the taboo against eating people when he argued in *A Modest Proposal* (1729), that the problem of the poverty as well as the overpopulation of Ireland could be solved by selling the children of the Irish peasantry to be served as delicacies on the tables of the rich in England:

> I have been assured by a very knowing American of my acquaintance in London, that a young healthy child well nurs'd is, at a year old, a most delicious, nourishing and wholesome food, whether stewed, roasted, baked or boiled; and make no doubt that it will equally well serve in a fricassee, or a ragoût.

In Evelyn Waugh's *Black Mischief* (1930), Basil Seal has an affair with Prudence, daughter of Sir Samson Courtenay, Envoy Extraordinary to Azania, and at one point in their embraces tells her that he loves he so much that he could eat her. When order breaks down in Azania, Basil effects his escape in the company of a number of tribal chiefs, while she is evacuated by the RAF. After her plane has crashed, and Basil has taken part in a hearty feast offered by his hosts, he recognizes the red beret which Prudence has earlier worn jauntily on her head; and realizes where the meat had come from. He is temporarily chastened, but is depicted in *Put Out More Flags* (1942) as having made a good recovery.

The witnesses quoted in Brian Marriner's *Cannibalism: The Last Taboo* (1992) say that human flesh tastes rather like pork. This is the impression given in Anthony Burgess's *The Wanting Seed* (1962), where a solution is found to the problems of overpopulation in warfare organized in order to provide human flesh. No charge was brought against the survivors of the air crash in the Andes in 1972 who had kept themselves alive by eating the flesh of the other passengers who had been killed when the plane came down. The charge brought against Dudley and Stephens in 1884 was one of murder, not of the wrongful disposal of a human body.

See **cannibalism** in I.

Lamb It is unusual for ruminants to be at the receiving end of taboos, certainly in the Middle East. The **camel**, forbidden in *Leviticus*, 11:4 on the ground that 'although he cheweth the cud' 'he divideth not the hoof', is also atypical as a ruminant in that it has a three-chambered and not a two-chambered stomach.

Sheep clearly satisfy the requirements of *Leviticus* in dividing the hoof and chewing the cud. They are also acceptable to Muslims, and it is only in the Far East that a refusal to eat them serves as a means of affirming a religious or cultural difference. They are rarely eaten in China, and it is unusual to find lamb dishes in Chinese restaurants in Europe or North America. Since the ethnic or Han Chinese are normally omnivorous (see **rodents**, below), it is hard to find any other explanation for the distaste which they have for lamb except the desire to distinguish themselves from the quite sizeable (13 million out of 1,110 million: 8 per cent) Muslim minority in China itself. This explanation is supported by the fact that it is equally unusual for Christians in the Philippines to eat mutton or lamb. The expanation most frequently given in conversation is that sheep, whether alive or dead, have an unpleasant smell. A more probable reason is that there is a 5 percent minority of Muslims in the Philippines, from which the Christian majority (86 per cent Catholic, 9 per cent Protestant) wish to distinguish themselves in as many ways as possible.[19]

In Judeo-Christian mythology, sheep and lambs have more positive connotations than any other animal (see above, **goat**). In addition to being acceptable under *Leviticus*, 11:3, sheep are more easily herded than pigs, and thus easier to move about, a feature which made them highly acceptable to the nomadic, pastoral economies of the Middle East. *Sura* VI.145 of the Koran allows them with modifications, while at the same time acknowledging one of the similarities between what are often presented as the twin religions of Islam and Judaism:

> And to those of Jewry We have forbidden
> every beast with claws; and of oxen and sheep
> We have forbidden them the fat of them, save
> what their backs carry, or their entrails
> or what is mingled with bone.

Sheep are also unusual among animals found in Europe and the Middle East in that they offer an annual supply of material that can be used for garments. The same is true of similar wool-bearing animals such as alpacas and llamas, which do not seem to have been at the receiving end of any taboos. This is not true of animals like pigs or cows, whose skin can be transformed into garments only after they are dead.

The tendency of sheep to misbehave through lack of guidance is in *Isaiah*, 53:6: 'All we like sheep have gone astray.' This should be seen as a reference to the authority which the Church is called upon to exercise over all sorts and conditions of men. *John*, 10:16 makes the situation quite clear: 'And other sheep I have, which are not of this fold: them also I must bring, and they shall hear my voice: and there shall be one fold, and one shepherd.'

Meat (i) The strict taboo on meat observed by vegetarians is based on a number of factors: compassion for animals, the evidence showing that the production of meat is ecologically wasteful, the conviction that meat is an unhealthy food for human beings to eat. Vegetarians also point to the dishonesty implied by the contradiction between our habit of continuing to eat meat and the current practice of hiding the slaughter of animals and their preparation for the table in places far removed from the public gaze. Were we actually to see an abattoir, argues Noellie Vialles in *Animal to Edible* (Cambridge University Press, Cambridge, 1996), we would all immediately become vegetarians.

The general case for vegetarianism is well argued in Richard H. Schwartz, *Judaism and Vegetarianism* (1988), with its insistence that 'the high ideal of God, the initial vegetarian dietary law, still stands supreme in the Bible for Jews and the whole world to see, an ultimate goal toward which all people should strive'. Although it was, Dr Schwartz argues, originally God's intention that we should all be vegetarians, He 'gave permission for meat to be eaten as a reluctant concession to people's weakness'.[20]

The semiotic function of taboos is particularly noticeable in the case of vegetarianism. People who refuse to eat meat are not as others are, and are happy for the difference to be noticed. George Orwell made the unkind remark in *The Road to Wigan Pier* (1937) that the typical Socialist is 'a prim little man with a white-collar job, usually a secret tee-totaller and often with vegetarian yearnings'. He thus tended to belong, Orwell suggested, to that band of

> fruit-juice drinkers, nudists, sandal-wearers, sex maniacs, Quakers, 'Nature Cure' quacks, pacifists and feminists whom the word 'Socialist' draws to it as with a magnetic force.

P. G. Wodehouse expressed an even more pointed criticism when he made Bingo Little, in the short story 'Jeeves and the Old School Chum' (1923), describe his wife Rosie's friend Laura Pyke as 'a food crank'. Bingo then explains to Bertie Wooster what this involves:

> She says we all eat too much and eat it too quickly, and, anyway, we ought not to be eating it at all but living on parsnips and similar muck. And Rosie, instead of telling the woman not to be a fathead, gazes at her in wide-eyed admiration, taking it in through the pores. The result is that the cuisine of this house has been shot to pieces, and I'm starving on my feet. Well, when I tell you that it's weeks since a beefsteak pudding raised its head in the home, you'll understand what I mean.[21]

(ii) According to the 1974 edition of the *Encyclopedia Britannica*, taboos on what people could eat served as very clear social markers in Imperial China. At the time of the Han dynasty (206 BC to AD 220), beef, mutton and pork were eaten by the emperor; beef by feudal lords; mutton by high-ranking state ministers; pork by lower ministers; fish by generals; and vegetables by everybody else. In the West, taboos on meat can perform a more openly semiotic function when they are defied or abandoned. In François Mauriac's *Le Noeud de Vipères* (1930; 'Nest of Vipers'), the central character, Louis, flaunts his staunchly anti-clerical principles by eating a chop every Friday to show how different he is from his wife, a practising Catholic, who follows what was then the ruling of the Church by eating only fish.

In *Natural Symbols* (1970), Mary Douglas contends that eating fish on Fridays was 'a minor condensed symbol for the exiled Irish in London, as abstinence from pork has become a symbol of the law for Jews everywhere'. She expressed considerable regret for the recent decision by the Vatican to remove the injunction on Catholics not to eat meat on Fridays. This had always, she argues, been 'no empty symbol', but a form of behaviour which 'meant allegiance to a humble home in Ireland and to a glorious tradition in Rome, something equivalent to the pipes and haggis for the exiled Scot, or what abstinence from pork had meant to the venerable Aleazar'. But now, she writes,

> Friday no longer rings the great cosmic symbols for expiation and atonement; it is not symbolic at all, but a practical day for the organisation of charity. Now, the English Catholics are like everyone else.[22]

Her remarks are an indication that the post which she held from 1970 to 1978 as Professor of Social Anthropology at University College London, an institution originally founded to provide a university education based on strictly secular principles, did not require her to write about certain issues in her discipline with complete ideological neutrality.

Mix The primary aim of the food taboos of the Old Testament was almost certainly to remind the Israelites of how different they were from the tribes around them. However, these taboos also had another function. They required the Israelites to consume only animals that belonged to the same pure, unmixed type which they could offer in sacrifice to their God. In *The Unauthorized Version: Truth and Fiction in the Bible* (1992), Robin Lane Fox argues that the interdiction on shellfish, snails and snakes in *Leviticus*, 11:10 stems from a comparable desire to divide the world into satisfactory intellectual categories. 'The ideal type of fish', he writes,'was one which had the most attributes of fishy appearance, with both fins and scales, not one or neither.'[23]

Mary Douglas maintains that the same concern for the ideal type applies to the land animals presented in *Leviticus* 11:3–7 as suitable for human consumption. They had to chew the cud and they had to divide the hoof. No omission of either quality was permitted. This made **camels**, rabbits and hares unclean, because though they chewed the cud they did not divide the hoof, and the swine unclean for the reasons set out in *Leviticus*, 11:7: 'though he divide the hoof, and be clovenfooted, yet he cheweth not the cud.' Sheep were acceptable, as were cows. They were ruminants, which both chewed and divided. Verse 21 also allowed **chicken**.

There is a parallel to this quest for the pure, unmixed type in the commandment in *Leviticus*, 19:19: 'Thou shalt not let thy cattle gender with a diverse kind: thou shalt not sow thy field with mingled seed; neither shall a garment mingled of linen and woollen come upon thee.' In *Judaism and Vegetarianism*, Richard H. Schwartz defends the rule in *Deuteronomy*, 22:10 not to plough with an ox and an ass together on humanitarian grounds, arguing that 'such an act would cause the weaker animal great pain in trying to keep up with the stronger.'[24] However, it is equally explicable by analogy with the rules against mixing different categories which recurs elsewhere in the Judaic taboo system. Oxen and asses visibly belonged to different groups. What mattered was the intellectual satisfaction provided by the ability to impose a consistent order on the natural world, and in this respect taboos had a taxonomic as well as a semiological function. They ensured that the categories remained as clearly defined and as separate from one another as possible.

This taxonomic ambition recurs in so wide a variety of contexts that it seems to echo a psychological need which cuts across the boundaries separating different cultures from one another. Like orthodox Jews, the Masai warriors of East Africa, who drink the blood of their cattle, will not mix meat and milk. Most Inuit tribes, unlike the diners in the 'Surf and Turf' restaurants of Australia or North America, refuse to eat the products of the sea and the land at the same meal.[25] A frequent objection against 'foreign food' voiced by traditionally minded Englishmen is that it is 'all messed up together'. There is a widespread belief in England and North America – though not in France – that mixing the grape and the grain produces a bad hangover. This is not necessarily true. A meal can quite well be preceded by a dry Martini, accompanied by claret, and driven home by a single malt, with no harmful effects except to the pocket book.

The French see the English as quite barbarous because of their insistence on eating mint sauce with lamb, and apple sauce with pork chops. They themselves, however, are quite happy to mix sweet with savoury in *canard à l'orange.* Where they are more scrupulous in avoiding other forms of mixing is in their attitude to vegetables, insisting on serving green salad, and sometimes even cooked vegetables, after the main course and not with it. One reason for the non-U status of the Belgians in the eyes of the French is that they, like the English, mix savoury and sweet (see above, **horse**).

When strictly followed, the currently fashionable Montignac diet does make people thinner. This may be because it bans the consumption of protein and carbohydrates at the same meal, and thus observes the taboo on mixing. An equally probable explanation is that it leads people to reduce their intake by drawing their attention to how much they are eating.

See above, **birds** and **duck**; and, below, **seafood**.

Pork (i) Anthropologists differ as to the precise reason why Jews and Muslims have a taboo against eating pork. What they do agree about is that the taboo did not originate in the requirements of hygiene. It is true that orthodox Jews have always enjoyed a high level of immunity from food poisoning. In the Middle Ages, this was so much the case in Russia and Eastern Europe that the instigators of pogroms would accuse the Jews of having poisoned the wells, arguing that the better health which they enjoyed stemmed from their knowledge of which water sources to avoid. It remains true that anyone eating only kosher foods, especially in a hot climate, is less likely to contract food poisoning than people who eat pork or shellfish. But as in the taboo on **incest** (see section I) it is important to distinguish between function and origin, and there are a number of reasons why it is improbable that the taboo was originally based on considerations of hygiene.

Thus there is archaeological evidence that the people of the Middle East who pre-dated the ancient Israelites kept pigs and ate their flesh. There is also a long incubation period for the disease most commonly attributed to eating inadequately cooked pork, trichinosis. This makes it unlikely that a nomadic people like the Israelites would, at the stage in their history when the taboo was being formulated, have established a cause-and-effect relationship between eating pork and falling ill. There are plenty of other countries with as hot a climate as the Middle East – parts of China, for example – where the main meat eaten is pork. There is also the question of why, if the flesh of the pig had originally been banned because it was unhealthy, it then ceased to be taboo for Christians. The early converts lived in exactly the same climate as their Jewish neighbours, and it is clear from the incident of the Gadarene swine in *Mark*, 5:11–14 and *Luke*, 8:32–3 that some of the neighbouring tribes did keep pigs, presumably to eat them. It is unlikely that the fact of converting to a new religion brought about a sudden immunity to the trichinella spiralis, the parasite which can be killed only by pork being eaten while still fresh and then thoroughly cooked. This parasite, in any case, is not carried by the wild pigs whom the Israelites are likely to have encountered in their wanderings in the Middle East.

In *Eat Not This Flesh* (1961), Frederick Simoons suggests that the immediate reason for the ban on pork set out in *Leviticus*, 11:7 was quite simply that the raising of pigs was very difficult in the pastoral, nomadic economy of the early Israelites.[26] Marvin Harris makes a different suggestion when he argues that the various dietary rules set out in *Leviticus*, 11 – as well as in *Deuteronomy*, 12 and 14 – served the function of 'demarcating or bounding Jewish ethnic minorities from other groups'. In other words, you showed that you were a Jew, and proud of it, by not eating certain foods. Mary Douglas offers an illustration of how this worked in practice in the story of Aleazar, or Eleazar, brother of Judas Maccabeus, in chapter 6 of the second book of Maccabees. In the second century BC, after the conquests of Alexander the Great had brought the Jews under Greek sovereignty, King Antiochus tried to make them give up their allegiance to the Law of Moses and accept the eating of pork. Aleazar, however, did more than reject the meat itself. He refused to fall in with a subterfuge which would have enabled him to appear to eat pork while in fact consuming food which was perfectly kosher. He was 90 at the time, and his abstention caused his death. But he had made his point: Jews do not eat pork; and it is this which gives them their status as 'a peculiar people unto himself, above all the nations that are upon the earth' (*Deuteronomy*, 14:2).[27]

The food taboos of the ancient Israelites thus seem to have had two functions, neither of which was originally connected with hygiene. They were taxonomic, in that they were a means of dividing the world into intellectually satisfying categories, separating, as it were, the sheep from the goats at table as well as in the fields. In order to be kosher, an animal had to chew the cud and it had to divide the hoof. A fish had to be a proper fish, swimming in the sea and with fins, scales and a tail. But the taboos were also semiological, offering for all to see a sign of how you belonged to a particular social group.

In this respect, St Paul's statement in I *Timothy*, 4:4 that 'every creature of God is good, and nothing to be refused, if it be received with thanksgiving' marked at the time a step towards a new kind of religion. Like his insistence in *Titus*, 1:15 that 'Unto the pure all things are pure: but unto them that are defiled and unbelieving is nothing pure; but even their mind and conscience is defiled', it emphasized how Christianity was not concerned with the formalities of dietary observances and the insistence on tribal differences. It taught, instead, that the best way to show that you belong to a particular religion is by improved moral behaviour and higher spiritual aspirations, and not by abstaining from certain foods. (See, however, the Jewish prayer quoted in **uncircumcised** in Section V.)

The custom whereby Christians proved their capacity for self-denial by abstaining from meat in Lent nevertheless lasted from the twelfth to the twentieth century, and it is hard for the modern observer not to feel both sympathy and admiration for the way that orthodox Jews continue to use the food taboos of the Old Testament as a means of affirming their cultural identity. In the experience of suffering brought about by persecution, the Jews are the undoubted and unrivalled experts. It ill behoves any Gentile to criticize the techniques they have evolved for dealing with it.

(ii) Syed Anwer Ali, in *Qur'an: The Fundamental Law of Human Life* (1982) offers a more direct explanation for the Muslim taboo on eating pork. He writes quite simply that

> even medically it is seen that the flesh of swine is injurious to the physical as well as the moral health of mankind due to its dirty habits and evil trait of sex-perversion. It is said that the

diseases of tape-worms, scrofula, cancer and encysted trichura are more common among pork-eating people.[28]

The entry on food in Cyril Glassé's *The Concise Encyclopedia of Islam* (1989) explains the prohibition on pork by saying that 'in early Islam the eating habits of the Arabs were the criteria for determining what could be eaten and what not'. This fits in with Wilfred Thesiger's observation in *Arabian Sands* that

> Arabs never distinguish between what is eatable and what is not, but always between food which is lawful and food which is forbidden. No Muslim may eat pork, blood, or the flesh of an animal which has not had its throat cut while still alive.[29]

Dr Glassé adds a rider to this by pointing out that 'when there is no alternative, in cases of necessity, even prohibited food may be eaten', and recalls the general injunction in Islam 'to be reasonable in all things'.

In England, diet-conscious Gentiles refuse pork pie for the same reasons that they reject **chips** and **fried** food: it makes you fat, and is associated with the eating habits of the lower-classes, and more particularly the lower classes in the north. Pork pies are also, if removed from the refrigerator some three hours before eating them so that they can be as *chambré* as a good claret, absolutely delicious.

See below, **seafood**; also **pigs** in IV.

Raw Support for the idea that taboos are to be valued because they reinforce the idea of deferred gratification is found in the ruling in *Exodus*, 22:31 not to eat any meat that is 'torn from the beast in the field' but to cast it to the dogs. Civilization involves cooking and preparing one's food, just as it involves not lapping water like a dog (see **bodily functions** in IV).

Rodents The taboo nature of rodents almost certainly stems from the fact that they are seen as pests, an explanation reflected by the fact that while most Western Europeans and some Europeans will eat rabbit, Australians are much more reluctant. It is only in China that rats are eaten as a matter of course, with the claim that a Cantonese cook can serve up as food any animal that turns its back to the heavens being borne out by the availability of crispy fried rat, braised rat with black pepper, salt-roasted rat, and even the supreme delicacy of rat kebab, consisting of skewered cubes of rat fillet, onion and hot pepper. It is nevertheless only in accounts of Roman banquets that there are references to eating mice, forbidden in *Leviticus*, 11:29.

Although both the rabbit and the hare are occasionally seen as emblems of fertility, the former because of its high breeding rate, the latter because of its behaviour in the spring, it is unusual for rodents to be associated with religious practices. The taboo status of rats and mice would thus seem to be unusual in stemming solely from considerations of health, as well as from a variant of the Rover complex in the case of home-bred rabbits. In the 1870 siege of Paris, however, rats were sold at the price of one day's wages for a working man, and found plenty of takers.

Salt Salt has very positive connotations in the Bible: 'Ye are the salt of the earth: but if the salt have lost his savour, wherewith shall it be salted? it is thenceforth good for nothing but to be cast out, and to be trodden under foot of men.' (*Matthew*, 5:13). However, dietary fashions in the Western world now give it a high taboo status. **Butter** served in fashionable restaurants is invariably unsalted. The taboo stems from a puritanical insistence that anything which heightens the pleasure we take in eating should be avoided, while also reflecting the view that processed food already contains so much salt that anyone anxious to avoid hardening their arteries or raising their blood pressure should avoid it. **Sugar** is equally taboo, for associated reasons. See also above, **fried**.

Seafood While it is true that seafood is very frequently a source of infection, especially in hot countries, the taboo on it in Judaic religion and practice probably originates more in the concern for the pure type mentioned in the entry **pork** above than in the awareness of the dangers of seafood, which must in any case have been something of a rarity for the ancient Israelites. *Leviticus*, 11:10 places a ban upon 'all that have not fins and scales in the seas, and in the rivers', and verse 12 declares that 'whatsoever hath no fins nor scales in the waters, that shall be an abomination unto you'. The interdict pronounced in 11:42 on 'whatsoever hath more feet among all creeping things that creep upon the earth' makes the matter even clearer.

The Koran allows (*Sura* V.97) 'the game of the sea and the food of it', but puts an implicit ban on lobsters by forbidding (*Sura* VI.147) 'every beast with claws'. This may however be mitigated by the statement in *Sura* XVI.116 that

> These things only has he forbidden you:
> carrion, blood, the flesh of swine,
> what has been hallowed to other than God.

As in secular matters, silence on the part of the law implies consent. Muslims differ from Jews in being able to eat seafood, just as they differ from Christians by not making a cult of chastity. Muhammad had nine wives.

See also **mix**.

Snails Forbidden in *Leviticus*, 11:30, alongside ferrets, chameleons, lizards and moles.

Sugar As Gwendolen Fairfax informs Cecily Cardew, in Act III of *The Importance of Being Earnest* (1895), 'Sugar is not fashionable any more', and in spite of the traditional offer of 'one lump or two?' it has remained very non-U (for a definition of this term, see **serviette** in III). In Scotland, where the habit of eating oatmeal originally developed, only salt is served on porridge. Even if brown or Demerara, sugar still rots your teeth and makes you **fat**.

In *Sex and Destiny: The Politics of Human Fertility* (1984), Germaine Greer puts forward another argument against eating sugar when she writes: 'perhaps we should impose the same penalties on the consumption of sugar, tobacco or tea as we do on heroin, to protect people brutalized by this kind of cultivation.'[30]

Swans May be eaten in England only by members of the royal family; and by Fellows of St John's College, Cambridge, each year on 25 June. A sanitized version of the traditional limerick offers a reminder:

> There once was a student of John's
> Who attempted to gobble the swans.
> The porter said 'Here!

You can't do that there!
Them swans is reserved for the dons!'

See above, **birds** and **duck**.

Watermelon One of the rare examples of a fruit or vegetable being taboo is in *The Concise Encyclopedia of Islam* (1989), where Cyril Glassé writes that 'Ibn Hanbal, founder of the School of Law, is said never to have eaten watermelon because he never found a precedent for it in the Sunnah of the Prophet'.

NOTES

1 The 'World's Classics' edition of the Koran, translated by A. J. Arberry, Oxford: Oxford University Press, 1964.
2 See the remark in Muhammad Zafrulla Khan's translation, published by the Curzon Press, London and Dublin, 1971, p. ix. See also A. J. Arberry's Introduction to his translation of *The Koran* in the World's Classics (see above n. 1), in which he presents his version as 'an interpretation, conceding the orthodox claim that the Koran (like other literary masterpieces) is untranslatable'. On a number of occasions (e.g. *Suras* XLII.5; XLIII.4; XLVI.10) emphasis is placed on the fact that it is 'an Arabic Koran', perhaps with the implication that its message is indeed untranslatable into another tongue.
3 See Noel Perrin, *Dr Bowdler's Legacy*, David R. Godine, Boston, 1992, p. 219. Noel Perrin notes how one of the editors of Thomas Hughes's novel 'also omitted the word "nasty", which he felt was'.
4 See P. Fussell, *Caste Marks: Style and Status in the USA*, Heinemann, London, 1984, p. 184.
5 Judith Martin, *Miss Manners' Guide to Excruciatingly Correct Behaviour*, Hamish Hamilton, London, 1983, p. 462.
6 One of the anthropologists to whom the typescript of this book was sent for assessment allowed the intensity of her/his disapproval of any discussion of taboos to lead her/him to make what has to be seen as a mistake. 'Re:apples', wrote the consulted anthropologist, 'the author should look up *malum* in his Latin dictionary.' I dutifully did so, and discovered that it does indeed mean 'any tree fruit fleshy on the outside and having a kernel.' However, it has nothing to do with *malus*, the adjective for evil, from which we derive the French *mal*. *Malum*, meaning an apple, is derived from the Doric, and has a long 'a'. *Malus* is of doubtful etymology, possibly from the Etruscan, and has a short 'a'. One of my classical colleagues whom I consulted on

the matter told me he was once sternly reproved by his tutor for confusing *malum* with a long 'a' and *malus* with a short 'a' in a piece of Latin verse. 'I am amazed', his tutor said, 'that a scholar of this college could make so egregious and elementary a blunder.'

7 See Robin Lane Fox, *The Unauthorized Version: Truth and Fiction in the Bible*, Knopf, New York, 1992, pp. 21–2.

8 Judy Chicago, *Through the Flower: My Struggle as a Woman Artist*, Women's Press, London and New York, 1982, p. 150.

9 J. Drew, *Travels in a Strange State*, Little, Brown, New York, 1994; Warner Books, London, 1995, p. 124. On p. 146, the author also quotes a passage from Mark Twain's *Letters from Hawaii* to the effect that when Captain Cook and his men landed on the island, 'no one in the party had had any movement of his bowels for eighteen days, several for twenty-five or thirty, one not for thirty-seven, and one not for forty-four days'. If true, Twain's comment casts doubt on the widely held view that Captain Cook was a successful innovator in the improvements he brought about in the general health of seamen, especially in the elimination of scurvy by the inclusion of citrus fruits in his crew's diet.

10 F. J. Simoons, *Eat Not This Flesh: Food Avoidances in the Old World*, University of Wisconsin Press, Madison, Wisc., 1961, p. 29.

11 Toni Morrison, *Tar Baby*, Knopf, New York, 1981; Signet edition, 1983, p. 140.

12 Quoted in Simoons, *Eat Not This Flesh*, p. 121.

13 F. Steiner, *Taboo*, Penguin, Harmondsworth, 1967, p. 91.

14 Cyril Glassé, *The Concise Encyclopedia of Islam*, Stacey, London, 1989, p. 102.

15 Hutton Webster, *Taboo: A Sociological Study*, Stanford University Press, Stanford, 1942, p. 118.

16 P. Shuttle and P. Redgrove, *The Wise Wound*, Penguin edition, Harmondsworth, 1980, p. 99.

17 N. Barley, *The Innocent Anthropologist*, British Museum Publications, London, 1986; and Penguin, Harmondsworth, 1987, p. 128.

18 A full account of the case, *Regina* v. *Dudley and Stephens*, is given in Sanford H. Kadish and others, *Criminal Law and Its Processes*, Little, Brown, Boston, 1983, pp. 182–6.

19 I am grateful to Brian and Beth Hook both for correcting my overhasty assertion that there are no taboos on lamb, and for the excellence of the meal at which the discussion of Chinese and Philippine cooking took place.

20 R. H. Schwartz, *Judaism and Vegetarianism*, the Free Press, Marblehead, MA, 1988, p. 12 and p. 95.

21 It will be recalled that Rosie M. Banks earns a comfortable living by writing novels such as *Mervyn Keane, Clubman*, *Only a Factory Girl*, and *A Red, Red Summer Rose*. Freudians attribute the importance of food in Wodehouse to an oral fixation which prevented him from proceeding to the genital phase. It is this, in their view, which explains why the male–female relationships in his work never take a strongly sexual form but remain at a purely romantic stage.

22 See M. Douglas, *Natural Symbols*, Barrie and Jenkins, London, 1970, pp. 29–30, 59–60 and 67.

23 Fox, *The Unauthorized Version*, p. 82.

24 Schwartz, *Judaism and Vegetarianism*, p. 16.

25 See Simoons, *Eat Not This Flesh*, p. 109. Experienced fishermen nevertheless greet with some scepticism Edward R. Leach's claim on p. 160 of William Lessa and Evan Vogt's *Reader in Comparative Religion: An Anthropological Approach*, Harper and Row, New York, 1979, that the salmon is the only common fish subject to killing and eating restrictions, and that this is because it is simultaneously a fresh- and a salt-water fish. Fresh-water trout cannot be caught all year round either, and there is a rational explanation in both cases: you have to preserve the supply by not taking the fish when they are too young.

26 For a well-informed discussion of the whole issue, see Simoons, *Eat Not This Flesh*, especially pp. 37–42.

27 See Douglas, *Natural Symbols*, pp. 61–2. For Marvin Harris, see *Culture, People, Native*, HarperCollins, New York and London, 1993, p. 406.

28 Syed Anwer Ali, *Qur'an: The Fundamental Law of Human Life*, Syed Publications, Karachi, Hamdard Foundation Press, 1982, Volume II, p. 469. In contrast to Cyril Glassé, whose *Encyclopedia of Islam* (1989) gives a portrait of an essentially tolerant, humane religion, Syed Anwer Ali represents the more extreme wing of contemporary Muslim thought. On p. xxxi, he quotes *Sura* XXII.15 as meaning that 'Every child is born in Islam. It is his parents who make him a Jew, a Christian or a Magian.' On p. 61, he claims that 'only through the word of Allah could we declare murder as unlawful . . . or flog the adulterer and adulteress with 100 lashes . . . or cut off the hand of the thief'.

His insistence on p. 196 that women are not allowed at *salaat* (worship at the mosque) when they are menstruating because they are impure, or his reminder that the Koran (*Sura*. II.283) requires two women witnesses if a man is not available, tends to confirm Charles Nissim's comment in *The American Anthropologist* for March 1989, p. 937 when he writes in his review of Clifford Geertz's *Islam Observed*, University of Chicago Press, Chicago, 1968: 'Women's exclusion from social life in Islam is well known. Discussing their participation would be like discussing Navajo seafaring.'

Sura IV.12 enjoins different treatment of women by Muslims making a will:

God charges you, concerning your children:
to the male the like of the portion
of two females, and if they be women
above two, then for them two-thirds
of what he leaves, but if she be one
then to her a half.

The Old Testament showed comparable prejudice against women. *Leviticus*, 12:2–6 states that a woman who has given birth to a male child remains unclean for seven days, while if she has born 'a maid child', the period is fourteen. See also **veil** in V.

29 See p. 162 of W. Thesiger, *Arabian Sands*, Longman, London, 1959; Penguin, Harmondsworth, 1964.

30 G. Greer, *Sex and Destiny: The Politics of Human Fertility* (1984), Picador, London, 1985, p. 415.

Section III

WORDS AND THEMES

'Don't say it and don't talk about it!'

Although many native speakers of English are still deeply offended by the public use of what Michael Swan describes in his *Practical English Usage* (1980) as 'taboo words', objecting strongly to terms such as 'cunt', 'prick' or 'shit', and finding nothing funny in W. C. Fields's remark 'Give him an evasive answer. Tell him to go fuck himself', it is hard to say what the legislator can do about it. In a democratic and secular society such as our own, arguments about verbal taboos concern matters of taste rather than of morality and law.

Some of the traditional taboos concern the oldest words in the language, and the existence of onomatopoeic expressions comparable to boo, coo and moo may suggest a time when speech may have conveyed meaning by something other than conventional signs. Traces of this hypothetical period in the development of human language are seen in the large number of fricatives and plosives ('**f**uck', '**f**art', '**b**alls', '**p**rick', '**sh**it') in the taboo words in English expressing anger, contempt or displeasure.

Abortion
Alcoholism
Arse
Balls
Bastard
Black
Bugger
Bullshit
Cancer
Children
Christmas
Clappers
Contraception
Coon
Cunt
Dago
Death
Ejaculate
Eskimo
Erection
Fart
Female sexuality
Fuck
Gay

God
Gollywog
Goolies
Handbag
Illness
Indian
Infertility
Loo
Macbeth
Military matters
Ministers of religion
Monarchy
Money
Mothers-in-law
Names
Nigger
Pagan
Pansy
Piss
Political correctness
Politics
Poofter
Prick
Primitive
Pussy
Queer
Redneck
Research into sexuality
Rubber
Sambo
Serviette
Sex and sport
Shibboleth
Shit
Sod
Suicide
Tenure
Tribe
Twat
Vagina
Wank
Wog
Women's language

Abortion In *Dr Bowdler's Legacy* (1992), Noel Perrin describes how, from 1967 onwards, the word 'abortion' was quietly removed from paperback editions of Ray Bradbury's *Fahrenheit 451* (1953), and comments on the irony of a text describing 'an oppressive society in which books are forbidden objects' being treated this way.

The term 'voluntary termination of pregnancy' is not merely a euphemism disguising the very real moral objections to the practice of not allowing a viable foetus to come to term. It also distinguishes between spontaneous abortions, in which a woman loses her baby involuntarily, and the conscious decision not to continue with the pregnancy.

Alcoholism In the Preface to his autobiography *It Doesn't Take a Hero* (1992), H. Norman Schwarzkopf describes how his mother's alcoholism was his family's 'great unspoken secret' which he carried with him for twenty-five years before being able to mention it even to friends. Since it is seen as a moral failing rather than a physical illness, its taboo status is heightened rather than diminished by the fact that you don't have to say who you are to be treated by Alcoholics Anonymous.

Arse (i) Non-taboo equivalents abound, and include US butt and fanny, together with derrière when referring to a woman in fashion contests; and, in the UK, buttocks, posterior and sit-upon. The initials b.t.m. are used to designate the semi-polite equivalent 'bottom' in Dylan Thomas's radio play *Under Milk Wood* (1954): 'teach him with a slipper on his b.t.m.'

The word retained its power to amuse by surprise in the concluding lines of Louis MacNeice's 'Bagpipe Music' (1932):

> Sit on your arse for forty years
> And hang your hat on a pension.

When, in March 1957, the text of John Osborne's play *The Entertainer* was submitted to the Lord Chamberlain's Office, the expression 'ass-upwards' was ruled unsuitable, and was omitted from the final version. The Lord Chamberlain's Office was abolished in 1968, and with it the attempt to maintain censorship on the British stage.

Knowledge of the expression 'does not know his arse from his elbow' among speakers of British English was presumed in 1985 in the remark in the BBC programme *Yes Minister* that the minister in question 'does not know his ACAS from his NALGO' (= Advisory, Conciliation and Arbitration Service; National and Local Government Officers' Association).

The joke would go less naturally in the USA, where 'ass' is frequently used to denote the female genitals, especially in the sexist phrase 'a nice piece of ass' to describe an attractive woman.

(ii) In his *Encyclopedia of Censorship* (1990), Jonathon Greene quotes the example of the American comedian George Carlin, who in October 1973 recorded a 12-minute monologue entitled 'Filthy Words'. This caused protests when repeated on the radio and led to a case being brought to the US Supreme Court which was not settled for seven years. The words were 'fuck, shit, piss, cunt, tits, cocksucker, motherfucker, fart, turd, cock, twat and ass'. It is instructive for the native speaker of British English not only to note the spelling 'ass', but also to read through the list and then gauge her or his objections to other taboo words which might have caused an even greater scandal if Carlin had used them in Great Britain. These include arsehole, balls, bastard, bollocks, bugger, bum, bumboy, clit, crap, damn, frig, hell, poofter, prick, sod, screw, wank, wanker, whore, wick and willy.

Most of them, as the entries below illustrate, are used in a metaphorical rather than a literal sense. Readers shocked at seeing them in print might like to reflect on whether they agree with Edmund Leach's remark in *Man* (1958) that 'everyone takes it for granted that verbal expletives in almost every language derive their magical potency from association either with sexual and excretory functions or with God'.[1]

Although published in full in the United States in 1927, Robert Graves's *Lars Porsena: A History of Swearing* was forbidden by the laws governing obscenity in the 1930s to appear in an uncut version in the United Kingdom in 1936. This led Graves to comment: 'I have yielded to the society in which I move, which is an obscene society: that is, it acquiesces emotionally in the validity of the taboo, while intellectually objecting to it.' Timothy Jay, of North Adams State College in Massachusetts, was more lucky. In 1992, after a five-year interval in which his dean forbade him to pursue research on the matter, he finally published his *Cursing in America*. 'As soon as I got tenure', he told an interviewer on the *Buffalo News*, 'I went back to dirty words.'[2]

See below, **clappers**, **fuck** and **poofter**.

Balls Like 'fuck', the word is used far more frequently in a metaphorical than in a literary sense. In addition to designating an argument which, as Jeeves observed of Nietzsche, is 'fundamentally unsound' – 'All balls, old boy' – it indicates defiance or disapproval. Only rarely does it refer to the testicles. The 'balls-up', or 'cock-up', theory of history is more convincing than the one which depicts it either as a conspiracy or as the working-out of providence.

Edward Sagarin claims in *The Anatomy of Dirty Words* (1968) that the complimentary phrase 'he's got balls' is, in the United States, 'almost unknown to middle- and upper-strata economic groups, and its use is largely confined to adolescents, students, and personnel of the armed forces'.[3] He suggests that the use of the expression in English may stem from the Spanish 'Que cojudo es!' when praising the courage of a bull-fighter. It is also perhaps a recollection of Hemingway's use of *cojones* as a synonym for courage in *For Whom the Bell Tolls* (1940).

The sexist nature of English is underlined by the fact that no equivalent phrase exists to indicate physical courage in a woman. 'Cuntish' evokes stupidity, just as 'womanish' – as opposed to 'manly', in polite language – denotes weakness. There is a similar contrast between the ideas evoked by words such as 'dame', 'governess', 'madame' or 'mistress', and those called to mind by the masculine equivalents of 'knight', 'governor' or 'master'.

The metaphorical usage of the word 'balls' gives rise to a well-established joke in the British Civil Service. When an under-secretary wrote 'Round Objects' in the margin of a colleague's Minute which he was passing on to an unstreetwise minister, his note elicited the question: 'Who is Round and why does he object?'

Bastard Another taboo word in modern English which is far more frequently used in a metaphorical than in a literal sense. 'You bastard' is merely the equivalent of 'you sod' or 'you bugger', both terms of general insult rather than of description, and used much more frequently in the UK than in the USA. The word 'bastard' is not used in either a metaphorical or a literal sense when speaking of a woman. As a metaphor, it is replaced by the milder term of 'basket'. In a society in which titles are still transmitted through the male line, it does not seem to matter whether a woman is legitimate or not.

Until the late eighteenth century, there was no taboo on the literal use of the word 'bastard'. Before he became William I of England, William the Conqueror (1027–87) was habitually referred to by medieval chroniclers as William the Bastard. It was a useful way of distinguishing him from the other, legitimate sons of his father, Robert, Duke of Normandy. Although Gloucester's illegitimate son Edmund rails in *King Lear* against being stigmatized as a bastard, everyone knows about his status, and his father follows what was clearly the custom in saying 'the whoreson must be acknowledged'.

Noel Perrin comments in *Dr Bowdler's Legacy* (1992) on how

'Jane Austen's novels have never been bowdlerised by anyone except Jane Austen herself'. The expurgation in question amounts to no more than removing one sentence about bastards from *Sense and Sensibility* (1813), in a scene which leads her to comment:

> Lady Middleton's delicacy was shocked; and in order to banish so improper a subject as the mention of a natural daughter, she actually took the trouble of saying something about the weather.[4]

See also below, **God**.

Black The problem of how best to describe someone with a black skin has been around for some time. In 1961, the title of Jean Genet's play *Les Nègres* was translated as *The Blacks* in order to emphasize its main theme, which was that of the positive values attached to what the Senegalese poet and politician Léopold Sédar Senghor had earlier called '*la négritude*'. This did not, however, quite free the word from the negative associations which linked it with terms such as **nigger**. In *The Official Politically Correct Dictionary and Handbook* (1992) Henry Beard and Christopher Cerf suggest replacing 'blacks of the African Diaspora' by 'African Americans or Caribbean Americans'. David Rowan, presenting his 'Glossary for the Nineties' on 29 July 1995, in *The Guardian Weekly* claimed that the term which best expressed the continuing trend towards multiculturalism and ethnic diversity in the United Kingdom was 'round midnight', a term for black already current in the 1920s in jazz circles in the United States. The politically correct terms are 'Afro-American' or 'African American', but these are used mainly by white liberals.

Two meanings of the word in French create problems for supporters of **political correctness**. In the publishing world, '*un nègre*' is a ghost writer, and there is as yet no acceptable equivalent. '*Une tête de nègre*' is a chocolate-covered meringue. In March 1995, Madame Esther Mukalay Bissouelenko, from the Ivory Coast, called for a ban on the term. A number of confectioners now refer to it as '*une meringue au chocolat*'.

See below, **nigger** and see **white** in V.

Bugger Again a word rarely used in a literal sense in modern English, and scarcely used at all in the USA, where the term is sodomy (see **homosexuality** in I and IV). It comes, through the Old French '*bougre*', from the attitude of the Roman Catholic Church in the Middle Ages to the Greek Orthodox Church, whose members were said to be Bulgarians, infected by the Albigensian heresy, and thus tending to practise unnatural vices. Since the Cathars made a special virtue of chastity, it was a shade unfair. However, since in the Middle Ages sodomy and buggery were linked to heresy as well as to witchcraft, it was perhaps only to be expected. In 1967, the word was used literally when critics of the Act legalizing homosexual behaviour between consenting adults in England and Wales referred to it as 'the buggers' charter'. Churchill once remarked that the indiscriminate nature of Tom Driberg's sexual behaviour 'brought the name of buggery into disrepute'.

Bullshit A term frequently used both in the USA and the UK to mean 'nonsense' or 'untruth'. In the UK, it also refers to the unnecessary regulations in dress imposed on recruits to the armed services, as in the expression 'Bullshit baffles brains'.

Cancer On Sunday 25 February 1995, BBC 2 began a series entitled the *Male Survival Guide* with a programme on testicular cancer, described by one speaker as 'the most taboo subject of all'. This status was variously explained by the extreme sensitivity which men have in that part of the body (see **uncircumcised** in V), by the unpredictability of the disease and by the lack of any apparent correlation with life-style. Unlike lung cancer or heart disease, it seemed to have nothing to do with smoking, lack of exercise, excessive drinking or being overweight. The traditional refusal to discuss it links taboos with superstitions.

See **illness** below and **ghosts** in IV.

Children (i) It is taboo to express the dislike which all reasonable adults feel for small children. Part of the enduring popularity of W. C. Fields stems from his remark that a man who hates children and dogs cannot be wholly bad. The remark may, however, also have been inspired by an old pro's understandable reluctance to see himself constantly upstaged. It also put the case for a welcome interdict on any return of the way children were presented in the cinema of the 1920s and 1930s. Freddie

Bartholomew had golden curls, and Jacky Cooper possessed the ability to make tears flow from his eyes the moment the director shouted 'Cry!'

The power of the taboo against criticizing another aspect of the popularity of child actors is illustrated by what happened to Graham Greene. In 1937 he got himself into serious trouble by suggesting in his review of *Wee Willie Winkie* in *Night and Day* that there was a strongly sexual element in Shirley Temple's popularity, and writing of her ability to excite her 'antique audience' as she 'measures a man with agile studio eyes, with dimpled depravity'. He was taken to court, lost the case, had to apologize profusely, and *Night and Day* ceased publication.[5]

(ii) An illustration of the misleading way in which the word 'taboo' can sometimes be used in contemporary English (see also **adultery** and **paedophilia** in I) was offered by Digby Anderson in an article in the *Daily Telegraph* for 12 June 1996 entitled 'We must put children to work'. Describing the 'pleasant and excellent service' offered by 8-year-old boys selling sesame bread on a Turkish beach, he asked why modern British society should not introduce comparable services and thus 'break the greatest taboo of all – and involve *children* in work'.

It would be as tedious to rehearse all the arguments against child labour as it would to enumerate all the disadvantages for children of legalized **paedophilia**. Without the Factory Act of 1833, few British adults would have been able to read Mr Anderson's article, let alone appreciate the force of his argument.

Christmas On 24 December 1995, Alistair Cooke reported in his 'Letter from America' on BBC Radio 4 that the Christmas tree traditionally put up in Times Square in New York had been taken down. Protesters from orthodox Jewish and fundamentalist Muslim groups had objected to it on the grounds that it broke the First Amendment by giving preferential expression to Christianity. Francis Fukuyama reported a comparable event in *The End of History* (1992) when he noted that the Supreme Court had 'decided that even the non-denominational assertion of "belief in God" may offend atheists, and is therefore impermissible in public schools'.[6]

See below, **political correctness**.

Clappers Although itself a euphemism for 'clap', in the sense of gonorrhoea, this was censored by the Lord Chamberlain when the text of John Osborne's *The Entertainer* was submitted for authorization in 1957. Archie's song 'The old church bells won't ring tonight, 'cos the Vicar's got the clappers' had to be replaced by ''cos the Vicar's dropped a clanger'.

See above, **arse**.

Contraception The French law of 1920 banning the sale of all artificial means of contraception also placed an absolute ban on any attempt to advertise their existence. Even in the United Kingdom, where no law was ever passed banning artificial methods of birth control, as many condoms were probably sold in barbers' shops as at the chemist's. Until the 1960s, the only form of advertisement for contraceptive devices ever heard by the vast majority of young men was the murmured 'Anything for the week-end, sir?' when the haircut was finally completed. Until the spread of the AIDS virus in the late 1980s, universities in the British Isles refused to allow machines selling condoms to be placed in the bar, lavatories and administrative offices of the Students' Union.

See **oral sex** in I.

Coon Etymologically from 'raccoon', and as late as the 1920s sufficiently acceptable for the first man to make a talking picture, Al Jolson, to describe himself as 'the singing Coon'. He was in fact Jewish, and the son of a rabbi. His first film, *The Jazz Singer* (1927), in which he pretended to be a Negro, exploited the popularity of the Nigger Minstrel Show. This popularity did not entirely disappear from the United Kingdom until the 1960s, when the *Black and White Minstrel Show* finally ceased to be shown on television. Noel Perrin points out in *Dr Bowdler's Legacy* that it was only in the late nineteenth century that 'coon' began to be applied to blacks. In the 1840s, it meant a member of the Whig party, and it was not unusual to hear a white frontiersman comment of himself: 'I'm a gone coon.'[7]

On 31 March 1995, *The Times Higher* reprinted photographs from the 1950s of establishments with names such as 'Coon Chicken Inn', which could be found not only in the Deep South but in Portland, Oregon and Salt Lake City. It also reported that Winston Churchill, in private conversation, frequently used terms such as 'blackamoor', 'nigger' and 'chink'. Even the gentle Aldous Huxley showed little hesitation in defying what has become one of our own most important linguistic taboos in writing in the 1920s about 'grinning blackamoors' and 'repulsive German Jews', and it was reported in the *Times Literary Supplement* for 28 June 1996 that Bronislaw Malinowski not only referred to the Melanesians as 'Niggs', and echoed one of Conrad's views when he said that he would like to '*exterminate the brutes*', but also, apparently, expressed the desire that his seminar at Oxford should attract someone who was 'not a Jew, a Dago, Pole or any of these exotic products'.[8]

In 1948, Huxley also referred in his letters from Hollywood to the 'all-powerful Jewish gentleman in charge of production', and the present taboo on the use of such words illustrates how we have become as sensitive to the question of race as the Victorians were in the area of sex. More importantly, however, the self-denying ordinance adopted on the use of racial insults reflects the historical experience of the twentieth century. Anyone who justifies talking about 'yids' by repeating the proverb 'Sticks and stones may break my bones/But words will never hurt me' does so in ignorance of the path which led from *The Protocols of the Elders of Zion* to the gas chambers at Auschwitz.

Cunt (i) Described by David Crystal in *The Cambridge Encyclopedia of Language* (1987) as being, with 'fuck', one of 'the two maximally taboo words' in the English language. Hamlet's question to Ophelia, 'Did you think I meant country matters?', after his explanation, 'I mean my head in your lap', suggests that the word was well known in Shakespeare's time, though no more openly permissible than it was when Fletcher – the example is quoted by Eric Partridge – wrote in *The Spanish Curate* (1622) 'they write *sunt* with a C, which is abominable'. Some critics argue that 'quaint' in Marvell's *Ode to his Coy Mistress* (1653) –

> Turn thy quaint honour into dust
> And into ashes all my lust

– is a euphemism for cunt (see below, **twat**). Eric Partridge points out that 'the late Sir James Murray courageously included the word, and spelt it out in full, in the great *Oxford English Dictionary* of 1928'.[9] Its place in Cockney rhyming slang forms the basis for the disparaging remark 'You berk' (Berkeley hunt = stupid cunt). In the *Guardian* for 2 November 1989, Katie Campbell mentioned the disparaging See You Next Tuesday as a description for an unreliable young man (= cunt), and commented: 'Imagine a word so powerful that it has to be disguised, even when used as a term of abuse.'

In 1968, Edward Sagarin attributed the use as swear words of terms connected with natural elimination and sexual intercourse to the persistence of 'a mid-Victorian puritanism all the more nefarious because it is masquerading under the guise of hedonistic abandon'.[10] His argument is that we use words such as 'cunt', 'fuck' and 'prick' in such a negative sense because of the feelings of shame about sex instilled in us by puritanism. This can be supported by the fact that modern Arabic, Chinese, Japanese and Welsh do not use sexual terms as swear words. However, languages such as French, German, Spanish and Italian do, and puritanism in its strictly religious form played only a limited role in the development of Latin and Germanic culture.

The ban on terms connected with sex and excretion suggests an anxiety to maintain the clear demarcation between nature and culture which can be seen as one of the considerations originally inspiring the **incest** taboo. This view is easy to sustain, as far as English is concerned, by the fact that most obscenities are of Anglo-Saxon origin, reflecting a less sophisticated and more plainly spoken society than the one imported by the Norman conquest or developed in imitation of Continental models. It is more difficult to apply this view to the use of rude words in languages, like French or Italian, that do not have a level which reflects an allegedly cruder society. The fact that swearing in modern English no longer tends to be blasphemous, but to refer almost exclusively to parts of the body considered unclean, is an indication of how modern taboos differ from those of the past. In pre-literate and pre-industrial societies, taboos did not merely refer to what was forbidden. They also hedged around what was sacred. This concept plays little part in modern taboos.

(ii) The taboo status of words connected with sex and excretion can also be seen as expressing a refusal to countenance any blurring of the difference separating human beings from animals. This may explain why men, in particular, tend to express anger or frustration by uttering what are seen as obscenities. These express a defiance of social rules which is as violent as the open challenge to God represented in the past by blasphemy. From this point of view, the uttering of obscenities becomes a kind of warning sign to other people: 'Watch out! I am so cross that I might start behaving like an animal!' Leo Stone put forward a comparable explanation in 1954 when he argued in the *International Journal of Psychoanalysis* that pornography tries to reach what is normally beyond or below the reach of language. 'This', he wrote,

> is a partial explanation of why pornography is also the home of forbidden, tabooed words. These are the stubborn, primitive words of the language; they undergo the least evolution and retain their original force. Their primeval power has much to do with the fact that in our minds, these words are minimally verbal, that they are still felt as acts.[11]

This theory would help to explain the feeling that a taboo is more violated when a woman utters obscenities than when a man does. Women have traditionally been seen as the gentler sex, and the custodians of civilized values. Since they are less prone to physical violence than men, the threat to resort to animal-type behaviour is more frightening because less frequent. When, for the first time in the cinema, Faye Dunaway used the words 'fuck' and 'cunt' in the film *Network* (1976), in which Peter Finch, a television commentator in danger of losing his audience, threatens to blow his brains out during a live show, she created a much greater shock than if the words had been uttered by a male actor.

In the 1990s, any feelings of shock have been sensibly attenuated. The film *Boys on the Side* (1995) contains a scene in which Whoopi Goldberg, playing the part of a black Lesbian, encourages a white, inhibited, HIV-infected yuppie to say the word 'cunt'. She starts tentatively, in a whisper, but repeats it with increasing enjoyment, in a near-musical solo.

(iii) Not all women feel happy in their role as guardians of polite linguistic behaviour. One of the aims of the various taboos of the past has been to keep women in what men think ought to be their place, and the breaking of taboos is a traditional means of rebellion. The American feminists Casey Miller and Kate Swift protest with some vehemence in *Words and Women* (1977) against the linguistic conventions imposed by what they call patronymical and patriarchal society. They quote with approval the remark by Ruth Tadasco in *An Intelligent Woman's Guide to Dirty Words* (1972): 'women's sexuality has been so tortured by patriarchy that the language does not exist to describe her sexual needs without prejudice to her person.'[12]

It was in a similar spirit of protest that the American artist Judy Chicago carried out a number of experiments in the 1960s which involved creating body symbols evoking male and female sexuality. The reaction of the critics was nevertheless so hostile that she had to hide her paintings, so that she ended up by producing what she called 'closed forms transformed into doughnuts, stars and revolving mounds representing cunts', and adding:

> I use the word 'cunt' deliberately, for it involves society's contempt for women. In turning the word around, I hope to turn society's definition of the female around and make it positive instead of negative. Because I had a cunt, I was despised by society. By making an image of the sensation of orgasm, I was trying to affirm my own femaleness and my own power and thus implicitly challenge male superiority'.[13]

While it is true that 'cunt' is rarely used in English except as an insult, the same is equally true of 'prick' and 'balls'. Men might therefore have equal reason to protest about these linguistic insults to their sexual identity.

(iv) One of the advantages of taboos is what can happen when you defy them. On 10 December 1896, the first performance of Alfred Jarry's *Ubu roi* at the Théâtre de l'Oeuvre began with a resounding '*Merdre*' (shitr), the first time the word had been used on the French stage. Keith Beaumont commented in his study of Jarry in 1984 that 'to be able to use, or hear "taboo" words in an unexpected context offers a release from normal constraints, a release which expresses itself in laughter – all the more so when these obscenities are compounded by word play and linguistic invention'.[14] It is a remark which also applies to a sketch by the music-hall comedian George Robey. This involved using a large screen to teach a rather dim and short-sighted person the alphabet. The punchline came with the remark: 'Oh you're so stupid. Every time I say "F", you see K.' It is a joke that would be unacceptable nowadays on the grounds that it is cruel as well as politically incorrect to make fun of those who are differently sighted and otherwise gifted.

The same objection does not apply to the Frank Harris limerick which goes:

> The Dowager Duchess of Bray
> Was not, I am sorry to say,
> Of the best education.
> In spite of her station
> She always spelt Cunt with a K.

See below, **female sexuality**, **twat** and **women's language**.

Dago An abusive term designating a Spaniard. It is more common in England than in North America, where the two main disparaging terms for native speakers of Spanish are 'spick', perhaps from 'You spik Ingleesh?', and the milder 'wetback', in the sense of an illegal immigrant still wet from having swum across the Rio Grande. The term 'dago' is derived from 'Dago', the alternative to the Spanish first name 'Diego'. It is taboo nowadays for the same reasons which might put Tennyson in danger of prosecution under the Race Relations Act for writing, in his poem 'The Revenge: A Ballad of the Fleet', (1878):

> Let us bang those dogs of Seville, the children of the Devil,
> For I never turned my back upon Don or Devil yet.

When, however, in 1994, the English politician Tristan Garel-Jones was criticized for making non-p.c. jokes, he replied, 'Oh, it's all right. My wife's a dago, you know.'

The more a term of racial abuse expresses the contempt which the dominant group in society feels towards those whom it exploits and oppresses, the more objectionable it is. This is why, in English-speaking society, dominated as it traditionally has been by White Anglo-Saxon Protestants, terms such **Coon**, 'Frog', 'Mick', **Nigger**, 'Polack', 'Wop', **Wog** and 'Yid', are highly offensive, while expressions such as 'Limey', 'Prod', **redneck** and 'Whitey' are much less so. There is also a difference between words expressing enmity and those conveying contempt. 'Boche', 'Hun' and 'Kraut' are certainly offensive. But they have a different feel to them from 'Chink', 'Eytie', or 'nignog'.

Death (i) In an article on the undertaking industry, Simon Kent wrote in the *Guardian* for 8 April 1995 that although an average of 750,000 people die in Britain every year 'death is a taboo subject'. However, he then proceeded to add that 'for 17,000 British workers, it's a way of life and of earning their daily crust'. On social occasions, undertakers are as coy about what they do for a living as tax inspectors, another instance of the non-rational nature of taboos. It would be as appalling to live in a society in which the state had no money to protect its citizens against external aggression or internal disorder, and no means of educating them or looking after them when they are ill or old, as it would be to walk about in the streets of a city which had no undertakers. Although we rarely talk openly about death, a third of the complaints received by hospitals concern the way somebody's death has been announced to their relatives.

The irrationality of our attitude towards death was brought out by Liam Hudson when he commented in his review in *The Times Literary Supplement* for 27 May 1994 of Sherwin B. Nuland's *How We Die* (1994) that while death is a major theme of entertainment, the normal act of physical dying is pushed away into a corner. Although it is extremely rare in Great Britain or North America for an adult not connected with the emergency or medical services to see a dead body, the average teenager will have seen over 10,000 fictional deaths enacted on television before the age of 18. Mourning rituals have ceased to play the same role in Britain which they did before the Second World War. The phrase 'She buried him with ham', implying a meal after the funeral at which no expense was spared, has no meaning for anyone under 50. The apocryphal report of a funeral in the *Cork Examiner* which contained the comment 'at the graveside, one of the guests slipped and broke a leg. This cast a gloom over the whole occasion' raises only a grudging smile even after it has been explained.

On 24 April 1994, *The Independent on Sunday* reported how the Enlightened Tobacco Company had produced a brand of cigarettes called DEATH, and quoted its marketing director, B. J. Cunningham, as saying 'death is a taboo, and taboos are there to be broken. Breaking the taboo about death and smoking is our unique selling point.' Later on in 1994, however, the Advertising Standards Authority made the insurance firm of Allied Dunbar withdraw an advertisement which showed a coffin's eye view of a burial with the slogan: 'Every two minutes, somebody dies of heart disease.'

(ii) In August 1995, Timothy Leary set out to challenge La Rochefoucauld's maxim 'Le soleil ni la mort ne peuvent se regarder fixement' (Men can gaze steadfastly neither at the sun nor at death). At the age of 74, the Harvard psychologist who had introduced Aldous Huxley to the use of mescaline in the 1950s, and later popularized LSD, was diagnosed as having prostate **cancer**. In an interview about his illness and coming death, he was reported in the *Guardian* for 29 August 1995, as saying:

> This is wonderful. This is such a taboo topic and here we are talking about it. I grew up in a culture where you never talked about how much money you made or about anything about death. I love topics the establishment says are taboo.

While there are social groups, and even whole societies, which seem to make a cult of death, it is unusual for them to do so in order to mark themselves out as different from other people in the way that Jews mark themselves out as different from other tribes by banning certain foods, or certain Nonconformist sects by refusing to allow their members to drink alcohol. The only exception is in the way Roman Catholics and Jews are less likely than Protestants or agnostics to have themselves cremated, and totally refuse the luxurious embalmments described by Evelyn Waugh in *The Loved One* (1947).

In the Middle Ages, as in the even grimmer period of the Reformation and Counter-Reformation, there was no taboo on mentioning death. Painters and sculptors took evident pleasure in depicting a triumphantly grinning skeleton using his scythe to urge the participants in the Dance of Death on towards the torments of Hell. Art of this kind was also an excellent means of discouraging members of the lower orders from stepping out of line. It cannot be a coincidence that a society in which there are as few controls over personal conduct as in our own is also one where people are not encouraged to think about death.

See also **venereal disease** in IV.

Ejaculation Because of its predominantly sexual sense, this tends to be replaced in modern English by 'exclaim', so that the verbal 'he ejaculated' almost always becomes 'he exclaimed'.

Erection The word has narrower associations in French than in English. As Flaubert commented on the entry 'Érection' in his *Dictionnaire des Idées reçues* (1880, Dictionary of Received Ideas): 'Ne se dit qu'en parlant de monuments historiques' (Used only when discussing historical monuments).

Eskimo The correct term is Inuit.

Fart Arthur Miller's aim in his play *The Crucible* (1953) was to analyse the phenomenon of McCarthyism by reference to seventeenth-century New England, and especially the Massachusetts witch trials of 1692. It was not to provoke a scandal by the words he used, and there was no criticism of the scene in which the old farmer Giles Corey gives Judge Danforth the straight reply: 'A fart on Thomas Putnam, that's what I say to that.'

The historical accuracy of Miller's play is borne out by a remark in Bill Bryson's *Made in America* (1994) to the effect that

> seventeenth- and eighteenth-century users of English, Puritan and non-Puritan alike, had none of the problems with expressive terms like *belly*, *fart* and *give titty* (for to *suckle*) that would so trouble their Victorians descendants. Even the King James Bible contained such indecorous terms as *piss*, *dung* and *bowels*.[15]

In the France of the late nineteenth and early twentieth centuries, a music-hall comedian called Joseph Pujol (1857–1945) won fame and fortune by being able, as the poem puts it, to

> Fart anything from 'God Save the King'
> To Beethoven's Moonlight Sonata.

He was known as 'le pétomane', from the French verb 'péter', to fart, and represents the comic advantages which can occasionally be derived from the conscious breaking of taboos. When, in 1914, he retired from the stage, it was because his speciality act of mock artillery bombardments had ceased to be funny. It was too reminiscent of what the Germans were doing in real life.

Female sexuality The belief of the Ainu tribe that if a woman happens to move during intercourse, even slightly, her husband will 'die a poor man'[16] echoes the legend of the Victorian husband who reproved his wife for her show of enthusiasm with the comment 'Ladies don't move'. On 19 January 1967, a reviewer in the *Times Literary Supplement* quoted a piece of advice from a nineteenth-century book on marriage to the effect that 'no nervous or feeble young man should therefore be deterred from matrimony by any exaggerated notion of the duties required of him'. In 1972, *Le rapport sur le comportement sexuel des Français* (The sexual behaviour of the French) quoted a remark made in 1956 by a professor of medicine at Oxford when he said: 'Speaking as a doctor, I can tell you that 9/10 women are indifferent to the sexual act or dislike it, while the 10th, who likes it, is a prostitute.'[17]

The number and variety of articles in women's magazines advising their readers on how best to secure orgasm suggest that this taboo has now been reversed. The belief that a woman submitted to her husband's sexual advances only through a sense of duty would also have surprised the authors of the myth of the blind prophet Tiresias. He had been both man and woman, and when asked which sex derived more pleasure from the sexual act, replied in two lines (from the sixth-century BC Hesiodic myth *Melamadia*):

> Of ten shares the man enjoys one.
> The woman by enjoying ten satisfies her mind.

According to the legend, Zeus's wife Hera then imposed a vigorous taboo on the idea. She struck Tiresias blind for speaking the truth. It is an aspect of the story which has an ambiguity characteristic of myth but lacking in most taboos. Since it may well have been a man or group of men who invented the myth, Tiresias's reply could just as easily be a reflection of the Greek male's pride in his own sexual prowess as the recognition of a reality which only those with the same experience as Tiresias have been in a position to verify.[18]

See also **masturbation** in I and **wank** in III, together with the comments by Mary McCarthy and others quoted in **hedonism** in I.

Fuck (i) There are few equivalents in English literature to the compliment in Toni Morrison's *Tar Baby* (1981) to the effect that Jadine's lover, Son, 'fucks like a star'. Like 'shit', and like the other 'maximally taboo word' in David Crystal's *The Cambridge Encyclopedia of Language* (1987), 'cunt', the word 'fuck' is rarely used literally in British English. As in the case of **shit** (see below), humour can therefore sometimes be produced by suddenly using in its literal sense a word normally used metaphorically. Eric Partridge illustrates this by quoting the traditional '"Fuck me",' said the Duchess, more in anger than in expectation', together with the Duke's weary rejoinder '"Oh, no, not again".' Anyone who admires the American sitcom *Cheers*, or who is tempted to think that the various soap operas which provide such excellent evening entertainment on British television are an accurate guide to the way people in Salford, Liverpool or the East End of London actually talk, should ask themselves when they last heard one of the characters in *Cheers*, *Coronation Street*, *Brookside* or *EastEnders* say 'fuck'.

In the 1984 edition of Eric Partridge's *Dictionary of Slang and Unconventional English* (the eighth; edited by Paul Beale), the word 'fuck' is described as being used as an intransitive verb by either sex, but as a transitive word designating an activity only when applied to men. By 1990, this restriction had disappeared. Julia Roberts, playing the role of a prostitute in the film *Pretty Woman*, uses the word in its literal as well as its metaphorical sense when she says to Richard Gere, who has become a millionaire by buying and breaking up companies, 'We're both the same then. We both fuck people for money.'

(ii) Ronald Wardhaugh notes in *An Introduction to Sociolinguistics* (1986) that the better the Creek Indians began to know English, the greater their avoidance became of their word '*fakki*', meaning 'earth', because of its resemblance to 'fuck' and there is a surprising unanimity among European languages that the word for sexual intercourse is also a powerful expression of displeasure. In English, it is also a word remarkable for its versatility, being used in almost every sense except its official one of 'to have sexual intercourse'. In 'Fuck me!' it can be used to express astonishment, and in 'Fuck you!' and 'Fuck off!' to give voice to a combination of aggression and contemptuous dismissal. It is a universal adverb of reinforcement, sometimes in an ironic way – 'Fucking marvellous, ain't it' – sometimes with total approval, as in 'he scored a fucking good goal'. The remark that we were 'fucked about from arsehole to breakfast-time' is typical of the metaphorical use of the verb. In the USA, and less frequently in the UK, 'fuck with' means 'mess with' or 'provoke', a usage which removes any sexual implications from the graffito on a New York subway station: 'If you fuck with the Rossville boys, you die.' It does not mean that they have AIDS, but that they are to be feared for their violence.

As Peter Trudghill and Lars-Gunnar Anderson explain in *Bad Language* (1990), the word can also express philosophical resignation, as in 'Who gives a fuck?'; despair, as in 'Fucked again!'; and querulous displeasure, as in 'What the fuck is going on?' Native speakers of English do not need to have been in the armed services to have heard an example of tmesis as well as blasphemy in the exclamation 'Jesus fucking Christ!' On 26 June 1995, an article in the *Guardian* described how the word was used so frequently in New York that there was even a T-shirt on sale with the instruction: 'How to use the F*** word'. However, a student from Baltimore commented that it was still very much a taboo word there. The universality of 'fuck' is a discouraging sign of a lack of linguistic inventiveness. So, too, is the fact that the sole function in popular speech of the gerund 'fucking' is to announce that an adjective or noun is about to follow. Purists may nevertheless draw comfort from Figaro's explanation to his master Almaviva in Beaumarchais's *Le Mariage de Figaro* (1784) that the basis of the English language is the expletive 'Goddam'. It is a word now virtually extinct from British English except for that one example, though still common in the USA.

(iii) The taboo against the use of the word 'fuck' in literature was strong enough in North America in the 1940s for Norman Mailer to write it as 'fug' in the first edition of his novel about American soldiers at war in the Pacific, *The Naked and the Dead* (1947). Dorothy Parker is said to have greeted him with the remark: 'Hi! So you're the guy that can't spell "Fuck".'. Had she wished to prove Norman Mailer's illiteracy by referring him to the spelling available in a dictionary, she would have had to wait for over twenty years. As Herbert C. Martin pointed out in a letter published in the *New York Review of Books* on 12 January 1995, it was only in 1969 that the word was first given official recognition in American English by being included in Chambers *American Heritage Dictionary*. An earlier editor, Philip B. Grove, had wished to include it in the 1950s, but been over-ruled by the company president, Gordon J. Gallant. On 12 December 1995, the *Guardian* reported that it had, together with 'spick' and 'wop', been removed from the official American dictionary of Scrabble.

When John Osborne's *The Entertainer* (1957) was revived in 1996, the little man who arrived in paradise in Archie Rice's closing monologue was allowed to express his surprise at its wonders by saying 'Fuck me'. This replaced the ' "only one thing I can say", said the little man, "and he said it!" ' of the original, censored version. When, in October 1960, Penguin Books were prosecuted for publishing *Lady Chatterley's Lover*, Mr Griffith-Jones questioned the probability of the word appearing with the frequency it did there, in a conversation in the England of the 1920s between the wife of a baronet and her husband's gamekeeper. On 13 November 1965, in an edition of the BBC TV satire programme 'BBC3' chaired by Robert Robinson, Kenneth Tynan caused a great sensation by saying:

> I don't think anyone would mind if they heard the word 'fuck' spoken in the theatre.

It was, as Mary McCarthy commented at the time, 'a historic moment', and Robert Robinson, writing about the incident over thirty years later in his autobiographical *Skip All That*, pointed out that the word 'was a taboo, and a universal one', arguing that 'if you defy such a magic prohibition you release the power it conceals which is then free to take on other shapes'. One of these, as he observed,

> turned out to be an even more irritating ju-ju, in which 'fuck' was now used as an emblem of sincerity,

and he added

> As to Tynan, having done it once he did it again, in the form of the entertainment called *Oh, Calcutta!* By this time the new orthodoxy had taken root and the show in which the actors wore no clothes treated the word as obligatory. The scenario was mostly sixty-nine ways of not quite having it, and brought the fuck into disrepute.[19]

The outcry in 1965 was nevertheless of such intensity that Stanley Reynolds, writing in the *Guardian*, wondered why 'that one simple word of four letters can provoke a greater reaction inside us than long and complex words like apartheid, rebellion, illegal, police state and treason', while Mrs Mary Whitehouse, who in 1964 had founded the 'Clean Up Television' campaign, subsequently called the 'National Viewers and Listeners Association', said that Tynan wanted his bottom smacked. It was a remark which was truer than she knew. Tynan was an enthusiastic sadomasochist, who in November 1971 wrote in a letter to his wife: 'My present theory is that I cough and laze because of insufficient hairbrush wielding – inhibitions in one area causing inhibitions in others.'[20]

In 1994, I read Philip Larkin's poem 'This Be the Verse' (*c* 1971), with its opening lines

> They fuck you up, your mum and dad,
> They may not mean to, but they do

to a group of students at Stanford University, California. This produced a feeling of intense embarrassment, explained to me afterwards by a student who said that she had never before heard what she called 'the f*** word' used by a professor, but perhaps also explicable by what happens when you read something which contains the word aloud to a group and 'the privacy which exists on the page between the writer and the individual reader is infringed'.[21]

A politically incorrect joke current in England during Mao Tse-tung's Cultural Revolution of the 1960s told how a steward on a train in China offered refreshments to a senior cadre with the query: 'You for coffee?'; only to receive the reply: 'No. Me Party Member. You fuck offee.'

See above, **arse** and **cunt** and the entry on *Lady Chatterley's Lover* in Section IV; also **women's language** below.

Gay See below, **prick** and **queer**.

God The commandment 'Thou shalt not take the name of the Lord thy God in vain: for the Lord will not hold him guiltless that taketh his name in vain' (*Exodus*, 20:7) survives in the refusal of the Quakers and other sects to take an oath on the Bible. Courts rarely refuse to accept that what they affirm to be the case is true.

The habit of printing 'by G–d' survived for a long time, and the avoidance of anything which might be held to be blasphemous was particularly noticeable in nineteenth-century America. Early editions of Jane Austen's novels frequently replaced 'Good Lord!' by 'Indeed!', and Captain Wentworth is not allowed to exclaim 'Good God!' when Louisa Musgrove slips and falls down when jumping from the Cobb in *Persuasion*.

See **bastard**, above and **blasphemy** in IV.

Gollywog Said to derive from 'Golly! A Wog', and used for many years on the label for Chivers marmalade. By the 1950s the woolly toy itself, as well as all representations of it, had become sufficiently taboo to disappear totally from North America. By 1977, the gollywogs in Enid Blyton's Noddy books had been replaced in the United Kingdom by white gnomes. In July 1994 a teacher, James Evans, was reinstated in his post with £30,000 damages after he had successfully proved that he had not said of a pupil with a name which he found difficult to pronounce: 'O.K. Let's call her "Gollywog".' In the 1950s, in certain schools in south-east England, a yellow gollywog badge was worn by girls as a sign that they were no longer virgins.

Goolies A poetic-sounding word for the testicles, though one not frequently heard in the drawing-room. It is apparently derived from the Hindi, with Eric Partridge quoting the phrase 'Beecham Sahib's Goolies' for Beecham's Pills.

Handbag The fondness of conservative thinkers for taboos is encapsulated in the similarity between two quotations: Bronislaw Malinowski's claim in *Ethnology and the Study of Society* (1922) that 'tradition is a fabric in which all the strands are so closely woven together that the destruction of one unmakes the whole'; and Lady Bracknell's reproof to Jack Worthing in *The Importance of Being Earnest* (1895):

> To be born, or at any rate bred, in a handbag, whether it had handles or not, seems to me to display a contempt for the ordinary decencies of family life that reminds one of the worst excesses of the French Revolution.

Illness North Americans are always surprised at the habit in many parts of the British Isles of opening the conversation in the doctor's consulting room with the remark: 'I'm sorry to bother you, Doctor.' Like Continental Europeans, Americans take the view that the doctor is there to be bothered, having chosen a not ill-paid and highly prestigious profession, and that there is consequently no need to feel guilty about coming to see him or her. The British attitude has parallels with the comment by Hutton Webster that 'to the savage, sickness is sin or the result of sin'; and very probably the result of breaking a taboo.[22] You are, as Sir George Sitwell was wont to observe, only ill because you allow yourself to be ill. His own excellent health, he would add, offered definitive proof by contrary example.

Some illnesses are more socially acceptable than others, and fashions can change. Albert Camus commented on the fact that in the French community of Algeria, before the Second World War, the tuberculosis from which he suffered could be mentioned only by euphemisms. The same was less true in the British Isles, where a sustained campaign was mounted from the 1920s onwards to detect and eradicate a disease which, at the end of the nineteenth century, accounted for the death of one Western European in seven. There was nevertheless a code term in the British Isles, 'weak lungs', and the reluctance to name the disease directly may lie partly in the fact that it was so difficult to cure. Tuberculosis also tended to affect the poor, who were more exposed than the rich to the cold and damp which favoured the spread of the disease. It was especially prevalent in Lancashire mill towns, where the cotton industry flourished in the damp climate. In the English folk song 'The Foggy, Foggy Dew', the main character is a weaver, and the 'foggy dew' is said to be a slang term for tuberculosis. It was not until 1882 that Koch identified the bacillus, and not until the 1950s that the increasing use of the BCG vaccine originally developed in France in the 1920s by Calmette and Guérin (hence **B**acille **C**almette–**G**uérin) offered an alternative to a treatment previously based largely on fresh air and better food.

Although the Mimi of *La Bohème* (Puccini,1896; based on Murger's *La Vie de Bohème*, 1845) is a good girl, who catches tuberculosis because of the cold, there are particular reasons why Violetta, in Alexandre Dumas *fils*'s *La Dame aux camélias* (1848) / Verdi's *La Traviata* (1853), suffers from the illness. In the 1840s, the plaster on the walls of the new and luxurious houses and apartments going up in fashionable Paris took a long time to dry out. Rather than live in them personally, and thus risk making themselves more likely to catch tuberculosis, the rich rented them to the *demi-mondaines* who, given the initial advantage of cheap accommodation in a chic area, were prepared to stay until the walls were dry enough for respectable members of the upper classes to live there in safety. Since the custom would have been familiar to the audiences who went to see Murger's play and Verdi's opera, they would have seen the nature of Violetta's illness as a further pointer as to the nature and drawbacks of her profession.

During the Romantic period, and for some time afterwards, writers and musicians seem to have been either particularly vulnerable to tuberculosis themselves or peculiarly interested in it as a theme. The disease thus tended occasionally to lose its taboo aura and become almost fashionable. An illness which killed Keats, Katherine Mansfield, D. H. Lawrence and Chopin could be seen as bringing with it something of their sensitivity and artistic powers. Although André Gide (1869–1951) recovered from an early attack of tuberculosis to live to a ripe and unregenerate old age (see **paedophilia** in I), his description of the euphoria accompanying the period of convalescence which followed his own recovery from the disease in the 1890s accounted for much of the appeal of his early work. As Thomas Mann showed in *The Magic Mountain* (1924), tuberculosis could also provide an appropriate setting for a group of intellectuals cut off from the normal world in a sanatorium. The disease itself could serve as a symbol for the modern world, while its unpredictable nature gave a high probability to the fact that some of the characters afflicted with it might survive and carry on talking for quite a long time.

During the Peloponnesian war (431–404 BC), Athenian comic playwrights observed a strict taboo on any mention of the plague which had broken out in the second year of the war and probably led to the death of Pericles. On a different note, Evelyn Waugh observed in his 'Open Letter to Nancy Mitford on a Very Serious Subject' at the time of the U and Non-U controversy in 1963 (see below, **serviette**), that 'sodomy and impotence are both socially OK, but birth control is flagrantly middle class'. The taboo on mentioning mental illness is still quite strong, and may stem from the belief that madness was caused by demonic possession. By mentioning the disease, you might bring yourself to the attention of the devils as well. It may also, as in the case of cancer or tuberculosis, have been due to what was then seen as the incurable nature of the disease. For many years, **cancer** was a taboo subject throughout the Western world. In the 1960s, John Wayne was seen as showing great courage by allowing it to be known that he was suffering from it. He also defied another taboo (see **political correctness** below and **Eurocentrism** in IV) by having the words 'Fuck Communism' engraved on his cigarette lighter.

One of the queries reprinted in *Miss Manners' Guide to Excruciatingly Correct Behaviour* (1983) concerned the problem of how a woman correspondent should inform the man from whom she had contracted what she called a 'social disease' that he was a passive carrier. The date of publication of the book suggests venereal disease rather than AIDS. Miss Manners's advice was that 'traditional etiquette has a rule for everything': the woman should inform her former lover of the fact by a note accompanied by a gift of flowers.[23] There was, however, no indication as to whether she should employ the same euphemism of 'a social disease', or whether she should break the linguistic taboo and specify whether the disease she had caught from her sometime lover was herpes, syphilis, gonorrhoea, or non-specific urethritis.

See above, **cancer**, **death**, and below, **names**. See also **venereal disease** in IV.

Indian The politically correct term for the people who used to be described as 'Red Indians' is 'Native Americans'. As late as 1960, Agatha Christie's murder mystery *Ten Little Niggers*, first published in 1939, was being reprinted under that title, before being changed first of all to *Ten Little Indians*, and subsequently to *And Then There Were Nine*. The action takes place on Nigger Island.

Infertility In the fourth of the programmes in its series *The Trouble with Men*, BBC2 dealt with what the *Daily Telegraph* television guide for 26 February 1996 described as 'another taboo subject: male infertility'. As in the case of testicular cancer (see above, **cancer**) this was a welcome break from the traditional inequality with which taboos affected men and women. Traditionally, it was the woman who was seen as solely responsible for an infertile marriage. In a number of peasant societies, marriage was postponed until a couple had lived together long enough for the woman to prove her fertility by becoming pregnant. If she remained barren, it was seen as her fault and the man chose another mate. Should the decline in sperm count persist among Caucasian males, this situation might be reversed, with the woman agreeing to marry her partner only after he has made her pregnant. Dr Harrell pointed out as long ago as 1981 in her article in *The American Anthropologist* on 'Lactation and Menstruation', that male infertility is the limiting factor in 40 per cent of American couples evaluated for failure to conceive.[24]

An article in *The Guardian* for 2 August 1996 described how women were trying to overcome the problem created by increased infertility among men in the former Soviet Union by having recourse to artificial insemination and *in vitro* fertilization, both of which were described 'socially taboo'. This may stem from the traditionally macho nature of Russian society, where the feeling is as strong as it is among many males in the West that infertility in males denotes a lack of virility bordering on impotence. While article 2375 of the 1992 Catechism of the Catholic Church encourages research aimed at reducing infertility as long as those involved respect God's will, and 'the inalienable rights and moral integrity of the human person', articles 2376 and 2377 condemn both artificial insemination and *in vitro* fertilization. The birth of a child should, in the teaching of the Church, come only from an act of love between husband and wife.

Although article 2376 states that artificial insemination is also wrong because it denies a child the right to know who its father is, article 2379 states that a husband and wife not blessed with children of their own can 'show their generosity by adopting abandoned children or carrying our demanding duties towards other people'. The phrasing of article 2379 shows the Church adopting a cooler attitude towards adoption than the Romans, for whom it was a common practice. In *Genesis*, 30:2–7 in which Rachel, in her barrenness, implores her husband Jacob to go in to her maid Bilhah that she may 'bear upon my knees'. Dan and Naphtali are both born of this union, and both know who their biological father and mother are, which is not the case with most adopted children in the modern world.

Two novels, both by women, anticipated the current worries about a decline in fertility: Margaret Atwood, *The Handmaid's Tale* (1985), which makes wide use of the Jacob–Rachel–Bilhah myth; and P. D. James, *The Children of Men* (1992).

See above, **illness**.

Loo (US john) (i) The impression given by Miss Manners, the best-known judge of correct social behaviour in the United States, is that the acceptable term for the lavatory in North America is, in a private house, the bathroom. In a restaurant or other public place, it is the restroom. Miss Manners's preference for 'bathroom' is implied in what she tells the correspondent who asked whether it was 'wrong to disturb your hostess by asking where the bathroom is because she is busy with her party duties'. Her reply – 'When Miss Manners asks such a question, she is not fooling around'[25] – is a clear indication that a lady's asking for the bathroom should be interpreted as meaning that she needs a pee fairly urgently.

In both England and America, 'the little girls' room' or 'the little boys' room' are regarded as rather twee, as is 'powder room'.

The twentieth-century taboos on performing the processes of natural elimination in public reflect what we see as common politeness. These and other taboos are nowadays so deeply ingrained in the core of the personality that it is unwise for anyone wishing to keep a keen appetite for dinner to read the illustrative examples in Norbert Elias's *The Civilising Process* (1938) when about to eat.

The idea that euphemisms are the product of seventeenth-century Puritanism, or the forces in Victorian society which produced Dr Bowdler or Anthony Comstock, is hard to sustain against Lawrence Knight's comment in his *Clean and Decent: The Fascinating History of the Bathroom and the Water Closet* (1960). There was, he observes, 'a taboo' already in force in medieval society on the use of the word 'closet'. He adds:

> one would have supposed an earthier way of speech to have ruled, even among nobles and monks, than such coy evasions as 'necessarium' or 'necessary house', or, more oddly, 'garderobe' (wardrobe), exactly as we whisper today of the 'cloakroom'.

Lawrence Knight also refutes the idea that euphemisms are a peculiarity of English-speaking culture by listing some of the alternative terms for *chaises percées* in seventeenth-century France: *chaises d'affaires*, *chaises pertuisées*, *chayères de retrait*, *chaises nécessaires* or simply *selles*.[26]

Euphemisms reflect the role which we see taboos playing in distinguishing between human and animal behaviour, an ambition which has not been constant throughout the ages. Louis XIV frequently received his ministers while on his 'chaise percée'. Only the act of wiping one's bottom was seen as needing to be performed in private. At Versailles, courtiers relieved themselves at the corners of the staircases and behind the tapestries. If Milan Kundera's *The Unbearable Lightness of Being* (1984) is to be believed, it was standard practice among Czech doctors in the 1960s to urinate in the washbasin.[27]

(ii) In the United Kingdom, the conventional term in middle-class and upper-middle-class society has become the loo. Partridge gives this as late twentieth-century and suggests different etymologies: either the French '*l'eau*', as in the expression 'Gardez loo' used in eighteenth-century Edinburgh when emptying the chamber pot out of the top-floor window; or an abbreviation derived from the railway station 'Waterloo' (French 'les waters' = the WC); or the *bourdaloue*, from Louis Bourdaloue, 'the fashionable and prolix preacher in Louis XIV's reign'.[28] If older male speakers in Britain have served in the navy, or wish to create the impression of having done so, they talk about going to the heads. The term 'the jakes', widely used in the RAF, is less acceptable, possibly because U speakers follow the example of Evelyn Waugh and see the RAF as socially inferior.[29] Partridge traces it back to 1530 and the French term 'Jacques'. This, in turn, is given by Random House as the origin of the US 'John'.

U female speakers in Britain generally talk about going to the loo. As Miss Manners makes clear, they ask in North America for the bathroom rather than the toilet. 'May I use the lavatory?' has, in Britain, a socially acceptable directness to it. U speakers recognize the meaning of the expression 'exploring the geography' while rarely using it themselves. Asking to 'wash one's hands' is not likely to lead to the same kind of situation in Britain or America as the request to '*se laver les mains*' is in France. There, the visitor may simply be taken to a washbasin and expected to continue the conversation. Everybody knows what a 'comfort stop' is in a coach or car.

See also **bodily functions** in IV.

Macbeth Always referred to in the theatre by the euphemism of 'the Scottish play', with a total taboo on mentioning the title or quoting any of the lines. Any actor who does so has to go out of the dressing-room, turn round three times, and knock in the hope of receiving permission to return. This is not always granted. The ban on pronouncing the title is another example of a taboo shading into a superstition. It originates either in the large number of unsuccessful productions of the play, or in the occasions when one of the actors playing either Macbeth or Macduff has been wounded in the fight in Act V; or in both.

Military matters (i) In number 12 of *Japanese Book News* (Winter 1995), Inose Naoki reported that 'a taboo' on anything connected with the military had prevailed in Japan since the end of the Second World War. One of its effects was the considerable delay in calling for help from self-defence forces personnel after the disaster of the Kobe earthquake on 17 January 1995.

It is understandable, after the events of 1937–45, that there should be a suspicion of the armed forces in Japan powerful enough to be called a taboo. However, this situation is not peculiar to the societies which lost the Second World War. One of the most famous episodes in the 1980s BBC television comedy series *Fawlty Towers* has the hotel-keeper, John Cleese, feverishly telling himself 'Don't talk about the war!' when awaiting a party of German tourists. The University of Bradford, England, has a Professor of Peace Studies. It is a politically correct way of referring to the person who concerns her/himself with the same matters as the Professor of War Studies at King's College, London, or the Head of the Department of Defence Studies at the nearby University of Leeds. In the United States, the Defence Department was known until 1947 as the War Department. During the 1960s, 1970s and even the 1980s, the reaction against the Vietnam war was strong enough in the United States for Officer Training Corps to become completely taboo on a number of American campuses. The domination of student politics by the broad left led to a similar situation in several universities in the United Kingdom.

The roots of this attitude go back a long way in British society, and pre-date the horrors of the 1914–18 war. Kipling's poem 'Tommy', with its phrase about 'makin' mock o' uniforms that guard you while you sleep', first appeared in *Barrack-Room Ballads* in 1892. The dislike of all things military grew stronger after the disasters of the Somme and Third Ypres. In Aldous Huxley's *Point Counter-Point* (1928), the character modelled on the poet Baudelaire, Maurice Spandrell, claims that the *Encyclopedia Britannica* discusses 'intelligence' under three headings: 'Animal', 'Human' and 'Military'. He then pauses for effect, before adding: 'My stepfather is an example of intelligence, military.'

(ii) There is no uniformity about taboos connected with military matters. *The Guardian* for 23 January 1996 carried an article originally printed in *The New York Times* in which Anthony Lewis described how what he called the 'bloated military budget' of the United States was protected by an 'untouchable taboo'. He suggested a number of reasons why the $260 million spent annually on defence should be seen as 'untouchable'. These included the conviction of the Clinton administration that the United States ought to be ready to fight two major regional wars simultaneously, a belief reminiscent of the 'two fleets' policy of the British admiralty before 1914, whereby the Royal Navy ought to have twice the fire-power of any two fleets likely to be ranged against it. Other factors in the size of the American defence budget were the amount of waste stemming from inadequate financial controls, the advantages which any political party derives from looking tough on foreign policy, and the need to placate Congressmen fearful of the unemployment likely to be created in their area by any reduction in military contracts.

The use of the word 'taboo' to introduce an article enumerating these reasons suggested that a number of them were to be seen as spurious. In that respect, the article represented the same suspicion of military men mentioned above. Taboos against the military tend to be less powerful in countries which, like France, have experienced foreign occupation.

See also **pansy** below and **clever** in V.

Ministers of religion The Scottish fishermen of Gardenstown, a village about forty miles north by north-west from Aberdeen, not only allowed no mention on board ship of salmon, pigs, rabbits or hare, but also forbade reference to 'ministers of religion and women of a certain kind'. At first sight these taboos seem not only unconnected but unmotivated; until, that is, one reads the explanation offered by Edward Knipe and Denis Bromley,[30] who point out that

> In a fishing village the fishermen are the primary producers of food and commodities for trade, while in commercial terms at least, women and ministers are unproductive. The taboo on mentioning women and ministers constitutes a prohibition on mixing the productive and the non-productive. Fishermen naturally regard themselves as men of the sea. The taboo on mentioning pigs and rabbits constitutes a prohibition on mixing the land and the sea.

Although the ban placed on any mention of salmon seems at first sight irrelevant to this explanation, it does underline the absence of hygienic considerations in the formulation of food taboos. Salmon has the healthiest of connotations, and no one who has eaten in a good kosher restaurant will forget how splendid the smoked salmon is. Indeed, there is no suggestion that the fishermen refused to eat salmon. The ban was on mentioning it, and the authors suggest an explanation for this particular interdict when they write:

> the land on which Gardenstown is located was originally granted to the Scottish equivalent of an English lord. Salmon, which historically has been one of the most prestigious fish, has long been regulated by the Crown or civil authorities. The taboo on mentioning salmon constitutes a prohibition on mixing the fishermen with their rulers.

The fishermen, while the productive centre of the village, were not the centre of power. They marked their consciousness of this alienation by the taboos on what they would mention.

See **mix** in II.

Monarchy Claudius's assertion in *Hamlet* that

> There's such divinity doth hedge a king
> That treason can but peep to what it would,
> Acts little of its will

combines the seventeenth-century doctrine of the divine right of kings with Freud's view, in *Totem and Taboo* (1919), that Court ceremonies are a survival of the taboos surrounding the sacred person of the monarch in pre-literate societies. In Sierra Leone, it was so difficult to persuade natives to become king that they had to choose foreigners.

In 1957, Malcolm Muggeridge published an article venturing to suggest that all was not perfect in every branch of the House of Windsor. He received a postbag of abusive letters, with one anonymous correspondent writing to his wife rejoicing that the Muggeridges' eldest child had recently been killed in a ski-ing accident.[31] Memories of the incident remained vivid for a long time. Donald Cameron Watt, commenting in May 1994 on the attempt by Clive Ponting and John Charmley to undermine 'the Churchill myth', described how they, like Muggeridge, had

> encountered that terrifying spate of pathological hatred and obscene malediction which lies geyser-like inches below the

surface of public life ready to erupt over anyone who happens to offend the taboos of public belief.[32]

Money Although General H. Norman Schwarzkopf's autobiography gives his salary on reaching the rank of major-general in 1986 as $68,700,[33] there are other areas of American life in which one does not mention precise sums. University professors will never say what their salary is. This is partly to avoid losing face if the person they are talking to gets more, partly to avoid arousing even more jealousy in the department, and partly perhaps in acknowledgement of the idea that they are not supposed to be in the business for the money.

Although Miss Manners comments that it is 'as vulgar as ever to enquire into, or confess, the state of personal finances',[34] the 1995 edition of Vanderbilt's *Complete Book of Etiquette* states that it is now socially acceptable in North America to discuss one's divorce settlement at the dinner table. Julian Barnes's observation in his 1995 analysis of the collapse of Lloyd's, that in Britain money is still surrounded by 'furious secrecy and lavatorial shame',[35] suggests there may be something in the Freudian assimilation of gold to faeces. The reluctance to talk about money may equally well be a hangover from a hypocrisy about the empire which expressed itself in fiction by the habit of presenting the nabobs such as Joseph Sedley in Thackeray's *Vanity Fair* (1847), who had acquired immense wealth in India, as figures of fun. Part of the success of the English public schools after the reforms introduced by Thomas Arnold at Rugby in the 1850s stemmed from the insistence that they trained boys to take over the running of the empire out of a sense of duty, not to make money. It was a view which reached its apotheosis in Kipling's poem 'The White Man's Burden', written in 1899 to mark the fact that the United States had taken over responsibility for the Philippines. Its opening lines

> Take up the White Man's Burden –
>   Send forth the best ye breed –
> Go bind your sons to exile
>   To serve your captives' need –

emphasized the idea that the Europeans and North Americans who went out to rule

> Your new-caught, sullen peoples,
> Half devil and half child

did not do it for the money.

When the meeting between Jacques Chirac and Helmut Kohl in late 1995 avoided any discussion of how the Franco-German relationship could suffer if the single European currency were launched under conditions unfavourable to France, *The Independent* for 27 October commented on how unfortunate it was that both statesmen considered monetary problems 'a taboo subject for public debate'.

See above, **death** (ii) and **usury** in I.

Mothers-in-law In *Primitive Peoples* (1975), David Charles comments of what he calls the 'happy Eskimos of the Arctic' that 'relatives also observe the custom whereby a man and his mother-in-law do not speak except in case of necessity', and also reports that 'a women does not speak to her mother-in-law unless she is addressed'. He makes a comparable observation of 'the disciplined Zulus of South Africa' to the effect that a man was 'required to shun his mother-in-law'. Similar comments are made by Hutton Webster. He reports how, among the Dusun of northern Borneo, you must not mention by name your father, your mother, your father-in-law or your mother-in-law.[36]

The widespread taboo on mentioning your mother-in-law by name supports the view that there are psychological reasons for the frequency of jokes about mothers-in-law in the working-class culture of the north of England. Such jokes almost always refer to the husband's attitude to his wife's mother. Only very rarely do they imply a hostility of the wife to her husband's mother. This may be because such jokes are told in working-class clubs frequented principally by men. Alternatively, they may indicate a fear on the husband's part of seeing his wife grow old, like her mother, and lose her sexual drive before he does. Or, again, they may be inspired by the husband's feelings of guilt at having intervened in the powerful emotional relationship which existed between his wife and her mother before he came along.

Another possibility is that jokes about mothers-in-law may stem from an unresolved Oedipus complex which makes the husband protest with a slightly suspect violence against feeling any deep affection for a woman to whom he now stands in a mother–son relationship. A common theme in pornographic literature is that of a sexual relationship between a man and his still attractive mother-in-law. The jokes expressing hostility may thus serve as a defence against an Oedipal-type desire which refuses to recognize itself as such. They may also be linked with the taboo on what the French anthropologist Françoise Héritier calls 'second-type' incest (for her thesis in *Les deux sœurs et leur mère*, 1994, see **incest** (iii) in I), the ruling which sees as incestuous any sexual relationship which a man may have with either his wife's sister or her mother.

The American sociologist Alice S. Rossi suggests an alternative explanation. Men, she claims, become more nurturing as they move into their fifties and sixties. Women, in contrast, become more assertive.[37] This leads them, in her view, to arouse a hostility in the young which is in marked contrast to the affection inspired by older men. If true, her view would also explain the scarcity of jokes about fathers-in-law.

Names (i) Popular mythology in the Arab world explains the superior expression on the face of the camel by the idea that it alone knows the 100th name of God.

In *Taboo: A Sociological Study* (1942), Hutton Webster describes engaged couples among the D'Encastreaux Indians as not using real names when speaking to one another, but 'fancy names' instead; not an unusual occurrence among couples in America or Britain, who habitually address each other as 'honey' or 'darling'. In the Old West, a cowboy's past and personal name were both regarded as his private property which he had the right to keep secret.[38]

(ii) Pericles observed in his funeral oration at the end of the second book of Thucydides's *The Peloponnesian War* that the greatest of all women is the one 'whose praise or blame is least bruited on the lips of men'. In his article 'The Woman Least Mentioned' (1987), David Schaps points out that it was indeed, in fifth-century Athens, very unusual to mention a woman's name unless she was dead, had a shady reputation, or was connected with one's opponent in a law-suit. He argues that this was 'a sort of taboo –

perhaps a fear of exposing the women to the evil eye, or the simple feeling that it was indecent to drag a woman's name into court'. It was also a reflection of the fact that Athenian women were expected to play a domestic rather than a public role. A woman could therefore be best referred to by the name of the man with whom she was most closely associated, either her husband, her father or brother, or the head of her clan. 'A woman', writes David Schaps, 'was not somebody to respect; but somebody's mother – or sister, or wife, or daughter – that was another matter.'[39] The taboo against mentioning a woman's name lasted long enough in Western culture to inspire the famous Victorian narrative picture *For He Had Spoken Lightly of a Woman's Name.* In *Thank You, Jeeves* (1934) Bertie says: 'The Woosters do not bandy a woman's name. Neither do the Jeeveses.' It remains a rule that there is no mention of a lady's name in the officers' mess in the British armed services.

(iii) In *Caste Marks: Style and Status in the USA* (1984) Paul Fussell notes how certain names, especially those of Nixon and Reagan, are 'mentioned only in horror'. His observation runs parallel to the discovery made by the English journalist Peregrine Worsthorne when he went to the United States in the 1950s and found that liberal-minded Americans could not forgive Richard Nixon for bringing Alger Hiss to book as a Russian spy. 'So far as they were concerned', he wrote in 1993, 'Nixon was truly the guilty man, not Hiss.'[40]

A frequent way of underlining the taboo nature of a conservative politician, whether in Britain or America, is to omit first names or titles. One does not say John Major, Michael Heseltine, Mrs Thatcher or President Nixon. Instead, one spits out 'Major', 'Heseltine', 'Thatcher' or 'Nixon'. It is hard to hiss the names 'Portillo' or 'Reagan', containing as they do no sibilant. However, academics teaching English or sociology can manage it quite easily. On the other side of the ideological divide, Franklin D. Roosevelt was frequently referred to in conservative circles in the United States in the 1930s and 1940s simply as 'that man'.

During the U and non-U controversy (see **serviette** below), it was alleged that first names such as Howard, Malcolm, Neville, Norman and Percy had acquired taboo status among the upper classes in Britain. This stemmed from the visible intention of upwardly socially mobile parents to hint at aristocratic connections by suggesting a link with one of the powerful families established in England after the Norman conquest or, in the case of Malcolm, with one of the Scottish clans.

Taboo names for girls, especially in France, include Connie, Debbie, Sue-Ellen and Tracy, and there is a general as well as a particular reason for this. On the one hand, it is seen as pretentious in more or less every country to give one's offspring names from a different culture, so that it is as non-U in France to call a boy Michael or Frederick, or a girl Patricia or Alice, as it is in England to name one's son Bertrand or Pierre, or one's daughter Michelle or Louise. In Kingsley Amis's *Lucky Jim* (1954), the main character dreams of being able to tie his professor up in a chair and 'beat him about the head and shoulders with a bottle until he disclosed why, without being French himself, he's given his sons French names', while in Christiane Rochefort's novel *Les petits enfants du siècle* (1961; *Josyane and the Welfare*, 1967) the French family, who have lots of children in order to benefit from the generous system of family allowances, call their appalling eldest son Patrick. There is something irresistibly comic in the fact that some of the characters in François Mauriac's early novels have names such as Harry Maucoudinat or Percy Larousselle. In France, obviously American names such as Sue-Ellen, Debbie or Tracy have the additional disadvantage of revealing an over-consumption of American soaps, just as Kevin, the most popular boy's name in France in the 1990s, evokes either an admiration for English-speaking footballers or an undue liking for the films of Kevin Costner. Anglo-Saxon as well as Celtic names stand out in uncomfortable contrast to the solidly bourgeois and impeccably home-grown Marie-France or Pierre-Henri, as well as to the genuinely aristocratic Anne-Aymone or Charles-Hubert. In England, it is unlikely that either Tracy or Raquel will ever overcome the disadvantage of having been popularized through their occurrence in *Coronation Street.*

See **serviette** below and **knives** in V.

Nigger In 'A Tankard of Sporting Taboos', one of the chapters in Ray B. Browne's *Forbidden Fruits: Taboos and Tabooism in Culture* (1984), Quentin Voigt quotes a remark made by Babe Ruth when he invaded the Giants' locker room after a game during the fiercely contested World Series of 1921 and complained: 'I don't mind being called a prick or a cocksucker or things like that, but lay off the personal stuff.'[41] By which, Voigt explains, he meant 'the hated epithet "nigger lips"'.

The word 'nigger' now has maximum taboo status among white liberals throughout North America, and Noel Perrin points out in *Dr Bowdler's Legacy* (1992) that it has been scrupulously removed from a number of editions of Mark Twain's *Huckleberry Finn* (1884) intended to be used in schools. This is an example both of **political correctness** and of Noel Perrin's contention that bowdlerization is self-censorship carried out to avoid offending the delicacy of feeling thought to characterize potential readers.

The evidence in the O. J. Simpson trial in 1995 suggests that the word was in common use in the Los Angeles Police Department in the 1990s. In one of its reports on the O. J. Simpson trial, *Newsweek* for 28 August 1995 did not print the word 'nigger'. It referred merely to the use by Detective Mark Fuhrman of 'the N*** word'. Similarly, one still occasionally sees 'the F*** word' for 'fuck'.

When Guy Burgess, who subsequently turned out to be a Soviet spy, arrived in Washington in 1947 as Second Secretary at the British Embassy, his head of section, Hector McNeill, told him to remember three things: not to be openly left-wing; not to get involved in race relations; and above all not to get mixed up in any homosexual incident. 'I understand, Hector,' said Burgess. 'What you mean is that I mustn't make a pass at Paul Robeson.'[42]

See above, **black** and **censorship** in IV.

Pagan On 24 July 1994, *The Guardian* reported Anthony Everitt, of the British Sociological Society, referring to the adjective pagan as 'a rather derogatory word'. This was certainly the way it was used by the Catalan-born Professor of Spanish at the Queen's University of Belfast in the 1950s who used to refer to the bowler hat worn by the Ulster Orange man as 'the last vestige of pagán savágery'. But it is no criticism of Albert Camus or D. H. Lawrence to describe their world-view as pagan. It merely brings out their refusal to admire Christianity, and their preference for a culture which gave greater importance to the values of the body.

In contemporary Britain, followers of 'ancient' religions such as Druidism use the word to describe themselves and their beliefs.

Pansy During the Second World War, the apocryphal regimental badge for the Intelligence Corps in the British army was, in heraldic terms, 'A pansy resting on its laurels'. It implied a link between intelligence, homosexuality, and a lack of physical courage which would have surprised T. E. Lawrence.

In *The Psychology of Military Incompetence* (1977), R. M. Dixon argued that the frequency with which military operations end in disaster does not result from the skill which enemies show in defeating their opponents. It is caused by the training given to military leaders. The most valuable quality in an officer when in battle is to sum up the situation correctly and take a swift initiative. The training traditionally received, in contrast, emphasizes obedience to existing orders, and places a taboo on analytical intelligence. This, in Dixon's view, is why 'the Nelson touch' has been used so sparingly by the armed forces of Great Britain.

See **military matters** above and **clever** in V.

Piss There is no imperative 'Piss off' in the USA. 'Get fucked' would be the nearest equivalent.

The term is more frequently used to denote bad temper or anger. When acting as MC in the 1996 Oscar ceremonies, Whoopi Goldberg expressed a frequent and fully justified reaction when she commented of the models who were displaying some of the nominated costumes: 'They get $10,000 an hour and still look pissed off.'

Political correctness Although the term is said to have occurred for the first time as an expression in *The New York Times* in 1990,[43] the attempt to ban phrases judged offensive by progressive thinkers goes back at least to the 1970s. Noel Perrin notes in *Dr Bowdler's Legacy* (1992) how he discovered, in 1976, that the Commissioner of Education in Texas had removed five dictionaries from the approved list for Texas schools. The removal was in response to pressure from the National Association for Women, which objected to the fact that the five dictionaries did not include some new words such as 'chairperson', and did include old terms such as 'womanish'.

However, both the term and the practice very soon became a target of satire, leading to the publication of Henry Beard's and Christopher Cerf's *The Official Politically Correct Dictionary and Handbook* (1992) and of James Finn Garner's *Politically Correct Bedtime Stories* (1994). Henry Beard and Christopher Cerf point out in the 1993 edition of their book that 'the term "politically correct", co-opted by the white power élite as a tool for attacking multiculturism, is no longer "politically correct"'. This confirms the impression of political correctness as a movement whose history recalls Max Beerbohm's comment on Bergson: 'It distresses me, this inability of mine to keep up with advanced modern thinkers as they vanish into oblivion.'

It is highly taboo to refer to the movement as 'p.c.', just as it is unwise to describe the women's movement as 'Women's Lib'. Other examples of the taboos created by the cult of political correctness can be found in this section under the entries **gay**, **primitive**, **queer**, **suicide** and **tribe**. It is also implied in other entries such as **Christmas** or **gollywog**. It recurs in **clarity** and **Eurocentrism** in IV, and its connection with the view that taboos are concerned with power is analysed in **heresy**, also in IV.

See above, **arse**.

Politics A taboo subject at some dinner tables because of the passions that can be aroused. As the rhyme in the couplet

> Confound their politics,
> Frustrate their knavish tricks

in the second verse of 'God Save the Queen' indicates, the word retained well into the eighteenth century the negative associations now suggested by the term 'politicking'.

In an article published in the *Daily Telegraph* on 12 August 1995 to mark the fiftieth anniversary of the publication of *Animal Farm*, Michael Shelden argued that Orwell was, in 1945, 'espousing a point of view that was taboo in the most important political and intellectual circles' of his day. It was, Shelden commented, Orwell's use of his 'Fairy Story' to criticize the Soviet Union that explained the problems he had in finding a publisher. These problems showed how powerful the taboos were at the time against depicting Stalin, as Orwell himself put it, as 'anything but a Christian gent whom it is not done to criticize'. After Orwell had seriously considered printing the book himself in what would have become a very early example of the *samizdat* editions later circulated in the Soviet Union, it was taken by the firm of Secker and Warburg. It was a decision that saved Secker and Warburg from bankruptcy and made a fortune for Orwell's heirs. By 1995, *Animal Farm* had sold over ten million copies. There is no case of a literary or intellectual taboo whose defiance has proved unprofitable.

Poofter Its status as the most frequent derogatory word for homosexuals in contemporary spoken English, corresponding to 'fairy' in the United States, stems from the macho image of themselves projected by Australian males. It was in Australia, according to Eric Partridge, that the word was first widely used. However, long before Australia began to offer macho role models for British men, the nickname for Alban Torel, the coward in Somerset Maugham's short story 'The Door of Opportunity' (1932), was 'Percy Powder Puff'. The pointedly aggressive way in which the word 'poofter' is nowadays used by some heterosexuals may point to the existence of a 'white backlash' against the Gay Rights movement. In 1957, the Lord Chamberlain objected to the word 'pouf' in the typescript of John Osborne's *The Entertainer*, and the term was omitted.

Prick In *The Anatomy of Dirty Words* (1968), Edward Sagarin writes:

> A man called a 'big prick' or 'a perfect prick' in a phallic-worshipping society would be a much admired individual with a high degree of self-control, who would exercise this quality particularly during social contacts with another, which he would turn into a mutually agreeable moment.[44]

This might perhaps become the case if such a society were ever to come into being, especially if the man in question were, as Mr Sagarin rather archly puts it, capable of 'rising to every occasion'. The Sapir-Whorf hypothesis that language shapes our perception of reality may be true. But there are few examples of a pressure group successfully using this hypothesis to change the vision of the world held by the community in general. It is easier to ban pejorative terms than to give a new meaning to established expressions, and the recently created taboo on words such as 'pakki', 'nigger', 'yid' and 'wop' may have helped to reduce racial prejudice.

See below, **queer**.

Primitive Although used by Freud throughout *Totem and Taboo* (1919), and frequent in works such as *The Golden Bough* (12 volumes, 1890–1915), or *Totemism and Exogamy* (1911), by Sir James Frazer, one of the founding fathers of anthropology, 'primitive' has in practice become a taboo word in modern anthropology. Acceptable terms include 'pre-industrial', 'pre-literate', 'non-Western' and 'non-European'.

This is partly because of the cult of **political correctness**. As John J. Honigman observed in *The Development of Anthropological Ideas* (1976), 'the anthropological concept of primitive culture serves neo-colonialism by projecting the idea of white people's comparatively high social standing versus that of others'.[45] Beard and Cerf do not include the word 'primitive' in their dictionary. Its political incorrectness is so obvious that the taboo does not need mentioning. *The Official Politically Correct Dictionary and Handbook* does, however, comment on the term 'culturally deprived'. This, it points out, can sometimes be advantageously replaced by 'culturally dispossessed', a term which does not automatically imply, as Beard and Cerf put it, that 'Eurocentric culture is preferable to that of the marginalized group that is supposedly being deprived'. 'Culturally dispossessed' also has another advantage: it 'unmasks the assimilationist character of mainstream American society'. The entry **queer** below suggests why assimilationism is wrong.

See below, **tribe**; also **cannibalism** in I and **Eurocentrism** in IV.

Pussy Eric Partridge's *Dictionary of Slang and Unconventional English* (1937; 1992) gives various expressions in which the noun 'pussy' is used to designate a woman. He does not, however, mention either its widespread use as a synonym/euphemism for the pudendum/pudenda, the external sexual organs of a woman, or its use in the term 'eating pussy' for cunnilingus. Until the mid-1930s, the crime writer Agatha Christie (1890–1976) quite frequently described elderly ladies as 'old pussies'; until, presumably, somebody told her, and she proceeded to refer to them as 'old dears'. In Ian Fleming's *Goldfinger* (1959) the leader of the Lesbian gangsters is known as Pussy Galore. Bond, however, converts her to heterosexuality.

See **Lesbianism** in I and IV; also **oral sex** in I.

Queer (i) On 27 July 1994, one of the leading spokespersons for the Gay Rights movement in the United Kingdom, Peter Tatchel, told the *Guardian* that he actually preferred the word 'queer' since, as he said, 'the derogatory meaning is subverted and its effectiveness as an insult undermined'. This could not happen with what he called 'the politeness of "gay"'. This matches the recommendation in Henry Beard's and Christopher Cerf's *The Official Politically Correct Dictionary and Handbook* (1992). They quote a 'spokeslesbian' for the American advocacy group Queer Nation as saying that the word gay 'reflects a certain kind of white, middle-class assimilationist'.

A general prejudice against homosexuals remains visible in the reluctance of popular speech to follow the example offered by the media and consistently use the word 'gay' to denote homosexuals. It is not unusual to hear regret that terms such as 'a gay bachelor' or 'the gaiety of nations' have been robbed of their original meaning. A lack of **political correctness** also inspires the comment that since so many homosexuals seem even sadder than their heterosexual counterparts, the term 'gay' is a particularly unfortunate misnomer.

(ii) There is a link between **political correctness** and existentialism. In *La Nausée* (1938; *Nausea*), Sartre's hero Antoine Roquentin refuses to allow what he calls the 'strong red blood of his violent rebellion' to be absorbed and neutralised by the all-encompassing and universally tolerant humanism of the man he calls the Autodidact. All that the Autodidact's humanism would do is neutralize Roquentin's revolt and water it down, just as the 'repressive tolerance' of bourgeois society has neutralized the revolt of the rebels who tried to overthrow it in the second half of the twentieth century, and especially in 1968. As Gayatri Chakravorty Spivak, Professor of English and Cultural Studies at Pittsburgh University, put it in 1989,

> Tolerance is a loaded virtue, because you have to have a base of power to practise it. You cannot ask certain people to 'tolerate' a culture that has historically ignored them, at the same time that their children are being indoctrinated into it.[46]

Later in his career, Sartre praised the black man who proudly termed himself a nigger and refused to be assimilated into white society. In his view, taboos should not be abolished. They should be exploited, so that what was originally an insult was transformed into a source of pride. In the 1980s, the attitude which involves saying that you are proud of what other people accuse you of being inspired the owners of a large general store in South East London to call it *The Pakki Shop*. It also gave birth to the movements known as 'Gay Pride' and 'Glad to be Gay'.

Redneck In 1989, C. Vann Woodward commented that this was the 'only opprobrious epithet for an ethnic minority still permitted in polite company'.

See above, **dago** and **nigger**; also **political correctness**.

Research into sexuality When Alfred Kinsey published *Sexual Behaviour in the Human Male* (1948) in the United States, he commented in his 'Historical Introduction', that

> human sexual behaviour represents one of the least explored segments of biology, psychology and sociology. Scientifically more has been known about the sexual behaviour of some of the farm and laboratory animals. In our Western European-American culture, sexual responses, more than any other physiological activities, have been subject to religious evaluation, social taboo and formal legislation. It is obvious that the failure to learn more about human sexual activity is the outcome of the influence which custom and the law have had upon scientists as individuals, and of the not immaterial restrictions which have been imposed upon scientific investigations in this field.[47]

Restrictions on research into what Kinsey called 'as taboo a subject as sex' are taking a long time to disappear. In 1989, it became known that a highly distinguished team of medical researchers, headed by Dr Anne Johnson of the Radcliffe hospital, and supported by the Medical Research Council, were making an enquiry into the sexual behaviour of the British population. Although the perceived need for such a study had been heightened by the outbreak of the AIDS epidemic, the government intervened to ensure that public funding was discontinued. The Prime Minister, Mrs Thatcher, let it be known that she regarded such enquiries as intrusive and unacceptable. It was only through a grant of £900,000 from the Wellcome Foundation that the research leading to the publication of *Sexual Attitudes and Life-Styles* (1994) by Blackwell Scientific Publications could be completed.

Rubber British visitors to the United States should avoid using this word when asking for what North Americans call an eraser. It means a condom.

See **fetishism** in IV.

Sambo Partridge traces this as a term for a Negro back to 1800, but gives no etymology. He notes that in the late twentieth century the term is 'insulting, and in polite circles, almost taboo'.

Helen Bannerman's *Little Black Sambo* was first published in 1899, and went on to have twenty-four separate editions up to 1954. A new edition was then published, and was reprinted in 1956, 1959 and 1961. There is an element of geographical improbability about the story of a very negroid-looking little boy, whose mother is Black Mumbo and whose father is Black Jumbo, and who meets five tigers, whom by a clever subterfuge he transforms into 'a great big pool of melted butter (or "ghi" as it is called in India)'.

Serviette (i) Nancy Mitford's claim that this word constituted 'the great linguistic dividing line between the classes in England' is less true than it was when she made it in 1954. It is virtually meaningless in the United States and never applied to the way social distinctions worked in Scotland, Wales or Ireland. She made the remark in the context of what was known at the time as the 'U and Non-U' (Upper-class and Non-Upper-class) controversy, which shows linguistic taboos serving as social markers.[48]

The U and Non-U debate also offers an example of the essential triviality of most taboos. Even in the England of the time, it no more mattered to the vast majority of the population whether somebody said 'serviette' and not 'napkin', 'home' and not 'house', or 'toilet paper' rather than 'lavatory paper', than it does to non-Jews whether Gentiles do or do not eat pork. The taboo on non-U words can also be seen as an example of the kind of snobbery that helps to create the same economic maladjustment in the United Kingdom of which Hutton Webster complained in 1942 when he commented on how taboos in pre-industrial societies 'slow up the pace of work' and 'diminish production'.[49]

The U and Non-U controversy illustrates another characteristic of taboos, and one which they share with myths: their anonymity. Just as we do not know who invented the myth of Oedipus, of Persephone, of Red Riding Hood or of Cinderella, so there was no known *arbiter elegantiae* who imposed on certain sections of English society the view that it is aristocratic to say 'cakes' but non-U to talk about 'pastries'. No individual ever had the power to decide that it was socially OK to talk about going on one's bike but non-U to use the word 'cycle'. There may, perhaps, have been a person who laid down the rule that a swift way of putting oneself beyond the social pale was to speak in the way Pip does in *Great Expectations* when he attracts the disdainful comment from Estella: 'He calls the knaves, Jacks, this boy!' But if there was, we do not know her or his name. Like myths, and like Topsy in *Uncle Tom's Cabin*, taboos are conventions which 'just growed'. But if there is a virtually total mystery about the origin of linguistic taboos, their principal function is quite clear. They work, as the word **shibboleth** does in *Judges*, 12:6 (see below), as a means of exclusion. Anyone who talked about 'serviettes' was automatically, in the eyes of U-speakers in the England of the 1950s, beyond the linguistic pale.

(ii) If the origin of the taboos involved in the U and Non-U debate is shrouded in as much mystery as that of the incest taboo, there is nothing inexplicable about the way they worked. In the England of the 1950s, social prestige was still linked to the ownership of land. The upper class had always spoken with the brutal directness of those whose life brought them into daily contact with birth, copulation and death. Norbert Elias quotes a piece of advice to the upwardly socially mobile going back to 1695: one does not say of a man that he is 'deceased' but that he is 'dead'.[50] Members of the landowning aristocracy and gentry saw as a fact of life the movements in men as well as in animals of the bladder and the bowels. Because they had no reason to wrap up such events in euphemisms, they effectively reversed the taboos which led middle-class and lower-middle-class speakers to avoid the mention of the processes of natural elimination, or indeed anything unpleasant or unduly physical. If an upper-class aunt went mad, her relatives said that she was mad, not 'mental', 'disturbed' or 'suffering from nerves'. They would be much more likely to say that she was bonkers. If a woman was pregnant, her family said so, not that she was 'in an interesting condition' or 'in the family way'. They might even describe her as being 'in pod'. They would also say 'napkin', or 'table napkin', and not 'serviette'; and there are two reasons why non-U speakers did the opposite.

Non-U speakers have always thought French words are more elegant than English ones. They are wrong. The landed aristocracy shares with its tenants a suspicion of foreign habits which is reflected in its preference for Anglo-Saxon over Latin terms. Members of the English upper class say chop and not cutlet, hall and not vestibule, jam and not preserves, pudding and not dessert. Similarly, Paul Fussell observes that in the United States, 'driver' is preferred to 'chauffeur', while Miss Manners advises her readers to say 'underwear' and not 'lingerie', 'curtains' instead of 'drapes', and to eschew with even greater rigour the solecism of 'draperies'.[51] The fact that 'serviette' is a French word is one reason why members of the British upper class would never think it was elegant to use it to refer to what they call a table napkin. The second is that they are not afraid, by using the word 'napkin', of accidentally evoking what is known in British English as a baby's nappy (US diaper).

There is nothing arbitrary about the linguistic taboos created by this upper-class avoidance of supposedly refined language. Taboos which take the form of euphemisms are observed in an exaggerated form by the petty bourgeoisie, a class whose members are obsessed by the fear of sinking down again into the foul-mouthed proletariat from which they have only recently risen. Members of the upper class, in contrast, are secure in their status, and totally indifferent to what other people might think of the way they talk. Unless, that is, they are caught out using a non-U term. The columnist and novelist Jilly Cooper claims to have heard an upper-class child say to one of its friends: 'Mother says that "pardon" is much worse than "fuck".'

See also the entries **forks** and **knives** in Section V.

Sex and sport Sex itself is so much a taboo topic that it is possible to analyse in one entry all the contexts in which it occurs. The list of headwords on p. 321 offers a guide as to its frequency, and readers will find particularly detailed treatment in the entries on **contraception**, **homosexuality**, **incest**, ***Lady Chatterley's Lover***, **masturbation** and **oral sex**.

A more unexpected taboo is analysed in Allen Guttmann's *The Erotic in Sports* (1996), a book which contrasts the openness with which the links between sex and athletics were acknowledged in classical times, and what he calls the 'confused obfuscation' which he claims has characterized 'most modern discussions of the phenomenon'. His own suggested answer to the question as to why the link between sex and athletics has been what he calls 'a taboo among lovers of sports' lays the blame far more on the Protestant ethic than on the spirit of capitalism. It is not, in other words, what he calls 'capitalism's alleged need continually to repress, sublimate, and exploit the instinctual self' which accounts for our reluctance to accept that both men and women athletes can be sexually attractive precisely because of the elegant and well-trained bodies which enable them to show athletic prowess. It is much more a hangover from the Christian suspicion of the body, and he points out that if capitalism were 'the explanation for the suppression of eros, as Herbert Marcuse averred in *Eros and Civilisation* (1955), we should feel the taboo more intensely than ever'. This is not, however, at all the case. For as he points out, 'what we have witnessed in the last quarter century is capitalism's eager exploitation of the economic potential of eros in sports as in every other sector of our increasingly hedonistic culture'.[52]

While this is undoubtedly true, the need which Allen Guttmann feels to give space to refuting the ideas of a Marxist whose reputation outside a very narrow circle is not high points to the existence of what might be called an 'anti-taboo': the requirement that certain ideas be mentioned even if they have only a tangential relevance to the topic under discussion. A comparable requirement to give weight to contemporary **shibboleths** is visible in his remark on the previous page about 'those on the political right who see athletes as the paladins of "family values" and those on the left who condemn athletes as the shock troops of "compulsory heterosexuality"'. Outside what is again the very narrow circle of proselytizers for 'Gay Rights', it is again highly unlikely that such accusations are ever formulated.

Shibboleth Just as 'taboo' came into English from the languages of Polynesia, and took on a range of meanings which it did not originally have, so 'shibboleth' is a Hebrew word which has been borrowed and undergone a comparable change.

Its origins lie in an incident related in *Judges*, 12. When the Gileadites were at war with the Ephraimites, the former managed to seize the ford over the River Jordan before the latter. And as the Ephraimites, defeated in battle, tried to cross the river and pretend that they were Gileadites, the Gileadites submitted them to a simple phonetic test: they made them pronounce the Hebrew word 'shibboleth', designating either an ear of corn or a stream of water. If an Ephraimite pretended not to belong to his tribe, the Gileadites said to him (*Judges*, 12:6):

> Say now Shibboleth: and he said Sibboleth: for he could not frame to pronounce it right. Then they took him, and slew him at the passages of Jordan: and there fell at that time of the Ephraimites forty and two thousand.

It was a vigorously imposed taboo on the mispronunciation of a key word, but one strictly limited to the immediate occasion. The sense which the word now has in English of what the *Oxford English Dictionary* calls 'a catchword or formula affected by a party or sect, by which their followers may be distinguished, and others excluded' is first attested in 1638. The word is frequently used nowadays to denote a totally unimportant item of belief which is nevertheless so important as to be beyond question, the equivalent of a sacred cow. Oddly enough, this meaning is not mentioned in the dictionaries.

In *The New York Review of Books* for 16 November 1995, Luc Sante used the word in an unusual sense when he wrote that by the time the exhibition *The Perfect Moment* had been closed by the police in Cincinnati, Robert Mapplethorpe (see **sadomasochism** in IV) had become 'known to everyone within range of a television set, although less as an artist than as a shibboleth'.

Shit In 1922, as Noel Perrin notes in *Dr Bowdler's Legacy* (1992), e.e. cummings's *The Enormous Room* was printed with the exclamation 'My father is dead! Shit. Oh, well, the war is over' left uncensored. However, John S. Sumner, Secretary of the New York Society for the Suppression of Vice, noticed it, and was calmed down only when a girl in the publisher's office inked out the offending word in every copy left in stock.

The description of Widmerpool in *Hearing Secret Harmonies* (1975), the last volume of Anthony Powell's *A Dance to the Music of Time*, as a 'château-bottled shit' reflects the later slackening in the earlier, virtually absolute taboo against the public use of the word. This slackening began in the English upper-class society in which the action of Powell's novels takes place. In the United Kingdom, it remains a feature of upper-middle-class speech rather than that of the petty bourgeoisie or proletariat. Andrew Marr, writing in *The Independent* for 27 June 1995, illustrated the virtual disappearance of the taboo from the quality press by writing of John Redwood, the contender for the leadership of the Conservative Party, that he was not 'the classic gold-plated shit', since 'when he says that he hasn't gone round being disloyal about the Prime Minister in private, he is telling the truth'. On 26 November 1996, a woman contributor to the BBC radio phone-in programme *Call Nick Ross* described Diana, Princess of Wales as 'an absolute shit'.

An example of humour produced by the sudden collocation of the literal and metaphorical sense of a word is offered by the story of the senior civil servant who had the habit of going to the loo punctually at ten-thirty every morning. In response to the order from one of his colleagues in the Treasury that he be brought to the telephone immediately, supplemented by the remark 'And I don't care where he is', his secretary knocked on the door of the loo and gave him the message; only to receive the reply: 'Tell him that I can only deal with one shit at a time.'

Sod Technically, an abbreviation for sodomite, but rarely used as such, and virtually unknown in the USA. It can function as a verb – 'Sod it!' – or as an insult – 'You sod'. Its severity depends very much on the tone of voice in which it is pronounced.

Suicide (i) The Greeks and Romans, like the Japanese, saw nothing wrong in a death which avoided dishonour, and Pliny said that the power of dying when you please is the best thing the gods have given to men amid all the sufferings of life. For most Christian denominations, however, and especially the Roman Catholic Church, suicide represents the ultimate sin of despair in God, the closing of the door on the possibility of a divine intervention which may save you while you are still alive. It is this teaching of the Catholic Church which Scobie risks damnation by defying in Graham Greene's novel *The Heart of the Matter* (1948). As Act V, scene i of *Hamlet* reminds us, suicides could not normally be buried in Christian ground. *Suras* I.77–9, XL.70 and XLIV.6 of the Koran can be interpreted as placing a ban on suicide. The verses are nevertheless given a different interpretation by certain followers of Islamic Jihad and the Hamas movement.

The general taboo against acknowledging that someone may have died by suicide remains strong in modern society, and the coroner's verdict in the United Kingdom still frequently adds the phrase 'while the balance of the mind was disturbed'. Even in an aggressively secular society like the former Soviet Union, it was maintained that Tchaikovsky (1840–93) died of cholera, when it is almost certain that he committed suicide, possibly out of despair at the effects which a public revelation of his **homosexuality** might have on his reputation.[53]

Edwin Scheidman points out in his article on suicide in Norman Farberow's *Taboo Topics* (1963) that taboos involve things you mustn't do, words you mustn't say and ideas you mustn't even think about, and continues:

> Suicide seems to cut across all three kinds of taboo: the prohibitions against it (as against murder) may be found more often in the first (action) and the third (thought) kinds of taboo, whereas the topics of heterosexuality and homosexuality may be found more in the second (discussion) type of taboo.[54]

This has not been my experience, since I live in a society in which **homosexuality** is quite frequently discussed, albeit not always in tones of approval. I can nevertheless sympathize with Edwin Schneidman's later comment on how frequently he was asked 'How did you come to be interested in the topic?': there was always what he calls the 'sly implication that it must be some grossly overdetermined interest or concern on the researcher's part'. This 'nudge nudge, wink wink' reaction, virtually inevitable when you are looking at anything with sexual implications, can be annoying. It remains a valuable indication that you have hit on a taboo topic.

(ii) Suicide remains an offence under the criminal law in the United Kingdom, though not in the United States. In the United Kingdom, the survivor of a suicide pact may in certain circumstances be charged with manslaughter.[55] While this is justified on the grounds that the law must punish those whose actions cause harm to others, the taboo against suicide itself has religious and not secular origins. According to Henry Beard's and Christopher Cerf's *The Official Politically Correct Dictionary and Handbook* (1992), the acceptable terms for it include 'autoeuthanasia', 'voluntary death' and 'spiritually dysfunctional'.

Suicide is not recommended by the Voluntary Euthanasia Society – Exit, whose address is 13, Prince of Wales Terrace, London, W8 5PG. This nevertheless provides a form in which those who are still of a sound mind and healthy body can instruct their family, their physician and all persons concerned, under certain very carefully defined conditions, not to 'subject them to any medical intervention or treatment aimed at prolonging or sustaining life' when it would be better for them to be allowed to die. The US equivalent is the Society for the Right to Die, 250 West 57th Street, New York, NY 10101, which provides Living Will and Health Care Proxy forms. There is also the Hemlock Society, P.O.

Box 101810, Denver, CO 80250–9932, which is more concerned with changing laws and attitudes.

Tenure On 28 April 1995, an article in *The Times Higher* stated that something which had previously been 'a taboo subject', the question of tenure in American universities, had now started to be openly discussed. Seven years earlier, Charles J. Sykes's *Profscam* (1988) had alleged that the teaching performance of tenured professors in some major American universities was frequently so poor as to deprive them of the right to any employment at all. The terms 'sacred cow' and **shibboleth** are often used in the same context.

In September and October 1995, the French government announced its intention of looking more closely at the privileges said to be enjoyed by civil servants. Supporters of the market economy made frequent use of the word '*tabou*' to claim that such privileges, and especially that of tenure, had already been protected from critical discussion for far too long.

Tribe In *The Official Politically Correct Dictionary and Handbook* (1992), Henry Beard and Christopher Cerf report Robert B. Moore as writing that the word 'tribe' should be avoided because it has 'assumed a connotation of primitiveness and backwardness'.[56]

See above, **primitive**.

Twat In *Dr Bowdler's Legacy* (1992), Noel Perrin quotes four lines from the end of Browning's *Pippa Passes* (1841) –

> Then, owls and bats,
> Cowls and twats,
> Monks and nuns, in a cloister's moods,
> Adjourn to the oak-stump pantry! –

and comments that the evidence they provide shows that the middle class had totally forgotten the well-attested meaning of 'twat' as the female pudenda, 'just as it has still forgotten "quaint", so that Marvell's pun on the two meanings in "To His Coy Mistress" has fallen flat for six or eight generations now'.

See above, **cunt**.

Vagina On 20 December 1995, the *Guardian* reported that London Underground had banned the use of the word 'vagina' in a series of advertisements planned by the Marie Stopes International as part of their seventy-fifth birthday celebrations. The exhibition was going to be entitled 'Lie Back and Think of Egypt'. It contained a brief history of contraception from the Ancient Egyptians to the present day. However, the group that sells advertising space on the London Underground, Transport Displays Incorporated, apparently operated a ban on what it called 'offensive words and phrases' such as 'vagina' and 'contraceptive pessary'. It also banned the expression 'cervical cap fitted over the cervix'.

See **contraception** in I.

Wank Without saying so implicitly, Partridge gives the impression that the term is used only of men, and it is not widely known in the USA. There, the term is 'jerk off', as used by John Travolta in *Pulp Fiction* (1994) to describe what he intends to do after seeing Uma Thurman safely home after their night out. When, however, she mistakenly sniffs pure heroin under the illusion that it is cocaine, his plans have to change.

In what is still the male-dominated world of rude words, a wanker is a social inadequate. This is because anybody who masturbates is seen as not only unable to find a woman to sleep with him, but lacking the self-control to wait until he does. However, the fact that among recruits to the RAF of the 1940s, the term 'wanker', or 'wanking pit', was synonymous with bed – 'He's still in his wanker, and it's eight o'clock' – echoes Dr Kinsey's findings that 83 per cent of American males indulged in the practice.

There was, in contrast, the universal supposition that any woman who wanted a man could have one in an instant and on the asking. She would therefore never be in a situation where she needed to masturbate, so the word would never be applied to her in any literal sense. According to an article in the London-based magazine *Time Out* in February 1996, the word is used nowadays of women as well as of men, though in a metaphorical rather than a literal sense. Peter Stuart, producer of *The Girlie Show* on Channel 4, was reported as saying of a well-known model who had been named 'wanker of the week', that the term was 'a tongue-in-cheek cultural critique of someone who is a sacred cow.'

See above, **prick**; and **masturbation** in I.

Wog Supposed etymology 'Western [or Wily] Oriental Gentleman'. Familiar to the over-fifties in England in a wider sense through the remark that while the wogs begin at Calais, the dagos start at Dover. Also used ironically in homosexual circles in the United States to denote the **W**rath **o**f **G**od **S**yndrome = AIDS. While in Australia, it designates what is referred to in England as Gyppo tummy, by English-speaking visitors to South America as Montezuma's revenge, and by U-speaking circles in England as 'the trots'.

Women's language In *Words and Women* (1977), Casey Miller and Kate Swift write:

> Three of the first authors of international standing to use the word *fuck* in their books after the courts made it legally permissible were women: Iris Murdoch, Doris Lessing and Carson McCullers. Many more probably had it edited out of their manuscripts by timorous male editors. In Sybille Bedford's report of the *Lady Chatterley* obscenity trial, where the taboo words were discussed in detail, *Esquire*, 'the magazine for men', let all the words stand but substituted 'that word' for *fuck*. Playboy, more aggressively all-male, used one 'f' and three dashes to represent the word as it was spoken by Helen Gurley Brown in an interview. Mrs Brown had been asked if she had any difficulty with editors in getting her *Sex and the Single Girl* into print as she wrote it. She replied that the only serious contretemps occurred when she discovered in the galley proof that 'Frig you!' had been substituted for 'Fuck you!' as the proper retort for a young woman to neighbours who criticised her for sleeping with a man when she was not married to him. Mrs Brown said that she was outraged and told the editor, 'No woman would ever use that word.'[57]

If the word in question was 'frig', it is an interesting example of a euphemism becoming more taboo than the word it was meant to replace.

See above, **fuck** and **serviette**.

NOTES

1 See *Man: the Journal of the Royal Anthropological Society of Great Britain and Ireland*, Vol. 88, 1958, p. 162.
2 See Bill Bryson, *Made in America*, Secker and Warburg, London, 1994, p. 381.
3 E. Sagarin, *The Anatomy of Dirty Words*, Lyle Stuart, New York, 1968. See p. 91.
4 Noel Perrin, *Dr Bowdler's Legacy*, David R. Godine, Boston, MA, 1992, p. 221.
5 For a fuller account, see Norman Sherry, *The Life of Graham Greene*, Volume 1, *1904–1939*, Jonathan Cape, London, 1989, p. 621.
6 F. Fukuyama, *The End of History and the Last Man*, Penguin, Harmondsworth, 1992, p. 326.
7 Perrin, *Dr Bowdler's Legacy*, 1992, p. 283.
8 Review of Helen Wayne, editor, *The Story of a Marriage: The Letters of Bronislaw Malinowski and Elsie Malinowski*, Routledge, London, 1996 and of George W. Stocking, *After Tylor: British Social Anthropology, 1888–1951*, Athlone Press, London, 1996. For the Conrad quotation, see Stocking, p. 253; and p. 261 for Malinowski's reasons for feeling such intense annoyance at the Melanesians.
9 See E. Partridge, *A Dictionary of Slang and Unconventional English: Colloquialisms and Catch Phrases, Fossilised Jokes and Puns, General Nicknames, Vulgarisms and Such Americanisms as have been Naturalised*, revised edn edited by Paul Beale, Routledge and Kegan Paul, London, 1984. First published in 1937, constantly revised, never out of print, this is the alpha and omega of all studies of taboo or supposedly taboo words.
10 Sagarin, *The Anatomy of Dirty Words*, p. 32.
11 *International Journal of Psychoanalysis*, Vol. 35 (1954), pp. 30–56. Quoted in Stephen Marcus, *The Other Victorians*, Weidenfeld and Nicolson, London, 1964, p. 240.
12 See Volume 1 of *A Feminist English Dictionary*, Loop Center YWCA, Chicago, 1973, quoted in Casey Miller and Kate Swift, *Words and Women*, Anchor Books, Doubleday, Garden City, NY, 1977, p. 103.
13 Quoted on p. 128 of Pat Caplan, *The Cultural Construction of Sexuality*, Routledge and Kegan Paul, London and New York, 1987.
14 Keith Beaumont, *Alfred Jarry: A Critical and Biographical Study*, Leicester University Press, Leicester, 1984, p. 116.
15 Bryson, *Made in America*, p. 362.
16 See Hutton Webster, *Taboo: A Sociological Study*, Stanford University Press, Stanford, CA, 1942, p. 157.
17 *Rapport sur le comportement sexuel des Français*, Julliard, Paris, 1972, p. 49. Alfred Kinsey reports the majority of prostitutes as uninterested in

sex, and refusing to indulge with their lover in any of the bizarre practices which they perform for money with their clients.

18 See Mary R. Lefkowitz, *Women in Greek Myth*, Duckworth, London, 1986, p. 10. She explains the myth by writing that

> as comparative anthropology suggests, it was intended as an explanation of why bards behaved and dressed in a female manner, and indeed to understand both male and female experience in order to prophesy accurately.

This interpretation also leads her to comment, rather surprisingly for a feminist, that the story of Tiresias 'puts female sexuality in a bad light'. She then goes on to suggest that it can be interpreted as suggesting 'rewards and reasons for acquiring female sexuality'.

19 Robert Robinson, *Skip All That*, Century, London, 1996, pp. 125–9.

20 See Kathleen Tynan, *The Life of Kenneth Tynan*, Weidenfeld and Nicolson, London, 1987; Phoenix paperback, London, 1995, p. 322. For a discussion of Tynan's use of 'fuck', see pp. 236–8.

21 Robert Robinson, in a private communication. On p. 128 of *Skip All That*, Mr Robinson also writes, of the furore created by Kenneth Tynan's use of the word:

> *The Express* had a headline which read THE BLOODIEST OUTRAGE OF ALL. Their use of an adjective that had itself been impermissible at one time was, in the circumstances, a residual irony, but the paper was obliged to refer to Tynan's word, and thus make it clear that they knew it existed: in admitting it existed, they were admitting we all knew it existed; thus they reinforced Tynan's fracturing of the taboo, since the operation of a taboo proscribes any reference to what the taboo forbids. I have a feeling this double-bind beefed up the fury of the newspapers and their readers; Tynan had given them no option but to take part, at one remove, in his act of impiety.

The fact that this extract from *Skip All That* appeared on 12 November 1996 in the *Daily Mail* is an indication of the frequency with which the concept of taboo, in its widest sense, is now discussed in the popular press. It also illustrates the disappearance of any inhibitions on the public use of the word 'fuck', just as the description of the Princess of Wales as 'an absolute shit' by a female contributor to the BBC Radio 4 phone-in programme *Call Nick Ross* on 26 November 1996 shows how completely other inhibitions have disappeared.

22 Webster, *Taboo*, p. 311. Pages 311–12 give further details of the view of illness as a punishment on the individual for the offences committed

by the whole of the group to which that individual belongs, and of the propitiation ceremonies which must then be performed. The remark about the custom in the Manta Island, where

> From time to time, doctors impose new taboos on their patients. A doctor frankly acknowledged that this practice accounted for the innumerable restrictions observed by the Manta people

offers implicit support to the view that one of the functions of taboos is to increase the power of those imposing them.

23 Judith Martin, *Miss Manners' Guide to Excruciatingly Correct Behaviour*, Hamish Hamilton, London, 1983, p. 192.

24 *The American Anthropologist*, 1981, pp. 796–823.

25 Martin, *Miss Manners' Guide*, p. 464.

26 Lawrence Wright, *Clean and Decent: The Fascinating History of the Bathroom and the WC*, Routledge and Kegan Paul, London, 1960, pp. 46 and 100–1.

27 M. Kundera's *The Unbearable Lightness of Being*, Faber and Faber, London, 1984, p. 206.

28 Because he spoke so long that you needed to go to the loo before he had finished. See the Appendix to Partridge, *A Dictionary of Slang and Unconventional English*.

29 As evinced in *Men at Arms* (1952), the first volume of the 'Sword of Honour' trilogy, by the brief but damning portrait of Daisy Leonard who dislikes the Halberdiers Mess and comments that 'You just settle down on an RAF station as though it was business with regular hours and a nice crowd'; by Guy Crouchback's inability to recognize the meaning of the stripes on Ian Kilbannock's sleeve; and by the remark that 'Few things were better calculated to arouse Jumbo's sympathy than the news that a Halberdier officer had fallen into the hands of the Air Force'.

Jumbo Trotter is one of Waugh's most sympathetically presented minor characters, and it may not be simply snobbery that informs his and Waugh's own dislike of the RAF. Foot soldiers or cavalry men, who may well have to prove their valour in hand-to-hand fighting, have always felt a distaste for those who kill with missiles launched from a distance. In the *Iliad*, Paris is an expert archer, but also a coward.

30 See 'Word Taboos among Scottish Fishermen' in Ray B. Browne, *Forbidden Fruits: Taboos and Tabooism in Culture*, Bowling Green University Press, Bowling Green, Ohio, 1984, pp. 183–91.

31 See Malcolm Muggeridge, *Tread Softly for You Tread on My Jokes*, Collins/Fontana, London, 1968, p. 255. The article was originally

published in America in the *Saturday Evening Post*, and reprinted in England in *The National Review*.

32 *The Times Literary Supplement*, 17 May 1994 in a review of *Churchill: The End of Glory* (1994) and *Churchill: a Political Biography*.

33 See N. Schwarzkopf, *It Doesn't Take a Hero*, Bantam Books, New York, 1992, p. 327.

34 Martin, *Miss Manners' Guide*, p. 168.

35 'The Deficit Millionaires', in J. Barnes, *Letters from London*, Picador, London, 1995, p. 192.

36 D. Charles, *Primitive Peoples*, Davis and Charles, Newton Abbot, 1975, pp. 56 and 61; Webster, *Taboo*, p. 153. The correct term for 'Eskimos', a term probably derived from a Native American word meaning flesh-eating, is Inuit.

37 See her article 'Seasons of a Woman's Life' in Bennett M. Berger's *Authors of Their Own Lives: Intellectual Autobiographies by Twenty American Sociologists*, University of California Press, Berkeley, 1990, p. 320.

38 See R. Adams. *The Old-Time Cowboy*, Macmillan, New York, 1961, p. 60.

39 See 'The Woman Least Mentioned: Etiquette and Women's Names', *Classical Quarterly*, 27, 1977, pp. 323–30.

40 P. Worsthorne, *Tricks of Memory*, Weidenfeld and Nicolson, London, 1993, p. 140.

41 See Browne, editor, *Forbidden Fruits*, p. 105

42 Quoted from Alan Bennett, *Writing Home*, Faber and Faber, London, 1994, p. 210.

43 According to an article in *Le Nouvel Observateur*, no. 1588, 13 April 1994, contrasting the cult of universal values characteristic of French civilization with the recognition and cult of differences found in the United States.

44 See Sagarin, *The Anatomy of Dirty Words*, p. 102.

45 J. J. Honigman, *The Development of Anthropological Ideas*, Dorsey Press, Homewood, Illinois, 1976, p. 398.

46 Quoted from p. 46 of 'Who Needs the Great Works?' forum, *Harper's Magazine*, September 1989, by Henry Beard and Christopher Cerf, *The Official Politically Correct Dictionary and Handbook*, (1992), updated edition, Random House, New York, 1993, p. 126.

47 Alfred Kinsey, and others, *Sexual Behaviour in the Human Male*, W. B. Saunders and Company, Philadelphia and London, 1948, p. 3.

48 The debate about what was or was not 'U' speech was sparked off by an article by A. S. C. Ross describing how members of the English upper class distinguished themselves from other people in the nineteenth century by the way they spoke. The article had originally

appeared in a Finnish journal of comparative philology, but was spotted by Nancy Mitford and republished in 1956 in *Encounter* under the title 'U and Non-U, an Essay in Sociological Linguistics'. The same issue of the magazine contained an article by Nancy Mitford herself called 'The English Aristocracy', and Evelyn Waugh replied to her in 'An Open Letter to the Hon[ble] Mrs Peter Rodd (Nancy Mitford) on a Very Serious Subject'. The three articles were republished by Penguin under the title *Noblesse Oblige* (1957), and the book became something of a best-seller. The volume also contained a poem by John Betjeman entitled 'How to get on in Society', which contains thirty-two non-U words in five stanzas, and showed how a number of Professor Ross's comments remained true in the mid-twentieth century.
See **knives** (ii) in V.

49 Webster, *Taboo*, p. 252.
50 N. Elias, *The Civilising Process* (1938), translated by Edmund Jephcott, Blackwell, Oxford, 1978, p. 109.
51 Martin, *Miss Manners' Guide*, pp. 193–4; and Paul Fussell, *Caste Marks*, Heinemann, London, 1984, p. 154. Fussell also notes other mistakes of meaning and mispronunciation which mark Americans as belonging to a particular class, and quotes Lord Melbourne's remark: 'The higher and lower classes, there's some good in them. But the middle classes are all affectation and conceit and pretence and concealment.'
52 A. Guttmann, *The Erotic in Sports*, Columbia University Press, New York, 1996, pp. 6–7.
53 The matter is discussed in some detail in Anthony Holden, *Tchaikovsky*, Transworld, London, 1995.
54 Norman L. Farberow, editor, *Taboo Topics*, Atherton Press, New York, 1963, p. 34.
55 This applies only to what might be called the active partner in the attempt. If a husband and wife decide to kill themselves by running the engine of the car in an enclosed space, and if the husband, having been the one who turns the key, happens to survive when his wife dies, he is liable to prosecution. If, however, he should die and his wife survive, she, having been only the passive partner in the attempt, is not.
56 See Beard and Cerf, *The Official Politically Correct Dictionary and Handbook*, p. 56, quoting from Robert B. Moore's article 'Racist Stereotyping in the English Language', reprinted in a collection edited by Paula S. Rothenberg, *Racism and Sexism: An Integrated Study*, St Martin's Press, New York, 1988, p. 276.
57 See Miller and Swift, *Words and Women*, p. 101.

Section IV

IDEAS, BOOKS AND PICTURES

'Don't think it, write about it, paint it, print it, or show it!'

The entries **cunt**, **fuck** and **shit** in Section III suggest that linguistic censorship, in the sense of taboos on the use of certain words, has virtually disappeared from Western society. The entries in this section on the Hays Code, James Joyce's *Ulysses*, Radclyffe Hall's *The Well of Loneliness*, and D. H. Lawrence's *Lady Chatterley's Lover*, are a guide as to the number of artistic and literary taboos which have disappeared in the second half of the twentieth century. Other entries reinforce the idea that a decline in the number of intellectual and political taboos which it enforces is a defining characteristic of the open society.

Apartheid On 1 May 1994, Nicholas Bagnall reported in *The Independent on Sunday* that the South African Broadcasting Corporation decided as early as 1961 that the word 'apartheid' would be used only when quoting what was actually said by politicians, journalists or foreign correspondents. In its own programmes, the corporation insisted on the use of the words 'separate development', a decision which Nicholas Bagnall described as leading it to 'sink even further into the Orwellian mire'.

Restrictions on the freedom of expression are a normal feature of totalitarian societies, as well as a common occurrence in authoritarian ones. In *Le Mariage de Figaro* (1784), Beaumarchais made his principal character describe how the government of Louis XVI allowed him total freedom to write whatever he wanted in the newspapers, on condition that he mentioned neither the Church, the monarchy, public affairs, religion nor finance. When Orwell's *Nineteen Eighty-Four* was circulated in samizdat in the former Soviet Union and its dependent satellites, its account of the taboos on what one could and could not say in the Oceania of Big Brother was immediately recognized as an accurate description of the situation behind the iron curtain. The ideal inspiring our own rejection of intellectual taboos was expressed in its most cogent form by John Stuart Mill when he pointed in his essay *On Liberty* (1859) to the link between agnosticism and tolerance:

> The beliefs which we have most warrant for have no safeguard to rest on but a standing invitation to the whole world to prove them unfounded. If the challenge is not accepted, or is accepted and the attempt fails, we are far enough from certainty still; but we have done the best that the existing state of human reason admits of; we have neglected nothing that could give truth a chance of reaching us; if the lists are kept open, we may hope that if there is a better truth, it will be found when the human mind is capable of receiving it; and in the meantime we may rely on having attained such approach to truth as is possible in our own day. This is the sole amount of certainty attainable by a fallible being, and this the sole way of attaining it.

In 1825, Thomas Jefferson expressed the same idea more succinctly when he placed on the portals of the University of Virginia the words:

> Here, we are not afraid to follow truth wherever it may lead, or to tolerate any error, so long as reason is left free to combat it.

It is hard to think of a point of view more hostile to the idea of a taboo.

See below, **censorship**.

Auschwitz (i) Ian Buruma writes in *The Wages of Guilt: Memories of War in Germany and Japan* (1985) that

> the virtual taboo against depicting Auschwitz was broken, not by German artists, but by a Hollywood soap opera, a work of skilful pop, which penetrated the German imagination in a way that nothing had done before. *Holocaust* was first shown in Germany in January 1989. It was seen by 20 million people, about half the adult population of the Federal Republic.[1]

Ian Buruma draws a contrast between the readiness of the general public as well as the authorities in the Federal Republic to acknowledge German guilt for the atrocities of the Nazi era, and what happened both in Japan and in what was officially known between 1948 and 1990 as the German Democratic Republic, referred to by most commentators as East Germany, and described by the ungodly (see **Eurocentrism** below) as the Russian occupied zone. In both East Germany and Japan, though for different reasons, the taboo on discussing what had happened before and during the Second World War remained in force for much longer than in the democratic west, and in a way which illustrates how the maintenance of certain taboos can embody both the political values of a society and its attitude towards its past.

When Ian Buruma visited Buchenwald in 1988, in what nobody knew at the time were the last days of the East German régime, he was given a guidebook which read:

> Destruction of Marxism, revenge for the lost provinces and brutal terror against all resisters, these were the stated aims of German fascism from the very start. What was really at stake was the interest of monopoly capitalism, lavishly used to promote the Nazi movement.

More than a taboo on a topic, it was a taboo on the free and open analysis of it, an illustration of how totalitarian societies can survive only by keeping the minds of their citizens rigorously closed. Ian Buruma also points out how, between 1945 and 1950, the East German authorities used the same buildings which had housed the victims of Nazism as accommodation for German prisoners of war brought back from Russia. However, as the director of the camp during that period, Dr Seidel, observed, 'What happened here between 1945 and 1950 was taboo. It could not possibly be discussed.'[2] In the former Soviet Union, as John L. H. Keep pointed out in *Last of the Empires* (1995), traditional Russian anti-semitism was strong enough to prevent any mention of the Holocaust until the poet Yevtushenko 'broke the taboo' in 1961 in his poem 'Babyi Iar'.[3]

Although critical of what he describes as Ruth Benedict's excessively abstract distinction in *The Chrysanthemum and the Sword* (1950) between the Christian-inspired 'guilt cultures' of the West and the 'shame culture' created by Confucianism and Shintoism in the East, Ian Buruma does see it as a possible key to explaining the difference between Japan and West Germany. It was, he points out, a Japanese Christian, Mayor Motoshima of Nagasaki, who broke a major taboo in Japanese society by acknowledging in 1975 that the emperor could be held responsible for Japanese policy between 1937 and 1945, and recognizing that at no point did the Japanese population as a whole fail in their loyalty to Hirohito. For them it was enough after the defeat of 1945 to comply with what the American occupying authorities wanted, something which the tradition of blind obedience to whomsoever happened to be in power enabled them to do without losing face. Nothing in their own culture inspired them with the desire to break the taboo on discussing their crimes by trying to find out, as the West Germans had begun to do immediately after 1945, just why they had committed them.

(ii) In her discussion in *Misogynies* (1989) of the success of *Sophie's Choice*, Joan Smith writes:

> more central to the book's success [is] the breaking of a taboo; its central theme, the holocaust, is a subject rarely addressed in fiction. Authors have, on the whole, left writing about the mass

murder of Jews, gypsies, homosexuals, members of various Resistance movements and others by the Nazis to historians and to survivors like Primo Levi.[4]

In her further discussion of what she criticizes as 'the eroticization of the Holocaust', she raises the question of the censorship which good taste might well lead authors to impose upon themselves when discussing certain topics. This links up with the point made below in the entry on the **Hays Code** about the case for the voluntary acceptance of certain taboos.

The issue is further discussed in the Conclusion; as, too, in the context of French society, is the question of how long a society can profit from a critical obsession with its past.

Blasphemy (i) The statement in the First Amendment that 'Congress shall make no law concerning the establishment of a religion' means that it is difficult to make blasphemy a federal offence in the United States. In 1952, a New York statute prohibiting the showing of sacrilegious films was held to be unconstitutional for vagueness.[5] In 1968, the Supreme Court ruled in *Epperson* v. *Arkansas* that the First Amendment 'does not permit the State to require that teaching and learning must be tailored to the principles or prohibitions of any religious sect or dogma'.[6] By thus declaring that laws banning the teaching of Darwinism in public schools were unconstitutional, the court made it very difficult to repeat the situation which arose in Tennessee in 1925, when the trial of John Scopes upheld the right of a state to forbid the teaching of the theory of evolution as established fact.

Its ruling also provided a constitutional framework for the discussion of the question which a taxi driver in the Midwest asked the anthropologist Mary Douglas when she told him what she did for a living. 'Ah', he said. 'Just the person we need to settle an argument in our Bible group. Which came first, Adam and Eve or the Dinosaurs?'[7] The Scopes trial formed the basis for the film *Inherit the Wind* (1960), in which the real-life William Jennings Bryan, who led for the prosecution, was played by Fredric March, and Clarence Darrow, for the defence, by Spencer Tracy.

(ii) Geoffrey Robertson, commenting on the situation in the United Kingdom, remarked in his *Obscenity* (1979) that it 'appears that the law of blasphemy no longer relates to attacks on or criticisms of Christian doctrine, but is concerned solely with indecent or offensive treatment of subjects sacred to Christian sympathizers'.[8] He was discussing what had happened in Britain when the magazine *Gay News* was found guilty of blasphemy in 1976 for publishing James Kirkup's poem 'The Love that Dares Not Speak Its Name', and the verdict confirmed on appeal by the House of Lords.

The original charge had been brought in a magistrate's court by Mrs Mary Whitehouse, who in 1964 founded the Clean Up Television Campaign, subsequently the National Viewers and Listeners Association, designed to censor radio and television in their depiction of sex and violence. Professor Hogan comments in *Criminal Law* (1986) on the unusual nature of the success which she obtained on this occasion in her attempt to make the law defend traditional religious belief. Theoretically, the law on blasphemy was based on the dictum of Sir James Fitzsimmons Stephen in his *History of the Criminal Law* (1885) that 'all proceed on the plain principle that the public importance of the Christian religion is so great that no one is allowed to deny its truth'. However, as Professor Hogan points out, there has been 'no recorded instance of a conviction for blasphemy where an element of contumely or ribaldry is absent'. He also comments on the way in which the verdict against *Gay News* went against the principle set out by the House of Lords in its judgment on the case of *Bowman* v. *Secular Society Ltd* in 1917, when it was held that blasphemous words are punishable

> for their manner, their violence or their ribaldry, or, more fully stated, for their tendency to endanger the peace there and then, to deprave public morality generally, to shake the fabric of society and to be a cause of civil strife.

Given the relatively low circulation of the magazine in which the poem alleging Christ to have been a homosexual was published, it was extremely unlikely – the word used by Professor Hogan is 'ludicrous' – that the poem could have any effect whatsoever on the fabric of society.

The *Gay News* case offers parallels with some of the views expressed in the Salman Rushdie case. While there was no approval outside fundamentalist Muslim circles for the death sentence pronounced by the Ayatollah Khomeini in his *fatwa* of 13 February 1989, it was argued that *The Satanic Verses* (1988) ought to be withdrawn from sale because of the spiritual suffering that it caused to a large number of sincere believers. The offence it gave, it was maintained, was particularly unfortunate in that the novel had been openly published and widely praised in a multi-racial society in which believers in all creeds were at the same time being encouraged to feel at home. Lord Scarman put the case for the maintenance of taboos on all attacks on religion when he wrote:

> I do not subscribe to the view that the common law offence of blasphemous libel serves no useful purpose in the modern law. On the contrary, I think there is a case for legislation extending it to protect the religious beliefs and feelings of non-Christians. The offence belongs to a group of criminal offences designed to safeguard the internal tranquillity of the Kingdom. In an increasingly plural society such as that of modern Britain, it is necessary not only to respect the differing religious beliefs and practices of all, but also to protect them from scurrility, vilification, ridicule and contempt.[9]

Lord Scarman did not say whether this protection should be extended to such religious systems as the cult of the People's Temple founded by Jim Jones, and which led on 18 November 1978 to the collective suicide of 923 people in Guyana; and a comparable point was illustrated by a more frivolous example in the BBC Radio 4 discussion programme *The Moral Maze* on 28 November 1996.

In a decision which was unusual in two respects, the European Court of Human Rights had just upheld the application by a British court of the law against blasphemy in order to ban a short video depicting Saint Theresa of Avila grappling erotically with a full-sized statue of Christ. It was, a contributor pointed out, unusual on purely statistical grounds for a ruling by a British court to be confirmed on appeal by any European court. Although the European Court of Human Rights sits at Strasbourg, and is totally separate from the Court of Justice of the European Union, which sits in Luxembourg, there is a general tendency for decisions given by all courts situated in Continental Europe to follow the legal customs prevailing in France. Since the establishment of a secular republic in 1905, it is no more possible to bring a prosecution on the grounds of blasphemy in France than it is in the United States of America (see above (i)).

The European Court of Human Rights had nevetheless been influenced in its decision by two factors: an unusual readiness to forfeit its right to overrule a national jurisdiction; and the view that the law had the right to protect the feelings of sincere believers against what was judged to be gratuitous offence. Little attention was given to the contributor to *The Moral Maze* who asked whether his views as a squirrel-worshipper could, would or should be given comparable protection, but there is no gainsaying the logic of his remark. Since there is no more evidence for the beliefs of the traditional religions than for the pagan beliefs which he wished to espouse, he had just as good a case on intellectual grounds as the Anglican believers who had originally brought the case in the British court. Only the beliefs of the Church of England as by law established can benefit from the British law against blasphemy. It was also pointed out that the law on blasphemy differs from the 1959 Act on obscenity (see below, *Lady Chatterley's Lover*) in that no defence is permissible on grounds of aesthetic quality.

There is nevertheless some support for Lord Scarman's view of the law on blasphemy in the contrast between what had happened in the *Gay News* case, and the refusal in 1991 of the chief stipendiary magistrate in London to take action against Salman Rushdie and the publishers of *The Satanic Verses*. What the magistrate argued was that it was only the established Church which could be said to be part of 'the fabric of society which it is the object of the law to protect'. In 1992, the Law Commission for England and Wales recommended that the law of blasphemy should be abolished but at the time of writing (1996) this has not yet happened. This continues to create a situation in which the Christian has a privilege in law denied to holders of other beliefs, whether Sikhs, Muslims or Jews, whose only protection in law would lie in an appeal under the Race Relations Act.

Salman Rushdie himself, in an article in the *Observer* for 22 January 1989, forecast what was going to happen to him when he said:

A powerful tribe of clerics has taken over Islam. These are the contemporary thought police. One may not discuss Muhammad as if he were human, with human virtues and weaknesses. One may not discuss the growth of Islam as a historical phenomenon, as an ideology born of its time. These are the taboos against which *The Satanic Verses* has transgressed.

See below, **censorship** and see **God** in III.

Bodily functions (i) There is an intriguing absence from the taboos set out in the Old Testament of any mention of defecation or urination. In the Koran, the only reference to these natural functions is in the instructions for preparation for prayer in *Sura* V.8:

> If you are defiled,
> purify yourselves; but if you are sick
> or on a journey, or if any of you
> comes from the privy, or you have touched
> women, and can find no water,
> then have recourse to wholesome dust
> and wipe your faces and hands with it.

Hutton Webster's exhaustive *Taboo: A Sociological Study* (1942), like the other books on taboos by anthropologists such as Mary Douglas, Sir James Frazer, Edmund Leach, Franz Steiner and Sir Edward Tylor, is equally free of any reference to the processes of natural elimination. The books of *Exodus* and *Leviticus* offer detailed advice on how to deal with cases of sores, leprosy, or issues of blood, and the authors of the taboos which characterized pre-literate and pre-industrial societies were extremely interested in **menstruation**. There are, it is true, instructions to Muslim men to remain standing when they relieve themselves. In other cultures, however, the emptying of the bladder or the bowels does not seem to have interested the authors of taboos. When one thinks of how many taboos there are about art, food, dress, entertainment, hair-styles, ideas, language, sex, thought and prayer, this absence of rules about emptying the bladder or the bowels seems at first sight as intriguing as the silence of the dog in the night-time in Conan Doyle's *Silver Blaze* (see **cannibalism** in I and **apples** in II).

There are two possible explanations for the absence of taboos governing the processes of natural elimination. Since the inventors of taboos were almost certainly men, they felt no inhibitions about laying down the law for women, and telling them what to do when they were menstruating. But since, as Montaigne puts it in the essay 'On Experience', 'kings shit, and ladies too', the priests and lawyers who created the first taboos were more coy, and even a shade embarrassed, about mentioning the way their own bodies were also subject to the demands of nature. Alternatively, the taboo-makers may have felt that there was something instinctive in human beings which would always make them show a greater sense of modesty when needing to relieve themselves than the beasts of the field, and that rules were simply not necessary.

What one might call the argument from embarrassment is supported by the large number of verbal taboos preventing any direct reference to emptying the bladder or the bowels. The euphemisms listed below under **loo** – going to the bathroom, exploring the geography, washing one's hands – are an indication of how reluctant people are to talk openly about the topic, and this reticence is echoed in the field of literature. Only very rarely, as Aldous Huxley points out in *Point Counter-Point* (1928), do novelists deign to mention the mundane details of daily life, such as how a satisfactory bowel movement can create a sense of euphoria which lasts well until lunch-time. There is, it is true, a welcome exception in James Joyce's account in *Ulysses* (1922) of how Mr Bloom begins his day by a gentle opening of the bowels, but few other novelists have followed his example. Gustave Flaubert, allegedly the master of French realism, makes Emma Bovary travel for seven hours in a cab with her young admirer Léon without either of them needing to get out for any purpose at all. And never, either in erotic, pornographic or realistic fiction, have I seen a mention of the importance for both parties of a preliminary emptying of the bladder before they make the beast with two backs.

There are, it is true, occasional exceptions. Rabelais quite openly describes how his characters piss and shit, and there is even one moment when those who have eaten a particular kind of grape think that they are only about to fart but find themselves quite involuntarily emptying their bowels. Novels such as Erich Maria Remarque's *All Quiet on the Western Front* (1929) are quite open about the fact that most men fill their pants when they are first under fire, and it may be that the absence from other fiction of any mention of going to the loo is explicable by the fact that it is irrelevant to the main action of the novel. An equally telling explanation is that the subject rapidly becomes a very boring one.

(ii) During his editorship of *The New Yorker*, from 1925 to 1950, Harold Ross banned all references to 'the Jewish question', to cancer, to homosexuality and to all bodily functions. He would have been as unusual among modern editors as the Australian aborigines whom Ruth P. Rubenstein reported in 1995 as being 'indifferent to being seen naked but profoundly embarrassed if seen eating'[10] would be in Europe or North America. The anthropologists Marshall and Suggs nevertheless found the same tendency among the Marquesan islanders of the South Pacific, describing them as being 'very casual in their sexual behaviour', but 'exhibiting the same kind of neurotic symptoms we normally ascribe to sex in all matters pertaining to food'.[11]

Judges, 7:5–7 offers an early description of the role played in the attainment of full humanity by the restraint we impose upon ourselves in the satisfaction of our appetites. In the selection process devised by Gideon to find the 300 warriors best fitted to fight the Midianites, it was the men who revealed their animal status by lapping like dogs who were rejected. Only those who lifted the water to their mouth by hand were deemed to have reached a level where they were human enough to serve the Lord. The incident is also mentioned favourably in *Sura* II.250 of the Koran. In his *De civilitate morum puerilium libellus* (1534; 'On the Behaviour of Boys') Erasmus of Rotterdam gave comparable advice when he wrote: 'Some people put their hands in the dishes the moment they have sat down. Wolves do that.'

A number of rules against performing other processes of natural elimination in public are more recent than the episode in the Book of Judges, which probably took place sometime before the end of the eighth century BC. Antoine de Courtin commented in 1672 that it was sufficient, if in the presence of people of rank, to put one's foot over the sputum one had just ejected. It was not until 1859 that a book of Victorian etiquette laid down that 'spitting is at all times a disgusting habit'; and even then the spittoon remained a common item of furniture in saloon bars until after the 1914–18 war. If, Erasmus advises his readers, they blow their nose with two fingers and something drops on the ground, they should simply tread on it.[12]

See also **menstruation** in I and below; also **loo** and **serviette** in III.

Censorship In *Dr Bowdler's Legacy: A History of Expurgated Books in England and America* (1992), Noel Perrin distinguishes between censorship and what he calls bowdlerism. While the former is generally done by governments for political reasons, bowdlerism is done by individuals for moral ones. While censorship is usually imposed on books before they are published, and leads to their being withdrawn, bowdlerism comes afterwards, and is a form of editing. The book in question still appears, but in a form judged suitable to what is seen as an audience needing protection.

Dr Thomas Bowdler (1754–1825) was medically qualified, but was happier working in the prison reform movement and dealing with books than treating patients. He is best known for producing, in 1807, an edition of Shakespeare purged of 'those words and expressions . . . which cannot with propriety be read aloud in a family', followed by a better-known one in 1818. Noel Perrin links the popularity of Dr Bowdler's endeavours to the rise of the Evangelical movement and to the increase in general readership in the United Kingdom from a few thousand at the beginning of the nineteenth century to at least half a million by the 1850s. The fact that middle-class wives were expected to stay at home encouraged the view that they needed protection from the wicked world, and the verbal taboos introduced by Bowdler and his disciples had the effect of other taboos (see **menstruation** in I) of keeping women in what men thought was their place.

His work was by no means unpopular, and Noel Perrin quotes Algernon Swinburne (see **sado-masochism**, below) as saying as late as 1894 that 'no man did better service to Shakespeare'. Bowdler's example led to various attempts to purge the Bible of any reference to words or incidents judged unsuitable to the weaker sex, as well as to the work of Noah Webster (1758–1843). In addition to compiling in *A Compendious Dictionary of the English*

Language (1806) a work intended to produce a specifically American version of English, Webster also became what Noel Perrin calls 'one of the most dedicated expurgators in history', producing in 1833 'the first and last avowed expurgation the Bible has ever had', taming *Ezekiel*, 16:25 'Thou . . . hast opened thy feet to every one that passed by, and multiplied thy whoredoms' to 'Thou . . . hast prostituted thyself to everyone that passed by and multiplied thy lewd deeds'. [13]

See also **homosexuality** in I; the entries above on **apartheid** and **blasphemy**; also, below, **eugenics**, **Hays Code**, **heresy**, **Lady Chatterley's Lover** and **sexual activity**.

Clarity In *Le degré zéro de l'écriture* (1953; *Writing Degree Zero*), the French structuralist critic Roland Barthes expressed what was to become a very fashionable attitude in the English-speaking as well as in the French literary world when he wrote:

> clarity is a purely rhetorical attribute, it is not a general quality of language, attainable at all times and in all places, but merely the ideal appendage to a certain discourse, the one subjected to a permanent attempt to persuade. It is because the pre-bourgeoisie of the period of the monarchy, and the bourgeoisie of the post-revolutionary period, using the same kind of *écriture*, have developed an essentialist mythology of men, that classical writing, one and universal, has given up all trembling in favour of an unbroken tissue, of which each element represented a voice, that is to say radical elimination of every possible in language.[14]

As Barthes himself insisted, this placing of a taboo on clarity was politically motivated. Because middle-class writers such as Voltaire or Anatole France had laid such insistence on the importance of the idea that prose should be immediately comprehensible, it was clearly necessary for advanced thinkers to write in a way capable of destroying the intellectual basis on which capitalist society was established. Barthes's precept was followed by writers such as Georges Bataille, Maurice Blanchot, Malcolm Bowrie, Hélène Cixous, Jacques Derrida, Stephen Heath, Luce Irigaray, Julia Kristeva, Jacques Lacan, J. Hillis Miller, Toril Moi, Gayatri Chakravorty Spivak, Philippe Sollers and many others in addition to Barthes himself. Indeed, it is so hard to grasp what these authors mean that one adopts the paradoxical position of reading the play, novel or poem supposedly under analysis in order to understand what the critic is saying.

See below, **empiricism**.

Contraception (i) When, in Stella Gibbons's *Cold Comfort Farm* (1932), Flora Poste undertakes the civilization of the Starkadders, one of her first actions is to instruct Meriam Beetle 'carefully, in detail, in cool phrases' 'how to forestall the disastrous effect of too much sukebind and too many long summer evenings upon the female system'. Meriam, who has already had four children out of wedlock by Seth Starkadder, listens wide-eyed before exclaiming: ' 'Tes wickedness! 'Tes flying in the face of Nature', and the initial reaction of her mother is the same; until, that is, she thinks more about it and decides that 'all the same, it might be worth tryin' '. Flora's first battle is on the way to being won; without, however, the reader being given any of the precise details vouchsafed to Meriam.

Direct mention of contraception is almost as rare in imaginative literature as references to certain basic **bodily functions** (see above) and to **menstruation** (see below). There are eighteenth-century cartoons of Casanova (1725–98) illustrating the resistant properties of condoms by blowing them up like balloons, and in letter 110 of Laclos's *Les Liaisons dangereuses*, Valmont writes to the Marquise de Merteuil, after his successful seduction of the young Cécile Volanges, 'je lui ai tout appris, jusqu'aux complaisances; je n'ai excepté que les précautions' (I taught her everything, including how to really please a man; I omitted only the precautions). Boswell's *London Journal* has a number of references to condoms, mostly in the context of their usefulness in avoiding venereal disease. But compared with the care which writers show in describing clothes, feelings or furniture, their indifference to a topic of such universal interest as how to make love without getting pregnant bears witness to the power of a peculiarly inexplicable taboo.

One outstanding exception is the English novelist David Lodge, who made the ban imposed by the Catholic Church on all artificial forms of contraception into the main theme of two of his novels, *The British Museum Is Falling Down* (1965), and *How Far Can You Go?* (1984; US title, *Snakes and Ladders*). The former contains a passage inspired by the Church's decision to allow married couples to use what was known officially as the 'rhythm method' and unofficially as Vatican roulette. The main character, Adam Appleby, composes for an imaginary encyclopedia compiled for the instruction of visiting Martians after life on earth has been destroyed by atomic warfare, an entry which begins:

> Roman Catholicism was, according to archaeological evidence, distributed fairly widely over the planet Earth in the twentieth century. As far as the Western hemisphere is concerned, it appears to have been characterized by a complex system of sexual taboos and rituals. Intercourse between married persons was restricted to certain limited periods determined by the calendar and the body temperature of the female.

As David Lodge points out in the Afterword to the 1983 Penguin edition, the subject was considered sufficiently delicate for the novel to be placed by the authorities in charge of the Reading Room of the British Museum in the category of books which could be consulted only in the North Library, and which he himself describes as 'that inner sanctum which (as a passage in the novel explains) is reserved for the perusal of books deemed to be either especially valuable or pornographic', adding: 'I have not ventured to inquire which of these criteria has been applied to my novel.'

(ii) Very few people in Victorian England seem to have known about contraception, with the queen herself complaining about the frequency with which she became pregnant, and Dickens being surprised and more than a little resentful at the number of children born to him by his wife Catherine. The mistress for whom he abandoned her, Ellen Ternan, must nevertheless have been a little more worldly wise. She had no children by him. Although Françoise Barret-Ducrocq claims in *Love in the Time of Victoria* (1989) that 'the tracts of Francis Place were widely diffused in the 1820s, and works by neo-Malthusians like Richard Carlile, Charles Knowlton, Robert Dale Owen and William Thomson were very popular', the details she gives of the frequency of abortion and of marriages made necessary by the impending arrival of an unwanted child suggest that the taboo on providing such information was still very strong.[15] Even a leading biologist such as T. H. Huxley wrote to a friend in 1858 that he wished that

> a revised version of the genus Homo would come out, at any rate as far as the female part of it is concerned – one half of them seem to me doomed to incessant misery so long as they are capable of childbirth.[16]

His grandson Aldous was one of the first writers to break the taboo against mentioning contraception in an English novel. In *Brave New World* (1932), all the women keep themselves available for instant but infertile sex by wearing a Malthusian belt, and this very matter-of-fact reference to contraception was one of the factors that led to the novel's being banned in Australia between 1932 and 1937. The main references to birth control by twentieth-century French writers are to *coitus interruptus*, especially in the work of Jean-Paul Sartre, and Françoise Barret-Ducrocq suggests that this technique was the one most frequently used in nineteenth-century England.[17] It was almost certainly what French Catholic preachers denounced in the nineteenth century as one of the '*pratiques néfastes*' (disastrous practices) which prevented the French population from growing at the same speed as that of its European neighbours (see **contraception** (i) in I).

In a passage which reveals either an acute sense of humour or a total lack of it, Simone de Beauvoir describes an encounter which took place in Geneva in 1946 between Sartre and a Swiss lady of mature years and irreproachable respectability. The lady was worried lest her son, who was having an affair with a girl who was no better than she ought to be, might make her pregnant, and wanted to know if Sartre could offer any advice. 'Apprenez-lui à se retirer,' (Teach him to withdraw) said Sartre. 'An excellent idea,' replied the Swiss lady. 'I'll tell him. Knowing that this advice comes from you will have a great effect on him.'[18]

See **contraception** in I and III; also **menstruation** below.

Empiricism In the 1960s, when the Women's Movement was at its height, suspicion of an empirical approach to social issues was so intense that Nellie Alden Franz had to have her detailed and scholarly *English Women Enter the Professions* (Cincinatti, Ohio,

1968) privately printed at her own expense. Empiricism remains a boo word in left-wing circles, especially if preceded by 'British' or 'English'.

Just as **clarity** has the disadvantage for the revolutionary temperament of requiring the world-shaker to think about what he or she really means, empiricism offers the additional drawback of requiring her or him to accumulate evidence and examples.

Eugenics Perhaps because of the slaughter of so many young men in the 1914–1918 war, there was widespread concern in the England of the 1920s and 1930s with breeding a healthy race. 'Any rational theory of eugenic mating', wrote the reviewer of M. M. Knight's *Taboo and Genetics* in *The Times Literary Supplement* for 1 December 1921, 'ought somehow to educate the right sort of man and the right sort of woman to become attractive to each other.' As early as 1900, W. B. Yeats had shown an obsession with the dangers of producing 'degenerate stock', and his views were echoed by T. S. Eliot and Aldous Huxley.[19]

Anyone expressing comparable ideas in the 1990s would rapidly find themselves at the receiving end of the same kind of taboo that the National Union of Students imposed in the United Kingdom between 1968 and 1989 when they prevented speakers such as Hans Eysenck, Enoch Powell and Burrhus Skinner from visiting university campuses. In 1973, the University of Leeds withdrew the offer of an honorary degree that it had earlier made to William Shockley, the physicist and electrical engineer who had won the Nobel Prize for physics in 1956 for his invention of the transistor. He had drawn attention to the results of intelligence tests conducted in the United States in which Asians came out on top, followed by Jews, followed by Caucasians, but with Negroes coming last. Although Shockley had expressed support for alternative action proposals, this was outweighed by his suggestion that any male of low intelligence, of whatever race, who agreed to a vasectomy, should receive a grant of $1000 for each point he scored below 100 in a recognized IQ rating.

The problem of a possible relationship between **race** and intelligence resurfaced in October 1994 when there was a violent reaction, both from readers and from certain members of staff, against the decision of the liberal American magazine *New Republic* to publish an article by the right-wing sociologist Charles Murray linking race with intelligence. This was based on a book entitled *The Bell Curve: Intelligence and Class Structure in American Life* (1994) which Charles Murray had written in collaboration with Richard Herrnstein, and which argued not only that intelligence is largely inherited but that a low IQ lies at the root of crime, welfare dependency and a host of other problems. In an article refuting the claims put forward by Charles Murray, Andrew Sullivan, the British-born editor of *New Republic*, described the question as 'a taboo issue, filled with potential for hurt and anger, lurking just beneath the surface of American life' and needing to be brought out into the open. The persistence of the 'banned in Boston' syndrome led to *The Bell Curve* becoming an instant best-seller.

See also **contraception** in I, the comments in the **Introduction** on Sir Paul Conlon's claim about the racial origin of London muggers, and the entry **race** below.

Eurocentrism (i) In *The Dictionary of Politically Correct Terms and Phrases* (1992), Henry Beard and Christopher Cerf quote an article by Bayo Oyebade in the *Journal of Black Studies* for December 1990 to illustrate their definition of this as

> the view that Europe was the focal point of human history and that, as a result, the white-male-heterosexual-dominated 'Western' culture is somehow superior to all other ways of life and deserves to hold a privileged place in society.

Twenty years earlier, in the Preface to *The Offshore Islanders* (1972), Paul Johnson had shown that this definition, though accurate, was a shade eclectic. For him, it was the British, and perhaps even the English, who had done most to further the progress of mankind. His contention was that it would be 'time to change the direction of our history' only when

> we are taught by the Russians and the Chinese how to improve the human condition, when the Japanese give us science, and the Africans a great literature, when the Arabs show us the road to prosperity and the Latin Americans freedom.[20]

Eurocentrists express an attitude which is equally taboo in progressive circles when they point out that Islam has developed no theatre, and that there has been no successor produced in the Arab world to the *Thousand and One Nights*. They are equally vulnerable to criticism by multiculturalists when they remind their readers of the fact that the idea of the presumption of innocence and of trial by jury, like that of consciously limiting the power of the state and requiring the government itself to submit to the rule of law, first appeared among English-speaking Protestants. It is equally Eurocentric to observe that no culture untouched by European ideas has applied technology to make everybody in society richer. Nobody but a Eurocentrist would remind her or his readers that the women's movement originated among the Protestant middle classes of the English-speaking and Scandinavian world.

(ii) Eurocentrism is not always a consistent doctrine. Although Roman Catholicism was developed in Europe, it is not Eurocentric to express admiration of it. Eurocentrism involves an appreciation of the role played by Protestant dissent in helping to break the monopoly on intellectual activity exercised by the Church in the Middle Ages. It is not therefore Eurocentric to express considerable enthusiasm for medieval civilization. This had the advantage of being free of the spirit of intellectual inquiry and the cult of the autonomous individual encouraged by Eurocentric modes of thought. Neither can medieval culture be deprived of the credit which it derives among left-wing intellectuals and literary critics from having had no association with capitalism. It remains the height of Eurocentrism to express approval for any aspect of the United States of America or to say that the West won the cold war.

It was quite common, before the movement for multiculturalism and **political correctness** made them taboo, for Eurocentric ideas to be even more openly expressed than they were by Paul Johnson. In his 1958 Presidential Address to the Royal Anthropological Institute, Lord Raglan acknowledged that there had been 'some intellectual activity in Arab countries before 1200'. However, he added, 'since then, no Arab has had a new idea'. He explained this by quoting a remark by Elie Kedourie in the *British Journal of Sociology* for 1957: 'In Islam, the truth is already established and the student is not encouraged to add to the store of intellectual truth.' Similarly, in 1961, the German orientalist von Grunebaum wrote of the 'basic antihumanism' of Islamic civilization, claiming that it was 'not vitally interested in analytical self-understanding' and 'even less interested in the structural study of other cultures, either as an end in itself or as a means towards a clearer understanding of its own character and history'. He attributed this lack of intellectual curiosity to the determination of Muslim civilization 'not to accept man to any extent whatsoever as the arbiter or the measure of things'.[21]

In a similar vein, though without linking this attitude to the desire of Western imperialism to keep Islamic culture in a state of perpetual subjugation, Lord Raglan also quoted John MacMurray in *The Boundaries of Science* (1939):

> The attitude of mind which was characteristic of the Middle Ages could not have produced science. It had no interest in doing so. Medieval Society did not want scientific questions asked and answered because it had no intention of modifying the traditional forms of life.[22]

See below, **heresy**, **images**, **poetry** and **theatre**, and see **political correctness** in III.

Fetishism While the *Encyclopedia Britannica* restricts its discussion of fetishism to the practice of magic, the *Encyclopedia Americana* deals with the sexual aspects as well. In the United Kingdom, earlier taboos on the discussion, presentation and practice of eccentric and non-procreative sex have virtually disappeared. On 30 October 1995, the annual 'rubber ball' was held in London at the Albert Hall. This was not, as American readers might think, part of an advertising campaign on the advantages of condoms as contraceptives. (See **rubber** in III.) It was an event whose participants dressed up in rubber or other fetish garments of their choice. It was attended by over 3000 people, and discussed in detail on the same day in the arts programme *Kaleidoscope* on BBC Radio 4.

In the opening chapter of *Female Fetishism* (1994), Lorraine Gamman and Merja Makinen say that 40 per cent of the purchasers of the magazine *Skin Two*, which they describe as 'opening the closet for "pervs"', are women. However, they later confirm the commonly held view of sexual fetishism as a male rather than a female taste by writing that 'in the West, whereas the majority of the sex fetishists are male, the majority of food fetishists are female'.[23]

See **fat** in V.

Fiction Until the early twentieth century, it was by no means uncommon for a taboo to be placed on reading novels in the morning. Only history or theology were seen as suitable reading matter when the mind was at its most alert, and Jane Austen was clearly taking this taboo as one of her targets when she defined a novel, in Chapter 5 of *Northanger Abbey* (1818), as

> only some work in which the greatest powers of the mind are displayed, in which the most thorough knowledge of human nature, the happiest delineation of its varieties, the liveliest effusions of wit and humour are conveyed to the world in the best chosen language.

George Orwell showed more than a touch of **Eurocentrism** and lack of **political correctness** when he argued in his essay 'The Prevention of Literature' (1946) that 'prose literature as we know it is the product of rationalism, of the Protestant centuries, of the autonomous individual'. In one of his footnotes to the closing chapter of *Dr Bowdler's Legacy* (1992), Noel Perrin also offered an indirect explanation of why imaginative literature in the Islamic world has not so far fulfilled the promise of *The Thousand and One Nights*: he quoted the head of the Morals Division in the Egyptian Interior Ministry as saying: 'Any part of our heritage which includes dirty words should be locked up in a museum, and an expurgated version should be made available to youth.'.[24]

See below, **theatre**.

Ghosts In an article in the *Daily Telegraph* for 17 February 1996, Stephen Pile commented on how attempts to sell the television adaptation of Kingsley Amis's novel *The Green Man* (1986) in the Far East failed because the story contained a ghost, 'which is taboo'.

This is an unexpected statement, since ghosts appear quite

frequently in Japanese literature and cinema. The film *Rashomon* (1951) has a dead man's spirit testifying through a medium.

Hays Code (i) The establishment of the Hays office in the United States of America in 1922, following on from the introduction of censorship into the cinema with creation of the British Board of Film Censors in 1912, meant that certain actions, situations, scenes, subjects and words acquired a taboo status. Sex was limited to kissing, a convention exploited to comic effect in *The Purple Rose of Cairo* (1985), where Mia Farrow, having acquired her whole education through the Hollywood films of the 1940s, does not know what to do when the hero steps out of the screen and indicates that he is available for something further.

If there was a double bed, the same rules had to apply as in billiards: players had to keep one foot on the floor. In the opening shots of *Psycho* (1960), Janet Leigh clearly has spent the afternoon celebrating her successful theft of $40,000 from her employer by indulging in the activity referred to in Stella Gibbons's *Cold Comfort Farm* (1933) as mollocking. However, though in company with her lover, she still has her bra on. Although crime couldn't pay, Goldie Hawn and Warren Beatty are finally allowed to get away with it in *The Heist* (1971; US title *Dollars*). Homosexuality, the theme of Tennessee Williams's play *Cat on a Hot Tin Roof* (1958), was alluded to with such discretion in the 1958 film that many cinema-goers thought that Paul Newman was simply playing an alcoholic. In *Gone with the Wind* (1939), Clark Gable was able to tell Vivien Leigh 'Frankly, my dear, I don't give a damn', only by placing the accent on the verb 'give'. When the film was screened with subtitles in France, my friend and former colleague Ralph Hester was most disappointed to see that this potentially taboo line had become simply: 'Franchement, mon amie, c'est le cadet de mes soucis' (= the least of my worries).

(ii) At the time of his appointment in March 1922 as President of the Motion Picture Producers and Distributors Association, Will H. Hays (1879–1954) was postmaster-general in the cabinet of President Warren G. Harding. He described himself as an 'unreconstructed Middle Westerner from the sticks', and promised that

> this industry must have towards that sacred thing, the mind of a child, towards that virgin thing, the unmarked slate, the same responsibility, the same care about the impressions made upon it, that the best clergyman or the most inspired teacher of youth would have.

He also said that the duty of the film was to 'reflect aspiration, achievement, optimism and kindly humour in its entertainment'.[25]

Hays's influence, reinforced in 1930 by the Motion Picture Production Code, itself the product of the Roman Catholic Legion of Decency, lasted until the late 1950s. Since the 1960s, however, as the 1935 Cole Porter song has it, 'Anything goes'; a phrase prefaced in the song by the remark that 'Good authors too who once knew better words / Now only use four-letter words'. In *Eva* (1962), Stanley Baker and Jeanne Moreau broke the taboo on the presentation of **sado-masochism**. The openness with which what Freud thought was the most frequent of all perversions can be evoked in the literary world is visible in the cover for the paperback edition of Elizabeth Gage's *A Glimpse of Stocking* (1989). It shows the back view of a woman's leg, clad in a black, high-heeled boot with a whip wrapped round it.

The theme of Lesbian sado-masochism was openly treated in the film *The Killing of Sister George* (1969). In 1977, this gave rise to an episode in the BBC comic television series *Me Mammy* that encapsulates the central case for the creation of new guidelines in public entertainment, if not the retention of some taboos. Milo O'Shea, a loyal but worried son looking for a suitable film that his very Catholic mother might enjoy on her visit to London, chooses *The Killing of Sister George* on the very reasonable grounds that it sounds as if it is about the martyrdom of a nun who chooses to die for her faith. They enter the cinema just as Beryl Reid is forcing Susannah York to show her sexual submission by eating the contents of an ash-tray.

In their article in Ray B. Browne's *Forbidden Fruits: Taboos and Tabooism in culture* (1984), Gershaw Kaufmann and Lev Raphael claim that 'just as sexuality was tabooed in Freud's time, shame is still under taboo to-day. The paradox is that there is shame about shame.' It may be that there are other adults who are as embarrassed as I am by sex scenes in the cinema or on television, and there is currently much discussion in the United States about the possibility of revising the present system of classification, especially since so many children under the age of 17 are successful in getting in to see the R-rated movies from which they are theoretically banned. It might indeed help viewers as squeamish as I am myself if a series of voluntary guidelines could be adopted in the classification of films. These could take the form of a series of symbols which went from

> o, indicating as much sex as there is in *Citizen Kane* (1941), *Casablanca* (1942), *Les Enfants du Paradis* (1944), *Brief Encounter* (1945); to
> *, indicating the degree of conventional and consensual sex to be found in *The Graduate* (1967); to
> **, warning the grandfather taking his grandchildren to see *Rob Roy* (1994) in the hope of finding the same entertaining and ritualized violence which makes the Errol Flynn version of *Robin Hood* (1938) so enjoyable, that he will also see Rob and his wife copulating in the heather with the woman on top, and Rob's wife being raped in the Italian fashion; through to
> *** for bondage, murder, and extensive shots of Sharon Stone in simulated orgasm in *Basic Instinct* (1992).

In addition to being signs whereby individuals and groups communicate with one another, taboos also offer society a way of expressing certain values. As with other signs, taboos can sometimes be eloquent by their absence. By allowing everything to be shown, we implicitly accept the equivalent in art and entertainment to the presumption of innocence which governs the criminal law. It is not the novelist, playwright or film-maker who has to show that a product is harmless. It is the state which has to prove the product has harmed specific individuals.[26]

Heresy The names which embody the difference between blasphemy and heresy are those of Giordano Bruno (1548–1600) and Galileo Galilei (1564–1642). The former did indeed teach what modern astronomists have every reason to think is the case: that space is boundless and our solar system only one of a vast number which we are not yet able to count. Where he differed from Galileo, as he differs from the modern scientist, was in moving from matters for which publicly ascertainable evidence is available, to maintaining, as he did in his *Spaccio della bestia* (1584), that there was no reason to worship God and that the scriptures are no more than fantasy. It was for this, as much as for his denial of the view that the earth is the centre of the universe, that Bruno was burned at the stake in Rome in 1600.

Bertold Brecht was probably right to argue, as he did in the second version of *Galileo Galilei* (1948), that Galileo was a kind of Vicar of Bray of the scientific world, a time-serving coward who failed by his refusal to stick to what he knew to be the case to place modern science on firm ethical foundations. For taboos do more than function as signs. They are also about power. They are ways of thinking developed and imposed in order to prevent people from developing certain ideas and experiencing certain emotions. Although there is no evidence that the societies analysed by Hutton Webster in *Taboo: A Sociological Study* (1942) were consciously seeking to impose their authority on their members, their taboos were just as much a means of social control as those later developed by the Catholic Church. It may have been their realization of this similarity which led the Polynesian islanders, almost immediately after they had been introduced to the Bible, to describe it as a book about taboos.[27]

In 1981, the Law Commission for England and Wales stated that the criminal law is not an appropriate vehicle for upholding religious tenets. It thus totally reversed the view which Justice Bayley had expressed in 1823 when he told Susannah Wright that 'Christianity is part and parcel of English law, and we cannot permit that point to be argued here'. It also invited a parallel with Hutton Webster's other remark that the taboo system, which reached the acme of its development in Polynesia, did not long survive the opening up of the islands to European settlement.[28] Intellectually organized Christian belief has, it is true, lasted rather longer in Western Europe and North America, even when exposed to the ideas of Galileo and Darwin. It is, however, unlikely ever to be quite the same again.

See above, **blasphemy**; and **political correctness** in III.

Homosexuality (i) By modern standards, the reference in the Old Testament to the sin which led the Lord to rain fire and brimstone on the towns of Sodom and Gomorrah is remarkably discreet. *Genesis*, 19 merely describes how the arrival of two angels in Sodom, leads to the incident described in verses 4 and 5:

> But before they lay down, the men of the city, even the men of Sodom, compassed the house round, both old and young, all the people from every quarter;
>
> And they called upon Lot, and said unto him, Where are the men which came in to thee this night? bring them out unto us, that we may know them.

Not all modern readers will be as well acquainted with the Biblical sense of the verb 'to know', in the sense of to 'enjoy sexually', as Mrs Sarah Kirkby Trimmer was when she undertook in 1782 to produce a version of the Bible which she called a *Sacred History*, and which would be suitable for children. She cut the phrase 'that we may know them', and, as Noel Perrin writes in *Dr Bowdler's Heirs*, 'continues the chapter unchanged until Lot offers the crowd his daughters instead, and that verse she removes entirely'.[29]

Mrs Trimmer's way of referring to the incident thus gives a different impression to the one left by Robert Alter in the essay 'Sodom as Nexus: The Web of Design in Biblical Narrative', which he contributed to Jonathan Goldberg's 1994 collection *Reclaiming Sodom*. What the verb 'to know' evokes in Robert Alter's mind is the spectacle of 'all the male inhabitants of Sodom, from adolescent to dodderer, banging on Lot's door and demanding the right to gang-rape the two strangers'.[30] It would nevertheless have been equally dramatic if the inhabitants of Sodom had accepted Lot's offer in *Genesis*, 19:8: 'Behold now, I have two daughters which have not known man: let me, I pray you, bring them out unto you, and do ye to them as is good in your eyes.'

It will be recalled that when the angels later succeed in persuading Lot to leave Sodom before it is destroyed, his wife turns back to take a last look at the city, and is turned into a pillar of salt (*Genesis*, 19:26). This incident inspired a short poem penned by the English poet Rober Liddell while he serving in the Western Desert during the Second World War:

> Where once Lot's wife looked back in horror,
> To see God's lightning blast Gomorrah,

Today the Sodom sunshine blisters
Queen Alexandra's nursing sisters.

Her fate leaves Lot alone with his daughters, whose husbands have refused to leave the city. Thinking that this will mean that they will never conceive, they make their father drunk so that he will sleep with them and thus enable them to have children. The incident inspired a number of biblical paintings, especially by Flemish artists interested in painting the pink plumpness of naked female flesh. It also forms the theme of Ward Moore's short story 'Lot', first published in 1953 in *The Magazine of Fantasy and Science Fiction.* Mr Jimmon, husband to Molly and father of two sons and one daughter, Erika, has planned what to do when the expected nuclear holocaust takes place. He leaves Los Angeles in a station wagon laden with steel bows, flints, lures, hooks, thread and other articles needed for survival in the subsequent collapse of civilized life. When well away from the city, he stops for gas at a remote filling station, and finds a pretext to leave Molly and his two sons behind. He then drives away with the attractively nubile Erika.

In the Old Testament narrative, **incest** performed in order to perpetuate the human race is nevertheless seen as wrong, just as 'survival cannibalism' is deplored in *Ezekiel*, 5:10 (see **cannibalism** in I). The child born to the elder of Lot's two daughters is Moab, that to the younger Ben Ammi, who becomes the father of the children of Ammon (*Genesis*, 19). References to Moab and Ammon are almost always unfavourable: 'Moab is my washpot; over Edom will I cast out my shoe' (*Psalms*, 60:8); 'Surely Moab shall be as Sodom, and the children of Ammon as Gomorrah, even the breeding of nettles, and saltpits, and a perpetual desolation' (*Zephaniah*, 2:9).

The Old Testament offers no explanation of why Lesbianism should come to have been associated with Gomorrah.

(ii) Edward Sagarin commented in *Societies of Deviants in America* (1969), speaking of homosexuality in general,

> few subjects for so long completely enshrouded in silence have so quickly become so widely discussed. It strains one's memory to recall that the word was literally banned from the pages of *The New York Times* in the 1950s, only to make its appearance there a few years later in the headlines.[31]

As Richard Kramer put it, writing in *The New York Times* on 3 February 1994, 'Mart Crowley's *The Boys in the Band* flung open a door 25 years ago. The gay closet hasn't been closed since.' As late as 1957, however, the Lord Chamberlain objected to the word 'camp' in the text of John Osborne's *The Entertainer*.

The openness with which homosexuality can now be mentioned has not been universally welcomed. Jonathon Green reported in his *Encyclopedia of Censorship* (1988) that the opponents of 'secular humanism' in the United States of America insist on a 'total taboo' in the classroom on all discussion of sex, 'and especially homosexuality'. In England, the persistence into the twentieth century of the taboo on the discussion or literary treatment of homosexuality can be gauged from the fact that nobody in Nancy Mitford's *The Pursuit of Love* (1945), a novel in which the action takes place in the 1920s and 1930s, can persuade Uncle Matthew to explain what Oscar Wilde is supposed to have done. In the first version of Terence Rattigan's *Separate Tables* (1954), the original offence of the disgraced major was homosexuality. It was in order to placate propriety that he was later made into a molester of women in cinemas.[32] It was a sensible decision, in that it did not distract the attention of the audience from the theme of failure which gives unity to the play. Somerset Maugham's *Of Human Bondage* (1915) derives comparable benefit from the fact that the object of Philip Carey's hopeless passion is a woman, Mildred Rogers, when the original was almost certainly a boy.

(iii) Oscar Wilde's claim that the love that dare not speak its name is

> such a great affection of an elder for a younger man as there was between David and Jonathan, such as Plato made the very basis of his philosophy and such as you will find in the sonnets of Michelangelo and Shakespeare

was made in a speech from the dock at the trial in 1895. It places him by the side of André Gide, the first author openly to proclaim himself a homosexual and justify his tastes by rational argument. The dialogues entitled *Corydon*, privately printed in 1909 and openly published in 1922, argued that the practice was perfectly natural and widely accepted in cultures in no way inferior to our own. There was no attempt to prosecute Gide, though it was noticed that some of the friends who gave total intellectual support to his campaign invited him less frequently to their houses when their sons reached puberty.

Gide's description in his autobiographical *Si le grain ne meurt* (1926; *Unless it die*) of how early his sexual tastes had showed themselves inspired another short poem:

> The best known work of André Gide
> Is called 'If Perish Not The Seed';
> Indeed, his own peculiar taste
> Ensures it does all go to waste.

See **homosexuality** and **paedophilia** in I, **Lesbianism** and the entry on *The Well of Loneliness* below.

Images In *Totem and Taboo* (1919), Freud quotes Sir James Frazer's view that prohibitions on making images of living things stemmed from the desire to ban magical practices. It was an attitude which lasted for some time. In Arthur Miller's *The Crucible* (1953), the possession of a 'poppet' was seen as clear proof of witchcraft. In seventeenth-century Massachusetts, dolls were not for playing with. They were for sticking pins into in order to make your enemies feel ill.

The belief in magic and witches played a disastrous role in the history of Christianity. However, it did not finally hinder the development in Christendom of either sculpture or painting. Initially, the Church followed the commandment in *Exodus*, 20:4: 'Thou shalt not make unto thee any graven image, or any likeness of any thing that is in heaven above, or that is in the earth beneath, or that is in the water under the earth.' The second-century theologian Origen (*c.* 185–254) confirmed the view also expressed in *Exodus*, 20:4 by arguing that 'painters are makers of images, an art which attracts the attention of foolish men, and which drags down the eyes of the soul from God to earth'. He even went so far as to glory in the accusation directed against the early Christians by their pagan opponents that they lacked altars, idols and temples.

However, Origen fell into disfavour for other reasons, possibly because he was suspected of pantheism, perhaps because he became one of those who 'made themselves eunuchs for the kingdom of heaven's sake' (*Matthew*, 19:12), but more probably because of the accusation that he interpreted scripture in too allegorical a manner.[33] This led the Council of Alexandria, in 399, to forbid Christians to own or to read his works, thus opening the way for Pope Gregory the Great (540–604) to proclaim that images could play a useful role in teaching laymen, especially if they were illiterate, to appreciate the Christian message.[34] The increasing acceptance of the visual arts by the Western Church was another factor in the division between Rome and Byzantium, where the iconoclasts of the eighth and ninth centuries became increasingly successful in imposing their views, so much so that in 726 there was an Imperial edict forbidding all religious images. In the West, however, the progress of the visual arts from the eleventh century onwards was subsequently encouraged in Catholic Europe by the movement known as the Counter-Reformation. The Council of Trent (1545–63) went even further when it positively recommended the use of images on the walls of churches and elsewhere in order to educate the faithful. The acceptability of the visual arts in a religious context was also strengthened by the popular belief, already current in the Middle Ages, that St Luke the Physician (*Colossians*, 4:14) had drawn pictures not only of the Virgin Mary but of Christ himself.[35] In 1653, Jan Vermeer (1632–75) was admitted to the guild of St Luke, of which he twice served as headman.

There is no ban on representational art in the text of the Koran, and even a legend that the Prophet specifically protected a mural of Mary with the infant Jesus on one of the buildings in Medina. However, Muhammad also began his career as a teacher and prophet by commanding that the idols at the shrine at Medina should be destroyed, and *Sura* V.65–6 of the Koran places idolaters on the same level as apes and swine. The traditional dates for Muhammad's life – 570 to 632 – put him relatively close to Gregory. As Muhammad Zafrulla Khan puts it in his introduction to the 1971 translation of the Koran, 'the Prophet himself was not conversant with reading and writing', [36] and he may not have known about the change in Christian teaching on the role that images could play in the education of the faithful. His followers were nevertheless as anxious as the Prophet himself had been to show that Muslims were different from Christians. A taboo on the representation of men or animals by the visual arts, which the Christians were now accepting, was a handy way of doing it. It was expressed in two of the *hadiths*, or sayings attributed to Muhammad, and which became current in the centuries immediately succeeding his death in 632. These read: 'Whosoever makes an image, him will Allah give as a punishment the task of blowing the breath of life into it'; and 'Those who make these pictures will be punished on the Day of Judgement by being told: "Make alive what you have created" '.[37]

The official rationale for the Islamic ban on representational art thus lay in the belief that it was presumptuous for men to carry out the process of creation which was the exclusive privilege of God. However, the ban was not absolute, and had much more effect on religious than on secular art. The depiction of human and animal figures was acceptable as decoration on small objects for daily use, so long as there were no shadows cast, and there was a parallel in this respect with the early art of the Christian world. H. W. Janson points out in his *History of Art* (1962) that the section of the *Très Riches Heures du Duc de Berry* (1410) illustrating what happens in the countryside in October contains the first example in the visual arts since the world of classical antiquity of figures which cast a shadow.

David Talbot Rice comments in *Islamic Art* (1965) that the effectiveness of the ban on representational art in a religious context from about 690 onwards can be judged from the fact that no figures are included in the mosques either of the Dome of the Rock or at Damascus. However, a more relaxed attitude can sometimes be found in parts of the Muslim world more distant from its original birthplace. As H. W. Janson points out, the Mongols who invaded Persia and Mesopotamia were familiar with the rich tradition of Buddhist religious art in India and China, and did not share the official horror at the very idea of a picture of Muhammad. There is a splendid sixteenth-century Persian portrait of the ascension of the Prophet into heaven, with 'only one small concession to Islamic iconoclasm: the prophet's face is left blank, evidently because it was thought too holy to be depicted'.[38]

The ban nevertheless had a clear influence on the evolution of the visual arts in the Islamic world, and had one very positive effect in the impetus it gave to the arts of calligraphy and carpet-making. The ban may have been easier to enforce because of the absence from the areas of Persia, Mesopotamia, Egypt and North Africa which adopted Islam as their major religion of the paints and pigments which provided the basis for the art of Western Europe. In that respect, the taboo was successful in emphasizing how Muslims differed from Christians, and also served to bring out an even more fundamental difference between what H. G. Wells called the 'communities of the Will' and the gentler cultures which accepted more feminine values. For as Kenneth Clarke observed in *Civilisation* (1969), the aggressive, nomadic cultures of Israel, Islam and the Protestant North, which conceived God as male, produced very little religious imagery, and in most cases positively forbade it. Hellenistic and Catholic culture, on the other hand, with their cult of the goddess Athena and of the Virgin Mary, helped to inspire a tradition in which the portrayal of the gods in human form has played a major role in the visual arts.[39]

Incest While incest as an activity may have attracted some of the strongest taboos, the same is not true of incest as a literary theme. While this may confirm Freud's view that 'the basis of taboo is a forbidden action for which there exists a strong inclination in the unconscious',[40] it is also a sign of the awareness which writers have always had that the best way to attract and retain an audience is by stories with what the advisers to potential authors of romantic novels call 'strong human interest'.

Imaginative literature is indeed rich in examples of the dramas of incest, from Sophocles's *Oedipus Rex* to Webster's *The Duchess of Malfi*, and from Sartre's *Les Séquestrés d'Altona* (1959; *Altona*) to the discovery by Muriel, in Alan Bennett's 'Soldiering On' (1987), that her late husband's relationship with their daughter Margaret went beyond a father's normal feelings for 'Daddy's little girl'.[41] Incest between brother and sister, with the passionate encounter between Sigmund and his sister Sieglinde leading to the birth of the hero Siegfried, is central to the plot of Wagner's Ring cycle, while two of the most virile heroes in European literature, Fielding's Tom Jones and Beaumarchais's Figaro, come close to marrying their mothers.

Other twentieth-century examples sometimes have an unexpected source, as in the short story 'Une Confession' published in 1930 by the very rationally minded French novelist Roger Martin du Gard, and the fiction of the twentieth-century English Catholic novelist, Evelyn Waugh.

The Martin du Gard short story describes a brief but very passionate affair between a biological brother and sister in which the point is very specifically made that the fact of having lived together for seventeen years, added to their natural ties of blood, immediately creates between them the same kind of physical intimacy enjoyed by couples who have been happily married for a comparable time.[42] In Evelyn Waugh's 1943 *Put Out More Flags*, Barbara Sothill has always been very fond of her brother, Basil Seal. The appalling young evacuee, Doris Connolly, who herself carries something of a flame for Basil, immediately notices this, and asks Barbara if Basil is 'her bloke'. When Barbara replies, 'But Mr Seal is my brother', Doris immediately replies, 'her pig eyes dark with the wisdom of the slums': 'But you fancy him don't you?'; a reply which attracts the indignant comment from Barbara that she 'really is an atrocious child'.

Barbara's comment follows so closely on Doris's remark that it is impossible for the reader not to suspect that her diligently repressed feelings for Basil Seal do go beyond mere sisterly affection. The episode in the 1943 novel takes on even more significance in the short story 'Basil Seal Rides Again', where Basil has to come down very firmly on the immediate sexual interest which Charles Albright, whom he has strong reasons for suspecting might be his illegitimate son, arouses in his daughter Barbara Seal, and Sonia Trumpingon speaks for the reader when she says:

> You Seals are so incestuous. Why do you suppose you are so keen on Barbara? Because she's just like Barbara Sothill. Why is Barbara keen on Charles? Because he's *you*.[43]

See **incest** in I, and **homosexuality** (i) above.

Lady Chatterley's Lover (i) Between October 1926 and January 1928, D. H. Lawrence wrote three versions of his most famous novel. He toned down his defiance of one taboo, but continued to reject two others. It was this rejection which was to make the 1960 trial of Penguin Books the most important test case for the history of literary censorship in the United Kingdom.

In the first version, Arthur Mellors was to have remained what he was in social terms: Clifford Chatterley's gamekeeper and nothing more. He would, therefore, have spoken all the time in broad Nottinghamshire dialect, and the novel would have broken the taboo which said that there was something wrong with passionate and sincerely felt sexual relationships between members of totally different social classes. This still existed in the England of the 1920s, and paralleled the attitude traditionally adopted in Balinese society. There, a relationship between a woman and a man from a lower caste was 'equated with bestiality, and the offence was treated with the same severity as primary incest'.[44] However, Lawrence's nerve failed him, and he gave Mellors a past history in which he had had a grammar school education, had learned French and had held a commission in the British Army during the First World War. He could therefore express himself in standard English when he chose or needed to do so. This slightly reduced the linguistic shock to English social prejudices.

The text of the novel which came up for trial in October 1960 nevertheless continued to break two other taboos: the one which said that sexual experiences, especially of women, could not be described in detail; and the one which banned from acceptable literature words such as 'shit' and 'piss'. In one of his fairly frequent lapses from grammar school English, Mellors uses these when he says to Constance: 'Tha'rt real tha art! Tha'rt real, even a bit of a bitch. Here tha shits an' here tha pisses: an' I lay my hand on 'em both an' like thee for it.' Mellors also uses the word 'cunt', whose meaning he has to explain to Constance. He also has to tell her what 'balls', in the sense of testicles, are. Whether somebody brought up in the country, as Constance had been, would really have been so linguistically innocent as Lawrence suggests is an open question. It is, however, fairly easy to believe that neither her husband nor her upper-class lovers had awoken her sexually, and this was the real point of the novel.

(ii) The importance of the *Lady Chatterley* trial in a legal context lay in the fact that it was the first case of its kind in which a book could be defended against the charge of obscenity

> if it is proved that the publication of the article in question is justified as being for the public good on the ground that it is in the interests of science, literature, art, or learning, or of other objects of general interest.

The Obscene Publications Act, the law in which this change had been incorporated, had been passed only recently, in 1959, and had been sponsored in the House of Commons by the liberal politician Roy Jenkins. The only prosecution so far brought under its other provisions was of a slim volume entitled *The Ladies Directory*, published by Frederick Charles Shaw. He had been charged and found guilty of publishing an article likely to 'deprave and corrupt' people having access to it. His defence was that anyone reading *The Ladies Directory*, a guide to London prostitutes, would already have been pretty corrupt anyway. However, this defence was not accepted, and he was sent to prison for nine months. A different but perhaps less honest defence was presented in the *Lady Chatterley* trial, and was accepted.

Penguin Books assembled an impressive array of literary witnesses, including Graham Hough, Helen Gardner, Richard Hoggart and Rebecca West, all of whom defended Lawrence's novel on the ground of its literary merit. They occasionally agreed with Mr Griffith-Jones, for the prosecution, that it was not Lawrence's best novel, and that certain passages in it were unconvincing. But they all contended that it was a major work by one of the best-known English writers of the twentieth century. Had Lawrence's most famous admirer, F. R. Leavis, agreed to appear in court as well, it is quite possible that the book would have been defended solely on the grounds that its overall literary merit outweighed any harm which its publication might do.

Leavis, however, declined to appear, and a different defence was presented. Richard Hoggart, faced by some quite stiff cross-questioning, stuck to his view that Lawrence was essentially a Puritan, while the Reverend Donald Tytler insisted that the novel was 'a most impressive statement of the Christian view of marriage'. It was statements of this kind which led to a certain ambiguity in the 'not guilty' verdict, and which underlined the similarity with Flaubert's acquittal in 1857. He had got off because of the argument presented by his lawyer that *Madame Bovary*, far from being an immoral book which might encourage a married woman to take a series of lovers, was a terrible warning against the dangers of adultery. The acquittal of Penguin Books was based on a comparably limited reading of *Lady Chatterley's Lover*, and the taboo on the presentation of sexual activity in the novel retained at least some official status. Such activity could be described, so long as the ideological framework of Christianity was respected.

For we shall never know whether the jury gave its 'not guilty' verdict because it thought that Lawrence's novel was thoroughly immoral, but was redeemed by its literary quality, or whether it agreed with the words of another witness that *Lady Chatterley's Lover* was 'a book that all Christians should read'. If that was the case, the publication of the book was justified not on the aesthetic grounds introduced by the 1959 Act, but because it was a highly respectable work of art, as conventional in its morality as *Madame Bovary* undoubtedly is in the depressing portrayal that it gives of extra-marital sex. If, however, *Lady Chatterley's Lover* is really to be judged 'a book that all Christians should read', the only way in which they could be seriously recommended to do so is in order to receive a rather curiously phrased warning.

The plot describes how Constance Chatterley, whose husband Clifford has been made impotent by a war wound, finds sexual satisfaction with his gamekeeper, Arthur Mellors. It tells how she falls in love with Mellors, becomes pregnant by him, and ends the novel by going off to live with him in Scotland. As an expression of the essentially pagan philosophy underlying all Lawrence's mature work, it is highly convincing. But Constance had married Clifford before the war, and before he had undergone the accident which, as Jake Barnes observes in Hemingway's *The Sun Also Rises* (1926), 'is supposed to be very funny'. She had therefore taken the vow to remain faithful to him 'for better for worse, for richer for poorer, in sickness and in health', and it is hard to see how a Christian could justify her breaking it. For anyone who had read both *Lady Chatterley's Lover* and the 1552 prayer book, the respect paid to the traditional Christian teaching on sex lay more in the breach than in the observance.

The defence was, of course, helped by the question put to the jury by Counsel for the Prosecution. For when Mr Griffith-Jones asked them: 'Is it a book that you would have lying around in your own house? Is it a book that you would even wish your wife or your servants to read?' he did more than reveal how different the world of senior barristers was from that of ordinary people. He reminded everyone that taboos on what you are allowed to read and think are the expression of the power which one group of people exercises over another. Penguin Books had been faithful to one of its traditions by publishing *Lady Chatterley's Lover* in a complete and unexpurgated edition. It had also put the novel on sale at 3*s* 6*d* (= 18 pence; 50 US cents), roughly the price in 1960 of a packet of cigarettes. The working class could no longer be protected even by its poverty from what Mr Griffith-Jones saw as its worst instincts and most depraved passions.

(iii) In an article published in *Encounter* in September 1961, Andrew Shonfield pointed to two passages in the novel which implied that Arthur Mellors had done more than give Constance Chatterley a number of highly enjoyable orgasms through normal vaginal intercourse. He had, if the text of the novel were studied carefully, broken a more serious taboo by buggering her as well, just as he had earlier buggered his now estranged wife, Bertha Coutts.

The passage which Andrew Shonfield quoted from Chapter 16, page 258 of the 1960 Penguin edition, does not impose this particular reading. What it says is that Mellors had made Constance experience a 'reckless, shameless sensuality' which 'shook her to her foundations, stripped her to the very last, and made a different woman of her'. The extreme vagueness as to what actually happened is one of the features which links *Lady Chatterley's Lover* to the 'amusing' books which Mr Norris lends William Bradshaw in Christopher Isherwood's *Mr Norris Changes Trains* (1934) and whose authors 'despite their sincere efforts to be pornographic, became irritatingly vague in the most important passages'.

It is also this vagueness, coupled with a remark by Sir Clifford Chatterley, which suggests a possible confusion, perhaps in Lawrence's own mind, between two very different types of sexual activity. For what Sir Clifford mentions in Chapter 17, on page 280 of the Penguin edition, is the rumour that Mellors had used his first wife 'in the Italian way'. This is a conventional term not for sodomy but merely for vaginal intercourse from the rear, a mode of making love so pleasurable that it was widely condemned by the medieval Church, and held to be so useful to the perpetuation of the species that it was recommended by Lucretius as an excellent means of ensuring conception.[45] The paintings on the Greek vases reproduced in K. J. Dover's *Greek Homosexuality* (1978) almost invariably show the man penetrating the woman from the rear. However, it is not clear whether this is vaginal intercourse or sodomy, the latter activity being a practice used in the ancient world and elsewhere as a means of contraception.

Andrew Shonfield's article set off a lively discussion in which John Sparrow maintained that Lawrence was endorsing the practice of buggery or sodomy, and thus recommending the revival of a practice closely associated in the past with devil worship. John Sparrow's contention inspired a short poem recited with some glee in the more frivolous Middle Common Rooms of the Oxford of the early 1960s:

> Stern guardian of our morals, Warden Sparrow,
> Pray keep us in the sexual straight and narrow;
> Teach us discretion in our sexual roles,
> As Warden of all bodies *and* All Souls.

See also **homosexuality** and **sado-masochism** in I.

Lesbianism K. J. Dover draws attention in *Greek Homosexuality* (1980) to the lack of any hard evidence that the poetess Sappho (*c.* 650 BC) had sexual relationships with her circle of pupils and admirers on the island of Lesbos.

The term does not appear in the standard dictionaries until the mid-1940s. Proust popularized the adjective 'saphique', and his two principal male characters, Charles Swann and the Narrator in *A la recherche du temps perdu* (1913–36; *Remembrance of Things Past*, or, more accurately, 'The Quest for Lost Time'), suffer torments of jealousy at the idea that the woman they love is enjoying sexual relationships with other women. By giving to Volumes 9 and 10 of the original fifteen-volume edition of *A la recherche du temps perdu* the title *Sodome et Gomorrhe* (*The Cities of the Plain*), Proust inspired the clerihew:

People thought with horror
Of Sodom and Gomorrah
Till they were given a boost
By Proust.

It was nevertheless not quite accurate, since he presents both male and female homosexuality with considerable disapproval.[46]

French literature had already taken the initiative in talking about a form of sexual activity apparently so prevalent in nineteenth-century Paris that Baudelaire considered giving the title *Les Lesbiennes* to the collection of poetry finally published under the title *Les Fleurs du Mal* (1857; *The Flowers of Evil*). In the posthumously published *La Religieuse* (1793; *The Nun*) Diderot presented Lesbianism as an unnatural but inevitable consequence of the seclusion of women in convents. In Laclos's *Les Liaisons dangereuses* (1784), the Marquise de Merteuil uses the attraction which she feels for the charms of the young Cécile Volanges as another weapon with which to taunt the Vicomte de Valmont and increase his jealousy.

There are a number of ways in which Madame de Merteuil can be seen as a forerunner of the more radical wing of the women's movement, and she would have had some sympathy with the **S**ociety for **C**utting **U**p **M**en founded by Valerie Solanas in the 1970s. In the late nineteenth century, as Elaine Showalter points out in *Sexual Anarchy* (1990), Lesbianism was closely linked in the popular mind with feminism. She quotes the English journalist Edward Carpenter as writing in 1887 that

> the movement among women towards their own liberation and emancipation, which is taking place all over the civilised world, has been accompanied by a marked development of the homogenic passions among the female sex.[47]

The intensity of the disapproval directed against Lesbianism in the nineteenth and early twentieth centuries may perhaps have stemmed from its association with the women's movement. It is equally tempting to explain it in Freudian terms. Lesbian displays are a standard attraction in brothels, and descriptions of Lesbian love-making a compulsory feature in pornographic literature. An article entitled 'Treading Hilariously on Taboo Turf', in the *Daily*

Telegraph for 1 March 1996, praised the treatment of Lesbianism in the film *Gazon Maudit* (1994), screened in London under the title *French Twist.* The anonymous reviewer picked out a remark by one of the male characters – 'I don't mind two women doing it, as long as they fit me in' – and commented that this 'echoed the view of virtually every red-blooded man since time began'. The frankness of this recognition confirms Freud's view that our fiercest condemnations are directed against those activities by which we are most attracted, and which we find most fascinating.

It would be hard to imagine a male equivalent to what the English novelist Simon Raven calls a 'queens' moll', in the sense of a woman who has a lot of male homosexual friends whom she would never consider as potential sexual partners. Men may have a more tolerant attitude to Lesbianism than most married women have towards homosexuals. Unlike women, they do not see them as potential home-breakers or seducers of their sons. But their general attitude is that Lesbianism is a waste of good talent, a challenge which they have little doubt of their ability to overcome.

See **Lesbianism** in I, **bugger** and **pussy** in III, and the entry below on *The Well of Loneliness.*

Menstruation On 5 July 1995, the *Guardian* commented of a programme entitled *First Sex*, to be presented that evening on Channel 4, that

> Apart from those coy and unreal ads involving blue dye, wings and roller skates, which must give many an innocent lad a very strange idea of girls' working, menstruation is usually a taboo subject on TV and indeed in the world at large.

References either to menstruation or to pre-menstrual tension are indeed rare in imaginative literature, especially in English, but they do exist. In letter 141 of Laclos's *Les Liaisons dangereuses* (1784), the Vicomte de Valmont makes it fairly clear to the Marquise de Merteuil that he is less occupied than usual with his new mistress, la Présidente de Tourvel, because she is having her period, and the ignorance about sexual matters which Cécile Volanges has retained throughout her convent education is underlined when she does not realize from the fact that she has not had her period that she is pregnant. In Marcel Aymé's comic novel *La Jument Verte* (1949; *The Green Mare*), the hostess of the local inn is propositioned by Napoleon III while he is on a state visit, but replies, 'Sire, je suis dans le sang' (Your Majesty, I'm having my monthlies). She was clearly not one of those women of whom Alex Comfort wrote in *The Joy of Sex* (1972) and who are at their randiest during menstruation.[48]

In *Of Human Bondage* (1915) Somerset Maugham was seen as very daring to make Philip Callow's mistress, Sally Athelny, think that she is pregnant because her period is late, but the taboo was not broken until the publication of David Lodge's *The British Museum Is Falling Down* (1965). There, the day which Adam Appleby spends in London is dominated by his worry that his wife, Barbara, by whom he has already had three children, may be pregnant again. Her period is three days late, and the tension is maintained until the very end of the novel. It was the first work in which Lodge dealt with the taboo which the Roman Catholic Church, into which he was born in London in 1933, placed on artificial methods of **contraception**. Lodge treated the same subject in greater depth and detail, and in a less consistently comic manner, in *How Far Can You Go* (1977; US title *Snakes and Ladders*). It is surprising, when one considers how many men and women must have been preoccupied since the beginning of time with whether or not an act of sexual congress has resulted in conception, that the subject had to wait for so long before being given a central place in a work of fiction. There are references in Zola's *Germinal* (1885) to the preference of the miners in the north of France for sex with girls who have not yet started to menstruate, and who therefore cannot become pregnant. However, there is no reference to menstruation in Flaubert's *Madame Bovary* (1857), in spite of the fact that his heroine visits her young lover, Léon, on a regular monthly basis.

See above, **bodily functions** and **contraception**; see also **menstruation** in I and **loo** in III.

Mixing In the French classical theatre of the seventeenth century, it was considered wrong to mix comedy with tragedy. The works of Corneille and Racine thus present nothing comparable with the Porter's scene in *Macbeth*.

While there are no rules in the contemporary cinema against any kind of mixing of themes or atmosphere, traces left by earlier conventions can be found in the almost audible shudder which runs through the audience when, at the ending of *Sunset Boulevard* (1950), it is suddenly revealed that Erich von Stroheim, who had been presented up to that point as Gloria Swanson's chauffeur, has also been one of her husbands.

See **mix** in II.

Music See below, **pigs**.

Nuclear weapons During the cold war, there was a virtual taboo among liberal intellectuals on any discussion of nuclear weapons in any terms other than those of horrified rejection.

It was an attitude which Hermann Kahn evoked when he wrote in *On Escalation* (1960) of how some people see the attempt to think rationally about such weapons as 'at best an academic and useless exercise, and at worst immoral if not psychopathic'.[49] The caricature of him in Stanley Kubrick's *Dr Strangelove or How I Learned to Stop Worrying and Love the Bomb* (1963) gave memorable expression to this attitude, and it is hard to find any film, novel or play which breaks the taboo described by Kahn. If by any chance any author does attempt it, as David Fraser did in *August 1988* (Collins, London, 1983), a total absence of reviews ensures that his book vanishes into oblivion.

Nudity (i) Although the Greek statues were painted, they were not clothed, any more than were the athletes who competed in the Olympic games. In his second volume of lyrical essays, *Noces* (1938, *Nuptials*) Albert Camus commented on how the naked body then disappeared from Western culture until the cultural revolution of the 1920s and 1930s brought it back to the beaches of the Mediterranean.

While this is not entirely true as far as art is concerned, the idea of appearing without any clothes on, or as scantily dressed as Europeans, Americans or Australasians now are on beaches and camp sites, does not seem to have become acceptable until the second half of the twentieth century. The Olympic games were religious festivals and nudity was a feature of daily life in classical

Greece only in the *gymnasion*, a word derived from the Greek adjective *gymnos*, 'naked'. The custom whereby men removed all their clothes before taking exercise in the *gymnasion* led it to perform an important semiotic function, especially in the Greek colonies of the third and second centuries BC. Natives who succeeded in proving their acceptability to the Greek-speaking governing class had to prove their alienation from their original background by exercising in the *gymnasion* naked.[50] While Roman statues were normally clothed, either in military uniform or a toga, Michelangelo's statue of David in Florence is quite naked, a fact which led the town council of Jerusalem, as *The Independent* for 22 July 1995, put it, to decline the gift of a replica for fear of offending 'the ultra-orthodox and Arab communities'. They preferred, instead, Andrea del Verrocchio's more modest and well-clothed bronze. The 1822 Achilles statue of the Duke of Wellington in London was originally naked, but the genitals were subsequently covered over.

While the taboo on presenting the male genitalia in repose has now virtually disappeared, it remains an offence under the United Kingdom Obscene Publications Act to show an erect penis. It was nevertheless reader pressure which compelled *Women: the magazine for women by women* to replace its centre pages of naked erect phalluses by unexcited men in their underpants. The *Guardian* for 27 January 1995 also reported how the magazine's readership had fallen from the 250,000 who had bought the first issue to 60,000, perhaps an indication that the search for sexual excitement through print and images is a male rather than a female characteristic.

(ii) The Judeo-Christian view that there is something shameful about the naked body goes back to the first discovery that Adam makes when he and Eve have eaten from the tree of the knowledge of good and evil. As the Lord God is 'walking in the garden in the cool of the day', they hide themselves from his presence and later (*Genesis*, 3:21) make coats of skin to clothe themselves. The link between the ban on nudity and the fear of sex is fairly visible in medieval art. While the child Christ is often depicted with no clothes on at all, there is invariably a veil round the loins of the male and female characters. When Michelangelo unveiled his *Last Judgement*, above the altar of the Sistine Chapel on 31 October

1541, he was subjected to violent criticism by the papal master of ceremonies, Biago de Cesana, who said that it was 'better suited to a bathroom or roadside wineshop than to the chapel of the Pope'. He consequently added draperies. As late as 1931, United States Customs at New York tried to ban a series of postcards of the original, undraped frescos, but lost their case on appeal.[51]

The idea that nudity is inseparable from sex, and therefore has something shameful about it, is a strange one. As James Laver points out in *Modesty in Dress* (1969), anyone visiting a nudist camp can testify that complete nakedness is totally anti-erotic once the initial shock has worn off. The idea nevertheless lasted a surprisingly long time, and recurs in totally pagan contexts. Joe Lampton, the hero of John Braine's *Room at the Top* (1957), goes into a frenzy of jealousy when his mistress, Alice Aisgill, accidentally reveals that she had, as a young woman, posed as an artist's model. His reaction would not have surprised either Arnold Bennett or his readers, and the remark in *The Pretty Lady* (1916) that the girls in the armament factory in the First World War 'have to take off stitch after stitch from their bodies in one room and run in their innocence and nothing else to another room where the special clothing is kept'[52] shows a taste for euphemism which offers an odd contrast with the taboo-free horrors taking place at the same time on the Western Front. As late as the 1940s, girls in French Catholic boarding schools had to wear large white sheets when they went to have a bath. A girl stepped in, spread the sheet round the rim of the bath and washed herself without catching sight of her own naked body.

While the depiction of female nudes has been one of the traditional functions of the visual arts in the West (though see below, **prostitution**), male nudity has been a much less common theme. In 1880, the painting of the back view of a naked man drying himself after his bath which the French impressionist Gustave Caillebotte (1848–94) submitted to the fifth Impressionist exhibition in Paris was not shown, and temporarily disappeared when sent to a later exhibition in Brussels.

Pigs 'Islamic countries', wrote Stephen Pile in an article in the *Daily Telegraph* on 17 February 1996 discussing the failure of the BBC to sell its programmes abroad, will not accept musicals or even plays with a lot of incidental music, and pigs are right out. You might get away with a pig crossing the road in the background, but a single close-up of a porker means the deal is off. The Arab states even rejected Miss Piggy. But then, they also reject anything controversial or that makes adverse comments on friendly governments. They also dislike kissing, nudity, divorce and mysticism.

See also **pork** in II.

Poetry The denunciation of poetry in Plato's *Republic* is based on the idea put forward in Book Ten that if a man 'really knew about the things he represented, he would devote himself to them and not to their representation'. It differs from the taboo on representational art in Islam only in the sense that there is no mention of a final day of judgement. Plato's insistence that 'the artist who makes an image of a thing knows nothing about the reality but only about the appearances' has the same implication that it is wrong to pretend to knowledge which you do not possess.

For Plato, all forms of representational art are to be discouraged. Art, in his view, can successfully imitate only vices. It is quite unable to reproduce 'the reasonable element and unvarying calm' of the virtuous man. Since we ought always to be able to control our emotions, there should be a ban on art on the grounds that it encourages us to give way to anger, lust or grief. Comic drama is particularly reprehensible since 'bad taste in the theatre may insensibly lead you into becoming a buffoon at home'. The contention in the closing section of Book Ten of the *Republic* is that 'the only poetry that should be allowed in a state is hymns to the gods and paeans in praise of good men'.[53] This supports Karl Popper's argument, in the first volume of *The Open Society and its Enemies* (1946), that Plato was a precursor of twentieth-century totalitarianism.

Aristotle shows a more circumspect attitude in restricting censorship to works likely to be seen by the young. When he asks in the *Poetics* whether we should 'carelessly allow children to hear any casual tales which may be devised by casual persons, and to receive into their minds ideas for the most part the very opposite of those we would wish them to have when they are grown up?', he is quite near the modern attitude which sees a justifiable role for censorship in the need to protect the young. His argument that 'anything received into the mind at that age is likely to become indelible and unalterable; so that it is most important that the tales which the young first hear should serve as models of virtuous thought' is frequently heard in discussions on the role of television.

See above, **images**.

Prostitution The Old Testament treats the presence of harlots as a fact of life. In *Genesis*, 38:15, not knowing who she is, Judah takes his daughter-in-law Tamar to be a harlot, and she conceives of him the twins Pharez and Zarah. In *Joshua*, 6:17, only the harlot Rahab, who has acted as a spy for the Children of Israel, is spared from the slaughter at the taking of Jericho. There is no doubt about what Doll Tearsheet does for a living in Henry IV Parts i and ii, and the entry **trousers** in V gives details of what the whores of Venice wore as a means of identification in the sixteenth century. However, in the nineteenth-century, matters changed. Although completed as early as 1897, George Bernard Shaw's *Mrs Warren's Profession* could be performed only privately at the Stage Society in 1902 and was not licensed for public performance until the 1920s. This may have been because it also included **incest** as one of its themes, though not, in spite of Shaw's admiration for Ibsen, the **venereal disease** which would have been a high professional risk both for Mrs Warren and her clients. In 1967, the Performing Arts Theatre at Michigan State University was dissuaded by the Dean's Office from printing the last word in the title of John Ford's *'Tis pity she's a whore* (1633). The omission was so intriguing that the play attracted large audiences. In the Paris of 1947, Jean-Paul Sartre's play *La Putain respectueuse* (*The Respectful Prostitute*) was also not allowed to be advertised under its full title. The version put on the advertising hoardings, *La P*** respectueuse*, quickly gave rise to the use of the term 'une respectueuse' to describe a prostitute.

One of the great *causes célèbres* of nineteenth-century French art concerned less the presentation of a naked woman in Edouard Manet's *Olympia* than the identity of the model. *Olympia* was exhibited at the 'Salon des Refusés' in 1865, and evoked such hostile criticism that two policemen had to be stationed in front of it to prevent enraged spectators from hitting the canvas with their walking-sticks. This was only partly because of a newly developed objection to the depiction of totally nude women. This had shown itself for the first time in the previous year when Manet's *Le Déjeuner sur l'herbe* had been criticized for depicting a naked women sitting with two fully clothed men, a feature of the painting which nowadays evokes criticism from certain feminists. There was, however, another and more important reason for the reaction to *Olympia*. The model was well enough known in the *demi-monde* of contemporary Paris for Mallarmé to describe her as a 'wan, wasted courtesan', and to praise Manet for his realism in 'showing to the public, for the first time, the non-traditional, unconventional nude'.[54]

From this point of view, Manet was the victim of the punishment said to be visited on any artist original enough to break the established taboos surrounding his subject-matter. There were at the time hundreds of pictures of naked women in the Louvre, and none of the canvases on which they figured had ever needed to be protected by the police. What the protests against *Olympia* expressed were the taboos which constantly threaten to transform the presentation of the world in the verbal and visual arts into a series of stereotypes. Oscar Wilde described the objections of the nineteenth-century critics of realism as 'the rage of Caliban seeing his face in the glass'. On 4 April 1986, Wlademar Januszlak's article on *Olympia* in the *Guardian* developed this idea in a way which offered a further explanation for the attempt by conservatively minded forces in society to use taboos to restrict artists' ability to choose their subjects and to write or paint as they please.

In *Olympia*, Januszlak argued, the waitress in the *Folies Bergère* has become the naked courtesan,

> and you, Mr 19th century bourgeois, have become her client. It is your flowers she is receiving. You are making the black cat on the bed bristle. You she looks up at.
>
> No wonder this Olympia was so famously rejected from the 1865 salon. The top-hatted bourgeois of Paris recognised himself as the accused, and it is perhaps because we the audience are still, technically speaking, the accused, that we continue to have difficulty in looking Manet's art squarely in the face.

For a Marxist critic, it is an example of an artistic taboo being used in the same way as intellectual and literary taboos are used: to keep a particular social group in power by denying other people the right to look critically at its pastimes, its privileges or its ideology.

See above, **heresy** and **nudity**, and **venereal disease** below.

Race There is nowadays an implicit taboo in the United Kingdom on mentioning the racial origin of anyone accused of a crime or brought before a court. It is also the height of **political incorrectness** to argue that certain characteristics are associated with particular races.

See **eugenics**, above; see also **dago** and **nigger** in III and **white** in V.

Rape What was then the strict taboo on mentioning the crime in print gave rise in 1957 to the seizure by the British Customs authorities of a book entitled *Rape round our Coasts*. The author commented: 'I hope they enjoy it. It's about soil erosion.' A comparable misunderstanding led in 1979 to the banning from a school library in the United States of a book called *Making it with Mademoiselle*, until it was discovered to contain a set of instructions about sewing.[55]

The taboo would have surprised pre-nineteenth-century writers. There is no doubt about what has happened to Lavinia when she comes back on stage in Act II of *Titus Andronicus*. The situation in the twentieth century has gone back to this less inhibited age. When Howard Brenton's *The Romans in Britain* was produced at the National Theatre in London in 1980, there were a number of protests about the scene in which one of the Roman soldiers tries to bugger one of the native Britons, only to comment 'Arseful of piles. Like fucking a fistful of marbles.'

The word occurs frequently among supporters of the campaign organized by Andrea Dworkin and Catharine MacKinnon against what they see as the threat to women contained in pornography. Their general thesis is that marriage is legalized rape, and in *Letters from a War Zone* (1988), Andrea Dworkin writes that 'Romance . . . is rape embellished with meaningful looks'. Catharine MacKinnon claims that 'To be about to be raped is to be gender female in the process of going about life as usual'.[56]

Sado-Masochism It is quite frequent for sado-masochism to be treated comically, which is perhaps another way of expressing its taboo status. The only example which I have come across of its being treated with sympathy and sensitivity is the radio play *Over the Hills and Far away*, broadcast on BBC Radio 4 in December 1983, and based on John Bird's 1976 biography of the Australian composer Percy Grainger. In Thomas Otway's *Venice Preserved* (1682), when Antonio, 'a fine speaker in the Senate', visits the courtesan Aquilena and pretends to be her dog so that she can whip him, the intention is clearly to make the audience laugh. The idea that sado-masochism – unlike **homosexuality** – is inherently funny is also central to Christopher Isherwood's *Mr Norris Changes Trains* (1934). It is equally the case with the character of Widmerpool in Anthony Powell's twelve-volume *A Dance to the Music of Time* (1951–75), and more directly in that of Somerset Lloyd-James in Simon Raven's ten-volume *Alms for Oblivion* sequence (1964–76).

There are nevertheless exceptions, especially in pornography, where the slightest hint of humour is always enough to ruin the effect. One of the best-known serious novels is Leopold von Sacher-Masoch's *Venus in Pelz* (1870; *Venus in Furs*). This is now easily available, and there is even an audio-tape. Indeed, as Gilles Deleuze observes, there is nothing to censor in it,[57] especially since the novel ends with the main character, Severin, being cured of what is finally presented as an illness. There are indeed few cases of sado-masochists 'coming out' and proclaiming the legitimacy of their sexual tastes in the way that homosexuals do. In the first volume of his *Confessions* (1782–1789), Jean-Jacques Rousseau takes himself with his customary seriousness when describing the emotions he felt when being chastised by Madame de Warens, but does not present his tastes as in any way to be imitated. The Marquis de Sade (1740–1814) preaches endlessly, but the sex is so overlaid by the philosophy that it is hard to take seriously. The most honest and most disturbing account of how a man acquired the taste for sexual ill-treatment is T. E. Lawrence's description in

The Seven Pillars of Wisdom (1926) of how he was flogged and buggered by his Turkish captors.

The poet Swinburne is quite humourless in *Lesbia Brandon* and other works which he published under various pseudonyms. No hint of humour is allowed to ruffle the narrative in the best-known work of masochistic flagellation, *Harriet Marwood, Governess*, originally published in Paris by Maurice Girodias's Olympia Press in 1960, and judged to have sufficient literary merit to be republished by the Grove Press, New York, in 1967. Homosexual sado-masochism had earlier been treated in French literature by Proust, who in *Le Temps retrouvé* (*Time Regained*, 1927) makes his narrator peep though a curtain in a homosexual brothel and see the Baron de Charlus being flogged. The scene is comic only by contrast to what the reader knows of how Charlus behaves elsewhere in the novel, and he himself insists on being taken absolutely seriously.

There has never been the same kind of taboo on either the practice or the presentation of **sado-masochism** as on homosexuality or Lesbianism. This may be because it has tended to be not only a minority taste but one pursued in private. 'Operation Slammer' described in the entry **sado-masochism** in I, is the only case to have come to court. The photographs of Robert Mapplethorpe gave homosexual sado-masochism a publicity which it had not before enjoyed, especially when Jesse Helms, the Republican Senator for North Carolina, destroyed a copy of the catalogue of the exhibition *The Perfect Moment* on the floor of the Senate in June 1995. This led to the cancellation of the exhibition that was to have been held in the Corcoran Gallery, Washington, DC, as well as to a court case brought by the sponsors of *The Perfect Moment* against the city of Cincinnati when it tried to cancel the exhibition as well. A largely working-class jury accepted the argument of a number of eminent art critics that Mapplethorpe's work was not pornographic, a decision which led Jeremy Bernstein, writing in *The New York Review of Books* for 16 November 1995 to comment, rather strangely, that

> cultural taboos have in the past century tended to collapse not long after a furious battle for their maintenance was apparently won, since the resulting exposure and publicity inoculated the

population against any possible shock, and eventually eroded fear.

The entries above on ***Lady Chatterley's Lover*** and below on ***Ulysses*** suggest that taboos of this kind collapse even more quickly after an appeal against their enforcement has succeeded in the courts.

See also the entry **sado-masochism** in I and on the **Hays Code** above.

Sexual activity The selective nature of taboos, and their tendency to concentrate on sex, soon made themselves felt when Herman Melville came to prepare the manuscript of *Typee* (1846). This was at one and the same time his first book and the first book to present the phenomenon of taboo to the American reading public. As Leon Howard commented in his notes to the 1968 Northwestern University Press edition, 'Melville was still in the stage of learning about taboos, and he may have discovered as many while revising *Typee* as when writing it'.

Most of the excisions that Melville had to make concerned the attitude which the inhabitants of the Polynesian island of Typee had towards sex. The relatively slight differences between the first, bowdlerized edition and the version now available is an indication of how sensitive American readers of the 1840s were assumed to be. (See **God** in III.) The sensitivity of the American public in this respect parallels the impression given in what was known as 'The Green Book' of how the British public was expected to react at the time when the BBC was being established. The Green Book was the creation of the first Director-General of the BBC, Lord Reith (1889–1971; held office from 1922 to 1938) and listed the topics seen as unsuitable for broadcasting. It was not withdrawn until 1963, and owed its name to the fact that it was bound in green covers. It stated that

> Programmes must at all costs be kept free of crudities. There can be no compromise with doubtful material. It must be cut. There is an absolute ban upon the following: jokes about lavatories, effeminacy in men, immorality of any kind, suggestive references to honeymooning couples, chambermaids, fig leaves, ladies' underwear (e.g. 'winter draws on'), animal habits (e.g.

'rabbits'), lodgers, commercial travellers. When in doubt – cut it out.

The entry on 'Broadcasting Censorship' in Jonathon Green's *Encyclopedia of Censorship* mentions other notes of guidance, dated as recently as 1973 and 1979, and which laid down what he calls 'taboo topics' in light entertainment and allied areas, including the royal family and the Church. In the United States, there was a comparable list of 'Do's and don'ts' drawn up in October 1927 by the Studio Relations Department on the advice of Will H. Hays (see above, **Hays Code**). These excluded pointed profanity, licentious or suggestive nudity, illegal drug trafficking, any suggestion of sexual perversion, white slavery, miscegenation, sex hygiene and venereal disease, actual childbirth, children's sex organs, ridicule of the clergy, and willed offence to any nation, race or creed. They were completed by twenty-six further topics, including under the 'Be Careful' category

> the use of the flag; a variety of larcenous crimes; murder; sympathy for criminals; sedition; rape; prostitution; women and men in bed together; wedding night scenes; surgical operations; seduction; the institution of marriage as a whole; anything to do with law enforcement and its officers, etc.[58]

Although the guidance for film-makers does implicitly recommend at least a partial ban on violence by the mention which it makes of murder, it is still sex which is the main target. This was also the case in the strict Calvinist tradition within which Lord Reith was brought up, where no taboo ever seems to have been placed on reading the chapters in the Bible in which, as I *Samuel*, 29:5 puts it 'Saul slew his thousands, and David his ten thousands'. There has also been no criticism in Islamic countries of the passage in *Sura* XLVII.4–8 of the Koran which reads

> When you meet the unbelievers, smite their necks,
> then, when you have made wide slaughter among them,
> tie fast the bonds

and which goes on to promise Paradise to 'those who are slain in the way of God'.

There have nevertheless been alterations to the order in which topics from which viewers are seen as needing protection are listed in a recent change to the 1984 Video Recordings Act. An amendment introduced by David Alton, the Liberal Democrat MP from Liverpool, means that the law now states that the British Board of Film Censors

> shall in making any determination as to the suitability of video work, have special regard, among other relevant factors, to any harm that may be caused to potential viewers' through their behaviour to society, by the manner in which the work deals with: a. criminal behaviour, b. illegal drugs, c. violent behaviour or incidents, d. horrific behaviour or incidents, e. human sexual activity.[59]

Sexual displays All forms of sexual behaviour constitute an offence if performed in public, the argument being that what is then termed 'an exhibition' is likely to cause a breach of the peace. Since this interdiction also applies to heterosexuals, homosexuals cannot claim to be victims of discrimination.

Theatre (i) In spite of the view of some of its moralists that the imitation of the passions by actors and actresses on stage might provoke a more serious imitation of them by members of the audience in real life, the Christian Church did not play a major role in inhibiting the development of the theatre. Indeed, the performance from the tenth century onwards of liturgical dramas, followed by the rise in the thirteenth and fourteenth centuries of the Miracle and Mystery Plays, created a tradition exploited to the full by the playwrights of the Renaissance.

Certain limitations were nevertheless imposed by the Church, and it was not until after the Restoration of 1660 that women were allowed to appear on the English stage. Shakespeare must have found some remarkably gifted boys to play Cleopatra and Lady Macbeth, to say nothing of Doll Tearsheet, Goneril and Regan, or Tamara Queen of the Goths in *Titus Andronicus*. In 1673, Molière could not be buried in consecrated ground, and even as late as 1730, Voltaire was moved to protest with great vehemence against the taboo which led to the corpse of the actress Adrienne Lecouvreur being disposed of in open ground under the cover of darkness. But Racine defied the teaching of the Jansenists to become France's greatest tragic dramatist, and it was only in the Cromwellian period that the theatres of England were closed for religious reasons.

(ii) The absence from the theatres of Western Europe or North America of plays originally written or performed in the Middle East does not betoken a lack of curiosity as to what happens elsewhere. Japanese No plays and Chinese opera are quite widely performed, and in the late 1980s the Hindu epic the *Mahabharata* was very popular in Australia as well as England. It is more a reflection of the effectiveness of the taboo on theatrical activity evoked by William O. Beeman's entry on the Middle East in the *Cambridge Guide to World Theatre*:

> The Islamic conquest of the region beginning in the 7th century marks a period with little mention of any dramatic or theatrical activity. Orthodox Islam tended to view dramatic presentation as suspect, since it involved the depiction of personages who were imaginary or deceased. Thus the most conservative religious officials labelled it idolatry, an illicit attempt to create an alternative reality to that created by God. Just as images of human beings and animals were banned from plastic and pictorial arts under Islam, human images were banned from depiction in public performance.

Although this may well have been true in the past, an obvious exception in the twentieth century is in the large number of films made and distributed by the Egyptian cinema.

See above, **fiction**.

Ulysses (i) James Joyce's most famous novel was published in Paris in 1921 by Sylvia Beach's Shakespeare Company, but banned from entering the United States until 1933 and the United Kingdom until 1937. In January 1923, 499 copies of the third printing of 500 sent to England from Paris to the Egoist Press, which had already distributed the first and second printings, were seized by the Customs authorities at Dover and burned in the presence of the publishers and their agent.

In the United States, however, Random House challenged the exclusion order in 1933, and their case was upheld by Federal Judge John M. Woolsey. It was confirmed in the Federal Court of Appeal by Justice Augustus Hand, who delivered the historic verdict that

> Art cannot advance under compulsion to traditional forms, and nothing in such a field is more stifling to progress than limitation of the right to experiment with a new technique. . . . We think *Ulysses* is a book of originality and sincerity of treatment and that it has not the effect of promoting lust.[60]

Welcome though the judgment was, the implication nevertheless remained that *Ulysses* would not have been licensed for import if it had had the effect of exciting lust. There is thus a similarity both with the verdict in the *Lady Chatterley* case and with the comment made by Justice Donahue in 1946 when he dismissed the attempt made by the state of Massachusetts to ban Kathleen Winsor's *Forever Amber*, namely that 'while the novel was conducive to sleep, it was not conducive to sleep with a member of the opposite sex'. D. H. Lawrence expressed a more vigorous disapproval of the treatment of sex in *Ulysses* when he wrote to his wife Frieda that 'the last part of it is the dirtiest, most indecent, obscene thing ever written'.[61]

According to Jonathon Green's *The Encyclopedia of Censorship* (1988), the acquittal on 6 July 1966 of Burrough's *The Naked Lunch* marked the end of the last attempted prosecution of a literary work in the United States.

See **hedonism** in I and **violence** below.

Venereal disease The openness with which AIDS is discussed contrasts with the refusal in the nineteenth century to allow any direct mention of venereal disease. Although the text of Ibsen's *Ghosts* (1881) contains some fairly broad hints that the disease from which Oswald is suffering is hereditary syphilis, the consensus among modern critics is that the play should be seen, as the entry in *The Cambridge Guide to World Theatre* (1988) puts it, as an analysis of 'the more insidious social diseases it exposes'. Nineteenth-century critics were less convinced of its symbolic meaning. In 1891, the suggestion in *Ghosts* that Oswald was suffering from venereal disease led the critic of the *Daily Telegraph* to describe it on 14 March as 'simply abominable' and to say that

> the play last night is 'simple' enough in plan and purpose, but simple only in the sense of an open drain; of a loathsome sore unbandaged; of a dirty act done publicly; or of a lazar house with all its doors and windows open.[62]

The interest aroused by Ibsen's play can be judged from the fact that over 500 articles were published on *Ghosts* within a year of its performance. Although the critics who attacked *Ghosts* were as chary as Ibsen himself of actually naming what one of Miss Manners's correspondents (see **illness** in III) calls 'a social disease', they had little hesitation in denouncing him for breaking what was clearly a powerful taboo. In 1917, Eugène Brieux's play *Les Avaries*, translated as *Damaged Goods*, and which also dealt with venereal disease, was initially banned. However, it later ran for almost 300 performances. During and after the Second World War, no punches were pulled in the films warning members of the British armed services against the dangers of contracting venereal disease. Some men, and not a few women, were put off sex for life. In 1919, according to the Royal Commission on Venereal Diseases, 450,000 people were infected with syphilis in London alone.

The virtual disappearance in the late twentieth century of taboos on the presentation of 'social diseases' in the theatre is visible in the success enjoyed both in the United Kingdom and the United States of Tony Kushner's *Angels in America* in the early 1990s. Subtitled 'A Gay Fantasia on National Themes', it dealt quite fully with the impact of AIDS on American society. In 1987, the American critic and biographer Edmund White had already commented that 'if Yeats was right in thinking sex and death were the only two topics worthy of adult consideration, then AIDS wins hands down'.[63] There has, so far, been only one attempt to ban *Angels in America*. It took place in Charlotte, South Carolina, in 1996, and failed.

See **oral sex** in I and **homosexuality** in I and above.

Violence (i) It is an illusion, argues Norbert Elias in *The Civilising Process* (1938), to think that we live in a violent society. It was not until the late seventeenth century that officially organized groups within Western society ceased to question what we now accept as being the state's monopoly on the use of force. Feudal aristocrats saw it as their right to exact vengeance in blood, and took a long time to accept the legitimacy of the charge that fighting a duel 'disturbed the King's peace'. In the Middle Ages, the nobility saw their delight in the joy of battle sanctified by the descriptions in the *Chansons de Geste* of how warriors hacked down trees, took castles by storm and massacred both their enemy and his dependants.

The violence of life in sixteenth- and seventeenth-century England is reflected in episodes such as the putting out of Gloucester's eyes in Act IV of *King Lear*, and the rape and mutilation of Lavinia in *Titus Andronicus*. We regard the taboos against violence as the norm, and are horrified when they are broken. Even after the triumphs of the middle class had put an end to the perpetual war of all against all, gentlemen in the West End of London in the late nineteenth century wore coats with heavy astrakhan collars to protect themselves from being garrotted as they walked from their club to the theatre.

(ii) In an article entitled 'Less Tarantino, more Chatterley', published in *The Independent* on 6 June 1995, Robert Dole linked an attack on the depiction of violence in films such as *Reservoir Dogs* with a defence of a more open depiction of sex in the cinema. 'The mistake which the Right makes', he wrote,

> is to lump violence along with sex. Sex is a completely different matter – and contrary to the views of the moralisers, there is nothing like enough of it in the cinema. By way of illustration, answer this simple query on American films of the last five years: how many times has the actor Tim Roth (a) had nookie; (b) killed people? Whereas decapitating people is illegal, immoral and unusual, sleeping with them is often beneficial, pleasurable and certainly universal. One is bad, the other is good.

See above, the entries on ***Lady Chatterley's Lover***, **sexual activity** and ***Ulysses***; **hedonism** and **oral sex** in I; the remarks about the insistence on sex in the second section of the Introduction and in the third section of the Conclusion; and the comment in **uncircumcised** in V about the ambition of the old to control the sexuality of the young.

Well of Loneliness, The The condemnation of Lesbianism in *Romans*, 1:26 is very discreetly worded – 'For this cause God gave them up unto vile affections: for even their women did change the natural use into that which is against nature' – and there is no explicit mention in *Genesis*, 13:10 or elsewhere in the Bible of female homosexuality as one of the sins which led the Lord to destroy Sodom and Gomorrah. Proust's use of the term '*gomorréenne*' as synonymous for Lesbian has not established a usage noted in any standard French dictionary.

The attraction exercised by certain tabooed activities may be an element in the frequency of Lesbian displays in brothels frequented by men. It may also have been the firmness with which this interest in female homosexuality is officially repressed which explains the violence of the reaction to *The Well of Loneliness.*

For when, in the summer of 1928, the relatively unknown novelist Radclyffe Hall published the first novel in English openly to describe female homosexuality, she gave full justification to Macaulay's remark that he knew of 'no spectacle so ridiculous as the British public in one of its periodical fits of morality'. James Douglas, in the *Sunday Express*, wrote that he would 'rather give a child a bottle of prussic acid to drink than allow him or her to read the book', and the publisher, Jonathan Cape, offered to withdraw it. The Home Secretary at the time was William Joynson-Hicks, the model for the character occupying the same functions in Evelyn Waugh's *Vile Bodies* (1930), and of whom the Customs officer comments when he impounds the manuscript of Adam Fenwick-Symes's autobiography at Dover: 'Particularly against literature the Home Secretary is. If we can't stamp out literature in the country, at least we can stop it being brought in from outside.'

An unexpurgated edition of *The Well of Loneliness* was prepared by the Pegasus Company in Paris, and could be ordered by post for 25*s*, more than half the weekly wage at the time of an elementary school teacher. When the first consignment of the book arrived at Dover, it was seized and both Jonathan Cape and Pegasus charged under the 1857 Obscene Publications Act, defined in 1869 by Lord Cockburn when he said:

> The test of obscenity is this, whether the tendency of the matter charged with obscenity is to deprave and corrupt those

whose minds are open to such immoral influences and into whose hands a publication of this sort may fall.

At the trial, at Bow Street Magistrates' Court on 8 November 1928, Sir Charles Biron refused to hear expert evidence as to the book's literary merit, and ordered the copies impounded to be destroyed. On appeal, at the Quarter Sessions, the case was again lost when Bernard Shaw's offer to produce for James Douglas one child, of either sex, one bottle of prussic acid and one copy of *The Well of Loneliness*, and see what he did, was not accepted.

Until 1949, the book could be read in England only in the version published by Covici-Friede in New York in 1928, and illegally imported. No ban was placed on it in America, where by 1934 it had been reprinted eighteen times. In her autobiography *Memories of a Catholic Childhood* (1967), the American novelist Mary McCarthy described how she satisfied the curiosity aroused in her grandmother and great-aunt by the wide press coverage of *The Well of Loneliness* in the United States by explaining to them what Lesbians did. This was not information she could have derived from the text of the novel.

The report that Sir Charles Biron was 'especially upset by a portrayal of Lesbianism "as giving these women extraordinary rest, contentment and pleasure"'[64] suggests that he had not read the book. Unlike her creator, the main character in the novel, Stephen Gordon, is rarely happy in her loves, and the story ends with her dying of the grief she causes herself by giving up her adored Mary Llewellyn in order to enable her to marry Martin Hallam. In 1949, the book was republished in England without causing any reported offence and without leading to any lawsuit. In 1957, an abridged version was read on the BBC radio programme *A Book at Bedtime.*

There is a contrast in this respect between radio and television. In January 1995, an episode of the Liverpool soap opera *Brookside* in which two women, Viv and Beth Jordache, exchange a passionate kiss, was broadcast shortly before nine in the evening, but censored before the programme was repeated in the omnibus edition the following Sunday afternoon.

NOTES

1 Ian Buruma, *The Wages of Guilt: Memories of War in Germany and Japan*, Vintage, London and New York, 1985, p. 88.
2 Buruma, *The Wages of Guilt*, pp. 211 and 215.
3 J. L. H. Keep, *Last of the Empires*, Oxford University Press, Oxford, 1995, p. 130.
4 Joan Smith, *Misogynies*, Faber and Faber, London, 1989, p. 87.
5 See Rollin M. Perkins and Ronald N. Boyce, *Criminal Law*, third edition, Foundation Press, Mineola, NY, 1982, p. 475.
6 See Ralph C. Chandler, *The Constitutional Law Dictionary*, ABC–CEIO Services, Santa Barbara, 1985, p. 86.
7 Mary Douglas, *Risk and Blame: Essays in Cultural Anthropology*, Routledge and Kegan Paul, London, 1994, p. 3.
8 Quoted in the article on 'Blasphemy' in Jonathon Greene's *Encyclopedia of Censorship* (New York, 1988), Facts on File, Oxford, 1992.
9 See Richard Webster, *A Brief History of Blasphemy*, Orwell Press, London, 1994, p. 64.
10 *London Review of Books*, 6 August 1995, review of Thomas Kunkel, *Genius in Disguise*, Random House, New York, 1955. Ruth P. Rubenstein, *Dress Codes: Meanings and Messages in American Culture*, Westview Press, Boulder, CO, 1995, p. 17.
11 Quoted in Kenneth Plummer, *Sexual Strategies: an Interactionist Account*, Routledge and Kegan Paul, London, 1975, p. 70.
12 See Norbert Elias, *The Civilising Process*, translated by Edmund Jephcott, Basil Blackwell, Oxford, 1978, pp. 149, 156 and 89.
13 Noel Perrin, *Dr. Bowdler's Legacy*, David Godine, Boston, 1992, pp. 134–5.
14 Collection 'Points', Éditions du Seuil, Paris, 1972, p. 43.
15 Françoise Barret-Ducrocq, *Love in the Time of Victoria* (1989), translated by John Howe, Penguin Books, Harmondsworth, 1992, pp. 127–35.
16 Letter quoted in Ronald Clarke, *The Huxleys*, Heinemann, London, 1968, p. 74.
17 Barret-Ducrocq, *Love in the Time of Victoria*, p. 127; for Sartre's novels and short stories, see Philip Thody, *Sartre*, Macmillan Modern Novelists, London, 1993, pp. 89–90.
18 See *La Force de l'âge*, Gallimard, Paris, 1963, p. 104. For more detail on the frequency of *coitus interruptus* in Sartre's fiction, see Thody, *Sartre*, pp. 89–90, 115, 127.
19 See John Carey, *The Intellectuals and the Masses: Pride and Prejudice among the Literary Intelligentsia 1880–1939*, Faber and Faber, London, 1992, and *The Hidden Huxley: Contempt and Compassion for the Masses*, edited by David Bradshaw, Faber and Faber, London, 1994.

20 First published by Weidenfeld and Nicolson, London, 1972; Penguin, Harmondworth, 1975, p. 22.
21 Quoted in Talal Asad, *Anthropology and the Colonial Encounter*, Humanities Press, Atlantic Highlands, NJ, 1973, p. 116.
22 *Man: the Journal of the Royal British Anthropological Institute*, Vol. 88, March 1958, pp. 142–7.
23 Lorraine Gamman and Merja Makinnen, *Female Fetishism*, Lawrence and Wishart, London, 1994, p. 146.
24 Perrin, *Dr Bowdler's Legacy*, p. 213.
25 See the entry Hays, Will H. in Greene's invaluable *Encyclopedia of Censorship*.
26 The relaxation of the rules which prevented British film-makers from presenting what they saw as an accurate and full account of human experience has been studied in detail by Anthony Aldgate in *Censorship and the Permissive Society: British Cinema and Theatre, 1955–1965*, Oxford University Press, Oxford, 1995. He underlines how much resistance there was to what we now see as a necessary and justified liberalization, and quotes Alan Sillitoe's view, expressed at the time that he was adapting his novel *Saturday Night and Sunday Morning* (1957) to the cinema, that 'censorship in the British film industry is in its own way as hidebound as that of the Soviet Union'.
27 Hutton Webster, *Taboo: A Sociological Study*, Stanford University Press, Stanford, CA, 1942, p. 368.
28 Webster, *Taboo*, p. 366.
29 Perrin, *Dr Bowdler's Legacy*, p. 117.
30 Jonathan Goldberg, editor, *Reclaiming Sodom*, Routledge, New York and London, 1994, p. 33.
31 Quoted from Edward Sagarin, *Society of Deviants*, Crown Publishers, New York, 1960, in Erving Goffman, *Stigma: Notes on the Management of Spoiled Identity* (Routledge, London, and Prentice Hall, New York, 1963), Penguin, Harmondsworth, 1968, p. 195.
32 See Geoffrey Mansell, *Terence Rattigan: A Biography*, Fourth Estate, London, 1995.
33 The matter is fully, not to say exhaustively, discussed in the *Catholic Encyclopedia*.
34 See E. H. Gombrich, *The Story of Art*, Phaidon, Oxford, 1950, Chapter VIII. For a fuller discussion of the question, see the entry 'Iconoclasts' in the 1911 edition of the *Encyclopedia Britannica*.
35 See H. W. Janson and Anthony F. Janson, *The History of Art* (1962), Harry N. Abrams, New York, 1991 edition, p. 178.
36 See *Quran*, translated by Muhammad Zafrulla Khan, Curzon Press, London and Dublin, 1971. Dr Khan points out that the word *quran* –

his transliteration of the Arabic – means that which is read, recited, rehearsed or otherwise carried by mouth, and that the book is 'literally the word of Allah'.

37 Quoted from Ron Landau, *Islam and the Arabs*, Allen and Unwin, London, 1958, p. 212.

38 Janson and Janson, *The History of Art*, p. 308.

39 See *Civilisation*, BBC Publications, London, 1969, p. 177.

40 *Totem and Taboo* (1919), Penguin Books, Harmondsworth, 1938, p. 54.

41 'Soldiering On' is one of the *Talking Heads* monologues, originally performed by Stephanie Cole and broadcast on BBC television. It is available in book form by Faber and Faber, London, 1990. In his autobiographical fragment *Les Mots* (1963; *Words*), Sartre speaks of his lifelong interest in brother–sister incest, and points out how it recurs in the relationship between Boris and Ivitch in *Les Chemins de la liberté*. He comments that Franz and Léni, in *Les Séquestrés d'Altona*, are the only characters in his work to do anything about it.

42 See the Pléiade edition of Martin du Gard's complete works, Paris, 1954, p. 1122.

43 Evelyn Waugh, *Basil Seal Rides Again* (1953), reprinted in *Work Suspended and other stories*, Penguin, Harmondsworth, 1982, p. 277. In spite of the physical and psychological similarities to his own younger self which Basil immediately notices in Charles Sothill, the reader is left in intriguing doubt as to whether Basil's warning to his daughter is not also the expression of a fatherly affection possessive enough to verge on the incestuous.

In a letter to his daughter Margaret Fitzherbert on 28 October 1963, Waugh wrote:

> Nancy Mitford says that no young girl would be put off marrying by the supposed discovery that she was engaged to her brother. True? Ask some of your wilder, irreligious friends so that I can refute her. I should have thought it was a deep-rooted taboo. (*The Letters of Evelyn Waugh*, edited by Mark Amory, Penguin, Harmondsworth, 1982, p. 612.)

44 See Margaret Mead's entry on incest in the *International Encyclopedia of the Social Sciences*, 1968.

45 See p. 18 of Richard Zachs, *History Laid Bare: Love, Sex and Perversity from the Ancient Etruscans to Warren G. Harding*, HarperCollins, New York, 1994 and p. 61 of Rattray Taylor, *Sex in History*, Panther Books, London, 1965. It will be recalled that when, in the 1995 film of *Rob Roy*, Archibald Cunningham rapes Rob Roy's wife, he does it from the rear, and she immediately becomes pregnant from that single encounter.

46 See my study of the issue in Philip Thody, *Marcel Proust*, Macmillan Modern Novelists, London, 1987, pp. 69–70. As I also point out in my *Jean Genet: A study of his novels and plays*, Hamish Hamilton, London, 1968, Proust is not the only homosexual author to write of his own tastes with considerable disapproval.

47 Elaine Showalter, *Sexual Anarchy* (1990), Bloomsbury, London, 1991, p. 23. The Manifesto for the Society for Cutting Up Men, published by the Olympia Press, Paris in 1971, argued that 'the male is an incomplete female, a walking abortion, aborted at the gene stage. To be male is to be deficient, emotionally limited; maleness is a deficiency disease and males are emotional cripples.'

48 Quoted in Penelope Shuttle and Peter Redgrove, *The Wise Wound*, Gollancz, London, 1978, p. 90.

49 Hermann Kahn, *On Escalation*, Pall Mall Press, London, 1983, p. 134.

50 *The Oxford Dictionary of the Classical World*, Oxford University Press, Oxford, 1986, p. 323.

51 See Greene, *Encyclopedia of Censorship*, p. 170.

52 Quoted by Otto Jespersen, *Language: Its Nature, Development and Origin*, Allen and Unwin, London, 1954, p. 246.

53 Plato, *The Republic*, translated by H. P. D Lee, Penguin Classics, Harmondsworth, 1955, p. 384. All other quotations are taken from this translation.

54 See the discussion of the painting in Francis Francina and Charles Harriman, *Modern Art and Modernism: A Critical Anthology*, Harper and Row, London, 1982, p. 97.

55 Ray B. Browne, editor, *Forbidden Fruits: Taboos and Tabooism in Culture*, Bowling Green University Press, Bowling Green, Ohio, 1984, p. 128. Also H. Montgomery Hyde, *A History of Pornography*, Dell Publishing Company, New York, 1965, p. 19. Other instances of mistakes made by what Montgomery Hyde calls 'an illiterate bureaucracy' include the prosecution in 1895 at Clay Center, Kansas of a man called Wise for sending obscene and pornographic material through the post, when the material in question consisted entirely of quotations from the Bible.

56 Quoted by Nadine Strossen, *Defending Pornography*, Simon and Schuster, New York, 1995, p. 110.

57 Gilles Deleuze, *Présentation de Sacher-Masoch*, Editions de Minuit, Paris, 1967, p. 23. Count Leopold von Sacher-Masoch (1836–95) wrote some 90 novels, of which *Venus in Furs* is the only one still in print. He was the mildest of men, particularly fond of children and cats; offering a parallel in this respect to the Marquis de Sade. He carried his disapproval of the death penalty to the point where, acting as a judge

in a revolutionary tribunal during the Terror of 1793–4, he dismissed the charges against his mother-in-law, who had originally been instrumental in sending him to the Bastille.

58 See Greene, *Encyclopedia of Censorship*, p. 194, under the entry 'Motion Picture Producers and Distributors Association'.

59 Quoted from an article by Nolan Fell in the April/May 1995 issues of *Rushes* deploring the reduction in the freedom of expression brought about by this amendment.

60 Quoted from Greene, *Encyclopedia of Censorship*, p. 321.

61 See Richard Ellmann, *James Joyce*, Oxford University Press, Oxford, 1959, p. 628.

62 Quoted from Michael Elgan, *Ibsen: The Critical History*, Routledge and Kegan Paul, London, 1972.

63 'The Artist and AIDS', *Horizon*, November 1987, p. 22.

64 Quoted in Greene's *Encyclopedia of Censorship*.

Section V

SIGNS

'Don't make yourself look like that!'

The entries in this concluding section offer more examples of how taboos work as signs. If people forbid certain actions or words which are, for the most part, morally neutral, it is to reinforce their sense of group identity by showing how different they are from their neighbours or rivals. Taboos are best studied in the context of the discipline known as semiology or semiotics. This is consistent with what Franz Steiner gives as the original meaning of the word, which was 'to mark clearly'.[1]

Arms Although women are now generally accepted bareheaded in most Christian churches, the widespread ban on their entering churches without covering arms bare to the shoulder (or in brief shorts or mini-skirts) is still enforced in some Mediterranean Catholic areas.

Beards When, in 1696, Peter the Great assumed effective power as Tsar of Russia, he personally shaved off the beard of any *boyar* (nobleman) who came to see him. It was a portent of the more ferocious and significant modernization he was to carry out in other fields, and one of the first examples of beards being seen as betokening an unacceptable difference of social attitude. In the West, the invention in 1901 of the safety razor by King Camp Gillette (1855–1932) marked the beginning of a period in which fewer and fewer men wore beards. In the 1920s, a taboo on beards was practised in the streets of London through the game 'Beaver'. This meant shouting out the word 'Beaver!' whenever one saw a man with a beard, and scoring twenty-five points for a full imperial, twenty for a flowing, artistic beard, and fifteen for a short, naval style.

The game was inspired partly by the plethora of beards worn by the rulers of Europe in 1914 who were judged responsible for the 1914–18 war. The arbitrary nature of the signs put out by facial hair was nevertheless illustrated by the fact that the wearing of a beard also became a feature of left-wing intellectuals rather than of businessmen and politicians. This may have been because of the beards worn by Lenin and Trotsky, and the mention of 'a bearded cove' by one of the highly conservative, upper-class characters in the Bulldog Drummond series of novels by Sapper is frequently a prelude to the supposed revolutionary being beaten up. The view of bearded characters as social dissidents against whom a rigorous taboo can be legitimately enforced fits in with Mary Douglas's suggestion, in *Natural Symbols* (1970), that whereas smooth men exercise immediate social control, shaggy ones do so only from a distance and on a more long-term basis.[2]

Professor Douglas illustrates this idea by the story of Jacob and Esau in *Genesis*, 27. It is Jacob, the smooth man, who tricks his father Isaac into giving him his blessing while Esau, the hairy man, is out in the fields. Unlike John the Baptist, whose coat of camel's hair emphasizes how he too is at home in the wilderness, Esau is not a prophet. But he has the unworldliness of the unkempt country-dweller, which is also the mark of those who bring strange messages from afar off. It would still be very unusual, in present-day Britain, for a man wearing a beard to be chosen to stand as a candidate for the Conservative Party. Beards were, however, a frequent feature of members of the left-wing splinter group known as Militant Tendency.

See below, **hair**.

Boots In the late 1960s and early 1970s, a number of schools in England refused to allow boys to attend classes if they were wearing pit boots. This ban on what, in a miner going to work, is perfectly normal footwear, arose because of the habit of urban hooligans in non-mining as well as mining areas of wearing heavy boots. They did so either as a sign of social disaffection or because boots were useful for kicking people.

The ban stemmed partly from the clothing worn by the 15-year-old tearaway Alex and his friends in the 1971 film of Anthony Burgess's novel *A Clockwork Orange* (1968), who dressed themselves up in white boiler suits and heavy black boots. The model which they offered to urban hooligans led to the unofficial establishment in a number of association football grounds of what was known as 'the *Clockwork Orange* corner'. Clothing and footwear of this kind are an example of how nobody can dress innocently.

See below, **hair** and **trousers**.

Chrysanthemums While grown all year round in England, these are autumnal flowers in France, cultivated specially to be placed on graves on All Souls Day, 1 November. They should not therefore be taken as gifts to your hostess if you are invited to lunch or dinner in France.

Clever There is still a basic truth in G. R. Love's comment in *Subways Are for Sleeping* (1957), that 'after seven-thirty in the evening, in order to read a book in Grand Central Station or Penn Central, a person either has to wear horn-rimmed spectacles or look exceptionally prosperous. Anyone else is apt to come under surveillance.' It parallels Auden's observation that

To the man in the street, who I'm sorry to say,
Is a keen observer of life,
The word 'intellectual' means straightaway
A man who's untrue to his wife

In 'Loggers Can't Cry; and Other Taboos of the Northwest Woods' (1984), Jack Estes wrote of how, in that particular macho community, it is 'taboo to read anything that hints of intellectual stimulation'.[3] There is only one way in which a man sitting reading a book in an airport lounge in an English-speaking country can make himself immune to interruption: by choosing one whose cover is decorated either by a man with a revolver or by a scantily clad woman. The situation of women is, of course, different; men need to protect themselves against the bore who wishes to tell his life-story or explain his views on sport, women to discourage the potential sexual predator.

The Hungarian humourist Georges Mikes pointed out in his *How to Be an Alien* (1949) that the official, dictionary meaning of 'clever' does not correspond to the way it is used by native speakers of English in England. According to the dictionary it means 'intelligent', 'ingenious', 'resourceful' or 'skilful'. In practice, it is synonymous with 'sly', 'deceitful', 'unreliable',' dishonest' and, above all, 'snobbish', 'over-confident' and 'impractical'. Lord Salisbury's 1960 remark that the then Foreign Secretary, Iain MacLeod, was 'too clever by half' gave a specific illustration of the mistrust of intelligence which is not exclusive to the English-speaking world. It can also stem from the fear that anyone who is clever will criticize society and try to bring about change. As a French nobleman remarked of Voltaire, Diderot and Rousseau: 'Cela veut raisonner de tout. Et cela n'a pas vingt mille livres de rente' (They have ideas about everything. And on less than twenty thousand a year).

An anecdote in Jonathan Gathorne-Hardy's *The Public School Phenomenon* (1977) suggests that the taboo on cleverness was stronger in England in the case of girls than of boys. A father entrusting his daughter to Roedean told the headmistress: 'I don't mind my girl taking one A-level so long as she doesn't look clever.' Another told the headmaster of Westminster School: 'Parents don't pay for good teaching. They pay for short hair.'[4] The first parent may have been thinking of Baudelaire's remark that only homosexuals fall in love with clever women: 'Aimer les femmes intelligentes, c'est un plaisir de pédéraste.' The reputation of public schools for nurturing homosexuals was not always undeserved.

See below, **tears**.

Colour (i) A crucial stage in the way men organized their appearance was reached when what J. C. Flugel, in *The Language of Clothes* (1930), called 'the great masculine renunciation' introduced a virtual taboo on use of colour in men's clothes. Until the early nineteenth century, men used colour in Western society as extravagantly as male animals do in nature, and often for a similar reason: to advertise their attractiveness to the opposite sex. However, with the industrial revolution, male sexual attractiveness moved to the ability to make money. This was what distinguished the new ruling class from the aristocracy, where inherited wealth remained consistent with an ostentatious style of dress. The signs of the ability to make money were diligence, perseverance and self-denial, all qualities incompatible with the flaunting of wealth through the wearing of colourful clothes.

The only exceptions allowed to the sober black of the industrious businessman, at least in English society, were ties, those badges of tribal membership whose origin is explained by anthropologists as relics of the penis shield still worn in Papua and New Guinea. An alternative view is that the tie is the direct descendant of the emblazoned shield of the knight in armour. In Westerns, gamblers or corrupt sheriffs wear a boot-lace tie. It emphasizes their tenuous claim to respectability. Because of the style affected by Edward VIII, British officers in civilian clothes never wear the double-knotted or 'Windsor' tie. When he abdicated on 11 December 1936 in order to marry Wallis Simpson, the Duke of Windsor forfeited the feudal chieftain's right to have his followers show their allegiance to him by wearing his colours.

Clothes were also signs of differences in social status. In the Middle Ages, damask, velvet and satin could be worn only by nobles, whose clothes proclaimed the hierarchical principle on which society had traditionally been founded. Broadcloth was reserved for burgers. The poor wore what they could find. Similarly, while cardinals wore scarlet, bishops purple and abbots green, white was reserved for the Supreme Pontiff.[5] What were known as 'sumptuary laws' continued to operate in many European countries until the French Revolution of 1789, with the ban on the use of certain colours and types of cloth playing the same function as the avoidance of alcohol or pork: to indicate membership of a group.

(ii) The very firm directive by Miss Manners to the effect that in the USA ladies wear white shoes only between Memorial Day (the last Monday in May) and Labor Day (the first Monday in September) reflects the view of white as a summer colour. Her warning 'otherwise, you will develop warts on your toes'[6] nevertheless gives her interdict the appearance of a genuine taboo. Its persistence is shown by the behaviour of Kathleen Turner in the film *Serial Mum* (1994). After a woman juror has helped to acquit her for an earlier series of crimes, in a trial which takes place after Labor Day, Kathleen Turner murders her because she had, during the trial, worn white shoes.

The taboo against white also forms part of the cult of **political correctness**. One asks for 'coffee with milk', not 'white coffee'. Taboos against other colours remained sufficiently vigorous in late-twentieth-century England to affect the not particularly ostentatious colour of brown. The *Daily Telegraph* for 17 June 1995 described how Sir Julian Critchley appalled the squirearchical element in the Tory party, what the article ironically described as 'great men like Colonel Sir Walter Bromley-Davenport, Brigadier Sir Otho Prior-Palmer and Sir Hugh Vere Muro Huntley Lucas-Tooth', by being seen wearing brown shoes in a public place within twenty miles of Charing Cross. Brown suits have never really caught on, and the man who is described in the music-hall monologue as having attended a Cockney funeral in brown boots is forgiven only because he gave his other boots away 'to a man who didn't have no boots at all'.

Confrontational Masao Miyamoto was reported in the *Guardian* for 14 June 1995 as saying: 'In Japan, confrontation is taboo, and the desire to avoid it is the most important element in our society.' It is this, combined with what Fukatsu Masumi referred to in the *Japan Quarterly* for 1995 as 'the taboo' on discussing Emperor Hirohito's accountability for Japanese foreign policy, that helps to explain why the Japanese found it so difficult to apologize for the atrocities committed by their soldiers between 1937 and 1945.[7]

The reluctance of a people who are so polite and apologetic to one another on a day-to-day basis to apologize for their behaviour as a nation offers another pointer as to the nature of taboos. In the shame culture inspired by Shintoism, as in the guilt-centred religion of Judeo-Christianity, taboos tend to affect only those aspects of human behaviour which are morally insignificant. It is easy to abstain from alcohol or pork, and to bow in humility to a social inferior. Signs, like politeness, cost nothing. It is less easy to say that you are sorry for the way your soldiers massacred civilians and tortured prisoners of war. It has taken the Christian sects a long time to abandon the use of violence against their ideological opponents. It has taken them even longer to apologize for their behaviour towards non-Christians.

See also **Auschwitz** in IV.

Cross-dressing (i) This practice is specifically forbidden in *Deuteronomy*, 22:5: 'The woman shall not wear that which pertaineth unto a man, neither shall a man put on a woman's garment: for all that do so are abomination unto the Lord'. One of the main charges brought against Joan of Arc at her trial in 1431 was that she wore men's clothes. It is still technically an offence to do so under French law, though not in the United Kingdom or the United States. Like the closing phrase in the condemnation of bestiality in *Leviticus* 18:23 – 'Neither shalt thou lie with any beast to defile thyself therewith: neither shall any woman stand before a beast to lie down thereto: it is confusion' – the ban on cross-dressing confirms the view that one of the aims of taboos is to establish clear distinctions and avoid all kinds of mixing.

The Independent on Sunday for 29 January 1995 quoted Rupaul Charles, a drag queen at Las Vegas, as saying: 'What was once taboo becomes another form of entertainment, of life-style.' There is evidence to support this claim in recent films such as *The Crying Game* (1992) and *Priscilla Queen of the Desert* (1993). There is, however, a clear difference between this kind of cross-dressing, and the peculiarly English entertainment of the Christmas pantomime. The films have analogies with the success of the one-man show put on by Quentin Crisp. His aim continues to be what it was when he put on make-up and dressed in a provocatively feminine style in the London of the 1930s: to disturb anyone who thinks he is totally heterosexual by presenting him with an image of what he might become if he let himself go. In the two films from the 1990s, there is the suggestion that the bisexuality associated with cross-dressing is not altogether a bad thing.

In the cross-dressing which accompanies the Christmas pantomime, as in the popularity of Barry Humphries as Dame Edna Everage, the aim is quite different. Just as there is never any question of Dame Edna actually being a woman, the pantomime dame continues to be played by a large and obviously heterosexual man. This reinforces the taboo against cross-dressing by constantly reminding the audience that cross-dressing is funny, and therefore not normal. The pantomime dame is a man whose masculinity is so great that nothing can disguise it. Similarly, in Raymond Queneau's novel *Zazie dans le métro* (1959), 'l'oncle Gabriel' is a large, hairy and obviously heterosexual man who earns his living by appearing in a comic turn as a transvestite in a homosexual bar.

Whatever the skill with which they disguise themselves physically as women and the brilliance with which they act the part, there is never any doubt in *Some Like It Hot* (1959) that Tony Curtis and Jack Lemmon are still very much men. The same is true of Dustin Hoffman's performance in *Tootsie* (1982) or Robin Williams in *Mrs Doubtfire* (1993). Dressing up as a woman may enable the former to achieve the professional success which had eluded him when he was trying to earn his living as an actor playing male parts, and Robin Williams is at least temporarily successful in being near his children. There is even the suggestion that men may become better people by pretending to change their sexual identity. But as with the pantomime dame, the reminder is always there that cross-dressing is not something which a heterosexual would do under normal circumstances. The taboo is reinforced. It is not defied.

Until the change described by Rupaul Charles began to come into effect, stage performances by men who looked as if they might well be women had to be followed by a kind of cleansing ceremony. The English female impersonator Danny la Rue, for example, always appeared in men's clothes to take the curtain call at the end of the show in which he had earlier been dressed in magnificent female attire. The audience could therefore leave the theatre fully reassured in their sense of sexual identity. Danny was a man, and it was all a joke. It was, however, Danny la Rue's performance in the 1969 BBC television version of Brandon Thomas's farce *Charley's Aunt* (1896) which marked the beginnings of the change in which the taboo against cross-dressing has come to be presented. When the English comedian Arthur Askey had to dress up as a woman in the 1940 film of *Charley's Aunt*, there was no doubt that he was a man. In the scene where he pulled up his long skirt in order to run away, you saw that he was still wearing plus-fours underneath. When Danny la Rue had to run, you saw shapely legs in silk stockings.

(ii) The latest edition of Leslie Halliwell's *Filmgoer's and Videoviewer's Companion* lists over thirty films in which men have been disguised as women, and a score or so in which women have been dressed as men. These range from the sinister switching of Anthony Perkins to his dead mother in *Psycho* (1960) to the comic performance of Alec Guinness, again in the tradition of the pantomime dame, in *Kind Hearts and Coronets* (1949). However, as in the tradition whereby the principal boy in the English pantomime is played by an actress, the sexual implications are not the same as those created when men play women. The actress playing the principal boy may not always be as nubile as she was but she is still sexually attractive as a woman. The pantomime dame, although undoubtedly heterosexual, is definitely not sexually attractive as a man. When Greta Garbo pretended to be a man in *Queen Christina* (1933), she was if anything more captivating than she was as a woman. The same was true of Marlene Dietrich in *Morocco* (1930) and *Seven Sinners* (1940).

This may reflect a difference in the nature and severity of the taboos against **homosexuality** and **Lesbianism**. Heterosexual women tend to be fairly hostile to homosexuals, whom they see as possible rivals, potential seducers of their sons, and a threat to the stability of the home. Their attitude towards Lesbians is not as openly hostile as the one which some men adopt towards homosexuals, but they are not keen on the idea. Heterosexual men have a more ambivalent attitude. They see Lesbians not as a threat but as a challenge. Their dream is to effect the same conversion that James Bond carries out on Pussy Galore in *Goldfinger* (book, 1959; film, 1964). It is this attitude which enables film producers to present women who increase their sexual attractiveness by dressing up as men. Men who have diligently suppressed their interest in boys can also indulge in some of their favourite fantasies without feeling guilty.

See **homosexuality** in I, **mix** in II, **pussy** in III, the entry on *The Well of Loneliness* in IV, and **trousers** below.

Degrees Miss Manners is critical of holders of a PhD from a Faculty of Arts, Humanities or Science who refer to themselves in private life or in the telephone directory as 'Doctor'. This creates a confusion with holders of a medical qualification which can lead to embarrassing incidents, as when an expert in medieval Catalan receives a telephone call in the middle of the night asking him to come and remove an inflamed appendix. The possession of a doctorate, advises Miss Manners, should be as private a source of satisfaction as the wearing of silk underwear. In the 1950s and 1960s, it was regarded as very non-U (see **serviette** in III) for scientists in the Bell telephone research laboratories to use the title 'Dr'. This may have been because many of the senior managers at the time did not possess a research degree.

In England, the addition of the abbreviation 'Hons', and even more of the code words 'Oxon.' or 'Cantab.', on the notice-board outside a school to designate the degree held by the headteacher is not a guarantee of academic respectability. Names such A. J. K. Blenkinsop-Carruthers, MA Hons (Oxon) or Hilary June Benedict de Bergerac, BA Hons (Cantab.) evoke the over-large rosette of the *Légion d'Honneur* worn in their button-hole by French confidence tricksters.

Different Erving Goffman wrote in *Stigma: Notes on the Management of Spoiled Identity* (1958) that 'in an important sense, there is only one complete unblushing male in America: a young, urban, northern, heterosexual Protestant father of college education, fully employed, of good complexion, weight and height and a recent record in sport'. Roland Barthes, a left-handed, Protestant homosexual with only a very basic university degree, made a similar observation in *Roland Barthes par Roland Barthes* (1975) when he wrote: 'Qui ne sent combien il est naturel en France d'être catholique, marié, et bien diplômé?' (Who does not feel how natural it is in France to be Catholic, married, and well qualified academically?)

In Tom Wolfe's *The Bonfire of the Vanities* (1988), the anxiety of Sherman McCoy's wife Judy about her social status reveals itself in her fear of looking different. In Chapter 15, she is deeply embarrassed at the party given by the Bavardages to be seen forming 'a minimal cluster with him, just the two of them'. Nothing could have more delighted Oriane, Duchesse de Guermantes, the embodiment of elegance in Proust's *A la recherche du temps perdu* (1913–27; *Remembrance of Things Past*). It would have been a sign for all to see that she and her husband Basin could find no one worthy of their company. It would thus have made the prestige which she derived from excluding most of the people she knew in society from her own social circle even greater. It would also have given her a chance of talking to Basin, something which the extent of her known social commitments normally prevented her from doing.

Dreadlocks Nobody living in a society ridden by taboos can abolish them. All anyone can do is decide whether or not to conform. When, in July 1995, Sir Paul Conlon broke what the *Daily Express* called a 'taboo' by claiming that 'most muggers are black', an interview in the *Guardian* for 8 July reported a 24-year old unemployed Londoner called Jason Joseph as saying: 'It's tough out there being a black man. Just try and get a job – people just look at you and don't want to know.'

Widespread though racialism undoubtedly is in England, Mr Joseph was not helping himself by wearing what the *Guardian* called 'thick gold bracelets and a mane of dreadlocks'. No one questions his right as a citizen of a pluralistic democracy to wear what he chooses and to look how he likes. Indeed, in 1986, a court in New York State ruled that it would 'needlessly infringe' the beliefs of a Rastafarian imprisoned in a state penitentiary to require him to shed his foot-long dreadlocks.[8] But there are also commercial taboos. No shop-keeper in the United Kingdom would employ a man with dreadlocks. It would discourage the customers. The irrationality of the taboo is evident in the fact that customers can be just as well served – or just as badly – by a Negro with long black hair as by a Caucasian with short back and sides. But it would be a brave shop-keeper anywhere who counted on this degree of broad-mindedness.

Elbows 'All joints on the table', as Nanny would say, 'will be carved.' However, in a letter to the *Daily Telegraph* on 28 November 1995, D. Cameron-Moore pointed out that in his youth, one elbow on the table was permitted if you had rounded Cape Horn, and two if you had sailed round the Cape of Good Hope as well.

English The tone of hostility and disapproval with which Rockmetteller Todd's aunt says to Bertie Wooster: 'You're English, aren't you?' in the short story 'The Aunt and the Sluggard' (1921) suggests that it was already not a very good idea to be audibly or visibly English in America if you could possibly avoid it. Authors of books intended to be sold in the United States are nowadays instructed to replace all reference to habits prevalent in England by what happens in North America; and are equally enjoined to replace the words 'England' or 'English' by 'Britain' or 'British'.

This latter piece of advice can certainly avoid some misunderstandings. It nevertheless neglects the taboo status which the words Britain and British have for a number of native speakers of English. Thanks to the popular press, to remarks by Labour politicians during the more severe economic crises of the 1960s and to the refrains of patriotic songs, both the noun and the adjective are associated with chauvinistic slogans and attitudes such as 'Let's make Britain Great', Harold Wilson's 'I'm Backing Britain', 'Standing up for Britain', and 'Britons never, never, never shall be slaves'. Orwell may have been talking about a past which was already mythical when he evoked, in his essay 'England, Your England' (1941), what he called 'the gentleness of English civilisation', our 'addiction to hobbies and spare-time occupations', our lack of interest in military matters, our old-fashioned outlook and 'mixture of bawdiness and hypocrisy', our 'deeply moral attitude to life', and 'the old maids biking to Holy Communion through the mists of the autumn mornings'.[9] But he was talking about the

English, not the Scots, the Welsh and the Northern Irish, just as Alan Bennett was when he commented in *Writing Home* (1993) on how, in contemporary America, 'English is invariably a word of abuse, representing smallness of mind, intimacy, gossip, charm. All the things Auden fled from.'[10]

A comparable indicator of the taboo status of England and the English in the United States is in the cinema. In *The Lion King* (1995), the villainous Scar speaks with a strong English accent. In Clint Eastwood's *The Unforgiven* (1992), it is the English actor Richard Harris who is beaten up by Gene Hackman and transformed from the hero he thinks he is into an object of ridicule. In Harrison Ford's *Patriot Games* (1992), the traitor is a very English higher civil servant with what was clearly considered the very English name of Geoffrey Watkins. The habit of casting English actors as villains in political dramas goes back at least to *The Manchurian Candidate* (1962). There, the English-born Angela Lansbury plays the wicked mother and the English actor Laurence Harvey the brain-washed baddie. The effect would be quite different if the accent of the actor or actress were Scottish, Irish or Welsh. For most North Americans, any accent linking a speaker of non-American English to one of the countries which have suffered at the hands of the Anglo-Saxon invader and exploiter has highly positive associations. This fits in with the alternative explanation for giving the role of the baddie to an Englishman: it avoids giving offence to racial groups whose past history makes them understandably more touchy than the formerly successful and unoppressed English.

One reason for the unpopularity of the English in contemporary America is underlined by Tom Wolfe's portrait of the journalist Peter Fallow in *The Bonfire of the Vanities* (1988). Fallow despises the Americans whose hospitality he enjoys, and makes a point of never paying for a meal or a drink. Kingsley Amis's description of the publisher Roger Micheldene in *One Fat Englishman* (1963) offers an equally valid explanation. Micheldene is condescending, supercilious and pompous, redeemed only by his lechery and greed.

Enthusiastic Between the revolution of 1789 and his death in 1838, Charles Maurice de Talleyrand failed to play an active role in French politics only when a display of courage might have brought him to the guillotine or before a firing squad. The advice he gave to his assistants was always the same: 'Surtout. Pas de zèle.' (Above all. No zeal.) A gentleman distinguished himself from upstart vulgarians by observing a total taboo on enthusiasm. This led Talleyrand to eschew the zeal for revolutionary purity which inspired Robespierre with such a passion for the guillotine that he used it to eliminate most of his former colleagues. The taboo on enthusiasm also helped Talleyrand to avoid the cult of military glory which brought about the downfall of Bonaparte. His advice echoed the other eighteenth-century view that excessive and visible piety was a very dangerous attitude to adopt in religious matters. The eulogy on the gravestone of one English cleric praised him for having, throughout his life, 'conducted Divine Service with Diligence but without Enthusiasm'; an emotion defined in the *Shorter Oxford Dictionary* as 'ill-regulated religious emotion or speculation'.

See the entry **work** in Section I for a comparable taboo placed by a society with aristocratic pretensions on all forms of visible effort.

Fat There is a marked contrast between the Duchess of Windsor's remark that a woman can never be too rich or too thin and the criteria observed by the Hima, a tribe of nomadic cattle breeders in Uganda. They are 'widely known for the long horns of their cattle and for the obesity of their women, who in the interests of loveliness gorge until they can hardly walk'.[11]

In *Female Fetishism* (1994), Lorraine Gammon and Merja Makinnen ask: 'Why should a creative and liberated black celebrity such as Oprah Winfrey consider that losing 70 lbs was one of her great achievements?' Part of the answer is that in the West, being fat betokens a tendency to gorge yourself on cakes and soft drinks. They are cheaper and offer more instant oral gratification than the high-fibre foods and fresh fruit favoured by the rich. It thus suggests poverty, either now or in the past. If you started out poor, and had to make a great effort to acquire your money, you are now openly rewarding yourself with food and drink to compensate for early privations.

Forks (i) The arrival of the fork from Byzantium in eleventh-century Venice was seen as such an impious novelty that the dogeresse was severely rebuked by the ecclesiastics, who called down divine wrath upon her. Until well into the Renaissance period, people ate out of a common dish, using either their hands or their knife to pick out the piece of meat they wished to eat. They then put it on the slice of bread known as a trencher; hence the expression 'a good trencherman'. The priests' hostility to the dogeresse's behaviour stemmed from the belief that such refinement showed too great a concern for the elegance and vanity of this fallen world.[12]

By the fourteenth century, it was beginning to be considered rude to put back the piece of meat you had initially chosen into the communal dish. However, Norbert Elias argues that 'a major part of the taboos that people gradually impose upon themselves in their dealings with one another, a far larger part than is usually thought, has not the slightest connection with hygiene'. This fits in with the remark in the *Collins Encyclopedia* that the Fijians cooked the flesh of their enemies apart from other food, and ate it 'with wooden forks which were taboo for other uses'. They did so not for health reasons but to stress the idea that this was special fare.

Even among twentieth-century Europeans and North Americans, Elias contended, what are now considered to be good manners were not originally concerned with hygiene. They stemmed from the observance of customs, and from what he calls 'delicacy of feeling'.[13] It was not because they might be dirty that people began to wash their hands before sitting down to table. It was to perform a '*rite de passage*', and indicate that they were going to take part in a different activity. Neither in the way people ate nor in the kind of food they consumed were taboos originally inspired by thoughts of health or hygiene. What mattered was the way such taboos marked you out as different from other people. Only uncircumcised Gentiles ate pork; only the vulgar stuck to a style of eating which had come to be regarded as uncivilized.

(ii) In the twentieth century, attempts to use forks as signs of the refinement expected of a member of the upper class tend to backfire. When the speaker in John Betjeman's poem 'How to Get On in Society' (1956) says to her guest

Now here is a fork for your pastries
And do use the couch for your feet

she commits three solecisms. U speakers avoid words of French origin. They do not say 'pastries' ('*des pâtisseries*') but cake. More inexplicably, they say sofa and not couch. The hostess is equally wrong to think that her guest will want to use a fork. Members of the upper class spurn such affectations of refinement, and eat cake with the fingers.

See below, **knives** and **newness**; also **serviette** in III.

Gloves (i) The *Hints on Etiquette and Usages of Society, With a Glance at Bad Habits* (1834) advises ladies 'never to dine with their gloves on, unless their hands are in too bad a state to be seen'. When Emma Bovary attends the dinner which precedes the ball at La Vaubyessard, which takes place some time in the 1840s, she notes with surprise that several of the ladies have not, when taking off their gloves, put them in their wineglasses. This means that they are going to drink wine, something which a well-brought-up girl born into a socially undistinguished farming family like the Rouaults, and recently married to an obscure country physician, would never do.

(ii) The lines in Frances Cornford's poem 'To a Fat Lady seen from the Train':

O fat white woman whom nobody loves,
Why do you walk through the fields in gloves . . .
Missing so much and so much?

attracted a vigorous response from G. K. Chesterton:

Oh why do you dash through the fields in trains
Fat-headed poet without any brains
Guessing so much and so much?

Chesterton's poem ended with the suggestion that the lover she was going to meet liked her to show that she was a lady by wearing gloves, especially in the country. In the England of the 1950s, a teacher at Cheltenham Ladies College was reproved by the headmistress for not putting on her gloves when going to post a letter. Leather gloves function as a sign of rank in the British armed services, where they must be carried at all times by commissioned officers in uniform. Other ranks are issued with woollen gloves, which they wear only if it is cold.

Hair (i) Charles Berg's thesis in *The Unconscious Significance of Hair* (1951) that head hair is a universal symbol for the genital organs offers an instructive way of looking at the story of Samson in *Judges*, chapters 14–16. It presents Delilah as the castrating woman who deprives a man of his sexual power by cutting off his hair. Edmund Leach comments in 'Magical Hair' (1958), in the anthropological journal *Man*, that 'almost the whole of psychoanalytical theory rests on the most glaring fallacies'.[14] He criticizes Dr Berg's thesis that 'head hair is widely used as a ritual symbol with genital and anal connections' by pointing to the number of societies in which it is patently not true. This scepticism highlights how the approach to taboos by anthropologists differs from the methods used to study them by psychoanalysts.

Psychoanalysts see taboos, especially those connected with hair and with sex, as reflecting tensions which are innate in all individuals, wherever they happen to live. The anthropologist, in contrast, assumes that what Dr Leach calls 'public ritual symbols' are 'given potency by society, and not by individuals'. In his 1974 article 'Hair, Sex and Dirt', P. Hershman gives an example of this difference of approach by pointing out that the refusal of Sikh men to cut their hair is one of the five symbols of Sikhism. The others are a refusal of circumcision, the wearing of shorts, and the carrying of a two-edged blade and a one-edged comb. Hair, Dr Hershman argues, attracts taboos because it can be seen not only to be 'at the "boundary" of the body but also to be a "structural anomaly" by being joined to it but apart from it'.[15]

Anthropologists thus emphasize the idea that the symbolism attached to hair, like sexual behaviour itself, is a social construct. This enables them to explain why both the symbolism and the behaviour vary so much from one society to another, and how each can have a different meaning in every case.

Sura XLVIII.28 of the Koran, which instructs believers to enter the mosque with their heads shaved and their hair cut short, offers a parallel in the custom whereby certain orders of Christian monks still remove most of the hair from their head. Holy men in

Hindu and Buddhist culture, in contrast, wear their hair very long.

American and British society has recently developed a strong set of taboos on female body hair. Models, gymnasts and skimpily attired performers generally remove hair from their armpits and from much of their pubic area. In some circles, a total lack of pubic hair in women is considered to make a woman extremely sexy. This contrasts with the attitude still adopted by Latin cultures, specially by the French. The description '*généreusement touffue*' (richly endowed with pubic hair) implies a high degree of erotic appreciation, and offers a parallel to the incident in John Braine's *Room at the Top* (1957), when Alice Aisgill tells Joe Lampton to stop wearing hair oil. It prevents her from running her hands through his hair when they are making love.

However, not all members of every culture recognize the sexual significance of hair. In the Eton of the 1920s, the only females whom the boys met in term time were mature ladies known as dames. In his book on the public schools, Jonathan Gathorne-Hardy describes how one of these lusted after one of the boys until finally,

> unable to contain her desires, she drew him ravenously into a room, locked the door, pulled down her knickers, pulled up her skirt and said: 'Here! What do you think of that?'
> 'Gosh, ma'am,' said the boy. 'Stand still. If you wait a minute, I'll run to my room, get my bat and kill it.'[16]

See **sado-masochism** in I, **beards** and **dreadlocks** above, **hats** and **moustaches** below

Hands (i) The habit of using the word 'taboo' in a context totally alien to the Polynesian culture where Captain Cook first heard it is offered by a remark in Brian Simon's and Ian Bradley's study of Victorian public schools:

> When in 1849 football rules were committed to writing at Eton, a principal rival, several were diametrically opposed to those recorded at Rugby a few years before. It is interesting to note that central among these is a taboo on the use of hands, now the main distinguishing mark of association football – soccer.[17]

It would not occur to most games players to refer to the rules of their particular game by the pejorative term 'taboos'. They are the conventions without which the game cannot be meaningfully played. The phrase about the 'taboo on the use of hands' again emphasizes how taboos serve as signs distinguishing one tribe from another. Etonians kick the ball but do not use their hands. It is a defining feature of the game as first played at Rugby that the hands are used.

Another justification for using the word 'taboo' in this context lies in the example of the advantages which can be derived from an act of defiance. A plaque at Rugby school records how, in 1823,

> William Webb Ellis, with a Fine Disregard for the
> Rules of Football, as Played in His Time,
> First Took the Ball in His Arms and Ran with It,
> Thus Originating the Distinctive Feature
> of the Rugby Game.

(ii) It has long been a sign of rudeness for a man to keep his hands in his pocket, almost as bad as keeping a pipe or cigarette in his mouth when talking to a lady. The attempt in 1863 to counteract 'the Harrow slouch' by forbidding boys to keep their hands in their pockets did not last long at Harrow itself. It nevertheless spread to other public schools, and was imitated at the local grammar schools, which followed their lead in other matters such as the wearing of school uniforms. There is still a great divide in education in the British Isles between those whose parents are rich enough to pay for them to go to an independent, fee-paying school and those who attend the local state school. The former know about the taboos governing polite behaviour, and break them only deliberately.

Hats (i) Taboos concerning headgear have a social as well as a religious significance, especially for men. When Edward VII was still Prince of Wales, he aroused comment in the late 1890s by wearing a brown bowler (US derby) in London during the Season. The general taboo on appearing hatless in public lasted until after the Second World War, with a trilby (US fedora) being included in every ex-serviceman's demobilization outfit. It disappeared in America in the 1950s, and President Kennedy's insistence in 1960 on appearing bareheaded at his inauguration in order to show off his splendid head of hair put an end to the hopes of a revival in the hat business.

Certain types of headgear are still worn in the United States, and can acquire a taboo status which they can equally rapidly lose. In his study of social distinctions in the United States, *Caste Marks* (1984), Paul Fussell is very scathing about the baseball cap worn back to front. However, by the 1990s, the association of the baseball cap with classlessness had made it an almost obligatory item of headgear for candidates for the US presidency. In the 1920s, part of Ataturk's attempt to modernize Turkey by making it a secular society took the form of banning the fez or tarbush. In French student restaurants of the 1950s, it was considered hilariously funny to bang on the table until anyone ignorant enough of conventions to come into the restaurant wearing a hat had removed it. Miss Manners reminds her readers that a gentleman removes his hat when entering an elevator.

(ii) Hats, especially in so far as they cover hair, also play a role in religious ceremonies. A Hindu man may enter a Sikh temple bareheaded because he wears his hair cut short. A Sikh, who observes the rule of not having his hair cut but winding it on the top of his head, must wear his turban at all times. A Punjabi woman must follow the same rule.[18] Jews, men and women alike, are punctilious about wearing hats both on their way to the synagogue and during the service. The custom whereby Christians, both men and women, also wore hats on their way to church now exists only in the more traditional parishes.

Heels The sumptuary laws in pre-revolutionary France placed a taboo on anyone except a male member of the upper nobility wearing shoes with red heels. Napoleon's remark that he was 'ni talon rouge ni bonnet rouge' (neither a red heel nor a red cap) exploited the associations of this taboo to claim that he represented the interests neither of the aristocracy in their elegant footwear nor of the revolutionary extremists in the red, Phrygian bonnet of the *sans-culottes* (see below, **trousers** (ii)).

A number of organizations in the 1960s and 1970s introduced a ban on women wearing stiletto heels. This was a rational measure to protect carpets and other floor covering. There are two reasons for the current taboo on high heels: respectable women do not wish to be mistaken for prostitutes; feminists object to sacrificing the comfort offered by lower or medium-sized heels to a purely masculine idea of what is elegant or attractive.

Infibulation In tribal Africa, as in parts of the Muslim world, uncircumcised women are socially unacceptable. According to an African myth recounted in the French poet Blaise Cendrars's *Anthologie Nègre* (1963), the origins of female circumcision lie in a decision by God to test the power of each sex to resist evil. First, he ordered the man to cut his wife's throat. The man refused, and threw the knife into the river. The woman, however, accepted, and was on the point of cutting her husband's throat when God intervened, telling her to desist and sentencing her never to touch iron again. The removal of the *labia minora* by an iron knife reflects her continued subjection to what, for her, then became a taboo material. The fact that it is a woman who carries out the operation is said to offer proof that women are subjected not to men but to iron itself.

The practice is not mentioned in the *Koran*, and according to Cyril Glassé's *The Concise Encyclopedia of Islam* (1989) 'practices such as clitoridectomy and/or removal of the labia are a grave offence against the person and are strictly forbidden in Islam'. The hidden nature of the mutilation makes it difficult to interpret as a badge of tribal identification, and it may be explained as an imitation of male circumcision. The barrier which it places on the woman's enjoyment means that she is never interested enough in sex to take a lover. She thus never risks requiring her husband to provide for children he has not fathered. Popular mythology in the Arab world credits woman with a sexual voracity which can be prevented from exhausting her partner only if brought under surgical control.

Elaine Showalter describes in *Sexual Anarchy* (1991) how, in the 1860s, the English physician Isaac Baker Brown pioneered the operation of clitoridectomy, or surgical excision of the clitoris, for female nervous disorders. 'A skilful surgeon,' she writes, 'he was much admired for the brilliant dexterity he displayed when using the left hand when operating on the female.'[19] A programme broadcast on the French television chain ARTE on 21 September

1995 described the existence in France before 1914 of a non-Muslim 'Société des orificilistes' which carried out female circumcision in order to prevent women becoming hysterical kleptomaniacs.

See below, **uncircumcised**.

Jeans In *Dress Codes: Meaning and Messages in American Culture* (1995), Ruth P. Rubenstein reports a memo being sent on 2 May 1995 to 143 assistant prosecutors in the US District Courthouse in Brooklyn telling them not to wear jeans. In his self-portrait film *JLG par JLG* (1994) the French film-maker Jean-Luc Godard explains his personal taboo on jeans by saying that they are a symbol of US imperialism.

Knives (i) When, in Chapter XXII of Dickens's *Great Expectations*, Herbert Pocket advises Pip that 'in London it is not the custom to put the knife in the mouth – for fear of accidents – and that while the fork is reserved for that use, it is not put further in than necessary' he is giving table manners a utilitarian function which Norbert Elias sees as different from their origin. The argument in *The Civilising Process* (1938) is that the taboo on using knives at table to do anything but cut the meat arose in a society in which people would have been sufficiently skilled in handling them not to run any danger of cutting themselves accidentally.

It remains customary to break the bread served with a meal and not to cut it with the knife. Mrs Humphrey, the author of *Manners for Men* (1897), tells the story of an absent-minded and short-sighted cleric who,

> with the remark 'My bread, I think', dug his fork into the white hand of a lady who sat beside him. He had been badly brought up, or he would not have used his fork, and the white hand would have experienced nothing worse than a sudden grasp.[20]

Elias writes that we find, in 'the present form of the knife ritual', what he calls 'an astonishing abundance of taboos of varying severity'. English visitors soon notice how North Americans cut up their food and then use only the fork to carry it to their mouths. Miss Manners issues a reminder that it is still taboo to cut up all the meat at one time, just as it would be to mash the food on one's plate. The meat, she advises, should be cut at intervals; and one should never carry more than three forkfuls of the same kind of food to one's mouth in succession. One etymology of the word 'taboo' gives it as 'to separate' or 'to mark clearly'. This is what one does when eating with what are currently seen as good manners.

Elias points out how shocked the Chinese are when they first come to the West and find the barbarous Europeans eating with swords, and a trace of their horror remains in the discomfort we feel when a fellow diner lifts his knife to his face; or, even worse, points at us with it. This, Elias argues, is less because we are afraid that he might cut himself or attack us than because of our realization that he is confusing the original function of the knife as a weapon with its present role as partner to the fork. The taboo status of knives also explains the Maori custom of eating with a specially pointed stick, as well as the Malay dish known as satay, which consists of meat on a wooden stick. *The Habits of Good Society* (1859) stated that 'no epicure ever put knife to apple' and advised that an orange should be peeled with a spoon.

(ii) When Betjeman's hostess begins with the lines

> Phone for the fish-knives, Norman
> As Cook is a little unnerved.

she reveals her non-U status in five ways. U speakers do not use abbreviations. They set themselves apart from the modern world by talking about motor-cars, television sets, telephones and wireless sets. They avoid male first names with obviously bogus aristocratic connections. They hint at feudal ties rather than at functions, referring to their cook as Mrs Brown, Jones or Jenkins. If 'Cook' is having hysterics, or has gone mad again, they say so, perhaps even using the term 'temporarily bonkers'. And they do not have fish-knives.

Although this is partly a result of the general taboo about knives at table analysed by Norbert Elias, another reason is given in *Hints on Etiquette and Usages of Society, With a Glance at Bad Habits* (1834). This states that 'fish does not require a knife, but should be divided by the aid of a piece of bread', and explains why: fish sauces are acidulated, and 'acids easily corrode steel and draw from it a disagreeable taste'. The authors add that 'in the North, where lemon or vinegar is very generally used for salmon and many other kinds of fish, the objection becomes more apparent'. The fact that acid does not have this effect on silver poses only an apparent problem. The only silver which is socially OK is Georgian or pre-Georgian. In *The Rituals of Dinner* (1991), Margaret Visser explains that fish-knives were a Victorian invention, and Miss Manners, quoting Debrett's most recent gloss on Nancy Mitford's *Noblesse Oblige*, agrees. They cannot therefore come from the right period, and could have been bought only by *parvenus* wishing to impress.[21] See above, **forks**; and below, **newness**.

Legs In the 1930s, a teacher sitting on the platform at Cheltenham Ladies College during a prize-giving ceremony received a note which read PLSDNT + LGS. The ban may stem from the need to avoid the untidy appearance of a row of people sitting some with the left leg over the right, some with the right leg over the left. A lady wearing a short skirt also runs the risk of showing her underwear, and Miss Manners advises a candidate about to sit her oral examination for a master's degree that

> Neither gentlemen nor ladies properly cross their knees and the fact that this is universally done does not make it right. A gentleman's at ease posture while seated is to place one ankle upon the opposite knee. A lady's is to cross her ankles. Take care that the examiners do not uncover such areas of ignorance in you.

This fits in with other taboos on body language by discouraging gestures which have a defensive air, such as folding the arms across the chest or placing your hands on the table in front of you with the fingers of the right hand entwined with those of the left. Any committee chairman noticing members adopting such a posture can expect disagreement.

Moustaches In the 1970s, it became customary for homosexuals in America and England to signal the fact by growing a moustache and by having their hair cut so short that their head appeared virtually shaved. The moustache was not the pencil-thin type of Adolphe Menjou, betokening continental sophistication, nor the neatly trimmed one which was used by men as different as George Orwell, David Niven and Clark Gable to express an essentially Anglo-Saxon virility. Neither, although the moustache worn by those who had chosen to 'come out' covered the whole of the upper lip, was it allowed to sprout like one of the bushy moustaches of RAF fighter pilots during the Second World War. It was, on the contrary, kept scrupulously short. The defiance which it expressed of heterosexual convention was, in this as in other respects, as carefully controlled as the bare upper lip of those men who soon became conscious of how they, in contrast, by shaving the whole of their face every day, were announcing their preference for women.

See above, **hair**.

Newness Since the 1960s, there has been a total taboo on any student appearing in jeans which are not stained with ink and torn across at least one knee. Newness is taboo here, as in other contexts, because it hints at a group membership which is sufficiently recent to be suspect. Undergraduates wearing tidy clothes show an inability to break with the school rules and integrate themselves into the world of the university or college. A comparable need to produce a suitably battered garment as a sign of group membership is evoked by Ruth Rubenstein when she writes that the Stetson of an authentic cowboy 'will have accumulated finger prints, for it is used as a water bucket, waved in the air to steer cattle, and tipped to keep off bugs and supply shade'.[22]

The need to have a battered Stetson or dirty jeans parallels the taboo which still forbids anyone appearing at a Hunt Ball in a pink jacket which has not already been worn. To do so is instantly to reveal one's status as a 'nouveau riche'. The English conservative politician Alan Clarke, who inherited at least one castle in addition to several other town and country houses, suggested that his erstwhile colleague Michael Heseltine might fall into this category. Heseltine was, he remarked uncharitably, the kind of man who had had to buy his own furniture.

Pens No gentleman allows a pen, and even less a comb, to protrude from the top pocket of his jacket. Just as a lady does not put on make-up in public, a gentleman combs his hair only in private. He thus avoids displaying the instrument he uses to do this, and is equally scrupulous in not wearing what is known in the

United States as a 'nerd pack', defined by Paul Fussell as 'that little plastic envelope, often with advertising on the outer flap, worn in the breast pocket of a shirt to prevent pens and pencils from soiling the acrylic'.[23]

This particular clothes taboo is linked with the taboo on **newness** analysed above and the one on **work** studied in I. It is the mark of a gentleman not to advertise what he does by his appearance. If he does need a pen or pencil for his work, he keeps it concealed in an inside pocket. Ideally, however, like Mr Darcy in *Pride and Prejudice*, he does nothing; and it will be recalled from Jane Austen's general portrait of English society in the early nineteenth century that few activities were more reprehensible than to be in trade. As Ruth Benedict observes of the Japan which she set out to explain to the Americans in *The Chrysanthemum and the Sword* (1946), commenting on the fact that the merchants ranked just above the outcasts, 'a merchant class is always disruptive of feudalism'.[24]

Perfect There is only an apparent contrast between the injunction in *Matthew*, 5:48 'Be ye therefore perfect, even as your Father which is in heaven is perfect' and the rule noted by Bernard Levin in *A World Elsewhere* (1994) when he writes that, in the Jewish or Muslim traditions,

> when a new synagogue or mosque is built, a brick is left out, or a patch of wood left unpainted, or some other tangible incompleteness is recorded. The reason is that God alone is perfect, and no mortal can aspire to Godhead.[25]

Christ is talking about moral perfection, and the Muslim and Judaic taboo on perfection is applied to purely human creations. Bernard Levin's thesis in *A World Elsewhere* is that the creators of utopias all have one feature in common: they wish to deny human beings the right to differ from their version of what constitutes the perfect life. This leads them to create imaginary societies with a large number of taboos. A similar point is made by Max Dublin in his *Futurehype: The Tyranny of Prophecy* (1990).

Pins In the 1970s and 1980s, the wearing of safety pins in the lobes of the ears became a sign of the social disaffection associated with the punk movement. Since safety pins are not normally visible, being used either to secure a baby's nappy (US diaper), or to hold up a garment when normal means of suspension have failed, the public wearing of them in a blatantly non-utilitarian context represented a deliberate inversion of values. Its rejection of the taboo on what is and what is not an appropriate style of dress was consistent with the cult of uglification by which punks rejected a society which they accused of rejecting them. In that respect, the movement had links with the idea of existentialist authenticity mentioned in the entry **nigger** in III.

See below, **studs**.

Skin The decorated vases and sculptured figures surviving from fifth-century Athens suggest that while men were more attractive if their outdoor activities had given them a healthy tan, a woman was expected to keep her skin white by staying out of the sun. After the end of the classical period, white skin became a sign for both sexes of the ability to earn one's living without working in the sun. It was not until the late nineteenth century that the rise of activities such as alpinism and organized sport made it desirable for men and women to look as if they had spent a lot of time in the open air. The realization that prolonged exposure to sunlight can cause skin cancer has not yet changed this fashion, and attempts to create a taboo on sunbathing have been marginally less effective than the campaign against tobacco.

Smell Lear's 'Give me an ounce of civet, good apothecary, to sweeten my imagination', like the repulsion which Casca feels in *Julius Caesar* for the 'sweaty night-caps' and 'bad breath' of the Roman mob, suggests that our own preoccupation with unpleasant smells is not a new phenomenon. The plethora of deodorants, mouthwashes, sprays and breath mints popularized by modern advertising techniques has nevertheless created a taboo against any kind of natural smell, an interdict satirized by the couplet 'The goat that reeks on yonder hill / Has browsed all day on chlorophyll'.

See below, **water**.

Socks There is probably no country in which a man wearing socks with sandals is not immediately identified as being what Paul Fussell calls an absolute nerd. It is nevertheless in Australia that it is the quickest way to lose status. It is described as 'a filthy Pom* habit', almost as bad as wearing ankle socks with bush shorts instead of socks which go right up to the knee.

In both cases, the taboo is explicable in terms of the ban on mingling two kinds of dress. Just as the Israelites were told in *Leviticus*, 19:19 not to let 'a garment mingled of linen and woollen' come upon them, so the Australian male must not confuse formal and informal dress. Socks are worn in the city, and are hidden by the shoes against which they protect the feet. Sandals are to be worn in the country, where it is healthy to let the fresh air play on and about the feet to keep them cool. It is consequently counter-productive to wear socks. Short socks are worn with tennis shoes. A man walking in the bush needs protection all the way up to his knee. This is provided by long socks and boots.

Studs The wearing of studs by young people, either in the nose or ear, or occasionally even in the nipples, tongue or genitals, has analogies with the wearing of **pins** (see above). It can also have a more complex ideological motivation. Some of the studs are similar to certain forms of jewellery worn by Hindu or Muslim women. When worn by female Caucasian undergraduates, they express sympathy and solidarity with a group said to be persecuted by Western society.

At the same time, the studs express the same rejection of the bourgeois norm as the safety pins of the punk. Wearing them defies the taboo which says you are not allowed to hurt yourself (see **sado-masochism** in I). At the same time, the wearer also issues a challenge to what the apostles of the **politically correct** movement call the cult of bourgeois rationality. It is, the wearer proclaims, a matter of total indifference to me whether what I wear does or does not make me uncomfortable or unhealthy. By breaking the rules on what may or may not be worn in a particular

* =English; frequently lengthened to 'Pommie bastard', or 'whingeing Pom', i.e. an English immigrant discontented with his lot and given to complaining; as well as to organizing trade union activities.

part of my body, I am showing how arbitrary the standards of beauty are in the society which happens to exist at the moment.

A less condemnatory approach characterized an article entitled 'Piercing Looks' by Anne Patch in the *Yorkshire Evening Post* for 27 February 1996. 'Skin piercing' she wrote,

> is not merely a follow up to the punk fashion of the seventies. This form of body adornment has its roots in Roman times. Ear piercing, the most popular, has been around since time immemorial, although at the turn of the century it was almost seen as barbaric. The Romans were into nipple piercing. Centurions wore nipple rings as a sign of virility and courage and to hold their capes in place. Many Victorian and French aristocratic women wore such rings to enhance the shape of their nipples. Amongst the ancient Egyptians, navel piercing was a sign of royalty. Commoners were forbidden to adopt the practice. Prince Albert gave his name to a 'dressing ring' used to secure the part of his anatomy which might spoil the line of the extremely tight trousers which were popular at the time.

Tears To weep in public became highly suspect for men at roughly the same time as the 'great masculine renunciation' (see **colour**, above) prevented them from wearing colourful clothes. In seventeenth-century France, aristocrats as battle-hardened as the Grand Condé, who marked the beginning of French military predominance in Europe by beating the Spaniards at Rocroi in 1643, wept openly at performances of Corneille's tragedies. In the second half of the eighteenth century, the impact of Rousseau led to a situation where the ability to weep in public was a sign not only of sensitivity but of virtue. This changed with the industrial revolution. The tears of men who wept might blur the figures on the balance sheet.

In most contemporary cultures, it remains a sign of effeminacy in men to be seen crying in public, just as one of the quickest ways to lose status in a macho, working-class community is to fail to express an obsessive and overwhelming interest in sport. In its comments on the improved standing of women in Japanese society, an article in the *Daily Telegraph* for 23 March 1996 commented on how jealous some Japanese men felt of the freedom which their wives, sisters or girlfriends enjoyed at not having to spend their time either working, drinking or watching sport.

See **work** in I and **alcohol** in II.

Trousers (i) When, in 1947, the women's junior common room at King's College, London, decreed that none of its members would wear trousers, the decision was first of all interpreted as a rejection of wartime austerity. It fitted in with a refusal to countenance the lack of elegance in dress reflected at the time by the use of the word 'slacks' for women's trousers, and with Elizabeth Williams's recollection in *Only Halfway to Paradise* that 'the Amazons, the women in trousers, the good comrades had had their glorious day. Gracious living beckoned once again.'[26] What nobody said openly, but what was obvious to early students of semiology, was that the women were not only trying to be more feminine. They were also indicating their approval of a new puritanism. It had long been an article of faith among the French provincial bourgeoisie that a woman who wears trousers is no better than she ought to be. This view was now spreading to England.

This suspicion of women in trousers was not entirely an invention of the French. In 1590, according to Cesare Veccellio, the whores of Venice wore men's breeches in order to make their profession instantly recognizable.[27] From a practical point of view, it was an odd choice. As a Frenchmen is said to have exclaimed, on first seeing a Scottish regiment in kilts: 'Pour la guerre, je ne sais pas. Mais pour l'amour! C'est magnifique!' (I don't know about war. But marvellous for love.) He would not have made the same comment if they had been wearing breeks.

Theoretically, the 'ordonnance du 16 brumaire An IX' (14 November 1803) forbidding women to wear trousers has never been revoked. In 1933 Marlene Dietrich was told by the French police that she would have to choose between wearing trousers and staying in Paris.[28] The ban on women wearing trousers, or men dressing themselves up in skirts, shows the same desire to keep the categories separate as the dietary laws forbidding orthodox Jews to eat meat and dairy products at the same meal. There are also sexual implications. Respectable women wear skirts. That is how they identify themselves as respectable, marking themselves out as different from the sexually predatory men who wear trousers.

(ii) The revolutionary *sans-culottes* of the 1790s were so called because they had replaced the knee breeches and stockings of the *ancien régime* aristocracy by the modern trousers already worn by the Parisian working class. They were indicating their revolutionary sympathies by dressing down, just as the middle-class radicals of the 1960s who wished to affect a stance of being 'prolier than thou' wore the black leather jackets popular with the Berlin working class in the 1920s and 1930s.

Leather has since acquired a set of more complex sexual associations, especially in the homosexual S/M scene. Before then, a more sinister note was struck in England by the 1981 BBC television adaptation of Malcolm Bradbury's *The History Man* (1978). In it, the 'radical's radical' Howard Kirk, splendidly played by Anthony Sher, wore the long black leather coat fashionable at the time among academics sympathetic to the hard left, but reminiscent of the very similar garments worn by SS officers in the 1930s and 1940s. This enabled it to serve as a reminder of how successful other revolutionaries had been in the recent past, and of how unwise it therefore was to criticize what conservatives called the fascism of the left.

In *Language: Its Nature, Development and Origins* (1922), Otto Jespersen quotes Dickens's remark in *Dombey and Son* about 'those manly garments which are rarely mentioned by name' as a characteristic euphemism for trousers. I have not, however, been able to find chapter and verse for the allegation that the Victorians put little frills round the legs of tables and piano stools.

See **cross-dressing** above.

Umbrellas (i) In mid-twentieth-century America, there was as strict a taboo on men carrying umbrellas as there was in England against their wearing galoshes, or over-shoes. In both cases, the taboo may be interpreted as a desire not to appear effeminate, with the ban on umbrellas also being explicable by the desire of American men not to look English. There may have been political motivations behind this, in that the umbrella was still associated with Neville Chamberlain and the appeasement policy which culminated in the Munich agreements of September 1938.

When, in the film *Crimson Tide* (1995), Gene Hackman held an umbrella above his head while addressing the crew of the nuclear submarine US *Alabama*, it was clear that any associations of the umbrella with a lack of aggressive virility could, on occasion, yield to purely practical considerations. It was pouring with rain at the time. The wartime taboo on British naval officers carrying umbrellas was also lifted when they were stationed in Sierra Leone and ran the risk of being caught in a torrential downpour.

(ii) Ruth Benedict reports that the sumptuary laws in feudal Japan emphasized the merchants' low social position, regulating 'the clothes they could wear, the umbrellas they could carry, the amount they could spend for a wedding or a funeral'.[29] The umbrella played a comparable role as one of the signs whereby boys at English public schools indicated their status in the school hierarchy. In nineteenth-century Harrow, juniors could not have their umbrella furled, while at Eton, only members of Pop had the right to carry a tightly rolled umbrella. Public schools are so called because they were, in the nineteenth century, publicly reformed, thus distinguishing themselves from the private schools which kept the rules designed by their individual proprietor. Pop is a self-elected group of boys who originally used to meet in a tuck shop known by its Latin name of *Popina*. Freudians see the tightly rolled umbrella as a sign of sexuality kept firmly under control, a penis wrapped in an easily transportable shield.

Uncircumcised (i) The importance in Jewish culture of the *bris* or *briss* ceremony conducted on the male child within eight days after birth means that circumcision is not the taboo topic that it tends to be among squeamish Gentiles. There, it is sometimes avoided as a subject of conversation with the same care as operations on the prostate gland.

Although there is no mention of circumcision in the Koran, its rejection by the early Christian Church offers a possible key as to why it is practised in certain Muslim societies. It was, apparently, a close-run thing whether circumcision should be a necessary precondition for membership of the whole of the Christian Church, as indeed it still is for the Church of Abyssinia. St Paul led the opposition, so that there is a note of not unjustified triumph in *Colossians*, 3:10–11:

> And have put on the new man, which is renewed in knowledge after the image of him that created him:
>
> Where there is neither Greek not Jew, circumcision nor uncircumcision, Barbarian, Scythian, bond nor free: but Christ is all, and in all.

One result of this statement by the man normally referred to by Jews as Paul of Tarsus was the introduction into the service performed in orthodox synagogues of the prayer:

> I thank God I was born; I thank God I was born a Jew and not a Gentile; and I thank God I was born a man and not a woman.

This took place in what Christians call the first-century AD and Jews in the United States occasionally refer to as the first century CE (= Christian Era). The timing of the prayer suggests that it was a conscious riposte to *Colossians* 3:11, and strenuous waving of the prayer shawl was another change introduced at the same time.

The description of the rite in *Genesis*, 17:9–14 makes it very clear that circumcision is a sign of group membership. In the Old Testament, 'the uncircumcised' is a term of intense opprobrium. I *Samuel*, 18:24–8 describes how David offers King Saul the foreskins of 200 Philistines in response to the challenge to prove his worthiness to marry the king's daughter Michal. The dislike of 'the uncircumcised' survived long enough for them to be addressed, as they are in *Acts*, 7:51, as the 'stiffnecked' who 'always resist the Holy Ghost'.

(ii) The custom itself may go back to the days when men went about naked. If this is the case, then circumcision was originally akin to tattooing or the making of facial incisions as a mark of tribal identity. It can therefore be seen as an illustration of Ruth P. Rubenstein's remark, in her *Dress Codes: Meanings and Messages in American Culture* (1995), that while there are many societies in which people are unclothed, there are none in which they are unadorned. When Charles Darwin, seeing the snow melting on their bare skins, gave blankets to the Yaggans of Tierra del Fuego, they tore them into strips and used them as decoration.

Circumcision goes back to the Egypt of 3000 BC, and sculptures on Greek vases clearly show the Egyptians as different from the

Athenians by being circumcised. Those who have undergone circumcision know that they are marked for life with the badge of membership of their tribe. Those, like the Sikhs, who pointedly refuse it, do so in order to show that they are different from the other cultures, especially that of Islam, with which they might come into contact.

In addition to its semiotic function, circumcision has a number of other features in common with taboos. It is cruel, irrational, denies any possibility of choice to the children or adolescents on whom it is inflicted, gives a privileged position to men, and bestows power on the elders of the tribe. When the ceremony is postponed until puberty, it emphasizes the control that the old exercise over the sexuality of the young. The taboo on retaining the foreskin is shared by a number of societies, including the Australian Aborigines, the Zulus, the Xhosa, and the natives of New Caledonia. It was also practised by the Aztecs.

In Book II of the *Histories*, Herodotus said that by practising circumcision the Egyptians differed from men of other nations, 'who leave their private parts alone'. He attributed the practice to hygienic reasons, writing that they 'preferred to be clean than comely'. If they thought this, the Egyptians were as mistaken about its effects as Herodotus was about their uniqueness in practising it. Circumcision came to be publicly justified on the grounds of health only in the late nineteenth century. The statistics which then purported to show that the wives of circumcised men had a lower incidence of cancer of the womb have since been revealed as misleading.

The ceremonies surrounded the public circumcision of boys are much more elaborate than when the operation is performed on a girl. This is because those societies which practise it when the boy is in his early teens use it as a '*rite de passage*', marking the period when the boy will no longer spend most of his time in the company of women but will join the men. In some societies, the boy goes to the ceremonies dressed in girl's clothes, and assumes full male attire only afterwards. Although the girl will always remain within the women's world, whether circumcised or not, there are societies in which, as among the Berti of Sudan studied by Ladislav Holy, she is unacceptable as a bride until the operation has been performed. Female circumcision is against the law in

France and one of the arguments put forward against allowing girls to wear the chadour or Muslim veil in the classroom is that such tolerance could be interpreted as a move towards the approval of less humane practices.

(iii) There are a number of reasons for seeing a strong sexual element in circumcision, and thus interpreting it as more than merely a sign of tribal membership. In *The Wise Wound* (1978), Peter Redgrove and Penelope Shuttle quote Bruno Bettelheim's *Symbolic Wounds: Puberty Rites and the Envious Male* (1955) to support their view that male circumcision is an attempt to obtain the blood which symbolizes the wisdom naturally vouchsafed to women by menstrual bleeding. 'Look!' they envisaged the elders of the tribe declaring. 'I too have a menstruating vagina.'[30] For the Dogon tribe of Mali, circumcision constitutes a necessary step in the fulfilment of male sexuality. They believe that every human being is born with both a male and a female soul. The male soul can be released only if the female soul, represented by the foreskin, is removed.[31]

Confirmation for John J. Honigman's view that 'circumcision, like blood-letting, was originally part of a private sacrifice which cemented the group to God'[32] is offered by the fourth chapter of *Exodus*. Moses has attracted the Lord's anger by not having his son circumcised. Zipporah, his wife, daughter of Jethro, has to take a sharp stone and circumcise her son, declaring; 'A bloody husband thou art, because of the circumcision', before the Lord agrees to release him. The evidence of those cultures which postpone circumcision until puberty, and which also practise female circumcision, or infibulation, reinforces its sexual connotations. *Exodus*, 4:22–6 also suggests that the practice may have originated either as a sacrifice to the goddess of fertility, or as a '*rite de passage*' from childhood to adolescence, with everything that this implies by way of sexual activity. The descriptions of the ceremonies, whether by anthropologists such as Ladislav Holy or travellers with as strong an admiration for the Arabs as Wilfred Thesiger, make it sound a highly painful ordeal.[33]

See above, **infibulation**.

Veil (i) The idea of women veiling their heads is common to all three religions which originated in the Middle East, and St Paul maintained the Judaic tradition as far as women were concerned when he wrote in I *Corinthians*, 11:5–6:

> But every woman that prayeth or prophesieth with her head uncovered dishonoureth her head: for that is even all one as if she were shaven.
>
> For if the woman be not covered, let her also be shorn: but if it be a shame for a woman to be shorn or shaven, let her be covered.

St Paul nevertheless broke with Judaism by writing in I *Corinthians*, 11:4 that 'Every man praying or prophesying, having his head covered, dishonoureth his head'. His ruling is still visible in the way that men attending a service in the Church of England take their hats off. In the more traditional parishes, however, women are still not expected to come to church without a hat.

Later in the same chapter, St Paul maintains that if a man has long hair, it is 'a shame unto him', whereas for a woman it is 'a glory to her', and the rules he lays down illustrate at one and the same time how taboos about headgear can function as signs indicating membership of a particular religion – orthodox Jewish men must wear a hat inside the synagogue as well as on their way to it – and how they had sexual connotations from the very beginning. For it is hard not to read I *Corinthians*, 11:9–10 –

> Neither was the man created for the woman; but the woman for the man.
>
> For this cause ought the woman to have power on her head because of the angels

– in anything but a sexual sense. Men control their sexuality by keeping their hair short while women indicate their sexual availability by keeping it long; except in church, where their minds should be on other things.

(ii) *Sura* 24.31 of the Koran, which instructs women not to reveal their beauty except to close relatives, creates what modern fundamentalism imposes as a taboo on their appearing unveiled in public. Although Cyril Glassé points out in *The Concise Encyclopedia of Islam* (1989) that 'the wearing of a veil is not a religious requirement of Islam but a matter of cultural milieu', some highly orthodox Muslim women interpret *Sura* 24.31 as commanding them to leave the house only when entirely shrouded in black. In the France of the late 1980s and the early 1990s, the wearing of the chadour gave rise to a quarrel about whether Muslim girls should or should not wear a head-scarf in class in the state schools.

Since 1881, state education has been strictly secular in France, and France itself a secular republic since 1905. Teachers must observe a strict neutrality on all religious and political matters, and there has always been a ban on any form of religious or political propaganda by the pupils themselves. Within the classroom, Catholics must not wear a crucifix, Jews the yarmulka, or Muslim women the chadour, since to do so could be interpreted as a sign inviting their fellow pupils to do likewise. In October 1989, Ernest Chenière, head teacher at the Collège Gabriel-Havez, at Creil in the outskirts of Paris, instructed five Muslim girls to remove their veils and appear in class bareheaded like everybody else.

Chenière's supporters argued that he was perfectly justified in excluding pupils who did not keep to the rules in this way. The Muslim families to whom these girls belonged had, after all, chosen to live in France, and were thus under the moral as well as the legal obligation to observe the law. The next step, it was argued, would be the refusal of orthodox Muslim parents to allow their children to attend classes in biology on the grounds that Darwinian evolutionism was against their faith, and to insist on separate classes for the teaching of history. Chenière's supporters replied to the accusation that the exclusion of these Muslim girls was a form of racism by pointing out that they were perfectly entitled to come to school if they kept the rules. They also drew the attention of anyone criticizing Chenière's behaviour as racist to the fact that he was from the French West Indies and black. This particular argument lost some of its force when Chenière later stood, unsuccessfully, as a candidate in a municipal election for Jean-Marie Le Pen's National Front, and the conflict between freedom of conscience and the secular ideal was less clear-cut than either side contended.

There is a contrast with the ruling given by the US Supreme Court in 1969 in the case of *Tinker* v. *Des Moines* School District. By a vote of seven to two it upheld the right of three high school students to wear black armbands in order to protest against government policy in Vietnam. A 'symbolic gesture' of this kind, the court ruled, constituted 'a silent expression of opinion, unaccompanied by any disorder or disturbance'. Gestures of this kind were in this respect judged to be 'a protected substitute for speech'. One of the ways in which Germaine Greer's *Sex and Destiny* (1984) offers support to ways of thinking which her earlier book, *The Female Eunuch* (1970) would have criticized as highly reactionary can be illustrated by her remark that in 1937, when the veil was banned in Iran, 'many older women refused to leave their houses because their self-image depended on being screened from the eyes of strangers'.[34]

Water The idea that a taboo on washing could actually exist is likely to inspire even more incredulity among modern readers than the notion that the ban on **pork** is not hygienic in origin, or that the taboo against **incest** was not originally inspired by the fear of producing unhealthy offspring. As George Orwell remarked in *The Road to Wigan Pier* (1937), everyone knew that 'the lower classes smell', and that the only way to avoid this terrible fate was to take a cold bath every morning. Similarly, it was an article of faith in nineteenth-century England that while Napoleon had weakened himself by taking a series of very hot baths, Wellington had retained enough vigour to win the battle of Waterloo by taking a cold bath every morning.

The sixteenth and seventeenth centuries nevertheless witnessed a revulsion against washing which contrasted with the Roman cult of the public bath and with its continuation into the Middle Ages. The taboo on washing yourself all over lasted in France at least to the middle of the nineteenth century, with a Dr Goulin being reported as having told his patients, in 1848, to follow the precept 'Saepe manus, rare pedes, nunquam caput' (the hands often, the feet rarely, the head never).[35] When a Miss Pardoe, visiting Lady Mary Wortley Montagu in Constantinople in the early eighteenth century, expressed surprise at the grubbiness of Lady Mary's hands, she received the immediate reply: 'Ah, madame, if you were to see my feet!' The fact that Nana, the high-class prostitute in Zola's *Les Rougon-Macquart* (1871–93), has a splendidly equipped bathroom is a sign of the contrast between the degraded nature of her profession and the luxury it makes possible. When, in the early twentieth century, the Ritz Carlton hotel in New York installed bidets, the management was immediately compelled to remove them by the League of Decency.[36]

The lack of hygiene in the Versailles of Louis XIV was not due to inadequate technology. The fountains worked, albeit intermittently, and the knowledge needed to install flushing toilets was certainly there. But as Nancy Mitford comments in *The Sun King* (1966), most houses and palaces relied until the twentieth century on the chamber-pot and the outside loo. When she herself was presented at Court in 1923, she writes, 'the only possibility offered was a chamber-pot behind a screen in the ladies' cloakroom'.[37] It was a question not of technology but of attitude. The various Christian Churches competed with one another to show a contempt for bodily comfort which was seen as a necessary condition for spiritual salvation. Christendom in general was also anxious to distinguish itself from an Islam in which bathing was an accepted part of life, and the Turkish bath is still considered by traditionally minded Englishmen as a decadent as well as an Oriental institution. In late nineteenth-century England, the adoption by the Salvation Army of the motto 'Soup, Soap and Salvation' emphasized its desire to carry the relatively recent view that cleanliness is next to godliness as far as or even further than any of its rivals.

In *The Independent* for 27 October 1995, the practice of washing the dishes after a meal was described as 'the nation's last taboo'. The article containing the phrase began with the remark: 'Washing up is a bit like sex. We all do it, we rarely talk about it in public, and although it may be humdrum, it can also be an extremely intense experience.' It is also an experience which tends to bring people together, especially in a family. Anyone not leaving the dining-room for the kitchen to help with the washing-up will soon become aware that they are losing out on the fun.

White The suggestion by Henry Beard and Christopher Cerf that this should be replaced by 'melanin impoverished' reflects the ambition of politically correct discourse to avoid any suggestion of moral or cultural superiority of the type implied by the words which Kipling puts into the mouth of Canada in the poem 'Our Lady of the Snows' (1897):

Soberly under the White Man's law
  My white men go their ways.

It is difficult, however, in the better-known 'Gunga Din', to suggest how Kipling can avoid using the taboo word 'white' in order to express the theme of the poem, which is the recognition by the white-skinned, British soldier of the moral superiority of the black-skinned, Indian water-carrier. Early in the poem, which ends with the line 'You're a better man than I am, Gunga Din!', the soldier declares:

An' for all 'is dirty 'ide,
'E was white, clear white, inside
When 'e went to tend the wounded under fire!

Kipling was a taboo author in the literary world of the 1930s, to be mentioned only with the kind of disapproval which Auden puts into his poem on the death of Yeats (1939), in which he argues that the ability of a poet to use language makes even the most unattractive political attitudes acceptable:

Time that with this strange excuse
Pardons Kipling, and his views,
And will pardon Paul Claudel
Pardons them for writing well.

See above, **colour**; also **black** in III and **race** in IV.

NOTES

1 See Franz Steiner, *Taboo*, Cohen and West, London, 1956; Penguin, Harmondsworth, 1967, p. 32. 'Only later', writes Steiner, 'did it come to signify sacred or prohibited in a secondary sense; because sacred things and places were commonly marked in a peculiar manner in order that everyone might know that they were sacred.'
2 Mary Douglas, *Natural Symbols*, Barrie and Jenkins, London, 1970, p. 102.
3 See Erving Goffman, *Stigma: Notes on the Management of Spoiled Identity*, Prentice Hall, New York, 1963; Penguin, Harmondsworth, 1968, p. 60; and Ray B. Browne, editor, *Forbidden Fruits: Taboos and Tabooism in Culture*, Bowling Green University Press, Bowling Green, Ohio, 1984, p. 179.

4 Jonathan Gathorne-Hardy, *The Public School Phenomenon*, Hodder and Stoughton, London, 1977, p. 234 and p. 401. 'A' levels correspond to graduation from an American high school, and a pass in at least two subjects is essential for entrance to a university.
5 See Ruth P. Rubenstein, *Dress Codes: Meanings and Messages in American Culture*, Westview Press, Boulder, CO, 1995, p. 33 and p. 76.
6 Judith Martin, *Miss Manner's Guide to Excruciatingly Correct Behaviour*, Hamish Hamilton, London, 1983, p. 544.
7 See 'The Eclipse of Showa Taboos and the Apology Resolution', *Japan Quarterly*, October–December 1995, pp. 419–23. For a further discussion of the issue, see Ian Buruma, *The Wages of Guilt: Memories of War in Germany and Japan*, Vintage, London and New York, 1985.
8 Rubenstein, *Dress Codes*, p. 242.
9 George Orwell, 'England, Your England' (1941), in *Selected Essays*, Penguin, Harmondsworth, 1957, p. 64. See also *The Complete Essays, Journalism and Letters of George Orwell*, Secker and Warburg, London, 1968, Volume II, 'My Country Right or Left', p. 70.
10 Alan Bennett, *Writing Home* (1993), Faber and Faber, London, 1994, p. 270.
11 See the review on p. 333 of *Man*, the journal of the Royal Anthropological Institute, New Series, Volume 9, 1974, of Yitzchak Elam's *The Social and Sexual Roles of Hima Women: a Study of Nomadic Cattle Breeders in Nyamushozi County, Ankole, Uganda*, Manchester University Press, Manchester, 1973. For Oprah Winfrey, see Lorraine Gamman and Merja Makinnen, *Female Fetishism*, Lawrence and Wishart, London, 1994, p. 158.
12 Norbert Elias, *The Civilising Process: The History of Manners* (1938), Basil Blackwell, Oxford, 1978, p. 68.
13 Elias, *The Civilising Process*, p. 115.
14 Edmund Leach, 'Magical Hair', *Man:* the journal of the Royal Anthropological Institute, Volume 88, 1958, pp. 147–62.
15 See P. Hershman, 'Hair, Sex and Dirt', *Man:* the journal of the Royal Anthropological Institute, New Series, Volume 9, 1974, pp. 274–98. For Edmund Leach, see *Man*, Old Series, Volume 29, pp. 147–64.
16 Gathorne-Hardy, *The Public School Phenomenon*, p. 177.
17 Brian Simon and Ian Bradley, *The Victorian Public School*, Gill and Macmillan, London, 1975, p. 175.
18 See Hershman, 'Hair, Sex and Dirt'.
19 Elaine Showalter, *Sexual Anarchy*, Bloomsbury, London, 1991, p. 130.
20 Mrs Humphrey, *Manners for Men*, James Bowden, London, 1897, pp. 67–8. The reprinting of this book in 1993 by Pryor Publications, Whitstable, Kent, like the reappearance in 1946 of the 1834 *Hints on*

Etiquette and Usages of Society: With a Glance at Bad Manners, points to an interest in the social taboos of the past that sees them as very funny.

21 Margaret Visser, *The Rituals of Dinner* (1991), Viking Penguin, London, 1992, p. 185 and Martin, *Miss Manners' Guide*, p. 148.

22 See p. 48 of Rubenstein, *Dress Codes.*

23 Paul Fussell, *Caste Marks: Style and Status in the U.S.A.*, Heinemann, London, 1984, p. 63.

24 Ruth Benedict, *The Chrysanthemum and the Sword*, Charles E. Tuttle, Vermont and Tokyo, 1946, p. 61.

25 Bernard Levin, *A World Elsewhere*, Jonathan Cape, London, 1994, p. 113.

26 Quoted in Elizabeth Rouse, *Understanding Fashion*, Blackwell Scientific Publications, Oxford, 1989, p. 190.

27 See p. 108 of Rubenstein, *Dress Codes.* In the previous century, the Venetians had already shown an anxiety to make their whores instantly identifiable. According to p. 71 of Paul Tabori's *Dress and Undress*, New English Library, London, 1969, they required them to sit with bare breasts in front of an open window, hoping that their charms would divert young men from the 'unnatural aberration' of homosexuality.

28 See p. 38 of Philippe Perrot, *Les Dessus et les Dessous de la bourgeoisie*, Fayard, Paris, 1980.

29 Benedict, *The Chrysanthemum and the Sword*, p. 62.

30 Penelope Shuttle and Peter Redgrove, *The Wise Wound* (1978), Penguin Books, Harmondsworth, 1980, p. 67.

31 See the entry 'prépuce' in Volume IV of Jean Chevalier and Alain Gheerbrant, *Dictionnaire des symboles*, Seghers, Paris, 1974.

32 John J. Honigman, *The Development of Anthropological Ideas*, Dorsey Press, Homewood, Illinois, 1976, p. 150.

33 See p. 105 of Wilfred Thesiger, *Arabian Sands*, Longman, London, 1959, Penguin, Harmondsworth, 1964, and the mention on p. 124 of widespread shame for a boy who cannot stand the pain:

> 'By God, Ali's son made a fuss when they cut him. He cried out like a woman.' The others laughed and some of them exclaimed: 'God blacken his face!' I realised that this wretched boy's failure would soon be known far and wide among the Bedu.

See also chapter 7 of Ladislav Holy, *Religion and Custom in a Muslim Society*, Cambridge University Press, Cambridge, 1991, especially the cold notation on p. 169: 'The circumcision of girls is of the pharaonic type and consists of the removal of the clitoris, labia minora and labia majora.' As Huxley says, one is all for religion until one has been to a really religious country.

34 Germaine Greer, *Sex and Destiny: The Politics of Human Fertility*, Secker and Warburg, London, 1984, p. 206.

35 Quoted by Philippe Perrot, *Le travail des apparences ou les transformations du corps féminin, XVIIIe et XIXe siècles*, Editions du Seuil, Paris, 1982, p. 121.

36 See Lawrence Wright, *Clean and Decent: The Fascinating History of the Bathroom and the WC*, Routledge and Kegan Paul, London, 1960, p. 118.

37 Nancy Mitford, *The Sun King*, Hamish Hamilton, London, 1969, p. 53.

CONCLUSION

A SENSE OF COMMUNITY

In *It Doesn't Take a Hero*, Norman H. Schwarzkopf describes how he ensured that all the troops taking part in the operation 'Desert Storm' in 1990 were well briefed on the need to commit no offence against the various customs of Arabic and Islamic society. His insistence that no one should drink alcohol, like the ban he imposed upon the import into Saudi Arabia of soft porn magazines, was primarily a reflection of the need to avoid alienating an essential political ally. If there was going to be a united front in the campaign to free Kuwait from military occupation by Iraq, the fire-power of the forces operating under the flag of the United Nations needed to be supplemented by a visible ideological unity. This could be achieved only by the readiness of the more open society of the West to accept, if even only on a temporary basis, the taboos of a society based on customs whose supernatural origin placed them beyond criticism or change.

General Schwarzkopf's assessment of the political needs of the campaign also reflected a basic common politeness. It is very ill bred to offend against the customs that enable the members of any society not only to communicate with one another but also to indicate how they differ from their friends as well as from their enemies. Taboos on alcohol or the presentation of semi-naked women may seem highly irrational. They remain one of the principal ways in which Islamic society maintains its sense of collective identity. The arguments in favour of taboos are not limited to the central issue of what role the law should play in modern society. There is more to it than Lord Devlin's contention that there is no such thing as private morality in sexual matters, and that the law has the duty to intervene to stop what the libertarian would see as self-regarding activities such as homosexual behaviour between adults. Taboos can be seen as a means whereby society tries to hold itself together against internal decay as well as external threats.

They can also be defended on practical grounds by the parallel with what happens in a community where adults are actively involved in a wide range of cultural and social activities. Children or adolescents living in such a community run a much lower risk of becoming delinquents than those whose parents, relatives and neighbours do nothing except go to work and watch television. The link is irrational in that there is no observable cause-and-effect relationship. It is not something that can be proved, and it has nothing to do with the intellectual or cultural level of the activities in which the adults choose to involve themselves. These can be bridge or church-going, amateur dramatics or work for a charitable organization, trade union activity or rugby league, soft ball or darts, model-making or gardening, the Workers Educational Association or the rotary club. Nor is it necessary for the young people themselves to be involved. There is a kind of moral equivalent to the 'trickle-down' effect which market economists present as increasing the general wealth of society by the tendency of the activities of the rich to create employment for the poor. What these activities bring about is the diffusion of a sense of community whose effects can be explained only by seeing society as an organic whole and not as a mechanistic association of individuals.

Taboos can sometimes be justified on the grounds that they play a very similar role. Just as there is a statistical link between a high level of social participation by adults and a low level of juvenile delinquency, so there is a tendency for members of sub groups that observe a large number of taboos to give very little trouble to the police. Orthodox Jews, fundamentalist Muslims, Seventh Day Adventists, members of the Free Presbyterian Church of Scotland, of the Plymouth Brethren or of the Salvation Army, all accept a high degree of control over their private behaviour. All have a strong sense of personal responsibility, stable families, and a virtually non-existent criminality. The theology on which their behaviour is based may be intellectually inadequate. It may give rise to restrictions on personal conduct which the libertarian would unhesitatingly dismiss as taboos. But there is no doubting the socially beneficial effects of the discipline that the taboos inseparable from such creeds impose upon their followers.

ARGUMENTS IN FAVOUR OF TABOOS

The above argument is different from the political case for taboos put forward by thinkers of a conservative persuasion. This involves the acceptance of a society where authority is clearly based on an established and unquestionable social hierarchy, and which draws its strength from taboos at the same time as it helps them to maintain their force. Shakespeare's Ulysses sets out the case for such a society in the first Act of *Troilus and Cressida* when he tells Nestor:

> Take but degree away, untune that string,
> And hark what discord follows! Each thing meets
> In mere oppugnancy: the bounded waters
> Should lift their bosoms higher than the shores,
> And make a sop of all this solid globe;
> Strength should be lord of imbecility
> And the rude son should strike the father dead;
> Force should be right, or, rather, right and wrong –
> Between whose endless jar justice resides –
> Should lose their names and so should justice too.
> Then everything includes itself in power,
> Power into will, will into appetite;
> And appetite, an universal wolf,
> So doubly seconded with will and power,
> Must make perforce an universal prey,
> And last eat up himself.

The argument that anarchy is the worst of all social evils is a powerful one. If taboos had been able to prevent the kind of chaos which broke out in Rwanda or the former Yugoslavia in the early 1990s, they would figure among the most valuable political inventions devised by men. Although it would nowadays be impossible to find rational arguments to justify a society based on the kind of hierarchy outlined by Ulysses, there is a strong case for having a community held together by something other than enlightened self-interest. There is, fortunately, little possibility of Western industrial society going back to the kind of society admired by Shakespeare's Ulysses. It was one in which what Edmund Burke called 'the principles of natural subordination' provided a kind of organic link between all its members, but at the high cost of complete social immobility.[1] That idea, together with the religious justification on which Burke's 'principles of natural subordination' were based – *Romans*, 13:1: 'Let every soul be subject unto the higher powers. For there is no power but of God: the powers that be are ordained of God' – belongs so thoroughly to the past that it can never be revived.

This does not, however, remove the case for having a set of moral rules which are accepted for other reasons than the protection they afford, through the legal system, to specific individuals and definable social groups. Arthur Koestler's Rubashov, in the novel *Darkness at Noon* (1940), makes exactly this point to himself as he paces up and down in his prison cell, awaiting execution as one of the victims of the purges whereby Stalin maintained his authority in the Soviet Union of the late 1930s:

> Looking back over his past, it seemed to him now that for forty years he had been running amuck – the running amuck of pure reason. Perhaps it did not suit man to be completely freed from old bonds, from the steadying brakes of 'Thou shalt not' and 'Thou mayst not', and be allowed to tear straight along towards the goal.[2]

You do not need to be an out-and-out reactionary to see the advantages of what George Orwell called, in his essay 'England, Your England' (1941), 'the strange mixture of reality and illusion, democracy and privilege, humbug and decency, the subtle network of compromises, by which the nation keeps itself in its familiar shape',[3] and to recognize that one of the uses of even the most apparently irrational taboos may be to help keep a society on an even keel.

It is also possible to argue that attitudes and practices which a later culture might dismiss as taboos, and regard as narrow-minded and hypocritical, did, in their day, perform an invaluable role for the dignity of those who adopted and followed them. 'It is not usual nowadays', wrote Steven Marcus in *The Other Victorians* (1964),

> to regard such values as chastity, modesty, propriety or even rigid prudery as positive moral values, but it is difficult to doubt that in the urban lower social classes they operated with positive force. The discipline and self-restraint which the exercise of such virtues required could not but be a giant step towards the humanization of a class of people who had traditionally been regarded as almost another species.[4]

There is an immediate if involuntary parallel here with the contention in Claude Lévi-Strauss's work that 'incest rules convert unregulated copulation present in nature into an orderly system of marriage characteristic of culture'.[5] In this respect, taboos embody something of the principle of deferred gratification which Freud sees as the first step towards the process of civilization. They thus represent a practice which any culture rejects completely only at its peril. The society described by Steven Marcus in *The Other Victorians* was one of extreme social inequality and great economic injustice. Working-class women may have used prudery and even frigidity as means of escaping from the animality in which men of their own class, as well as members of the aristocracy and bourgeoisie, tried to imprison them by the forms of sexual behaviour in which they expected and required them to take part.

These are tempting arguments, comparable in weight with the practical benefits offered by a society with a strong sense of corporate identity. This identity does not draw much strength from a legal system based solely on rational concepts of punishment and deterrence. It can, in contrast, receive powerful reinforcement from certain forms of religious belief. There is something odd about the claim made by the American jurist Sanford H. Kadish when he said:

> Thurman Arnold surely had it right when he observed that certain laws 'are unenforced because we want to continue our conduct, and unrepealed because we want to preserve our morals'.[6]

It is true that Lord Devlin can be interpreted as giving the law a semiotic function as well as a punitive or deterrent role. At the same time as the law defines the penalties attached to anti-social actions, it is also a set of signs setting out the values that society thinks are important. It does this, in particular, when judges choose to deliver what is called an exemplary sentence in order to express the abhorrence in which the actions of a particular individual are held. But the signs of more general disapproval which the law gives out when it punishes other offences cannot function without a content. There is no point in having laws which, as Thurman Arnold suggests might be the case, are never enforced.

There is also a case, in the private as well as in the public sphere, for having taboos which place limits on the discussion of certain topics and on the expression of certain ideas. It is best expressed in literature in Ibsen's *The Wild Duck* (1884), with its portrait of the disasters produced by an idealist who insists on requiring all the members of a problem family to face up to the truth about themselves. Most private relationships benefit from having a series of private, often unspoken taboos about what can be openly said or frankly discussed, and not all societies derive profit from the removal of every taboo on what can be revealed about their past. The remark that Irish history is something which all Irishmen should forget and all Englishmen remember can be applied to other countries with a comparable history of invasion, oppression and civil war. Some taboos are best left in place, and it is often hard to see what purpose is served by the constant raking-over of the coals of French history between 1940 and 1944 in order to see who did and who did not support the Vichy government. The unity established by Tito in the former Yugoslavia may have been based on a myth, and on a series of taboos which prevented the expression of Serbian, Bosnian or Croatian nationalism. But it was certainly preferable to what happened after his death. We may be right to laugh at the euphemisms with which the Victorians surrounded such natural events as sexual intercourse and pregnancy. There are nevertheless days when one feels that a few more euphemisms, and a few more taboos upon the sexual questions which can be openly discussed, would be very welcome on British television.

These arguments in favour of taboos are nevertheless not irrefutable, and there are at least nine reasons to resist any feelings of nostalgia for a society governed by more taboos than are formally recognized in the culture and the legal system of the United

States and the United Kingdom in the late twentieth century. It is the soundness of these reasons which provides the intellectual basis for the pejorative overtones which the word 'taboo' has acquired in modern English, and to which I referred in my Introduction. The habit of using the word primarily in an ironic sense does not stem from a purely frivolous rejection of the stricter morality of the past. It reflects the ideal of a society in which controls on action and expression are reduced to a minimum consistent with public safety.

REASONS TO RESIST NOSTALGIA FOR TABOOS

The first and most important of the reasons for feeling suspicious of any desire to resuscitate the taboos of the past lies in the Sermon on the Mount. Hutton Webster defines a taboo as 'an imperative Thou Shalt Not in the presence of dangers apprehended'.[7] Taboos tell people what not to do, generally without explaining to them why. What characterizes the teaching of Christ in *Matthew*, 5 is the positive commandment to behave with love and charity towards our neighbours. It places the moral responsibility for virtuous action on the individual, and explains that this is the way to a more perfect life. Our Lord spends far more time telling people what they should do than what they should not, and his message coincides with the ethical teaching of the other higher religions. The institution of marriage has no need to be protected by what Peregrine Worsthorne calls sexual taboos, and which he rather disappointingly fails to define. It is founded on a sense of responsibility towards one's partner, towards one's children and towards oneself. This responsibility may be difficult to exercise, but there is no doubt about the soundness of its intellectual basis. It does not need reinforcing by anything so irrational as a taboo.

The second reason for being suspicious of any return of a taboo-dominated society lies in the realization that any long-term and satisfactory improvement in the condition of the Victorian women described by Steven Marcus lay not in more taboos but in greater social justice. He himself argues that the sexual revolution which has taken place in the Western world since the 1960s came about as a substitute for the economic and social revolution which failed to materialize after 1945. It would be small consolation to those who are still at the bottom of the pile to make them go back to the often highly repressive Victorian values which went hand in hand with the even greater social inequalities of the nineteenth century.

The third reason for not wishing to bring back the taboos of the past is that they tended to ban activities which do not particularly matter, while leaving important ones completely untouched. There are, it is true, ancient and well-established taboos against killing members of one's own tribe, and these support Hutton Webster's contention in *Taboo: A Sociological Study* (1942) that murder is comparatively rare among the pre-literate societies where taboos are most numerous. But human beings as a whole have been singularly indifferent to developing taboos against killing members of their own species who do not belong to their own particular tribe. Warriors who have killed a tribal enemy may, as among the Fijians or the Mekeo tribes of British New Guinea, have to submit to a series of purification ceremonies before being allowed to resume full membership of their community. They were required to eat special food in a place set aside for them, as well as to abstain from sexual intercourse.[8] But no culture has yet evolved a set of taboos which totally ban human beings from killing one another.

There have, in contrast, been a large number of taboos against various forms of sexual activity. It is hard not to see this as an unconscious tribute to the power of sex as a means whereby human beings escape from the pressure of society and enjoy themselves as individuals. In so far as such taboos have tended to encourage monogamy and marital fidelity, there is clearly a strong case for maintaining them. But since such taboos have also been directed against forms of sexual activity which, like oral sex, are perfectly compatible with a stable relationship within marriage, it is very tempting to see them in a less favourable light. Taboos are about power. Taboos on sexual activity are a means whereby a group with a particular concept of what sex ought to be like tries to impose its views on everybody else. For all the demographic and theological arguments surrounding them, this is especially true of the taboos on **contraception**, **homosexuality** and **oral sex** discussed in section I. The ambition to prevent people from enjoying themselves too much seems to be a permanent feature of human beings, and to be as common among those who have no effective power in society as among those who have taken on the responsibilities of leadership. Indeed, in the United Kingdom at any rate, newspapers aimed at a popular readership are much more censorious than those aimed at a more intellectual public, and revolutionaries do not need to be successful to exhibit a strong tendency towards puritanism, especially in sexual matters. Christ set very high standards in *Matthew*, 5:28 – 'whosoever looketh on a woman to lust after her hath committed adultery with her already in his heart' – and life would have not been very amusing in fifteenth-century Florence if Savonarola's ideas had been allowed to triumph. Cromwell, Robespierre, Lenin, Stalin and Castro all tried to divert to political activity the energy which most human beings, when left to themselves, prefer to spend on sex.

It is equally tempting to see the number and variety of taboos about sex as a substitute for the failure of society to control genuinely anti-social behaviour. It is very difficult to prevent people from killing their fellows. They do so in armed bands, whose activities are sometimes dangerous to resist. When such bands are integrated into society, they constitute powerful pressure groups. It is hard to resist their arguments in favour of a preventive strike against a potential enemy, and it is a matter of common experience that societies which try to keep themselves to themselves are only occasionally successful in holding off predatory neighbours. When human beings are enjoying sex, on the other hand, they are behaving with all the vulnerability of isolated individuals seeking nothing but their own pleasure. This offers an irresistible opportunity to try to stop them. Freud may or may not have been right to argue that we seek to repress with most fervour those activities by which we are most tempted. The multiplicity of taboos against sex suggests that he was right to see taboos as a means whereby people sought to restrict the ability of their fellows to enjoy themselves.

It is, in this respect, the contrast between the relative lack of importance of most of the activities forbidden by taboos and the extreme gravity of those they have left untouched which is one of the best arguments against trying to revive them. From an ethical point of view, it really does not matter whether one does or does not abstain from pork, beef or alcohol. Neither is it a moral offence to use rude words, or to read the kind of books in the reserved section of the British Museum which were once waggishly described as having been weighed in the balance and found wanton. Such activities have so little impact on other people that it often seems as though human beings invented taboos about sex, food or drink, or about religious belief, correct language and appropriate forms of literary expression in order to avoid having to ask themselves serious questions about genuine moral issues. In *Totem and Taboo* (1919), Freud quotes the German psychologist Wilhelm Mundt's claim that taboos are 'the oldest unwritten code of humanity', one which is 'older that the gods and goes back to a pre-religious age'. In so far as they predate the invention not only of religion but also of laws and philosophical speculation, they are indeed a relict of a pre-ethical stage in the evolution of human thought.

This feature of taboos is closely linked to the fourth reason for feeling less than enthusiastic about any attempt to reintroduce them. Both in their ancient and in their modern form, they are a means whereby one group in society exercises power over another. This is visible in what anthropologists present as the oldest taboo, the one against incest. It was always the men who decided to exchange their women, not the other way round. The women seem to have had as little choice in the matter as they did when the taboo against menstruation required them to abstain from certain foods, or to remove themselves from society during the period in which men judged that they were unclean.

At first sight, the linguistic taboos introduced by the movement for political correctness have the distinct advantage of trying to create a more equal society, and especially of redressing the traditional imbalance in the exercise of power by men and women. From another point of view, however, this movement shows a taste for the exercise of power by certain groups which is comparable to the ideology inspiring the Holy Office. The only difference is that the ambition to prevent the expression of heretical ideas no longer comes solely from the conservative organs of the right. It now also characterizes those who would style themselves as belonging to the left.

George Orwell identified this tendency as early as 1946 when he wrote in an essay entitled 'The Prevention of Literature':

> Fifteen years ago, when one defended the freedom of the intellect, one had to defend it against Conservatives and against Catholics, and to some extent – although they were not important – against Fascists. Now, one has to defend it against Communists and 'fellow travellers'.

In 1969, Herbert Marcuse, one of the intellectual heroes of the student rebellion of 1968, showed how accurate Orwell's diagnosis remained. 'The whole post-fascist period', he wrote,

> is one of clear and present danger. Consequently, true pacification requires the withdrawal of tolerance before the deed, at the stage of communication in word and picture. Such extreme suspension of the right of free speech is indeed justified only if the whole of society is in extreme danger. I maintain that our society is in such an emergency situation, and that it has become the normal state of affairs.[9]

One of the great disadvantages of all taboos is the power which they put into the hands of zealots. The movement for political correctness is unlikely to have the kind of influence exercised by the thought police in *Nineteen Eighty-Four* or the Inquisition in sixteenth-century Spain. It has, from the very beginning, made itself too vulnerable to ridicule. It nevertheless shows how permanent the appetite for power is in all societies, and is a reminder of the fifth reason for being suspicious of all taboos: that they are, at best, a substitute for laws that are rationally conceived, impersonally applied, and do not try to privilege one group in society at the expense of others.

It may be possible to argue that some of the taboos of the past were so necessary a step in the evolution of society that they should be jettisoned only with the greatest caution. This is what the Polish-born anthropologist Bronislaw Malinowski claimed when he wrote in 1922: 'Destroy tradition, and you will deprive the collective organism of its protective shell and give it over to the slow individual process of dying out.'[10] This runs parallel to Lord Devlin's contention in *The Enforcement of Morals* (1959) that 'society is not something that is kept together physically; it is held by the invisible bonds of common thought. If these bonds were too far relaxed the members would drift apart.' It is a superficially attractive proposition. But while laws can be changed to take account of the different and evolving needs of a society, as well as of the changes in its moral attitudes, taboos cannot. With them, it is all or nothing at all, with a total immunity to rational argument protecting them against any possibility of change.

The sixth reason for resisting any nostalgia for taboos is a social and historical one. When, in 1940, Koestler published *Darkness at Noon*, Hitler's fascism was an even greater threat to Western civilization than the 'running amuck of pure reason' involved in the attempt to create scientific communism in the Soviet Union. But as Francis Fukuyama argued in his *The End of History and the Last Man* (1992), a book which it immediately became taboo to praise in English-speaking academia, Western society has shown a quite remarkable resilience in seeing off the challenge of both forms of totalitarianism, and has held off the threat of communism with even great success than it did that of fascism. It has, moreover, done so without ever needing to keep its citizens under control by the revival and imposition of ancient taboos.

The suggestions current in the 1940s and 1950s for a return to the certainties of traditional religion as the only means of saving Western society from the threat of left-wing totalitarianism proved unnecessary. The liberal capitalism of the industrialized West has showed itself quite capable of surviving, and even of prospering, without abandoning any of its hostility to the authoritarianism inseparable from the concept of taboo. Whether it will be able to maintain this prosperity in the face of the competition from the newly industrialized countries of Asia is naturally an open question. It is often argued, especially by conservatively minded critics, that this competition is all the more formidable in that the societies from which it comes, like Malaysia or Singapore, have retained a greater sense of family loyalty and social responsibility than Western Europe or North America, and have done so precisely because they have not jettisoned the taboos of the past.

The best reply to this argument lies in the seventh reason for feeling less than enthusiastic about any attempt to reimpose traditional taboos. It was expressed by Aldous Huxley when he commented in *Jesting Pilate* (1926) that 'One is all for religion until one visits a really religious country. Then, one is all for drains, machinery and the minimum wage.' When you look at what has been banned in the past, and remains forbidden in many non-European societies of the present day, you feel an extraordinary sense of gratitude for living in Western Europe or North America in the late twentieth century. Admiration for the kind of society established in Malaysia is unlikely to survive prolonged exposure to it.

The eighth reason is that taboos are at one and the same time the expression of a static society and a means of refusing social change. Anthropologists most frequently use the word when talking about societies which, mainly for geographical reasons, have experienced little or no contact with other cultures, and have not been affected by the social changes brought about by advances in technology. Such societies existed in the islands of the South Pacific where Captain Cook first came across the word 'taboo', among the Aborigine tribes of Australia, or in Africa and the less accessible parts of Asia. They did not, however, long survive in the same form once their members saw that life could be run on different principles. It is an instructive as well as a cheering experience to move from a book such as Hutton Webster's *Taboo: A Sociological Survey*, with its unending list of gloomy interdicts and dire threats of unavoidable calamities, to the world of the two volumes of Robert Graves's *The Greek Myths* (1954).

The myths analysed by Graves do not depict an idyllic humanity, and there is no lack of beliefs that we can see to be irrational. But at least the society that produced these myths, and which, in Graves's interpretation of them, they served to express, was a society on the move. It may be possible to argue that some taboos developed into rationally defensible laws, and even to sympathize with Sir James Frazer's contention that 'taboos prohibiting contact with things, regardless of the purposes for which they were observed, fostered concepts of property rights'.[11] But there is no doubting the truth of the remark in the 1974 edition of the *Encyclopedia Britannica* to the effect that 'taboos and other regulations in connection with food are incompatible with the idea of an open society'.

It may well be true, as William Lessa and Evon Vogt suggested in 1979, that societies with many taboos contain few neurotics.

Either, they argue, the neuroses which find victims in more open societies find a 'harmless outlet' in taboos, or non-neurotics look benevolently at the customs observed by their fellows and decide that they do not concern them.[12] This observation runs parallel to the frequently noted fact that the suicide rate drops rapidly in wartime. This is scarcely a good reason for having wars. Lessa and Vogt's remark about the benevolence of the non-neurotic also misses the point about the very real restraints which taboos place upon everybody's freedom of thought and action. It is not a sign of neurosis to wish to limit one's family while retaining a vigorous sex life, to make love to a member of one's own sex, or to find descriptions of other people's sexual experience both entertaining and instructive.

The ninth and final reason for not wishing to bring back the taboos of the past is that you can't do it. Once the kind of society admired by Orwell has gone, it cannot be put back into place. 'La plus belle fille au monde', as Paul Valéry once remarked, 'ne peut donner que ce qu'elle a. Mieux vaut parfois qu'elle le garde.' (The most beautiful girl in the world can give only what she has. It is sometimes better for her to keep it.) Taboos can sometimes last a long time. But once gone, they are like the fragile quality of virginity: they can never be restored.

Only in some of the performing arts, and particularly the theatre and the cinema, is there a case for the adoption of a number of what I describe in Section IV as modified taboos. These would not be imposed from outside, and would be more accurately described not as taboos but as self-denying ordinances inspired by consideration for other people's feelings. They would thus be very different from the taboos of the past, and would resemble them in only one way: they, too, would lack the ability required of laws to be justified by open debate as well as by reason and experience. Like some of the verbal taboos which can be defended by a desire not to devalue the linguistic currency, they would require for their acceptance a modicum of good taste as well as a sense of freely accepted personal responsibility on the part of all members of society. Since, however, both good taste and personal responsibility were qualities conspicuously lacking in many of the interdicts known as taboos in the past, it would be convenient to be able to borrow another word to describe the rules which would protect people's feelings without unduly restricting their freedom.

NOTES

1 Thus the closing peroration of Burke's *Reflections on the Revolution in France* (1790) runs:

> To be enabled to acquire, the people, without being servile, must be tractable and obedient. The magistrate must have his reverence, the laws their authority. The body of the people must not find the principles of natural subordination by art rooted out of their minds. They must respect that property of which they cannot partake. They must labour to obtain what by labour may be obtained; and when they find, as they commonly do, the success disproportioned to the endeavour, they must be taught their consolation in the final proportions of eternal justice.

2 See the paperback edition of Arthur Koestler, *Darkness at Noon* (1940), Penguin, Harmondsworth, 1945, p. 228.

3 George Orwell, *Selected Essays*, Penguin, Harmondsworth, 1957, p. 72.

4 Steven Marcus, *The Other Victorians*, Weidenfeld and Nicolson, London, 1964, p. 146.

5 Quoted from John J. Honigman, *The Development of Anthropological Ideas*, Dorsey Press, Homewood, Illinois, 1976.

6 Stanford H. Kadish and others, *Criminal Law and Its Processes: Cases and Materials*, 4th edition, Little, Brown, Boston, MA, 1983, p. 243.

7 Hutton Webster, *Taboo: A Sociological Study*, Stanford University Press, Stanford, CA, 1942, p. 17.

8 Webster, *Taboo: A Sociological Study*, pp. 206–10.

9 See *Student Power: Problems, Diagnosis, Action*, edited by Alexander Coburn and Robin Blackburn, Penguin Education, Harmondsworth, 1969, p. 372.

10 Quoted on p. 250 of Raymond Firth, editor, *Man and Culture: An Evaluation of the Work of Bronislaw Malinowski*, Routledge and Kegan Paul, London, 1957.

11 Quoted in Honigman, *The Development of Anthropological Ideas*, p. 159.

12 William Lessa and Evon Vogt, *A Reader in Comparative Religion: An Anthropological Approach*, Harper and Row, New York, 1979, p. 23.

Select List of Themes and Topics

blood and **pork** in II; **Hays Code** and **images** in IV; section V, *passim*, but especially **forks**, **hands**, **uncircumcised**, **water**.

Social markers, taboos serving as: **smoking** in I; **alcohol**, **beef, chips, fried** in II; **serviette** in III.

Superstitions, taboos often similar to: **incest** (iii) in I; **whistle** in I; **bananas** in II; **cancer**, **Macbeth** and **salmon** in III.

Taxonomic (= classificatory) function of taboos: **bestiality**, **doors**, **incest** (iii), **intermarriage**, **oral sex** (ii), **paedophilia** in I; **birds**, **camels**, **mix**, **pork**, **seafood (duck** as an uncertain example) in II; **cunt** in III; **trousers** in V.

Women, taboos indifferent to welfare of: **bestiality** in I, **sado-masochism** in IV; **apples** in II; directed against: **menstruation**, **trespass** in I; **bananas** in II; **cunt** in III; **bodily functions** and **censorship**in IV; **infibulation** in V (especially endnotes 19 and 33).

Index of Headwords

Selective Index of Names

Select Bibliography

Andersson, Lars-Gunmar and Trudgill, Peter, *Bad Language*, Penguin Books, Harmondsworth, 1990.

Ardrey, Robert, *The Territorial Imperative*, Fontana, London, 1969.

Arens, William, *The Man-Eating Myth: Anthropology and Anthropophagy*, Oxford University Press, Oxford, 1979.

Ariès, Philippe and Béjin, André, editors, *Western Sexuality: Practice and Precept in Past and Present Times*, translated by Anthony Foster, Basil Blackwell, Oxford, 1985.

Ariès, Philippe and Duby, Georges, *A History of the Private Life from Pagan Rome to Byzantium*, translated by Arthur Goldhammer, Belknap Press, Harvard University Press, Cambridge, MA, 1990.

Asad, Talal, *Anthropology and the Colonial Encounter*, Humanities Press, Atlantic Highlands, NJ, 1973.

Barley, Nigel, *The Innocent Anthropologist*, British Museum Publications, London, 1986; Penguin Books, Harmondsworth, 1988.

Barret-Ducrocq, Françoise, *Love in the Time of Victoria* (1989), translated by John Howe, Penguin Books, Harmondsworth, 1992.

Beard, Henry and Cerf, Christopher, *The Official Politically Correct Dictionary and Handbook*, Random house, New York, 1993.

Bell, Vikki, *Interrogating Incest: Feminism, Foucault and the Law*, Pluto Press, London, 1993.

Benedict, Ruth, *The Chrysanthemum and the Sword*, Charles E. Tuttle, Vermont and Tokyo, 1946.

Bennett, Alan, *Writing Home*, Faber and Faber, London, 1994.

Berger, Bennett M., editor, *Authors of Their Own Lives: Intellectual Autobiographies by Twenty American Sociologists*, University of California Press, Berkeley, 1990.

Bodmell, W. F. and Cavalli-Sforza, G., *Genetics, Evolution and Man*, W. H. Freeman and Co., San Francisco, 1976.

Bowden, James, *Manners for Men* (1897), Prior Publications, Whitstable, Kent, 1993.

Braine, John, *Room at the Top*, Eyre and Spottiswoode, London, 1957.

Brown, Paula, and Tuzin, Donald, editors, *The Ethnography of Cannibalism*, published by the Society for Psychological Anthropology, Washington, DC, 1983.

Brown, Peter, *The Body and Society: Men, Women and Sexual Renunciation in Early Christianity*, Columbia University Press, New York, 1988.

Browne, Ray B., editor, *Forbidden Fruits: Taboos and Tabooism in Culture*, Bowling Green University Press, Bowling Green, Ohio, 1984.
Bryson, Bill, *Made in America*, Secker and Warburg, London, 1994.
Buruma, Ian, *The Wages of Guilt. Memories of War in Germany and Japan*, Vintage, London and New York, 1985.
Catechism of the Catholic Church, Latin text, Libreria Editrice Vaticana, Citta del Vatticano, 1992.
Chandler, Ralph C., *The Constitutional Law Dictionary*, ABC–CEIO Services, Santa Barbara, 1985.
Chicago, Judy, *Through the Flower: My Struggle as a Woman Artist*, Women's Press, London and New York, 1982.
Clarke, Ronald, *The Huxleys*, Heinemann, London, 1968.
Conley, Carolyn, *The Unwritten Law: Criminal Justice in Victorian Kent*, Oxford University Press, Oxford, 1991.
Cory, Donald Webster, *The Homosexual in America: A Subjective Approach*, Greenberg, New York, 1951.
Cruden's Complete Concordance to the Old and New Testaments, edited by C. H. Irwin and others, Lutterworth Press, Cambridge, 1941.
Cruickshank, Margaret, *The Gay and Lesbian Liberation Movement*, Routledge, London, 1992.
Dawkins, Richard, *The Selfish Gene*, Oxford University Press, Oxford, 1976; new edition, 1989.
Devlin, Lord, *The Enforcement of Morals*, Oxford University Press, Oxford, 1965.
Diamond, Jared, *The Rise and Fall of the Third Chimpanzee* (1991), Vintage, London, 1992.
Douglas, Mary, *Purity and Danger*, Barrie and Jenkins, London, 1966.
—— *Natural Symbols: Explanation in Cosmology*, Barrie and Jenkins, London, 1970.
—— *Risk and Blame: Essays in Cultural Anthropology*, Routledge and Kegan Paul, London, 1994.
Dover, K. J., *Greek Homosexuality*, Duckworth, London, 1978.
Dublin, Max, *Futurehype: The Tyranny of Prophecy*, Penguin Books, Harmondsworth, 1989.
Elias, Norbert, *The Civilising Process: the history of Manners* (1938), translated by Edmund Jephcott, Blackwell, Oxford, 1978.
Ellmann, Richard, *Oscar Wilde*, Hamish Hamilton, London, 1987.
Farberow, Norman, editor, *Taboo Topics*, Atherton Press, New York, 1963.
Ford, Clellan and Beach, Frank A., *Patterns of Sexual Behaviour*, Eyre and Spottiswoode, London, 1952.
Foucault, Michel, *The History of Sexuality*, translated by Robert Hurley, Pantheon, New York, 1980.

Fox, Robin, *The Red Lamp of Incest*, Notre Dame Press, Notre Dame, IN, 1983.

—— *The Unauthorized Version: Truth and Fiction in the Bible*, Knopf, New York, 1992.

Franz, Nellie Alden, *English Women Enter the Professions*, Cincinatti, Ohio, 1968; privately printed for the author.

Fraser, George Macdonald, editor, *The World of the Public School*, Weidenfeld and Nicolson, London, 1977.

Frazer, Sir James, *The Illustrated Golden Bough*, edited by Mary Douglas, Macmillan, 1978.

Freud, Sigmund, *Totem and Taboo: Resemblances between the Psychic Lives of Savages and Neurotics* (1919), Penguin Books, Harmondsworth, 1938.

Fukuyama, Francis, *The End of History and the Last Man*, Hamish Hamilton, London, 1992; Penguin Books, Harmondsworth, 1992.

Fussell, Paul, *Caste Marks: Style and Status in the USA*, Heinemann, London, 1984.

Gamman, Lorraine and Makinnen, Merja, *Female Fetishism*, Lawrence and Wishart, London, 1994.

Garner, James Finn, *Politically Correct Bedtime Stories*, Macmillan Publishing Company, New York, 1994.

Gathorne-Hardy, Jonathan, *The Public School Phenomenon*, Hodder and Stoughton, London, 1977.

Glassé, Cyril, *The Concise Encyclopedia of Islam*, Stacey Publications, London, 1989.

Goffman, Erving, *Stigma: Notes on the Management of Spoiled Identity*, Prentice Hall, New York, 1963; Penguin Books, Harmondsworth, 1968.

Goldberg, Jonathan, editor, *Reclaiming Sodom*, Routledge, New York and London, 1994.

Gombrich, E. H., *The Story of Art*, Phaidon, Oxford, 1950.

Graves, Robert, *The Greek Myths*, Penguin Books, Harmondsworth, 1954.

Greenberg, David F., *The Construction of Homosexuality*, University of Chicago Press, Chicago and London, 1988.

Greene, Jonathon, *The Encyclopedia of Censorship* (New York, 1988), Facts on File, Oxford, 1990.

Greer, Germaine, *Sex and Destiny: The Politics of Human Fertility*, Secker and Warburg, London, 1984; Picador, London, 1989.

Guttmann, Allen, *The Erotic in Sports*, Columbia University Press, New York, 1996.

Hall, Radclyffe, *The Well of Loneliness*, Covici-Friede, New York, 1928.

Halliwell, Leslie, *Halliwell's Filmgoer's and Videoviewer's Companion*, 10th edn, Paladin, London, 1993.

Harris, Marvin, *Culture, People, Nature*, HarperCollins, New York and London, 1993.

Héritier, Françoise, *Les deux soeurs et leur mère: Anthropologie de l'inceste*, Editions Odile Jacob, Paris, 1994.

Herodotus, *The Histories* (*c.* 490 BC), Penguin Classics, Harmondsworth, 1954.

Hinsch, Bret, *Passions of the Cut Sleeve: The Male Homosexual Tradition in China*, University of California Press, Berkeley and Oxford, 1990.

Hints on Etiquette and Usages of Society: With a Glance at Bad Habits (1834), republished in 1946.

Hite, Shere, *The Hite Report: A Nationwide Study of Female Sexuality*, Macmillan, New York, 1976; Collier/Macmillan, London, 1976.

—— *The Hite Report on Male Sexuality*, Macmillan, New York, 1978.

Honigman, John J., *The Development of Anthropological Ideas*, Dorsey Press, Homewood, Illinois, 1976.

Huxley, Aldous, *Point Counter-Point*, Chatto and Windus, London, 1928.

—— *Brave New World*, Chatto and Windus, London, 1932.

—— *Ends and Means*, Chatto and Windus, London, 1937.

Jespersen, Otto, *Language: Its Nature, Development and Origin* (1922), Allen and Unwin, London, 1954 edition.

Johnson, Anne M., Wadsworth, Joan, Welling, Kay and Field, Julia, *Sexual Attitudes and Life-Styles*, Blackwell's Scientific Publications, Oxford, 1994.

Johnson, Paul, *The Offshore Islanders*, Weidenfeld and Nicolson, London, 1972; Penguin Books, Harmondsworth, 1975.

Kadish, Sanford H., and others, *The Criminal Law and Its Processes: Cases and Materials*, 4th edn, Little, Brown and Company, Boston, MA, 1983.

Kinsey, Alfred, and others, *Sexual Behaviour in the Human Male*, W. B. Saunders and Company, Philadelphia and London, 1948.

Koestler, Arthur, *Darkness at Noon*, Jonathan Cape, London, 1940; Penguin Books, Harmondsworth, 1946.

The Koran, translated with an Introduction by Arthur J. Arberry, Allen and Unwin, London, 1955, The World's Classics, Oxford University Press, Oxford, 1983.

Landau, Ron, *Islam and the Arabs*, Allen and Unwin, London, 1958.

Leach, Edmund, *Lévi-Strauss*, Fontana Modern Masters, Collins, London, 1970.

Lefkowitz, Mary, *Women in Greek Myth*, Duckworth, London, 1986.

Lessa, William, and Vogt, Evon, *A Reader in Comparative Religion: An Anthropological Approach*, Harper and Row, New York, 1979.

Levin, Bernard, *A World Elsewhere*, Jonathan Cape, London, 1994.

Lewis, I. M., *Social Anthropology in Perspective*, Penguin, Harmondsworth, 1976.

Lodge, David, *The British Museum is Falling Down*, Secker and Warburg, London, 1965

—— *Changing Places*, Secker and Warburg, London, 1975.

—— *How Far Can You Go?* (US *Snakes and Ladders*), Secker and Warburg, London, 1980.

Malinowski, Bronislaw, *The Sexual Life of Savages* (1929), Routledge, London, 1970.

Marcus, Steven, *The Other Victorians*, Weidenfeld and Nicolson, London, 1964.

Marriner, Brian, *Cannibalism: The Last Taboo!*, Arrow Books, London, 1992.

Martin, Judith, *Miss Manners' Guide to Excruciatingly Correct Behaviour*, Hamish Hamilton, London, 1983.

McCarthy, Mary, *Memories of a Catholic Childhood*, Penguin Books, Harmondsworth, 1957.

Melville, Herman, *Typee: A Peep at Polynesian Life* (1846), Northwestern University Press and the Newberry Library, Evanston and Chicago, 1968.

Miller, Casey and Swift, Kate, *Words and Women*, Anchor Books, Doubleday, Garden City, NY, 1977.

Mitford, Nancy, and others, *Noblesse Oblige*, Penguin Books, Harmondsworth, 1957.

—— *The Sun King*, Hamish Hamilton, London, 1966.

Moore, John A., *Heredity and Development*, Oxford University Press, Oxford, 1972.

Nye, Ivan and Bernardo, Felix M., *The Family: Its Structure and Interaction*, Macmillan Company, New York, 1973.

Orwell, George, *The Collected Essays, Journalism and Letters of George Orwell*, Secker and Warburg, London, 1968.

Partridge Eric, *A Dictionary of Slang and Unconventional English: Colloquialisms and Catch Phrases, Fossilised Jokes and Puns, General Nicknames, Vulgarisms and Such Americanisms as Have Been Naturalised* (1937), revised edition by Paul Beale, Routledge and Kegan Paul, London, 1984.

Perkins, Rollin M. and Boyce, Ronald N., *Criminal Law*, 3rd edn, Foundation Press, Mineola, NY, 1982.

Perrin, Noel, *Dr Bowdler's Legacy: A history of Expurgated Books in England and America*, David R. Godine, Boston, MA, 1992.

Perrot, Philippe, *Les Dessus and les Dessous de la bourgeoisie*, Fayard, Paris, 1980.

—— *Le travail des apparences, ou les transformations du corps féminin, XVIIIe et XIXe siècles*, Éditions du Seuil, Paris, 1984

Pornography: The Longford Report, Coronet Books, London, 1972.
Rice, David Talbot, *Islamic Art*, Thames and Hudson, London, 1965; revised edn, 1975.
Rolph, C. H., editor, *The Trial of Lady Chatterley*, Penguin Books, Harmondsworth, 1961.
Rose, Michael, *Homosexuality: A Philosophical Inquiry*, Basil Blackwell, Oxford, 1988.
Rouse, Elizabeth, *Understanding Fashion*, Blackwell Scientific Publications, Oxford, 1989.
Rubenstein, Ruth P., *Dress Codes: Meanings and Messages in American Culture*, Westview Press, Boulder, CO, 1995.
Sagarin, Edward, *The Anatomy of Dirty Words*, Lyle Stuart, New York, 1968.
Sampson, Adam, *Acts of Abuse: Sex Offenders and the Criminal Justice System*, Routledge, London, 1994.
Schwartz, Richard H., *Judaism and Vegetarianism*, the Free Press, Marblehead, MA, 1988.
Schwarzkopf, Norman, *It Doesn't Take a Hero*, Bantam Books, New York, 1992.
Shuttle, Penelope and Redgrove, Peter, *The Wise Wound: Menstruation and Everywoman*, Gollancz, London, 1978; Penguin Books, Harmondsworth, 1980.
Simons, G. L., *The Book of World Sexual Records*, Star edn, London, 1975; revised edn, Corgi, London, 1983.
Simoons, Frederick J., *Eat Not This Flesh. Food Avoidances in the Old World*, University of Wisconsin Press, Madison, Wis. 1961.
Smith, Joan, *Misogynies*, Faber and Faber, London, 1989.
Smith, J. C., and Hogan, Brian, *Criminal Law*, Butterworth, London, 1987; new edn, 1992.
Steiner, Franz, *Taboo*, Cohen and West, London, 1956; Penguin, Harmondsworth, 1967.
Strossen, Nadine, *Defending Pornography: Free Speech, Sex and the Fight for Women's Rights*, Simon and Schuster, New York, 1995; Abacus, London, 1996.
Syed Anwer Ali, *Qur'an: The Fundamental Law of Human Life*, Syed Publications, Karachi, Hamdard Foundation Press, 1982.
Taylor, G. Rattray, *Sex in History*, Thames and Hudson, London, 1953; Panther, London, 1965.
Thesiger, Wilfred, *Arabian Sands*, Longman, London, 1959; Penguin Books, Harmondsworth, 1964.
Twitchell, James B., *Forbidden Partners: The Incest Taboo in Modern Culture*, Columbia University Press, New York, 1987.

Visser, Margaret, *The Rituals of Dinner*, Viking Penguin, London, 1992.
Wardaugh, Ronald, *An Introduction to Sociolinguistics*, Blackwell, Oxford, 1986.
Warner, Marina, *Managing Monsters: Six Myths of Our Times*, Vintage, London, 1994.
Waugh, Evelyn, *Black Mischief*, Chapman and Hall, London, 1930.
Webster, Hutton, *Taboo: A Sociological Study*, Stanford University Press, Stanford, CA, 1942.
Webster, Richard, *A Brief History of Blasphemy*, Orwell Press, London, 1994.
Weeks, Jeffrey, *The Construction of Homosexuality: Sex, Politics and Society since 1880*, Longman, New York, 1990.
Wildeblood, Peter, *Against the Law*, Penguin Books, Harmondsworth, 1957 [1956].
Wodehouse, P. G., *The World of Jeeves*, Herbert Jenkins, London, 1967.
Wolfe, Tom, *The Purple Decades*, Farrar, Straus and Giroux, New York, 1982; Picador, London, 1993.
—— *The Bonfire of the Vanities*, Jonathan Cape, London, 1987; Picador, London, 1988
Wright, Laurence, *Clean and Decent: The Fascinating History of the Bathroom and the WC*, Routledge and Kegan Paul, London, 1960.
Zachs, Richard, *History Laid Bare: Love, Sex and Perversity from the Ancient Etruscans to Warren G. Harding*, HarperCollins, New York, 1994.
Zilbergerld, Bernie, *The New Male Sexuality*, Bantam Books, New York and London, 1992.